GRADUATE TEXTS IN COMPUTER SCIENCE

Editors
David Gries
Fred B. Schneider

Springer
New York
Berlin
Heidelberg
Barcelona
Budapest
Hong Kong
London
Milan
Paris
Singapore
Tokyo

GRADUATE TEXTS IN COMPUTER SCIENCE

V.S. Alagar   K. Periyasamy

SPECIFICATION OF SOFTWARE SYSTEMS

With 88 Illustrations

Springer

V.S. Alagar
Department of Computer Science
Concordia University
Montreal, Quebec A3G 1M8, Canada

K. Periyasamy
Department of Computer Science
University of Manitoba
Winnipeg, Manitoba R3T 2N2, Canada

Series Editors

David Gries
Fred B. Schneider

Department of Computer Science
Cornell University
Upson Hall
Ithaca, NY 14853-7501, USA

Library of Congress Cataloging-in-Publication Data
Alagar, Vangalur S., 1940–
        Specification of software systems / V.S. Alagar and K. Periyasamy.
            p.   cm. — (Graduate texts in computer science)
        Includes bibliographical references and index.
        ISBN 0-387-98430-5 (hardcover : alk. paper)
        1. Software engineering.   2. Computer software—Specifications.
    I. Periyasamy, K.   II. Title.   III. Series: Graduate texts in
    computer science (Springer-Verlag New York, Inc.)
    QA76.758.A42   1998
    005.1—dc21   98-16912

Printed on acid-free paper.

Production managed by Victoria Evarretta; manufacturing supervised by Jeffrey Taub.
Photocomposed copy prepared from the authors' LAT$_E$X files.
Printed and bound by Hamilton Printing Co., Rensselaer, NY.
Printed in the United States of America.

9 8 7 6 5 4 3 2 1

ISBN 0-387-98430-5 Springer-Verlag New York Berlin Heidelberg   SPIN 10658033

Preface

This is a textbook on **software specification** emphasizing formal methods that are relevant to requirements and design stages of software development. The aim of the book is to teach the fundamental principles of formal methods in the construction of modular and verifiable formal specifications. The book introduces several formal specification techniques and illustrates the expressive power of each technique with a number of examples.

General Characteristics

Traditional textbooks on software engineering discuss the difficulties and challenges that lie on the path from requirements analysis to implementation of a software product. Most of these books describe some techniques in detail and give hints on implementation of these techniques. Only a few among them deal with important software engineering principles and techniques, and discuss how a particular technique may be used to implement a given principle. There is very little exposure in these books to a rigorous approach to, or a systematic study of, the construction of verifiable software. Those who have acquired an understanding of the fundamental principles of software engineering from traditional textbooks will find the following characteristics of this book quite relevant to the practice of software engineering:

- *The book deals with specification.*
  The principal characteristic of this book is to discuss formalisms that provide a theoretical foundation for the principles of software engineering, and are appropriate to the requirements and design stages of software development.

We discuss the concept of abstraction, the need for formalism in software development, the mathematical basis of formal methods, components of a formal system, specification languages, different levels of rigor in applying languages, and the need for tool support to use formal methods for different stages of software development. We discuss the relationship between specifications and implementations, as well as subjecting specifications to rigorous analyses and formal proofs.

- *The book emphasizes mathematical principles.*
  Formal approaches to software development can be understood and practiced by studying the mathematics they use. A primary objective of the book is to relate discrete mathematical structures to the study of abstract data types, and to bring students to the level of mathematical maturity where they can write and reason about small specifications. Once the students acquire the basic mathematical skills that a formalism is based on, mastery of formal specification languages, techniques for refinements, and proofs become easy to understand and apply. We believe that the use of tools and techniques become effective when their underlying principles are properly understood.

- *The book teaches formal specification languages.*
  Unlike many recent books that are devoted to one formal specification language, we discuss four specification languages to emphasize their design philosophies and their practical applicability. We also discuss formal specifications based on set theory and logic without regard to any specification language. The purpose here is to teach the reader that these mathematical abstractions form the formal basis of the four specification languages. The languages discussed in the book are OBJ3, VDM, Z, and Larch. We illustrate their expressive power for different classes of applications. We expect that our treatment of the subject will prepare the reader to learn more sophisticated languages and tools that may be developed in the future. It is our belief that mastery of these languages will allow the reader to choose the language that is suitable for a given application.

- *The book presents proofs.*
  Informal arguments conducted in conjunction with a formal specification often lead to a proof construction, which can be presented in a justifiable manner. Proofs ensure a measure of certainty on claims that can be made of specified system properties. We present proofs in rigorous as well as in formal styles. We avoid lengthy proofs, and put more emphasis on modeling, specification, and rigorous reasoning of the specifications.

- *The book presents engineering principles.*
  This book discusses the general principles for data refinement, operation refinement, and interface specification, and illustrates how these are constructed for particular specification languages. The presentation in the book aims to enable the reader to understand *why* a particular technique is important and *how* to apply the technique.

Audience

This book is designed to be used as a textbook by students of computer science, software engineering, and information engineering. Software professionals who want to learn formal specification languages and use formal methods in their work will find the material in the book useful for serious self-study. The sections on bibliographic notes give a broad account of work related to the topic discussed in each chapter; this should help software professionals to identify industrial applications and learn from the experience reported on the use of tools.

Background Knowledge

The book is designed for undergraduates, and beginning graduate-level students in computer science, computer engineering, software engineering, and information engineering. We assume that the reader has completed an undergraduate course in discrete mathematics. The reader must be fluent in programming and must have completed or be doing a course in software engineering. An exposure to undergraduate-level theoretical computer science course, or attainment of a certain level of *mathematical maturity*—which enables the reader to abstract, conceptualize, and analytically reason about abstracted concepts—will be an asset.

Organization and Content

Several specification languages, formal methods, and tools based on them have been developed by different research groups. Some of these methods are practiced by industries and government organizations such as NASA. Books devoted to one particular specification language or method have been published recently. Organizing the essential material to explore four specification languages in one textbook poses a challenge. We have organized this textbook based on the view that a reader should learn the following:

- where and how to integrate formalism in the development process,
- a mathematical basis, and
- the formal specification methods.

These are organized as follows:

- The first three chapters debate the questions: Why do we study formal specification? How do we integrate formal methods in a development process? and What are the attributes for a formal specification language?

- Chapters 4 and 5 introduce the concept of abstraction and formalism, and discuss extensions to BNF and finite-state machines, the two formal notations that the reader might have used in earlier courses.

- Chapters 6 and 7 discuss specifications based on logic, set theory and relations, and include material on proofs. Although the examples subjected to proofs are small, the structure of formal proofs is brought out clearly. These two chapters must be read carefully by those readers who want to review their mathematical knowledge.

- Chapters 8–11 describe the specification languages OBJ3, VDM, Z and Larch. We discuss the algebraic specification methodology in Chapter 8, and include a tutorial on OBJ3. In Chapter 9, we introduce VDM, a model-based specification language. Chapter 10 deals with Z, another leading model-based notation built around set theoretical foundation. In Chapter 11, we discuss Larch and Larch/C++ specification languages. Our goal is to treat specification languages from abstract to concrete levels. Whereas representational details are ignored in an algebraic specification language, VDM and Z specification languages use abstract data types as models for representing information of software systems. The Larch family of languages are geared towards interface specification, and clearly separate the sharable abstraction from the programming language details. In our opinion, these four languages are representatives of several specification languages used for specifying sequential systems, and their features can be utilized in different application areas.

While the material in the first seven chapters should withstand the passage of time, it is likely that some of the material in Chapters 8–11 may become outdated because of changes to the specification languages. The language OBJ3 has been around for a number of years, and its design principles are sound. The reader is expected to learn these principles; the syntax of the language or how OBJ3 system interprets a specification are secondary. We have used the ISO standardized notation for VDM in this book. The Z notation is also being standardized by ISO; however, the standardization process is not yet complete. Therefore, we have adopted an earlier version of Z. The Larch Shared Language (LSL), in which abstractions are developed, resembles an algebraic specification language. However, the semantics of LSL is based on first-order logic. Given the impressive LSL library constructed by Guttag and Horning, we do not expect the syntax and the semantics of traits in the library to change much. However, the Larch/C++ interface specification language may undergo changes. The reader is advised to refer to the web page for Larch/C++ maintained by Gary Leavens for any update on the language. Since interface specification must be related to programming, and C++ is widely used in industry, we hope that the choice of Larch/C++ bridges the gap between design and implementation issues to be resolved by software professionals.

Exercises

All chapters include a section on exercises. There are three types:

- Exercises based on the basic concepts and aimed at extending the basic knowledge; these exercises include specifications and simple proofs.
- Extensions to examples discussed in the chapter; these require integration of the material discussed in the chapter.
- Project-oriented exercises that require complete specifications and proofs.

Case Studies

Case studies are used in Chapters 8–11 to illustrate the features of OBJ3, VDM, Z, and Larch specification approaches. Each case study is chosen to demonstrate the integration of different concepts and features from a particular specification language. For example, the *Window* specification discussed in Chapter 8 demonstrates the integrated use of modular development and parametric specification concepts in OBJ3. This specification can be incrementally extended with additional operations, views, and theories towards reusing it in the design of another window management system. The *Network* example given in Chapter 9 is a simple version of a communication network. We have given a rigorous proof that the specification supports safe communication of messages between any two nodes in the network. The *Automated billing system* example presented in Chapter 10 is an instance of a real-life commercial application, which can be extended to suit a more complex situation. The case study in Chapter 11 presents Larch/C++ interface specifications for the two Rogue Wave library classes RWZone, and RWFile. These two examples are chosen to illustrate the applicability of Larch/C++ specification language to software products in commercial class libraries. The case studies may be read at different times and may be adapted or reused for different purposes.

Lab Components

The material in Chapters 8–11 may be taught with tool-supported laboratory projects. In order to ensure that the students use the tool effectively, the instructors must (1) provide a solid foundation on theoretical issues, and (2) give assignments on simple specifications which can be done by pencil and paper. This will give students sufficient familiarity with the subject matter before they start learning to use the tools. The differences in syntactic conventions, and even minor differences in semantics between the specification language and the language employed by the tool, must be overcome by the student. This implies that laboratory projects may only be introduced closer to the end of teaching the language; only then can the students' knowledge be expected to grow.

How to Use the Book

This book has evolved from the lecture notes prepared by the first author eight years ago. The notes were revised every year both for content and style. From the experience gained by both of us from the same notes in teaching different courses at different universities, we made extensive revisions to the notes in the last two years. However, the overall structure of the notes has not changed. Since the structure has withstood changes to the specification language details, such as syntax, we are confident that the different sequences as suggested below would fit different curriculum needs:

1. Chapters 1 through 3 are required for further reading of the book.
2. Chapters 4 and 5 may be read partially as well as simultaneously.
3. Based on the first seven chapters, a one-semester (13-14 weeks) undergraduate course within a software engineering program or computer science program or computer engineering program can be given.
4. Depending on the mathematical background of students in an information engineering program, material from Chapters 1 through 7 may be selected and supplemented with basic mathematics to offer a one-semester course.
5. A two-semester course for graduates or senior undergraduates in software engineering, computer engineering, computer science, and information engineering programs can be given as follows:
   (a) Chapters 1 through 7 may be covered in semester I. One of the following sequences for semester II may be followed:
      - Chapters 8, 9
      - Chapters 8, 10
      - Chapters 9, 11
      - Chapters 10, 11
6. An advanced graduate-level course can be given by choosing the material from Chapters 8 through 11 and supplementing it with intensive laboratory sessions requiring the verified development of a large project. This type of course requires tool support; for example, LP can be used with Larch, a theorem prover such as EVES or PVS may be used with Z or VDM. The material in the book may be supplemented with published papers in the area.

Acknowledgments

Our sincere thanks go to the many students and people who have helped us to create this book. We are grateful to the students of COMP 648 Systems Requirements Specification at Concordia University, and 74.716 Formal Specifications and Design at the University of Manitoba, for pointing out many of the errors in previous versions of the lecture notes.

Our deepest sense of gratitude go to Darmalingum Muthiayen, who critically read the entire book, and gave us valuable feedback and corrections. His thorough reading and suggestions for presentable style have contributed greatly to the current version of the book.

We sincerely express our thanks to Dennis Lovie, Jonathan Jacky, and Randolph Johnson for reading and providing critical reviews on the Z notation. In particular, we greatly appreciate Randolph Johnson's comments on the semantics of some of the notations which helped us improve the chapter to its current version. We followed up Dennis Lovie's suggestions on uniformity of names and descriptions in the examples, which enhanced the readability of the chapter.

Jimmy Cheng and David So helped us in typesetting the first version of lecture notes eight years ago. Many of the LaTeX commands defined by them have been used in typesetting the current version of the book.

Finally, our thanks go toward everyone whose work has inspired us in writing this book.

Contents

1

The Role of Specification

Software continues to play a prominant and critical role in large business applications, technical endeavors in space missions, and control systems for airlines, railways, and telecommunications. Software for managing these applications is complex to construct. The source of complexity of a software product lies in the set of stringent requirements, system integrity constraints, and the vast amount of knowledge necessary to adequately describe the expected interaction of the software with its environment. When all requirements are not properly understood, recorded, and communicated within the development team, there is a gap between the documented requirements and the requirements actually needed for correct functioning of the system. The inability in mastering the complexity leads to this discrepancy, which is the root cause of software errors. Precise documentation of requirements with sufficient detail to cover unexpected worst-case scenarios is a good defense against system errors.

More than two decades ago, Brooks [3] recognized the difficulties in developing large complex software and likened the development of large system software to a great beast thrashing in a tar pit. It was relatively easy to get hold of any particular component of the software, but pulling the whole out of the tar was nearly impossible. Twelve years later, Brooks [4] wrote that not only has there been little change, but there is not even a "silver bullet" in sight: a method, a software tool, development in technology, or management technique that would dramatically improve productivity. This situation was attributed to the *essential* difficulties that are inherent in the nature of software: *invisibility, complexity, conformity, changeability.* Accepting that there may be no "silver bullet" in this area, one of the promising attacks on these essential difficulties is to rigorously deal with the problem of gathering and *specifying* the requirements of a software product.

Requirements engineering and domain analysis deal with gathering and analysis of requirements which eventually lead to a decision on "what to build." Each deserves serious studies in its own right. We turn our attention to a study of specification as a means of dealing with the inherent difficulties stated above. After a discussion on software complexity, we explain the notion of specification and explain what aspects of software complexity can be controlled. The chapter concludes with a critique on natural language specification.

1.1   Software Complexity

Very large software systems contain several million lines of source code and voluminous documentation. In the future, rarely will such systems be built from scratch. They will incorporate existing software components and will require numerous intermediate steps in putting them together. This process is reliable only when the behavior and interface of the integrated pieces are well understood. The details of such a large design cannot be comprehended by one single person. Curtis et al. [6] define this scenario as psychological complexity. Basili [2] defines software complexity as "...*a measure of the resources expended by another system while interacting with a piece of software.*" Both authors remark that the underuse of structured programming techniques seems to increase the difficulty of comprehension of a software engineer. Unfortunately, structured programming has not adequately addressed all the issues. We discuss below factors that contribute to software complexity. An understanding of the sources of complexity will help the software developer to look for means of reducing the overall complexity in the construction of large software systems.

Structured programming techniques, which promoted the use of pre- and post-conditions, Hoare axioms, predicate transformers, and top-down design methodologies, provided some help to practitioners of those classical"formal" techniques. However, these new techniques have not totally eliminated all the problems afflicting software development. The main reason is that these methods do not provide the structuring and encapsulation necessary to synthesize large-grain software components. Although new design and development methods are being practiced today, it still remains difficult to ensure the expected performance of a system in a context where the system will be used. This is attributed to the ever-increasing complexity of developing software.

In order to be deemed useful, every software system should exhibit a certain behavior that is observable when the system is functioning in its environment. This observational behavior is the external projection of its internal effect. The behavior of the components and their interactions within the system structure cause the external behavior. When the components can be modeled in a simple way and the interactions are governed by well-defined deterministic rules, the overall behavior of the system becomes predictable to a high degree of accuracy. A system whose behavior is completely predictable is a *simple* system. Simplicity in this context does not rule out algorithmic complexity or software complexity, as defined by Basili [2] and Curtis [6]; simple systems are characterized by total predictability and short programs.

In contrast to simple systems, there are systems whose behavior is not completely predictable. When some of the components are difficult to model accurately or the interactions are governed by laws that are not well-defined, overall behavior can only be predicted with some degree of uncertainty. Clearly, such systems are *complex* systems. According to Parnas [14], a system is complex if the shortest description of the system is long. Different complex systems behave with varying degrees of complexity. For example, a weather forecasting system is complex due to the difficulty of formulating laws governing atmospheric storms; a software for monitoring and predicting the performance of stocks is complex because there is no accurate model for economic trends. When such uncertainties are based on information-theoretic interpretation, the definition of complexity given by Parnas [14] matches the notion of (un)predictability applied to these systems.

1.1.1 Size Complexity

Large software systems are built with a number of parts (modules). The behavior of such systems is determined by the behavior of the individual parts as well as the collective interaction among the parts. The properties of these parts and the laws governing their interactions must be understood before linking other parts that interact with them. The classical "formal" techniques used for small programs do not scale up to suit the production of large software systems. Size is also an important factor causing technical and psychological setbacks in the early stages of the software life cycle. The vast amount of information to be gathered and analyzed during the requirements specification stage can cause incorrect and incomplete information to leak through the review process. According to Leveson [10], almost all accidents involving computerized process control systems are due to this kind of error caused by the size factor. In fact, understanding the dynamics and the conditions under which software systems grow is a major challenge for the information technology industry.

1.1.2 Structural Complexity

There are two aspects to structural complexity: management and technical. Software process models suggest only the highest level system decomposition. Each phase in a life cycle is assigned a specific goal. People assigned to the different phases interact and oversee the production of products as dictated by the dependency among the phases. Within each phase, the target product may be developed either in a top-down manner or by reusing and combining existing software. The breadth and depth of the hierarchy of the development team organizing and managing the development activities determine the structural complexity of managing the system. In addition, traditions and policies in a software development firm may regulate information flow between certain groups, thereby increasing the structural complexity.

The level of interaction, known as coupling, among the modules of a software system is another measure of its structural complexity. The number of levels in the hierarchy of coupling and the span of control reflect the amount of changes that may be required in dependent modules due to changing requirements. The way that modules are connected determines the structural complexity and it has a great impact on the usability, modifiability, and performance of the system.

1.1.3   Environmental Complexity

The environment (context) in which the software system is to be utilized must be well understood. The execution of a program affects the environment in which it is effective. A client of a software may be another program or a human. In either case, a clear prescription of the purposes for which the software can be used must be made available. When the client is another program, such a prescription may be a set of rules. For embedded systems, such as *reactive systems* that constantly interact with the environment, a complete set of rules must be stated for proper use by the client. However, systems such as telephony, flight guidance systems in space navigation, and patient monitoring systems are better understood only when the system is successfully operating in its environment. The following are the major factors contributing to the complexity of embedded systems:

1. stringent time-dependent actions
2. the eventuality that validation of the integrated software is difficult to perform
3. lack of knowledge about the properties of the environment

1.1.4   Application Domain Complexity

The objects manipulated by the software are only models of the real objects belonging to the application domain. How do we abstract those aspects of reality that should be part of the model on which the software construction can be based? For some application domains, the models can only be approximate. This may be due to an incomplete knowledge of the domain objects, or a severe limitation of the model, or a combination of both. Engineering applications use well-tested models that are supported by sound scientific theories. However, there is no cognitive model for a user; there is no exact model to represent the geometry, topology, and properties of physical objects; there may not be an exact final model for weather as characterized by atmospheric ambiguities. In the absence of exact knowledge, it is very likely that many aspects of the domain may not be observable in the software; moreover, a number of observations projected by the software constructed from approximate models may not reflect reality.

1.1.5   Communication Complexity

Due to the size, the large number of internal structures, and the heterogeneous nature of application domains, a group of people rather than a single person will be assigned the task of developing a software system. Each person may play one or more roles in the activities associated with the development process. It is important that people involved in different phases communicate among themselves without ambiguity. The medium of communication can be one or more of verbal, graphical, or textual. Sometimes, much of the information required during the early stages of software development is *tacit*. When natural language is used for "written" technical reports, it is difficult to precisely state all the essential attributes of the product under development. When specification is expressed in a natural language and the design contains graphical constructs, it becomes difficult to relate descriptions in different media. When people use different notations within one phase, or different notations are used for different phases, errors creep in due to semantic differences of the notation. When errors arise at early stages of the software life cycle, it is very likely that they remain undetected until later stages and get amplified in the development process. Several empirical studies have confirmed that errors made in the requirements analysis phase are indeed significant. Moreover, design errors triggered by errors in the requirements analysis phase are more difficult to detect and correct; in fact, they cannot be fixed without first identifying their source in the requirements and then correcting the source.

1.2   Software Specification

Can software complexity be controlled by any systematic technique? We answer this question in two parts: (1) a proper specification can control and adequately contain certain types of complexity; (2) without specification, software complexity is uncontrollable. The second part of the answer is justified by the remarks of Brooks [4]. To justify the first part of the answer, we discuss below "what is a specification" without demonstrating how it should be presented.

1.2.1   What Is a Specification?

According to Chambers 20th Century Dictionary, "specific" means "that pertaining to a particular species," "specify" means "to be specific," and "specification" is the "act of specifying." In physical sciences, terms such as "specific gravity," "specific heat," and "specific inductive capacity" are defined to convey particular properties and characterize the behavior of physical substances in any context of their usage. In engineering and in architecture, "specification" refers to a statement of particulars describing the structural and behavioral details of the product to be developed. In the context of software development, all of the above meanings for specification can be carried over. In particular, software specification denotes a precise description of the system objects, a set of methods to manipulate them, and a statement on their collective behavior for the duration of their existence in the system to be developed.

One of the main goals of software engineering is the production of software that successfully works in the environment where it is intended to be used. The development process of a large, complex software system necessitates the gathering and the management of a vast amount of data on the application domain, processes, people, and product descriptions. In order to cope with the numerous objects that arise and the enormous amount of information generated while managing them, *abstraction* and *decomposition* have been found to be useful tools. The principle of decomposition ensures that properties of the whole system follow from the properties of its parts. Abstraction principles, which are discussed in greater detail in Chapter 4, ensure that the specification has only key features, without a description on how they can be realized. For example, when several people work on a software project, decomposition and abstraction of tasks would bring forth precision and simplicity in expressing the interdependence and communication among objects.

Software life cycle models decompose the entire development process into a series of phases and associate a specific task with each phase. Although the boundaries and the ordering of these phases differ in different models, the specification activity in each phase produces a more *precise definition* of system attributes. Since *object* description, *properties* of the object, and *operations* must be dealt with as a whole for every object in the system during its entire evolution, we may regard specification as a multistage activity rather than a one-time activity.

Figure 1.1 represents a simplified life cycle model. After the first phase of requirements gathering and analysis, a *software requirements document* (SRD) is prepared. This serves as a *contract* between the customer and the supplier. The first level software specification based on the objectives stated in the SRD is a precise and unambiguous description of the *behavior* of the desired system in terms of externally observable functional characteristics. Constraints of the system, if any, can also be specified as properties of the system. These remain *independent* of any implementation or execution of the system. This first level specification is termed *behavioral specification*, shown as BS in Figure 1.1.

Following the behavioral specification, which describes WHAT is expected of the system, the next stage is to specify the *operational* characteristics and the *internal structure* of the system. This specification level contains *more details* than the behavioral specification; however, every care must be taken to ensure that external

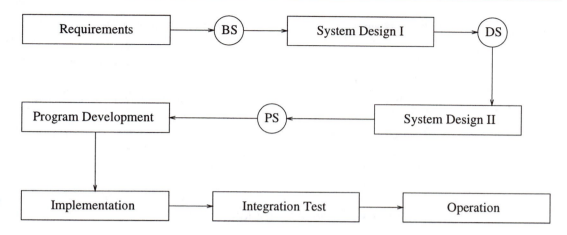

FIGURE 1.1. A simple life cycle model with specification phases.

behavior as defined earlier is preserved. This specification level, called *design specification* (DS), preserves the properties stated in the previous specification level, contains more details, probably motivated by certain needs, and provides mechanisms needed to produce such a behavior. We may view this specification as a more concrete description of the behavioral specification.

The first level design specification can be *refined* further by adding more and more details on data, action, control, and exception. Moreover, for each component in the design, interaction between components and component interfaces can be specified in more detail and further refined into a series of specifications. We consequently arrive at an interface specification and a detailed design specification, which can be implemented as a program. The implementation language and the hardware configuration for its installation are chosen at the interface specification stage. Thus the specification exercise encompasses more than one phase of the software life cycle. We must keep in mind that modifying existing specifications and/or including new specifications may become necessary during any stage of system evolution. Specifications are subject to validation to ensure that they remain faithful to the intended need, as expressed in the requirements document and as required by the usage context.

The essential properties that characterize specifications created during the software development cycle are summarized as follows:

1. It must be possible to define the observable behavior.
2. The interface of a software component must be precise and simple.
3. The behavior of the whole must be expressible in terms of the behavior of the parts. Stated otherwise, it must be possible to compose specifications.

4. It must be possible to develop a program from the detailed design specification.

5. The design specification must contain a description of all behaviors expressed by the behavioral specification.

6. It must be possible to test for conformance—that a program satisfies its specification.

7. It must be possible to subject a specification to rigorous analysis; for example, given a specification and a property, it must be possible to determine whether or not the property is a consequence of the specification.

1.2.2   How to Control Complexity?

The most common and effective technique for dealing with complexity is *abstraction*. The software development team does not have much control over environment and application domain complexities. Requirements may emerge during the software development process or when the software is operational. Domain experts and environmental scientists should provide support for reconstructing evolving requirements. Application domain models and knowledge-based support for environmental theories can also assist in reducing complexity at this level.

Software developers can deal with size and structural complexities through specifications that are precise and abstract. For example, to describe a collection of similar objects having some common attributes, one can use the notion of *sets*, without concern for the representation. Using quantified expressions, the developer can iterate over set members without resorting to any specific search procedure. Thus, the statement $\forall x \in X \bullet do\ f(x)$ describes a sequence of function computations for members of set X.

Modular decomposition techniques can be used to partition the world of objects. This allows us to understand the individual and the collective behavior of objects at a sufficiently high level of abstraction. Another approach is to use top-down functional decomposition with recursive definitions for abstracting the depth of a hierarchy in a structure chart. The depth of the hierarchy can be reduced by resorting to *incremental* modeling. In this approach, the developer creates only the most critical details and then expands the model with additional details to promote user understanding and system needs. Another effective means to deal with size and structural complexities is to *reuse* well-defined, well-understood, and well-tested software components. What is important here is the simplicity and correctness of interface specifications so that reusable components are best understood by examining their interfaces, without having to know how they are implemented.

Humans can follow organizational rules if they are clearly stated. However, rules for software development are subject to different interpretations. In order to ensure uniform interpretation of requirements, it is essential that the development team learns effective modes of communication that include precise notations to communicate different views for the same entity. Ad-hoc notations, natural language intercepted with graphics, and/or pseudocode are not sufficient to discharge the demands placed on a design team. With natural languages and graphics, it is very easy to miss some situations, initial and boundary cases, and exceptions.

1.2.3   A Critique of Natural Language Specification

Specification must be documented using a representation technique that can unequivocally be understood and acted upon by all software engineers involved in the production of software. The discussion in Section 1.2.1 underlies that specification is not a one-time activity, and clients of the specified product are different at different stages of the development cycle. There are several drawbacks to using an informal approach and a natural language description to specify software components intended for these clients. Natural languages are expressive but imprecise. It is possible to express any software property in a natural language, but the expression may be given different interpretations, or not understood at all. Natural language descriptions carry lot of noise, ambiguities, and contradictions, as pointed out by Meyer [11]. Noise refers to the usage of different words in a text to denote the same concept. For example, "non-empty sequence" of items is the same as "one or more" items. Although repetition is avoided in literary writing, in a technical document, observes Meyer, the same concept should be denoted by the same words, lest the reader be confused. Silence refers to undefined terms and undefined features of defined terms in a text. It is hard to analyze a natural language specification to detect this kind of error. Statements such as "event a happens after event b" is ambiguous, since the terms "happens" and "after" can be interpreted in more than one way. Another example is the usage of "up to" in the statement "an identifier can have up to 8 characters." Informal descriptions, such as diagrams, have no inherent semantics unless accompanied by precise annotations. After illustrating these pitfalls of natural language descriptions through the text processing example first developed by Naur [13] and subsequently corrected by Goodenough and Gerhart [7], Meyer shows how the specification can significantly be improved through reasonable use of more formal specifications. We take up the study of formal specifications in later chapters.

Exercises

1. Give a natural language description of the features and functionalities of any two text editors you have used. How many deficiencies, as described in the text and in Meyer's paper [11], are found in your natural language specification?

2. Take a recipe description from a cookbook. Determine the ambiguities, omissions, imprecision, and contradictions in it. How would you make it more precise? What environmental assumptions are necessary to implement the recipes ("bake the cookies," for example)?

3. Review a term project you have done and examine the stability of its design when a few of the requirements are changed. Are you able to do it from your design documentation and requirements specification? Explain the difficulties.

Bibliographic Notes

Complex software systems are created by the combined efforts of many people, and one person cannot have a thorough understanding of the interaction of the entire system. Hence, as pointed out by Brooks [4], one has to accept that there is no silver bullet in this area. The seminal book by Brooks [3] had a significant impact on software engineering development practices. The attitude of software developers has changed over the years, and now they are calling for more systematic approaches: more mathematics, science, and engineering in what they practice. This is described in the recent report [5] issued by the Computer Science Technology Board.

With regard to views on complexity and specifying software requirements for complex systems, Heninger et al. [8, 9] provide useful checklists. These two papers describe the difficulties encountered in writing requirements specification for large and complex systems and discuss the specification techniques that are used for making requirements precise, unambiguous, consistent, and complete. Myers [12] and Parnas [14] discusses complexity in the context of developing software for strategic applications and provides practical approaches to follow.

Alford [1] describes his Requirements Driven Development (RDD) method of system development based on a set of graphical and textual representations for capturing requirements and design. This method to systems engineering is supported by a set of tools for traceability analysis, to record design decisions, check consistency, and conduct reviews. It is believed that this method is widely practiced in industries.

A good critique of natural language specification has been given by Meyer [11]. This article explains the "seven sins" of a specifier in using a natural language, reviews the types of errors uncovered in published papers [7, 13], and proposes a formal specification approach. The message of this paper is that a natural language specification, even when corrected and cleaned up by experts, will have flaws.

References

[1] M. Alford, "SREM at the Age of Eight," *IEEE Computer*, Vol. 18, No. 4, April 1985, pp. 36–46.

[2] V.R. Basili, "Quantitative Software Complexity Models: A Panel Summary" in V.R. Basili (Ed.), *Tutorial on Models and Methods for Software Management and Engineering*, IEEE Computer Society Press, Los Alamitos, CA, 1980.

[3] F.P. Brooks, Jr., *The Mythical Man-Month: Essays on Software Engineering*, Addison-Wesley Publishing Company, Reading, MA, 1975.

[4] F.P. Brooks, Jr., "No Silver Bullet: Essence and Accidents of Software Engineering," *IEEE Computer*, Vol. 20, No. 4, April 1987, pp. 10–19.

[5] Computer Science Technology Board, "Scaling up: A Research Agenda for Software Engineering," *Communications of the ACM*, Vol. 33, No. 3, 1990, pp. 281–293.

[6] B. Curtis, S.B. Sheppard, P. Milliman, M.N. Borst, and T. Love, "Measuring the Psychological Complexity of Software Maintenance Tasks with the Halstead and McCabe Metrics," *IEEE Transactions on Software Engineering*, Vol. SE-5, No. 2, February 1979, pp. 96–104.

[7] J.B. Goodenough and S. Gerhart, "Towards a Theory of Test Data Selection Criteria," in R.T. Yeh (Ed.), *Current Trends in Programming Methodology*, Vol. 2, Prentice-Hall, Englewood Cliffs, NJ, 1977, pp. 44–79.

[8] K.L. Heninger, "Specifying Software Requirements for Complex Systems: New Techniques and Their Application," *IEEE Transactions on Software Engineering*, Vol. SE-6, No. 1, January 1989, pp. 2–12.

[9] K.L. Heninger, J.W. Kallander, J.E. Shore, and D.L. Parnas, "Software Requirements for the A-7E Aircraft," (second printing), NRL Memorandum Report No. 3876, Naval Research Laboratories, Washington, D.C., 1980.

[10] N.G. Leveson, "Software Safety in Embedded Computer Systems," *Communications of the ACM*, Vol. 34, No. 2, 1991, pp. 35–46.

[11] B. Meyer, "On Formalism in Specifications," *IEEE Software*, Vol. 2, No. 1, January 1985, pp. 6–26.

[12] W. Myers, "Can Software for the Strategic Defense Initiative ever be Error-free?" *IEEE Computer*, Vol. 19, No. 11, November 1986.

[13] P. Naur, "Programming in Action Clusters," *BIT*, Vol. 9, No. 3, 1969, pp. 250–258.

[14] D.L. Parnas, "Fighting Complexity," Invited Talk, *International Conference on Engineering Complex Computer Systems (ICECCS'95)*, Fort Lauderdale, Florida, November 1995.

2

Specification Activities

The previous chapter provides a general discussion of the different stages of specification in the software development process. It was assumed that the discrete steps of the development process have been well-defined. That is, the activities, deliverables, reviews, and analysis procedures associated with each step have already been established. It was suggested that a specification of the products and processes can be added to each step of such a well-defined development process. This chapter addresses specific issues that should be considered, activities that should be initiated, and the roles that are to be assumed when specifications are *formal* due to the integration of *formal methods* into the existing software life cycle process for a given project.

Formal methods refer to the use of techniques founded on mathematics, in particular on discrete mathematics and logic, in the representation of information necessary for the construction of software systems. The emphasis is not on the notations, but in their ability to adequately specify information. The techniques include syntactic and semantic analyses for specifications written in a formal specification language, traceability analyses, specification validation, and formal verification. These techniques can be applied to the products generated in each step of the development process.

A formal specification language is a mathematically based language, which has a well-defined syntax and semantics. Formal specifications written using a formal specification language provide abstract and precise descriptions of system behavior and properties. A formal specification may or may not be subject to the techniques of formal methods. The potential benefits of applying the techniques of formal methods to a specification include clarity, removal of ambiguity, and an understanding of system properties based on appropriate formal reasoning. We study formal systems, formal specification languages, and proof techniques in later chapters. At this stage, we want to study the impact of formal specification on the activities involved in every life cycle phase revolving around the triangular web *people, product,* and *process.*

2.1   Integrating Formal Methods into the Software Life Cycle

Formal methods can be applied to any or all steps in the software development process. Behavioral specification, design specification, and program specification can all be formalized. Formal specifications may be emulated to provide the developers an early view of system behavior. In addition, formal reviews of formal specifications to check consistency and coverage may be conducted.

It is necessary to determine the benefit-to-cost ratio of applying formal methods to a given project prior to integrating formal methods in the development process. The following technical factors [5] influence the benefit-to-cost ratio.

Type of Application

Formal methods may not be suitable for all types of applications. The characteristics of the problem domain and the complexity of their modeling should be evaluated to determine the suitability of applying formal methods to a project. If the project involves domains of high complexity, as discussed in the previous chapter, it may be advantageous to apply formal methods. However, problems over simple domains are usually less complex and do not warrant formal methods. In the mathematical domain, software requiring real-valued numerical calculations are difficult to formalize, whereas applications in logic and discrete mathematics lend to easier formalization.

Size and Structure

Size and structural complexities should be evaluated prior to adopting formal methods in a project. A measure of application size used in industries is KSLOC, thousands of source lines of code. The NASA report [5] gives the following statistics:

> Programs with size under 10 KSLOC have been subjected to verification. Most of the subsystems that have been subjected to design-level specification and verification are in the range 10 KSLOC to 100 KSLOC. However, precise size figures for requirements specification are lacking. A reasonable estimate is that formal specification of requirements have been attempted on systems that eventually lead to systems on the order of 100 KSLOC.

From these figures we may conclude that formal methods are effectively applied to systems of moderate size. It is also reported in [5] that formal methods cannot be applied in full to systems that use conventional programming techniques. To reap the full benefits of formal methods applied to large systems, they must be well-structured, and remain decomposable into well-defined components so that those of them that are critical may only be subjected to formal methods. When a system is composed of only loosely related components that lack cohesion, formalization activity cannot be expected to be fruitful. Greater benefits result when formal reasoning conducted on each component can be composed to draw conclusions on the composite behavior of the system.

Choice of Formal Method and Type of Analysis

The objectives for applying a formal method to a project must be clearly identified and documented. The development of safety-critical systems require the use of formal methods for specifying and analyzing critical components and their properties. An application which primarily uses the traditional structured development techniques may use formal methods only for the purpose of documenting data dictionaries. The objectives of these applications will have different impacts on the development process and consequently will influence different choices of formal methods.

Level of Formality

Methods such as manual inspection and walkthroughs conducted with the help of documents written in a natural language and supplemented by diagrams, equations, and pseudocode are not formal. Table-based specifications and diagrams used for object-oriented modeling [14] add more precision to natural language descriptions. These are only semi-formal notations. Specification languages such as Larch [7], VDM [10], and Z [15] have formal syntax and semantics, and also provide some mechanized support for syntax checking, semantic analysis, and proofs. Methods such as PVS [13], EVES [1], and HOL [6] provide support for developing formal specifications that can be subjected to rigorous semantic analysis and mechanized formal proof methods. From the objectives of a given project, criticality of the application, project size, and available resources, the degree of formality suitable for the project must be determined and a choice be made from the above possibilities.

Scope of Use

Formal methods can be used in one or more dimensions of the development process. The degree of formality may also be varied across the different dimensions.

1. *Selecting development stages:* Although formal methods can be applied to all stages of the development process, it is usual to apply it only selectively.

Depending upon the level of verification rigor appropriate to a project, a subset of requirements and high-level design may be chosen to undergo the techniques of a formal method. Integrating formal methods during the requirements and design stages has the advantage of enhancing the quality of the software. This is because errors can be detected during the early stages of the development process, and the precision injected early on leads to formal verification and validation. Due to the semantic gap between languages used for specification and proof and those used for programming, it is difficult to synthesize formal methods into the later stages of the development process. Tool support and good expertise are required to refine designs into programmable modules and conduct proofs on the correctness of refinements.

2. *Choice of components:* Higher levels of rigor may be called for to assess the quality of safety-critical components. To construct such components, formalism is not only necessary but a high degree of formality should be applied. Components that are not critical may be subjected to lower levels of rigor.

3. *System functionality:* A proof of correctness is required to establish that the system has the important properties required of it. Whenever the objectives of a project include such strict requirements, the functionalities of those components designed to meet such requirements should be formally verified.

Tool

It is not possible to apply formal methods with pencil and paper. To apply it with sufficient rigor, tool support is necessary. Since a tool may address one or more of the issues, developing a formal specification, syntax checking, semantic analysis, and theorem proving, the choice of tools for a project depends on all the factors discussed above.

2.2   Administrative and Technical Roles

Once a decision has been reached on adopting a formal method to a project, general guidelines can be put in place to implement this decision before the project begins. The guidelines include mechanisms for documentation standards for improved communication, configuration management, and reuse of specifications. When the existing development process has well-defined steps, formal methods can be inserted at relevant steps in the entire process or it can be applied on a small scale to some of the steps. A pilot study may also be done to integrate formal methods to understand the steps where it is most effective and train staff for these activities. An effective use of formal methods requires experts in application domain and people with formal methods expertise. People may have to be trained on the tools appropriate for the applications encountered in the project. Only well-trained staff will be able to choose the level of formality appropriate for an application. The roles and activities of the staff are identified below.

2.2.1   Specification Roles

Formal specifications are developed by a group of people who have a good understanding of the formal language used for the specification. A person may be the author, analyzer, user, or implementor for a specification unit. The author constructs the specification corresponding to a process or a product in a formal language. This activity involves a good understanding of language abstractions and the properties of the product or process. The analyzer demonstrates the inherence of desired properties in the specification. In particular, the analyzer resolves inconsistencies and demonstrates the coherence of the specification. A specification may be refined to include more information. Whenever a specification is refined, it is required to establish the satisfaction of the refined specification to its source. This can be done by an informal analysis; however, within a strict formal framework, a proof is required.

It is expected that the staff assigned for developing formal specifications have the expertise to translate the informally stated requirements into a formal text and act as advisors to users of the specification document. They are expected to field questions about tools, domain issues, and sufficiency of coverage, which arise during formalization and validation. Part of the role is also to help customers understand the formal documentation. This may be done through natural language expositions and graphical illustrations to express the meaning of formal constructs. In a typical walkthrough session, the specification staff shall demonstrate to the user that there exist requirements in the SRD corresponding to every formal specification unit and vice versa. The goal of such sessions is to have demonstrated to the user that the formal specification document fully captures the requirements stated in SRD. To earn the customer's confidence, the staff must develop and provide appropriate tools to the user for traceability and reuse of specifications.

A formal specification, however, is not a panacea. It will not, on its own, insure that no errors will be made, nor that the final product will be free of errors. Since errors in a specification will have a detrimental effect on all future stages of software development, the specification must be analyzed to eliminate all errors. There are two kinds of errors to look for: errors due to misuse of the specification language, and logical errors that incorrectly translate requirements. The role to be played here is to accumulate sufficient evidence to show that the formal specification is free of these two types of errors. This role, commonly known as *to validate*, must be played with the collaboration of the user. Ideally, the specification staff validate the specification by *executing* the specification in the presence of the customer.

Another important activity that the specification staff must undertake is to assist the test team in understanding and using the specification for designing functional tests for the product. Since, after validation, the specification contains expected and correct functionalities of the product, the test team has all required information for testing the final product. The main advantage in playing out this activity is that the large amount of work involved during *a posteriori* error detection is replaced by a more scientific effort spent *a priori* during the construction of software.

2.2.2 Design Roles

The role of a design engineer in a software development process is important. Design is concerned with constructing artifacts and assembling them together to produce the intended effect of a software product. The process of designing is inherently complex. It requires a combination of technical, intellectual, and cognitive skills. An object may be referred to as being "well-designed," when it excels the expectations in the context of its usage. In the absence of any scientific metric, the quality of a design is often assessed by attributes that cannot be quantified, such as user satisfaction.

Kapor [11] likens software designers to architects. The rationale is that architects have the overall responsibility for constructing buildings and engineers play a vital role in the process of construction. It is the architect who, upon receiving the requirements for constructing a house, produces a design that ultimately produces a "good" building that "pleases" the client. Engineers, taking directions from the architect, put things together by choosing components that are well-tested. Similarly, in software systems, the designer is the architect who receives the validated requirements specification and produces a design to meet the overall needs of the user. The selection of various components to construct the system begins during the design process.

Although the design of the system begins with system requirements analysis, the design activity takes shape only after the components to be used in building the system are identified. The design activity proceeds according to project guidelines and technical considerations planned for integrating formal methods in this stage. A good design is one that can withstand changes in the requirements and the environment. Towards achieving a good design, the design team may have to periodically meet with clients and specification staff to confirm changes in design caused by changes in specification. Thus, design staff play a pivotal role in software construction—they interact with clients, specification staff, and programming teams.

If the requirements specification and the design are both expressible in the formal language of the chosen formal method, then one can attempt to formally prove that the design satisfies the requirements. The multistage specification framework is an endeavor in this direction. The formal design paradigm incorporating formal proofs, which originated with the seminal works of Floyd [4] and Hoare [9], is relevant to the role of design staff.

A design usually contains more technical details than a requirements specification. It includes detailed design of components, and a user-interface design. Since design activity involves understanding requirements, observing how the design will be used by the clients of the system, and imagining what it is like while designing it, we may conclude that some heuristics beyond the tool support afforded by a formal method may be necessary in design construction.

2.2.3 Programming Roles

A programmer who assumes the programming role takes the designer's output and writes programs consistent with the detailed design. It is the programmer's responsibility to ensure both correctness and efficiency in translating the design decisions into source code. The basic assumption of the programmer is that every aspect of the design is implementable. However, it may happen that certain aspects of the design are difficult or impossible to implement. The programmer brings those design aspects that cannot be implemented to the attention of the design and specification staff. The rationale for unimplementable design aspects is traced back to the requirements and rectified.

Programs, formal specifications, and formal design documents are *formal* objects. The behavior of a computer is formal, in the sense that syntactic structures are manipulated according to well-defined semantics. These structures are self-contained so that every description is explicit in the respective formal language, although a design language may be different from the programming language used for its implementation. Therefore, some translation is necessary to obtain a program from its design specification. This activity often requires human intervention and consequently may not be described in a strictly formal manner.

The programmer and the test engineer who developed specification-based testing collaborate in testing programs. The outcome of testing determines whether or not a program correctly interprets the requirements of the customer. In case of errors, the specification team is brought in for consultation. In particular, the programmer does not make changes until the specification staff and the design team work out a new design.

Exercises

1. Explain how you would use the informal specification of a text editor given in Meyer [12] to generate test cases.

2. Using the diagrams in Rumbaugh et al. [14], give a design for the text editor satisfying the specification in Meyer [12]. Do you consider your design formal or informal? Give reasons.

Bibliographic Notes

The factors to be considered for choosing specific tasks for formal methods application are discussed in the NASA report [5]. This report outlines the technical and administrative considerations that must be reviewed before integrating formal methods into a development process. The report states that for an effective application of formal methods to a project, the team responsible for applying formal methods must be trained in formal methods and tools. An understanding of the activities, skills, and responsibilities associated with the roles involved in software development using formal methods is essential for the successful integration of formal methods into the development process.

Analysis and interpretation of formal specifications are enhanced with the help of tools. Tools for VDM and Z are provided by a variety of sources and are not integrated into a single toolset. See the VDM web page

(file://hermes:ifad.dk/pub/docs/vdm.html)

and Z web page

(http://www.comlab.ox.ac.uk/archive/z.html)

for details. For Larch specifications, Guttag et al. [7] describes a syntax checker and a theorem prover. Larch Prover (LP) is a proof assistant incorporating several proof techniques for rewrite-rule theory. EVES [1], and PVS [13] are more specialized tools allowing full semantic analysis and mechanized proof procedures. In addition to the automatic deduction component, EVES provides a number of commands to direct the theorem prover. PVS provides an integrated environment for the analysis and development of formal specifications. Tool components include parser, type checker, browser, specification libraries, and integrated proof checker.

Dick and Faivre [3] give a good introduction to black-box testing based on VDM specifications. Hierons [8] discusses a method to generate test cases from Z specifications. This method rewrites Z specifications to a form from which test cases can be generated and the testing process can be controlled. However, no tool support exists for conducting black-box testing based on formal specifications.

Two excellent treatises on design are the book by Winograd [16], which is a collection of articles showing the diverse perspectives of software design, and the book by Dasgupta [2], which explores the logic and methodology of design from the computer science perspective.

References

[1] D. Craigen, S. Kromodimoeljo, I. Meisels, B. Pase, and M. Saaltnik, "EVES: An Overview," *VDM'91: Formal Software Development Methods*; published as S. Prehn

and W.S. Toetenel (Eds.), *Lecture Notes in Computer Science*, Vol. 551, Springer-Verlag, Noordwijkerhout, The Netherlands, October 1991, pp. 389–405.

[2] S. Dasgupta, *Design Theory and Computer Science*, Cambridge Tracts in Computer Science, Cambridge University Press, Cambridge, England, 1991.

[3] J. Dick and A. Faivre, "Automating the Generation and Sequencing of Test Cases from Model-based Specifications," *FME93: Industrial-Strength Formal Methods, Formal Methods Europe*; published as J.C.P. Woodcock and P.G. Larsen (Eds.), *Lecture Notes in Computer Science*, Vol. 670, Springer-Verlag, April 1993, pp. 268–284.

[4] R.W. Floyd, "Assigning Meaning to Programs," *Mathematical Aspects of Computer Science*, American Mathematical Society, Providence, RI, 1967.

[5] *Formal Methods Specification and Verification Guidebook for Software and Computer Systems: Volume I Planning and Technology Insertion*, NASA Report NASA-GB-002-95, Release 1.0, July 1995.

[6] M.J.C. Gordon and T.F. Melham (Eds.), *Introduction to HOL*, Cambridge University Press, Cambridge, England, 1993.

[7] J.V. Guttag, J.J. Horning, with S.J. Garland, K.D. Jones, A. Modet, and J.M. Wing, *Larch: Languages and Tools for Formal Specifications*, Springer-Verlag, New York, NY, 1993.

[8] R.M. Hierons, "Testing from a Z Specification," *Software Testing, Verification and Reliability*, Vol. 7, 1997, pp. 19–33.

[9] C.A.R. Hoare, "An Axiomatic Approach to Computer Programming," *Communications of the ACM*, Vol. 12, No. 10, 1969, pp. 576–583.

[10] C.B. Jones, *Systematic Software Development Using VDM (second edition)*, Prentice-Hall International (UK), 1990.

[11] M. Kapor, "A Software Design Manifesto," in T. Winograd (Ed.), *Bringing Design to Software*, ACM Press, New York, NY, 1996, pp. 1–9.

[12] B. Meyer, "On Formalisms in Specifications," *IEEE Software*, Vol. 2, No. 1, January 1985, pp. 6–26.

[13] S. Owre, J.M. Rushby, and N. Shankar, "PVS: A Prototype Verification System," in D. Kapur (Ed.), *Proceedings of the Eleventh International Conference on Automated Deduction (CADE)*, Saratoga, NY, June 1992; published as *Lecture Notes in Artificial Intelligence*, Vol. 607, Springer-Verlag, New York, NY, pp. 748–752.

[14] J. Rumbaugh, M. Blaha, W. Pramerlani, F. Eddy, and W. Lorenson, *Object-oriented Modeling and Design*, Prentice-Hall, Englewood Cliffs, NJ, 1991.

[15] J.M. Spivey, *Understanding Z: A Specification Language and its Formal Semantics*, Cambridge University Press, Cambridge, England, 1988.

[16] T. Winograd, *Bringing Design to Software*, ACM Press, New York, NY, 1996.

3

Specification Qualities

Specifications arise from a need and are used to fulfill that need. A fair discussion of the principles of specification evolves around three fundamental questions: *Why specification? What to specify?* and *How to specify?* The answers to these questions lead to a resolution of the set of attributes of specification languages. The quality of a specification document written using a specification language with the right set of attributes should also be assessed. Since a specification can be regarded as a predicate whose truth value depends on a set of acceptable behaviors, a specification is neither inherently wrong nor perfectly correct; a specification is either relevant and consistent or irrelevant with respect to the stated purpose. In addition, a specification must be *understandable, verifiable*, and *maintainable* in order to be useful. This chapter explores ways of recognizing these traits in a specification through answers to two questions: What principles govern specifications? and What are the attributes of a specification language?

3.1 Principles of Software Specifications

A software engineer is motivated by several factors to specify a software product or a process:

- To succintly state that a property holds
- To precisely describe the interface of a component
- To contain design complexity
- To analyze hidden behaviors
- To demonstrate that all required behaviors are inherent in the design

- To localize the effects of change
- To prove that a final product meets its requirements

The starting point for a specification engineer is to get a firm grasp over the objects of the application domain that need to be represented in the system. This addresses the issue *"What to specify?"* Ideally, the customer is expected to have a good understanding of the application domain and is expected to develop the initial set of requirements in collaboration with the specification engineer. However, it invariably happens that the customer cannot provide a good view of the application domain. The customer usually has an imprecise notion of the requirements and may have a naive view of what is feasible. The vagueness is partly attributed to the complexity of the application domain itself. Unless the customer is an expert in the application domain, an adequate view of the domain cannot be conceptualized. For example, one possible view of a self-service gas station is a gas pump with its display unit and a cashier who monitors and receives payments. This view is consistent with the observation of a user who wants to fill up gas at the gas station. However, there is another broader view that includes the above view and takes into account storage tanks for gas, an accounting system, and an employee payroll. This extended view is essential for the management of the gas station. The proper choice of the application domain view determines the set of functionalities included in the behavioral specification.

The cycle of activities involved in deciding what to specify at the behavioral specification level is comprised of the following:

- Gather domain-specific knowledge.
- Develop notions to be expressed.
- Formulate an entity-relationship (E-R) diagram in which the notions are entities, properties are the attributes of entities, and relationships are the labeled arcs joining the entities; Figure 3.1 is a description of gas station system entities.
- Identify primitive notions, derived notions, and laws for deriving them.
- Check whether the chosen view of the application domain is broad enough to infer all required behavior; if not, enlarge the view and repeat the steps.

When the customer, domain expert, and software engineer iterate through this cycle of activities, a good understanding of the system to be designed will emerge. As the requirements become more and more understandable, it also becomes easier for the software engineer to examine whether adequate test sets can be generated from the specification. When there are doubts about adequate functional testability, the requirements and consequently the domain view may have to be changed with the agreement of the customer. The entire process is repeated with the revised view.

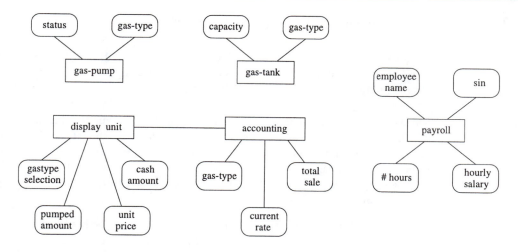

FIGURE 3.1. Entity relationship diagram for one view of gas station.

The next stage is to decide *"How to specify?"* The behavioral specification is a strict description of WHAT is desired and should not be biased towards HOW to realize it. Its descriptions must be definitional and not operational in character. The desired effects of each task must be enumerated with appropriate assertions restraining their validity. That is, a desired effect must be described as an assertion and not as a computation. Although behavioral specification is not imposing any specific realization, it must contain adequate information to generate possible behaviors among which an implementation can be found. This principle holds for every specification in the life cycle. In spite of following the iterative process to choose the right view of the application domain, because of the complexity of the environment, the chosen view may not adequately satisfy the goals. In such a situation, the behavioral specification will inevitably be the result of an incomplete or inappropriate view. Test procedures should be aware of this incompleteness and the possibility that the specification may be modified to reflect changing views.

In summary, the answers to *why*, *what*, and *how* lead to defining the notions of *view, model,* and *behavior* in a specification. A view is the result of an abstraction. A model exhibits the behavior of the object of interest. The observable behavior is derived only through a deductive mechanism within the formalism that underlies a specification language. A model may not exhibit the full behavior of the object of interest. The usefulness of a model depends on the choice of entities and properties in the model. From this discussion, it follows that a specification language must support abstractions to create the model and provide a means of predicting and observing behavior. In order for humans to learn and communicate about evolving system requirements, the specification language must remain easily understandable.

3.2   Attributes for Specification Languages

Each engineering field has developed its own formal system; however, the basis of all engineering formalisms is mathematics. Engineering is result-oriented and consequently, the end product is tangible. The specification of a tangible product and the product itself exist in two different media. For example, the specification of a bridge is an annotated diagram with measurements accompanied by mathematical equations supporting stress analysis. Software being invisible and intangible is hard to grasp by the mind. Both a software product and its specification belong to the same medium, namely the descriptive medium consisting of symbolic languages. The two objects may even use the same symbol to denote different entities; their only distinguishing feature is *semantics*.

Both a specification and the program that it specifies portray the behavior of some phenomena; the only difference between the portrayals is with respect to the level of detail. Whereas a specification describes a property through a desired effect, a program conforming to this specification achieves the desired effect, thereby demonstrating the presence of the desired property in the final product. This subtle relationship between a specification and a program satisfying it should be maintained during all the stages of software development.

Specification languages require formal semantics in order to produce a unique meaning for an expression. Semantics relates to assigning *meaning* (or *value*) to language constructs. Using the semantics of a language, one can make precise statements and assert certain properties about a specification written in the language. The question that arises at this stage is the following: Is there a language and its associated formal semantics such that formal descriptions in the language can be regarded as either specifications or programs? If one exists, its use at the different stages of system development eliminates the need for the software engineer to remember the particulars of several languages. The drawback of such a language is that the software engineer will have the tendency to introduce implementation-oriented details too early, unless the language itself effectively forbids this at an early stage and hence bias the specification towards a specific implementation. However, by controlling the level of detail and carefully choosing the declarative constructs in the language, a specification can be constructed. When a specification written in the language is enriched with implementation-oriented data structures and control constructs in the language, the specification becomes a program in that language. The distinction between a program and a specification in such languages is one of detail. The concept of *wide-spectrum language* was introduced by Bauer [4, 5] to serve this purpose. Declarative constructs in the language are used to write specifications, and subsequent refinements towards concrete programs are obtained through binding and transformation. In essence, a wide-spectrum language consists of a base language plus syntactic extensions for various high-level constructs. The two-level framework is based on formal semantics. It is machine-representable and interpretable. Programs in the verification system EVES [6] are specified, implemented, and proved using the wide-spectrum language Verdi, a variant of classical set theory and an imperative programming language. One drawback with wide-spectrum languages is that they require many diverse language constructs to be defined within the same language consistently.

LISP programs are declarative and consequently may be regarded as specifications. Such specifications, considered as *functional programs*, are executable. Historically, LISP has proved itself most useful in the task of creating working versions (prototypes) of complex systems. The language can be learned easily and can be used effectively in describing complex problems and their solutions. Nondeterminism, selection, and recursion are expressible in LISP. Moreover, LISP provides a small set of powerful constructs that can be combined to produce an abstract program. Such an abstract program is a high-level model with no consideration of control, sequencing, or choice implied in an implementation. Functions written in this style have no side effects. They correspond to the mathematical notion of a function, namely, "a function produces the same value whenever invoked with the same arguments." A specification in pure LISP is easy to construct, understand, and modify. It is easy to construct because of the small number of language constructs and rules. It is easy to understand because every use of a variable, within certain limits, yields the same value. This property, known as *referential transparency*, is a fundamental convention in the use of mathematical functions and expressions. Consequently, complex data flow analysis is not required to determine what value a particular usage of that variable represents. This provides a conducive foundation for reasoning and verification. Another major advantage of pure LISP specification is its declarative nature—there is no overspecification. In particular, unnecessary sequentiality will not be expressed. This, combined with nondeterminism, facilitates the introduction of parallelism in lower-level programs.

In spite of several attractive features, neither a wide-spectrum language nor LISP can adequately serve as a language for specifying software systems. They both lack *encapsulation, modularity,* and *extensibility*, which are essential to contain design complexity.

In contrast to LISP, imperative programming languages require algorithmic details, execution sequence, and data structure representations to be explicit in program descriptions. The program formally states a particular solution to the problem and may even state how the solution should be delivered to the user. We can consider a program as a model expressing the behavior of some entity — an algebraic formula, the square root function, a banking system, or an animation. Even at this level, the program is a behavioral specification of its execution. Despite being a formal object, the program is a string of symbols providing a concrete representation of its modeled behavior. The syntactic structure of the program can be analyzed by a *parser* and a *parse tree* showing the structure of expressions, and their relationships can be obtained. In turn, the parse tree becomes an *abstract* representation of the program. So, programming languages are also specification languages at a certain level of abstraction. However, they cannot be used as specification languages throughout the software development process, for the following reasons:

1. Procedural programming languages do not separate functionality from implementation.

2. There is no referential transparency in imperative programming.

3. The data manipulated by a program must have a particular representation. If the representation is changed, a different program may be required. The representation of data has consequences on its access.

4. Both data and control spaces are deterministic. For example, the semantic interpretation of the abstract parse tree of a program can generate behavior and execution sequences only if data and control information are complete. An analysis of the program with partial description is impossible.

5. Even if a program is modular and parameterized, strict type conformance may prevent the program from being extendible or reusable.

6. Over-specification is an aftermath in programming languages.

From the above discussion and the specification activities discussed in Chapter 2, we conclude that specification languages embody the following characteristics:

- *Formalism:* The language is based on well-defined syntax and a formal semantics for constructs.

- *Abstraction:* The language has powerful primitives for defining and manipulating data at the logical level. Logical data definition should not imply any particular data representation. The language provides the definition of objects independent of the notions of "value" or "boundary." It should be possible to define an object by the set of associations through which it interacts with other objects. The language provides abstract operations that create, destroy, access, and relate objects.

- *Modularity:* The language provides constructs for extending a specification through *enrichment* and *composition*. These features allow the construction of large and complex specifications by assembling smaller specifications; they also support modular design.

- *Modeling:* The language supports a model to maintain objects, their interactions, and the consequential system laws. The model defines the actions that an active object is allowed to perform.

- *Nondeterminism:* The language may provide nondeterministic constructs for indirect data access and unrestricted choice from a specific list of actions. Descriptive reference for data is a nondeterministic construct in which the reference to an object is made through a list of attributes.

- *Inference mechanism:* The language allows inference of the behavior of objects in the model using system laws and defined actions. The inference mechanism evaluates well-formed expressions in the language and provides meaning to the behavior displayed by the system.

- *Historical references:* The language may provide facilities for time-dependent object or action specification. This capability requires the ability to specify *time*, and associate time with object operations. By suitable extension, it may be possible to describe and analyze sequences of system states and further reason about temporal system properties at some or all future states.

Most specification languages include a subset of these attributes. Consequently, it may be impossible to express all the properties or behaviors of a system in a certain specification language. The language may simply be too weak, or it may not have the necessary constructs for specifying a particular feature of a particular system. It is therefore essential to diligently choose an appropriate language to specify the problem on hand. When a language having sufficiently many attributes is chosen and applied to the development process, the resulting benefit is that the specification can be rigorously assessed for the following qualities:

1. *Type correctness:* The specification is free of syntax and semantic errors.

2. *Sufficient completeness:* Everything that needs to be described is expressed within the confinement of the specification language.

3. *Precision:* The specification precisely and accurately portrays the characteristics of the problem.

4. *Consistency:* The specification is consistent; that is, the specification does not contain contradictory expressions.

5. *Operational completeness:* Every operation in the specification eventually leads to an implementation. In other words, there is a value, a result, or an observable state change for every specified action.

6. *Logical reasoning:* It is possible to conduct logical calculations from the specification to ascertain whether certain properties are consequences of the requirements, and whether requirements have been interpreted correctly in the derivation of design and programs.

Exercises

1. Construct a view of an automated banking system using E-R diagram. What entities should be represented and what are their essential attributes?

2. Why can C++ not be considered a specification language? What subset of C++, if any, can serve as a specification language? Illustrate with examples.

Bibliographic Notes

The classic work on determining the goals of specification languages is [3]. Major motivation in writing this chapter came from this work. Several requirements specification languages developed in the 70s are described in [1]. These include

- the language of Structured Analysis (SA) which was combined with a development methodology to form the Structured Analysis and Design Technique (SADT)
- PSL/PSA developed in the mid-1960s which was based on database facilities for exploring system requirements and validating various relationships and
- SRM, built on PSL/PSA rational database core, with added specification capability based on finite state machine and Petri net.

The Program Development System (PDS) [7], based on EL1 (Extensible Language 1), is similar in spirit to Bauer's work [4] on wide-spectrum languages. Their major difference is their design principle—PDS provides an integrated prototyping environment, and Bauer's language leads to an implementation. Several notions on (in)completeness in specifications are examined in [2]. This paper gives a classification of incompleteness based on the potential sources of errors in specifications.

References

[1] R.J. Abbot and D.K. Moorehead, "Software Requirements and Specifications: A Survey of Needs and Languages," *The Journal of Systems and Software*, 1981, pp. 297–316.

[2] V.S. Alagar and D. Kourkopoulos, "(In)completeness in Specifications," *Information and Software Technology*, Vol. 36, No. 6, 1994, pp. 331–342.

[3] R. Balzer and N. Goldman, "Principles of Good Software Specification and Their Implications for Specification Languages," National Computer Conference, Chicago, IL, 1981, pp. 393–400.

[4] F.L. Bauer, "Programming as an Evolutionary Process," *Proceedings of the Second International Conference on Software Engineering*, San Francisco, CA, 1976, pp. 223–234.

[5] F.L. Bauer, M. Bauer, P. Partsch, and P. Pepper, "Report on a Wide-spectrum Language for Program Specification and Development," Technical Report TUM-18104, Technical University, Munich, Germany, May 1981.

[6] D. Craigen, *The Verdi Reference Manual*, Technical Report TR-90-S429-09, Odyssey Research Associates, Ottawa, Canada, February 1990.

[7] A. Klausner and T.E. Konchan, "Rapid Prototyping and Requirements Specification Using PDS," in N. Gehani and A.D. McGettrick (Eds.), *Software Specification Techniques*, Addison-Wesley Publishing Company, Reading, MA, 1980.

4

Abstraction

The concept of abstraction is imprecise. It cannot possibly be defined, but the notion of abstraction can be explained, illustrated, modeled, and understood. The goal of this chapter is to discuss the different kinds of abstraction that have been proposed in mathematics and computer science and to emphasize the necessity of abstractions and difficulty of bringing out abstraction for software engineering.

4.1   What Is Abstraction?

Some of the common forms for communicating our thoughts are speech, text, and graphics. Of course there are other means of communications such as sign language. Thoughts are *abstract* and exist in a subtle abstract medium. Spoken words, textual writings, and drawings are concrete expressions of thoughts. Abstraction is inherent to human nature. The issues involved in developing an abstraction can be summarized as follows. Spoken words, textual writings, and drawings denoting the same object can be traced back to one thought. In other words, abstraction is a *one-to-many* map. The medium in which an abstract object is specified has more constraints. For example, the syntax and semantics of the language used to describe the object impose certain constraints on the description. Consequently, representational *details are ignored* in abstractions. Finally, an abstraction cannot be fully understood by an observer unless the context in which the object originates is properly depicted. That is, abstraction implies *generality* and exists in an idealized mental state of the creator of the abstraction.

The need to create abstraction has existed for a long time. Abstraction has enabled philosophers, mathematicians, and scientists to capture essential features pervading several phenomena in abstract concepts. In modern times, engineers and business experts have realized that abstraction is a vital tool in coping with the design of large complex systems. The principal advantages of abstraction in software engineering are the attainments of *simplicity, generality,* and *precision* in the software development process, and *completeness* and *correctness* in the resulting product.

4.2   Abstractions in Mathematics

Abstractions by themselves have very little practical value until they are contextually related to real-world entities. In mathematics, abstract notations and concepts are invented to generalize and unify more concrete concepts. For example, in "abstract algebra" all the unifying properties of real numbers, complex numbers, and rational numbers are studied under the banner "fields"; the abstract generalization of algebraic properties of integers is studied under the title "rings." These are idealized abstractions. Real numbers correspond to mental idealizations of a mathematician; there is no tangible manifestation of a real number. The essential property of real numbers that states "in between any two real numbers there is a real number" cannot realistically hold for angles, distances, and time intervals that we measure in practice.

As opposed to idealized abstractions, there are mathematical abstractions that provide precision and expressivity to scientific and engineering descriptions. Concepts such as point, line, and natural numbers are abstractions of the physical concepts "atom," "light rays," and "age." Vectors and tensors are abstractions used to deal with force and elasticity in engineering. These kinds of abstraction serve as *mathematical models* for certain aspects of real world phenomena.

4.3   Fundamental Abstractions in Computing

The three most fundamental abstract concepts in computing are *algorithm, Turing machines,* and *computability.* An algorithm is an idealization of a systematic mechanical process. The concept can be traced back to as far as the time of Euclid (300 B.C.). It is remarkable that such a mechanical procedure had been conceptualized several centuries before computers were invented. In spite of its antiquity, the concept of algorithm came to be understood in a more universal fashion only after Alan Turing (1937) described this computational abstraction with the *Turing machine.*

A Turing machine is a piece of abstract mathematics and does not bear any resemblance to a physical machine. This *abstract machine* is obtained by ignoring all structural and physical properties of computing devices and focusing only on the common useful functionalities of these devices. Turing invented this abstraction to solve Hilbert's tenth problem characterized by the question "Does there exist a general mechanical procedure that can solve any well-defined mathematical problem stated in a suitable format?" Turing gave a *specification* for stating the components of abstract machines and the rules governing the operations that can be performed on the machines corresponding to stated problems. Following the specification mechanically for any specific problem, the Turing machine for solving that problem can be realized. For example, Turing machines for performing arithmetic operations, symbolic comparisons, or any other complicated task can be constructed from a Turing specification, provided that these tasks can be described within the Turing abstraction framework. By composing such constructions, Turing specified a universal machine that can simulate the behavior of any particular Turing machine. Finally, Turing showed that there is no mechanical procedure for deciding whether or not the universal Turing machine stops. The conclusion arrived at is that there can be no *one* algorithm applicable to *all* problems, nor for *all* Turing machines and for *all* their input. Thus, Turing concluded that Hilbert's tenth problem has no solution. This conclusion has a profound impact on related mathematical issues. For computer scientists and engineers, the significant implications are the following:

- Abstraction leads to insight for a family of problems and a class of algorithms.
- Abstraction is the basis for specification.
- Simple solutions can be composed to obtain a result of far-reaching consequences.

The specification of a Turing machine uses terms such as "tape" and "internal states" that seem to correspond to the magnetic tape and the states of a real computer. This analogy helps us define a sequence of abstract machines $(m_0, m_1, \ldots, m_k)$. Each abstract machine consists, as in the case of Turing machines, of a set of states and transformations for affecting state changes. In a programming language, the state is the set of program variables and the transformations are the statements affecting the states. Thus, Turing machines are not only abstract machines, but they also serve as abstract models of programming languages and operational models of the algorithm concept.

The concepts abstract machine, abstract program, abstract propramming language, specification, and algorithm are all related to one another. Moreover, the concept of *computability* formulated by the logician Alonzo Church [1] is also related to the above concepts. The notion of "mechanical procedure" is fully abstracted in Church's thesis. The computability notion is a powerful functional and data abstraction that is achievable through "lambda calculus." Using this notion, abstract programs can be written as functions. The effect of these functions are derived from the rules of lambda calculus.

To capture computational behavior in a layer unconstrained by considerations of a machine architecture, Church considered a universe of objects called *functions* and provided a syntax for writing them. The arguments of functions are themselves functions. That is, functions and data are treated with no distinction. There exists a set of rewriting rules for manipulating function applications. Thus $f = gh$ implies that the result of the function g applied to the function h is another function f. This extends to self-application of a function. So, the lambda-calculus approach demonstrates the effect of recursion without explictly writing recursive equations.

The Greek letter λ (lambda) is used to denote the abstraction of a function from the argument used to evaluate it. The letter x immediately following λ is a dummy variable in the expression $\lambda x \cdot f(x)$, and lambda binds this variable with its occurrences within its scope. That is, x is a place-holder into which any other entity (e.g., function) may be substituted.

Thus, the notation $\lambda x \cdot f(x)$ abstracts the function f, which when acting on an argument a in the domain of f yields $f(a)$. That is,

$$(\lambda x \cdot f(x))(a) = f(a),$$

and consequently $\lambda x \cdot f(x) = f$. This captures the *function* for a range of values of the *datum* x; in Church's theory, the datum is viewed as a function. Similarly, $\lambda f \cdot f(x)$ abstracts the datum x and allows the set of functions to vary. Thus, lambda expressions provide both function and data abstraction. For the expression $f(x)$, the lambda binding serves both syntactic and semantic roles. It states what is to remain *fixed* and what is allowed to vary. Because both syntax and semantics are succintly conveyed, the lambda notation is formal and function application becomes a mechanical procedure.

The notation $\lambda x \cdot f(x)$ gives rise to abstraction by parameterization at the program level. For example, the expression $\lambda x \cdot (x^3)$ abstracts the "cubing" function for which there is no standard mathematical notation. However, if we set $C = \lambda x \cdot (x^3)$, then $C(a) = a^3$, $C(a+2) = (a+2)^3 = a^3 + 6a^2 + 12a + 8$. So we can interpret C to be the body of a *procedure* that evaluates the cube of its argument, and x to be its *formal parameter*. We can move towards more concrete notions by requiring the values of x to be integers and write the cubing function for integers by the lambda expression $\lambda x :$ integer $\cdot (x^3)$.

As remarked earlier, the power of lambda calculus lies in its ability to treat all objects as functions. A function can be composed with itself in a nested function. For example, the expression $\lambda f \cdot \lambda x \cdot f(f(x))$ abstracts x first and then abstracts f. As a consequence, it denotes a function which when applied to arguments g and a produces $g(g(a))$. Let us call this function TWO; that is,

$$\begin{aligned}
\text{TWO} &= \lambda f \cdot \lambda x \cdot f(f(x)), \\
(\text{TWO}(g))(a) &= \lambda x \cdot g(g(x))(a) \\
&= g(g(a)).
\end{aligned}$$

If $g = C$, then $(\mathrm{TWO}(C))(a) = C(C(a)) = C(a^3) = (a^3)^3 = a^9$.

Using these abstractions, Church showed that every mechanical operation done in a Turing machine can also be done by using a suitable lambda expression. Hence, Church's notion of computability, which is functional, is the same as that of Turing's mechanical operation which is operational. This establishes a fundamental relationship between machines and functions.

4.4 Abstractions for Software Construction

The abstraction process contributes mostly to the activities of system modeling, specification building, system design, and programming. Because of the heterogeneous nature of objects involved in software development process, no uniform method of abstraction can be practiced in software engineering. According to Jackson [2],

> Abstractions are inverses of interpretations and provide a bridge between the informal domain and the abstract machine. The bridge must be carefully sited and chosen as narrow as possible.

In general, abstractions in software engineering are more difficult to create and apply.

During the initial stages of system design, the application domain and the environment where the software is to function have to be understood. The initial system specification therefore requires problem and environment abstractions. At this stage, the *essential* properties must be identified and *unnecessary* details must be ignored. Although this is the most conventional meaning of abstraction, the interpretation of essential—as opposed to irrelevant—varies among software engineers. The issues to be studied include

- What entities and which properties of the entities should be abstracted?
- How a chosen entity is abstracted?
- What aspects cannot be abstracted and should be left to human interpretation?

The producer and the consumer arrive at a conceptual boundary around the environment and problem domain so that the abstraction takes place within this boundary. Consequently, this boundary limits the functionalities and the performance of the proposed system. For example, assume the environment to include engineers, robotic assembly lines, administrative staff, and showroom personnel for an airplane manufacturing company. An engineer working on the assembly line is concerned with the capabilities of the engine, including its size and performance, the brakes, the instrumentation panel, weather monitoring and navigation systems, and the aerodynamics of the body of the airplane. These correspond to an engineer's abstraction of the airplane. The abstractions of a pilot include communication systems, shape, and orientation of seats and brakes. A salesperson will choose seat color, seat adjustments, manufacturing date, and payload capacity as the abstractions of the airplane. For an administrative officer, the people who work in the company become the objects of interest. So, abstractions include employee name, employee identification, and employee salary. These abstractions should be represented in the formalism of the chosen specification language.

The chosen abstraction of the environment, called the view, characterizes the domain for subsequent study. The choice limits the information available in succeeding stages of the software development process. The critical consequence of this choice is a form of *incompleteness* — that is, the system would not be able to provide information on aspects that have not been included in this view.

Having abstracted the *entities* of the application domain, the next step is to explicitly state the relationship among the entities and their properties. This abstraction process is referred to as *building models and theories*. The next chapter discusses formal models and theories. The behavioral specification is the result of extending this abstraction process.

Abstraction is also essential in deriving design specification and program specification. Appropriate notations must be carefully chosen for design and implementation. As mentioned in Chapter 3, specification languages must support suitable constructs to distinguish a specification from its implementation. In practice, function abstraction leads to parameterized procedures, while abstracting data leads to *classes* of object. Function and data abstractions determine different paradigms for programming associated with partitioning a computation into various reusable parts. When function abstraction is predominant, it turns out that subsequent layers of abstraction are to be created so that each layer realizes the abstract actions of the previous layer; that is, details of actions are added at subsequent levels. With data abstraction prevailing, data objects are refined by adding more and more representational details. When operational details of functions or representational details of a data are added, we are effectively adding more and more instructions to an abstract machine.

Many system requirement specifications can be presented as a set of sequentially ordered steps of action. Each step is simple enough to be comprehended individually. In each step, the state of the system is transformed by the performance of an action. The overall behavior of the system is understood by following the steps in the sequence. Such a sequence of steps is called a *thread of control*. A process is an abstraction of a single thread of control. Thus a *process abstraction* can be viewed as the superposition of control abstraction on function and data abstractions.

Process abstraction describes *what an abstract machine does* and not *how it works*. Control abstractions must be included to explain the relevant flow of information. We reckon generality of control constructs in two ways:

1. Support familiar programming language control constructs (such as *for, if then else, while,* and *repeat*) over arbitrary data types; and

2. Provide facilities for defining new constructs whose implementation details are postponed to later stages.

For example, the construct "$\forall\, x \in S \wedge P(x) \bullet do\, A$" defines the action A for those elements in the set S satisfying a predicate P. The type of x is not of concern here.

The main difference between a process abstraction and a data abstraction is that the former is active, whereas the latter is passive. All operations in a data abstraction can be passively accessed. However, process abstraction controls when or where an operation can be accessed. Both data and process abstractions require that access be made only through explicit interfaces. The interface specification of an abstraction describes the unchanging aspects of that abstraction.

Abstraction is also an invaluable tool for *program specification* (PS), in which algorithmic and implementation-level data structures and controls need to be specified. A suitable choice of notation for algorithm specification is a combination of data abstraction, control abstraction, function abstraction, and elements of logic. An implementation specification, often termed as pseudocode, can be written in the implementation language without strictly following the syntactic rules of the language. When the missing syntactic details and the input/output functions are inserted, the implementation specification becomes the source code in the chosen language.

Exercises

1. Give definitions using lambda abstraction for the following functions:

   (a) one third of cubing

   (b) THREE, which takes a function f as an argument and produces a function which applies three times to itself

   (c) addition, multiplication, and raising to power n

   (d) composition of functions

   (e) characteristic function Ψ, which associates for every subset A of X the predicate whose value is true over A and false otherwise

2. Provide iterators for an abstract binary tree data structure.

3. Give an outline of a method that can be used to merge two related views of an application into one view integrating both. For example, consider integrating a coin-changing machine with a conventional vending machine.

Bibliographic Notes

Abstraction for different stages of software development activity is discussed by Zimmer [7]. An account of abstraction process for software engineers in setting up the relationship among specification, application, and program is given by Turski and Maibaum [6]. Abstraction is described by Jackson [2] as a link between a description and the phenomena it describes. It should help the developer to look inward at the descriptions from the application domains and justify that the descriptions are faithful.

An excellent account of Turing machine and Church's lambda calculus abstractions can be found in Penrose [4]. For an understanding of the seminal works of Turing [5], and Church [1], the reader can refer to any text book on theory of computation or formal languages; a rigorous treatment is available in the book by Lewis and Papadimitriou [3].

References

[1] A. Church, "The Calculi of Lambda-conversion," *Annals of Mathematical Studies*, Cambridge, MA, 1941.

[2] M. Jackson, "Description is Our Business," Invited Talk, *VDM'91 Formal Software Development Methods*; published as S. Prehn and W.J. Toetenel (Eds.), *Lecture Notes in Computer Science*, Vol. 551, Springer-Verlag, Noordwijkerhout, The Netherlands, October 1991.

[3] H. Lewis and C. Papadimitriou, *Elements of the Theory of Computation*, Prentice-Hall, Englewood Cliffs, NJ, 1984.

[4] R. Penrose, *The Emperor's New Mind*, Oxford University Press, Oxford, England, 1989.

[5] A. Turing, "On Computable Numbers, with an Application to Entscheidungsproblem," *Proceedings of the London Mathematical Society (ser. 2)*, Vol. 42, 1937, pp. 230–265.

[6] W.M. Turski and T. Maibaum, *The Specification of Computer Programs*, Addison-Wesley Publishing Company, Reading, MA, 1987.

[7] J.A. Zimmer, *Abstraction for Programmers*, McGraw-Hill, New York, NY, 1985.

5

Formal Systems

Scientific experiments are of two kinds: (1) processes undertaken to discover things not yet known, (E1); and, (2) processes undertaken to demonstrate things that are known, (E2). Scientific properties that have been observed will hold whenever the experiments are repeated with the same specifications, and under the same conditions. The results are independent of the scale on which the experiments are performed. Demonstrating the properties of a software system is analogous to conducting experiments of type E2. This can be done on a small scale, while establishing the properties of the software system through experiments on a reduced model of the system. However, the software development process is analogous to conducting experiments of type E1. This cannot be done on a small scale, or by employing a reduced model of the system. It is almost impossible to establish all the properties of a software system through the reduced model. It is therefore essential that software engineers get a direct exposure of the full-scale development process. On the other hand, a direct exposure of the full-scale development process may not be sufficient to reveal hidden properties of the system. A midway alternative is to adopt a certain degree of formality in software development. The motivation to espouse formal systems is driven by the quest for a foundation that is theoretically sound. A framework grounded on this foundation would contain the size and structural complexity of the system, provide a precise and unequivocal notation for specifying software components, and support a rigorous analysis of the relevant system properties. Based on these observations, we believe that adopting a formal approach to software development may prove beneficial.

A formal system consists of a *formal language* and a *deductive system*. The language may be introduced either informally or using a *metalanguage*. The syntax of the language provides representational abstraction for objects in the conceptual domain. The semantics of the language characterizes those statements in the language that are valid for the conceptual domain. A deductive system is a machinery for conducting inferences in the construction of proofs for logical assertions. A sound deductive approach must include only correct representations and correct mathematical reasoning.

In the pursuit of formalization of mathematical systems, several paradoxes, such as Russel's Paradox, were encountered. In the context of constructing formal systems, paradoxical statements may arise due to fuzzy boundaries between the formal language and the metalanguage. A paradoxical situation in the formal system will lead to self-contradictory conclusions in the deductive process. The challenge is to build formal systems in which syntax, semantics, and deductive mechanism do not allow contradictions to arise.

This chapter outlines the essential characteristics of a formal system. After a brief review of some of the formal systems studied in mathematics, science, and engineering, we discuss the components and properties of formal systems. This is followed by a description of two simple formal notations. The chapter concludes with a classification of formal specification methods.

5.1   Peano's Axiomatization of Naturals

Recall that abstraction "ignores details" and "generalizes" the domain being studied. With generalization, abstraction eliminates representational details; for example, Peano's axioms generalize natural numbers. The formal system of Peano [16], as stated below, uses set theory as the formal language, and logical axioms as the basis of inference.

Example 5.1   From the general point of view, natural numbers are the counting numbers. Our experience tells us that the set of natural numbers is infinite, and that for every natural number there is a unique next element. These observations are generalized by Peano's axioms, which postulate the existence of a set P together with the map $succ : P \to P$ satisfying the following axioms:

A1 (axiom of infinity)   The map $succ$ is injective but not surjective. There is a bijection between P and P', where $P' = \{y \mid y = succ(x), x \in P\}$.

A2 (axiom of induction)   If $S \subseteq P, S \not\subseteq P'$ and $S' \subset S$, then $S = P$, where $S' = \{y \mid y = succ(x), x \in S\}$.

To understand the meaning of these axioms, one needs to invoke the semantics of terms such as injective, surjective, and subset from the language of set theory and derive conclusions. There are four characteristics revealed in axiom A1:

1. P cannot be the empty set, because the empty set has no proper subsets.

2. An injective map from a finite set X to itself is also surjective. So, P cannot be finite.

3. Each element $x \in P$ is uniquely determined by the image $succ(x)$, since $succ$ is injective.

4. $P - P'$ is nonempty, for the map $succ$ is not surjective.

The following four facts can be derived from axiom A2:

1. Since $S' \subset S$, S cannot be finite.

2. Since $S \not\subset P'$, S contains an initial segment of P.

3. S has a least element.

4. If $x \in S$, the integer $succ(x)$ also lies in S. The conclusion is that S must be all of P.   ∎

Different kinds of logic, set theory, and algebra are formalisms that are used in designing formal specification languages. We study their fundamental aspects in later chapters.

5.2   Model and Theory

One of the roles of abstraction is to produce a mathemetical *model* of the object of concern. In mathematics, formal models are produced through generalizations; in natural science, physical science and engineering, formal models are built by ignoring irrelevant details.

5.2.1   Formalization in Engineering

The foundation for building theories in engineering is applied mathematics. For example, a mechanical engineer studies fluid dynamics using Navier-Stokes equation relating the velocity, density, pressure, and the viscosity of a fluid. The formal representation of these physical quantities is sufficient to understand the properties of fluid flow. Being non-linear, this differential equation is difficult to solve, even with the use of powerful computers. Supercomputers are being used as dedicated processors to analyze, understand, and predict the behavior of fluid motion modeled by this equation. This is an example where the validation of a model is extremely difficult and can only be approximate. The difficulty can be attributed to approximate modeling and incomplete knowledge of the relationship that exists among the attributes of a fluid flow.

5.2.2   Formalization in Science

Scientists start their experiments by creating a formal representation of the domain. The representation includes a description of the domain objects and a rule-based discussion of the observed properties and behavior of domain objects. The descriptive part is the *model* of the domain and the rule-based discussion part represents the *theory* for the domain model. Informally, the theory of a model is a set of statements that can be made about the modeled domain. In practice, the set of all facts may be too large to enumerate. Consequently, only a subset of the facts is explicitly stated in the theory; the rest can be derived by exercising the rules underlying the model. Confidence in the model grows as theory predictions coincide with observed facts. Whenever a new observation contradicts the theory, both the theory and the model need to be modified or abandoned in favor of new ones.

An ancient model of the universe due to Ptolemy considered the earth as stationary with the sun, the moon, the planets, and the stars moving in circular orbits around the earth. The theory of this model did not match the observed positions of the planets. The Ptolemic model was then replaced by the Copernicus model, in which the sun was considered stationary and the earth and the planets moved around the sun in circular orbits. Subsequently, Kepler modified the theory of Copernicus by postulating that the earth and the planets moved in elliptic orbits around the sun. The theory predictions of this revised model closely matched the celestial observations. Newton's laws of motion and theory of gravity generalized the previous predictive schemes. The axioms of Newton's theory of gravity were verified through experiments on the dynamics of terrestrial bodies, as well as through the observed outcomes in celestial mechanics. Other theories, such as Einstein's theory of relativity, accurately predicted the outcome of experiments well before the experiments became feasible. This evolutionary formalization process shows that scientific theories are acceptable only if they are found to be sound and free of contradictions.

Models in social sciences and economics may also be formal, although they may lack accurate predictive power because of approximate modeling and incomplete knowledge. A naive solution is to exhaustively capture all the features of the modeled objects. Such a model goes against the principles of abstraction and defeats the purpose of theory building; the theory may even include contradictions. Hence, one has to compromise between the simplicity of the model on one hand, wherein only essential objects are modeled, and essential axioms are stated, and robustness of the model on the other hand, wherein the detailed features of the conceptual domain are captured.

5.2.3   Formalization Process in Software Engineering

The problem description, the specification of domain objects and their interdependence, and the program satisfying the specification represent models at different levels of abstraction. There is an underlying relationship among the models: A program characterizes how a solution to the given problem is derived. The specification is a higher-level representation of the program it specifies. Representational and control details included in the program are not described by the specification. The problem description is part of the model describing the solution. It is integrated in the specification layer; that is, the specification layer describes both the model and the theory underlying the problem and its solution.

The specification thus serves the same purpose as a physicist's or an engineer's model. Therefore, a framework for building models and theories for software systems must be formal. The adequacy of the constructed model and theory must be established by showing that every intended behavior implied in the requirements is captured by the theory.

Formal specification in software engineering is a multistep activity:

1. Choose a formal framework within which specifications are to be built.

2. Construct a specification within the constraints of the syntax and semantics of the specification language.

3. Validate the specification against the requirements it is supposed to capture. If the intended properties are not consequent from the theory, the specification is modified, and the validation process is repeated until all the properties can be inferred from the specification. If a property cannot be deduced from the specification, step 2 is repeated. If a requirement or property cannot be captured by the model, then the formalism is inadequate. In such a case, we go back to step 1 to choose another formalism.

5.3 Components of a Formal System

A formal system includes three basic components: the syntax of the formal language, the semantics of the formal language, and the deductive mechanism of the formal system. The language of the formal system can be introduced either informally, or through a metalanguage. Sometimes, the term "object language" is used to distinguish the formal language from the metalanguage used to define it. The metalanguage is distinguished in our discussion either by explicit notational convention, or informally.

5.3.1 Syntax

The syntax of a formal language is described by its *grammar*. This represents a set of rules depicting how basic objects, called *alphabet*, and constructs of the language, called *sentences*, are resolved and how more complex expressions, called *well-formed formulas*, may be constructed.

We use the following convention for metalanguage notation: an alphabet is specified by writing the symbols within curly brackets {...}, separated by commas. If an alphabet is clear from the context, we omit it in the description. The grammar for a language is described by a number of rules. A rule introduces and defines a structural entity within the language. Each entity is introduced with a unique name, solely for the purpose of referring to it in other rules; the names are *not* part of the formal language. The name of an entity is followed by the symbol '=', the definition for the entity, and a semicolon. A definition may consist of a sequence of items, where each item is either an alphabet or an entity, and the items are separated by commas. A symbol from the alphabet is written within double quotes. When an entity can be defined in more than one way, the different possibilities are listed and are separated by the symbol '|'. Examples 5.2, 5.3, and 5.4 introduce different elements of a formal language.

Example 5.2   The entities *digit* and *digits* describe strings with one or more digits.

> *digit* = "0" | "1" | "2" | ... | "9" | ;
> *digits* = *digit* | *digit, digits*;   ■

Example 5.3   The entities *twodigits* and *threedigits* describe strings of a specific length.

> *digit*   = "0" | "1" | "2" | ... | "9" | ;
> *twodigits*   = *digit, digit*;
> *threedigits* = *digit, twodigits*;   ■

We need $n + 1$ rules to generate strings of length n > 1. However, we use a concise notation to denote strings of a specific length; for example, *digits(10)* denotes strings of exactly 10 digits.

We use meaningful identifiers to denote certain entities in the examples to follow. They are constructed according to the formal definition given in Example 5.4.

Example 5.4   We define two entities, *letter* and *digit*, and use them to create the entity *identifier*.

> *letter*   = "a" | "b" | "c" | ... | "z" | ;
> *digit*   = "0" | "1" | "2" | ... | "9" | ;
> *identifier* = *letter* | *identifier, digit* | *identifier, identifier*;   ■

5.3.2 Semantics

The syntax of a language defines the set of sentences that are consistent with the grammar. These sentences need to be attributed some meaning if they are to be of any use. A formal system is useful only if each symbol and construct of its language component are meaningful. The *semantics* of a language determines how well-formed formulas can characterize certain properties by distinguishing those statements that are true of the conceptual domain. The definition of semantics boils down to a relationship between sentences and expressions specified in such a way that their truth values can be systematically extended to any statement in the language. In a programming language context, the structure of a program is determined by the syntax, and the nature of the computations is determined by the semantics of the language. However, the semantics of the language component of a formal system has more implications than programming language semantics. An important issue in the use of formal systems is *pragmatics*, which refers to the way in which the formal system is used. It is concerned with the different interpretations that can be given to associations between entities in the abstract model within the formal system and real-world objects. An interpretation of the formalization can be deemed faithful to its corresponding real entity only if each property of that entity has been assigned a truth value by the semantics. In essence, the semantics of a language L is given by a structure (U, I), where U is the universe of values (e.g., integers, real numbers, Boolean) and the interpretation I is a mapping $I : L \rightarrow U$.

In Example 5.2, we interpret each digit to correspond to the natural number it represents, and interpret a digit next to another as the usual decimal system. Under this interpretation the well-formed formulas become the set of all natural numbers. However, other interpretations can be given to this language. Consider the case where we interpret each digit as a character and the adjacent symbols as a concatenation of characters. This interpretation assigns a value from the domain of sequences to each well-formed formula of the language. However, every interpretation must remain consistent with the way the objects are manipulated according to the semantics of the language.

5.3.3   Inference Mechanism

The syntactic manipulation of well-formed formulas with little concern for their meaning is achieved by adding a deductive mechanism to the formal language. This deductive capability allows the derivation of new well-formed formulas from those that are present in the language. Deductive systems of interest for validation of system specifications are called *axiom systems*. The two components of an axiom system are the *axioms* and the *inference rules*. An axiom is a well-formed formula that is inherently valid within the formal system; it can be specified without reference to any other well-formed formula. The set of axioms forms a *basis* of the formal system, allowing any other valid formula to be generated from the set by a systematic mechanical application of inference rules. An inference rule permits the generation of well-formed formulas as a consequence of other well-formed formulas.

Let L denote a formal language, and $x \in L$ be an axiom or any other well-formed formula. When applied to x, the inference rules produce zero or more well-formed formulas in L. We choose an arbitrary expression x from the resulting language L, and repeat the process of applying inference rules. This will result in either an infinite number of new well-formed formulas being added to L, or the process to terminate after a finite number of iterations. We are interested only in those formal systems for which the language L is closed under this process. In this case, the resulting set L is called the *consequence closure* of the formal system.

Let σ denote the consequence closure operator, such that $\forall x \in L$, $\sigma(x)$ denotes the set of all well-formed formulas that can be derived from x through successive applications of the inference rules. Clearly σ maps sets of well-formed formulas in L into sets of well-formed formulas in the consequence closure of L. The following properties hold on σ:

- Containment $\forall A \subset L, A \subseteq \sigma(A)$
- Monotonicity $\forall A, B \subset L, \text{ if } A \subseteq B \text{ then } \sigma(A) \subseteq \sigma(B)$
- Closure $\forall A \subset L, \sigma(A) = \sigma(\sigma(A))$

A *theory* in a formal system is a set of statements A, $A \subseteq L$, such that $\sigma(A) = A$.

Example 5.5 We define a formal system to describe the *unary* representation for integers and addition and multiplication laws. The alphabet consists of the symbols 1, e, $+$, and $\circ$. The well-formed formulas are defined by the following grammar:

nat	$= e \mid$ *string of ones*;
string of ones	$= suc(e) \mid suc(string\ of\ ones)$;
suc(e)	$= 1$;
suc(string of ones)	$=$ *string of ones*, 1;
sentence	$= (nat = nat + nat;) \mid (nat = nat \circ nat); \mid (sentence)$;

Axioms

1. $a = e + a$

2. $e = e \circ a$

3. $(x\ 1) \circ a = x \circ a + a$

4. $(x\ 1) + a = (x + a\ 1)$

Inference Rules

1. If $a + b = c$ is a well-formed formula, then (1) $suc(a) + b = suc(c)$, and (2) $a + suc(b) = suc(c)$ are also well-formed formulas.

2. If $a \circ b = c$ is a well-formed formula, then (1) $a \circ suc(b) = c + a$ and (2) $suc(a) \circ b = c + b$ are also well-formed formulas.

The sentence $111 = 11 + 1$ is a well-formed formula in the language. By the first inference rule we have $suc(11) + 1 = suc(111)$. An application of the grammar rule gives the well-formed formula $111 + 1 = 1111$. This is therefore an immediate consequence of the assumption that $111 = 11 + 1$ is a well-formed formula. From the second part of the first inference rule, another immediate consequence is that $1111 = 11 + 11$ is also a well-formed formula. Assuming that $11 \circ 111 = 111111$ is a well-formed formula, an application of the second rule gives $11 \circ suc(111) = 111111 + 11$. By expanding $suc(111)$ and using Axiom 4 twice, we get $11 \circ 1111 = 11111111$ as another well-formed formula in the language. If we interpret e to be the digit *zero*, "1" to be the digit 1, and a sequence of n 1's to be the natural number n, then it is straightforward to verify that $+$ and $\circ$ as defined here correspond to the addition and multiplication operations over natural numbers. ∎

As remarked earlier, the consequence closure of a formal system is the union of a set of axioms and a set of derivations of every subset for well-formed formulas using inference rules. The subset of well-formed formulas that we start with is called *premises* or *hypothesis*, and the well-formed formulas obtained by direct consequence of applying inference rules are called *derivations*. A statement is *provable* in a formal system if it has a proof constructed from the axioms using the inference rules. Within a formal system, the text of a formal *proof* consists of the hypothesis and the derivations, with logical steps representing the application of inference rules in between. Each logical step is an axiom or an immediate consequence of a previous step as determined by an inference rule. The conclusion represented by the last step of the proof is called a *theorem*. All axioms are true statements within the formal system. Every theorem other than an axiom requires a formal proof.

Example 5.6 Prove the theorem

$$111 \circ 111 = 111111111$$

within the formal system of Example 1.5.

Proof.

Step 1	$(x\ 1) \circ a = x \circ a + a$	Axiom 3
Step 2	$(e\ 1) \circ 111 = e \circ 111 + 111$	Substitution for $x(= e)$ and $a(= 111)$
Step 3	$(e\ 1) \circ 111 = e + 111$	Axiom 2
Step 4	$(e\ 1) \circ 111 = 111$	Axiom 1
Step 5	$1 \circ 111 = 111$	Definition of e
Step 6	$suc(1) \circ 111 = 111 + 111$	Inference Rule 2 applied to Step 5
Step 7	$(11) \circ 111 = 111 + 111$	Definition of suc
Step 8	$(11) \circ 111 = 11 + 1111$	Axiom 4
Step 9	$(11) \circ 111 = 1 + 11111$	Axiom 4
Step 10	$(11) \circ 111 = e\ 1 + 11111$	Definition of e
Step 11	$(11) \circ 111 = e + 111111$	Axiom 4
Step 12	$(11) \circ 111 = 111111$	Axiom 1
Step 13	$suc(11) \circ 111 = 111111 + 111$	Inference Rule 2 applied to Step 12
Step 14	$111 \circ 111 = 111111 + 111$	Definition of suc

Now apply Axiom 4 repeatedly to Step 14 and finally use definition of *e* followed by Axiom 1 to get the final result.

It is clear from this example that the well-formed formulas are manipulated strictly according to the grammar rules, axioms, and inference rules. That is, there is no interpretation assigned to the structures or their derivations. When the meaning for a string of *n* 1's is provided as the natural number *n* and *e* denotes 0, the formal operations provide the usual laws of addition and multiplication on natural numbers.   ∎

5.4   Properties of Formal Systems

A formal system is often constructed to fulfill a *need* and consequently the specifications within the system are subjective. The usefulness and validity of a formal system depend on the circumstances that called for the system. As opposed to mathematical models that do not actually exist, entities within a formal system model real-world objects. In software engineering context, properties of a formal system such as consistency, completeness, and decidability, determine the expressiveness of abstractions, as well as the ability to infer properties of conceptual domain objects from the deductive mechanism of the formal system.

An essential feature of a formal system, as discussed earlier, is its use in deriving a formal proof for certain assertions that can be made within the system. The primary advantage of a formal proof is that each step in the proof is a derivation of one of the available well-formed formulas and consequently the proof process can be automated. In other words, checking the validity of a proof is a computable process. It can be done algorithmically, and no evidence external to the formalized notions should be considered in deriving a proof. The consequence closure contains all the truth statements relevant to the formal system. However, it may not be complete in the sense that what is known to be true may not be provable within the formal system. Two factors contribute to this characteristic of incompleteness. The first comes from an incomplete formalization of knowledge about the application domain. The second is a form of incompleteness that is inherent in every formal system. These notions give rise to three important concepts: *consistency*, *completeness*, and *decidability*.

5.4.1   Consistency

The inference mechanism associated with a formal system enables us to determine whether or not a sentence *x* is derivable as a consequence of well-formed formulas in the formal system. Consider a formal system $F = (L, \sigma)$, where L is the formal language and σ is the consequence closure operator. If $x \in \sigma(L)$, we write $F \vdash x$. The symbol $\vdash$ is called the *syntactic turnstile*. A formal system is said to be *syntactically consistent* if for any given sentence x, $F \vdash x$ and $F \vdash \sim x$ cannot occur simultaneously. In other words, *at most* one of the sentences x or $\sim x$ can be deduced in F. In general, syntactic consistency is hard to establish. A formal system is *semantically consistent* if for each interpretation of a sentence there exists no mapping whose result produces both *true* and *false*. Semantic consistency is in general impossible to establish. Consequently, from a practical point of view, tool support is essential for ensuring consistency.

5.4.2 Completeness

It may happen that neither x nor $\sim x$ belongs to $\sigma(L)$. This occurs when x is a property not captured within the formal system. In such cases, we say x is *independent* of F. Whenever an essential property x is independent of F, x can be included in the formal system F, as an axiom, without violating the consistency of F. Thus, F can be extended by including sentences that are independent of F. Because axioms in F form a basis for F, a state is ultimately reached where the addition of one more axiom will violate the syntactic consistency of F. Every sentence in F is either derivable or refutable. This leads to the concept of *syntactic completeness*. That is, F is syntactically complete if for any given sentence x, either $F \vdash x$ or $F \vdash \sim x$. A formal system is *semantically complete* if for each interpretation of a sentence, every mapping of the sentence is either *true* or *false*. Completeness relates to the extensibility of a formal system, and consequently, its ablity to capture more meaningful entities from its conceptual domain. Evaluating the completeness of a formal system is indeed a daunting task.

5.4.3 Decidability

In 1931, Gödel showed that any reasonable formal theory contains sentences that could not be proved or disproved. This implies that it is impossible to certify that a formal system does not contain statements that are neither provable nor disprovable through its inference mechanism. There is no decision procedure to provide proofs for all true statements in a formal system, and some true statements do not have a proof within the system. Thus, the truth values of such sentences is *undecidable*. This result sets limits on deductive reasoning capabilities as applied to formal specifications. At the same time, the undecidability result guides the software engineer in specification building and reasoning. The software engineer cannot reject anything that is not deducible from axioms. On the contrary, a useful property that is not a consequence of the axioms should be added to the system specification and checked for consistency. If the added information is never used in subsequent design stages of the formal system, then it can be removed. Since the formal system must necessarily be broad, and hence is bound to be incomplete in Gödel's terms, the goal in designing a formal system focuses on consistency rather than on completeness. The construction of a formal system starts with a small and consistent set of axioms. The process progresses by discovering unspecified facts through formal deduction, gathering more knowledge on the domain, determining the independence of new facts, and augmenting the system with new facts.

5.5   Two Formal Notations

A formal notation differs from a formal system: a formal notation has formal syntax and semantics, but does not have an inference mechanism. For specifying certain tasks, we do not need the inference mechanism; a formal notation is sufficient. In this section, we discuss two formal notations: an extension to the syntactic metalanguage used in the previous section, and a notation based on an extended finite state machine. Both notations are quite expressive and useful.

5.5.1   Extended Syntactic Metalanguage

The extensions to the syntactic metalanguage consist of adding one or more of the following items with each grammar rule: (1) an action; (2) a predicate; (3) meta-symbols. We use upper case letters for the metasymbol; for example, DIGITS(6), CHAR(10), and CIRCLE. These denote predefined object types. We assume that the grammar generating these entities has been defined already and is available for use in creating other entities. Another abbreviation used is $\{\ \}^n$, which denotes $n \geq 1$ repetitions of the symbol within curly parentheses. Thus, $\{WORDS\}^n$ denotes an entity representing a sequence of n WORDS.

The commercial product *Idea Processor* was introduced by Hershey [13] to collect notes in the form of chunks of text, and rearrange them in groups to form an outline for an eventual expansion into a report. The structure of an *Idea Processor* document as simplified by Henderson [12] is defined as a collection of related ideas under a single title. Example 5.7 introduces an extended metalanguage notation for formalizing the notion of ideas, and valid documents that can be processed by an Idea Processor.

Example 5.7   An idea within a document is a header and its associated text. The header is composed of an identifier and a name. The text associated with an idea consists of subideas, and one or more paragraphs with text and diagrams. Each diagram has an identifier and a caption. An idea may have zero or more subideas, where each subidea has the same structure as that of an idea. A set of keywords is associated with an idea. For example, the following notes might be present in an idea processor document:

1. "specification in a natural language"

2. "ambiguities in natural language specifications"

$$
\begin{aligned}
document &= \text{NL , } DOC\_TITLE, \text{NL, } \{idea\}^n; \\
idea &= header, \text{NL, } text, \text{NL, } keyword; \\
header &= HEADER\_NUMBER, HEADER\_NAME; \\
text &= \{subidea \mid paragraph, diagram \mid diagram, paragraph\}^n; \\
subidea &= \text{T, } idea; \\
keyword &= \{WORDS\}^n; \\
paragraph &= line \mid line, \text{NL, } paragraph; \\
line &= WORDS \mid WORDS, line; \\
diagram &= drawing, \text{NL, } DIAG\_ID, diag\_cap; \\
drawing &= CIRCLE \mid RECTANGLE \mid DFD \mid FLOWCHART; \\
diag\_cap &= \{WORDS\}^4;
\end{aligned}
$$

TABLE 5.1. Grammar for Idea Processor documents.

3. "algebraic specification method"

   - "syntax and semantics of an algebraic specification language"

   - "an example"

   - "executing algebraic specifications"

The notes may include diagrams for illustration. The following interpretation is assumed for the upper case symbols used in the formalism shown in Table 5.1: NL denotes a new line; T denotes a tab (indentation). These actions are not explicitly described in the grammar. All other upper case symbols are meaningful identifiers for predefined entities; for example, DIAG_ID means diagram identifier. The formal definition of document given in Example 5.7 cannot be used for semantic purposes; it is useful only to identify structurally correct documents. We return to the semantic issues for this example in Chapter 8, and give an algebraic specification for *Idea Processor* documents and their operations.   ∎

The next example introduces a formal language for specifying *electronic forms*. In this example, an electronic form is a visual interface entity used for recording laboratory test results for the patients of a hospital.

Example 5.8   An electronic form, called *test_request_form*, records information on patients, labs, and tests, as well as the relationships among them. Although the details regarding the visual display of these forms may vary, their essential format can be abstracted sufficiently well to provide a screen specification for an electronic form. A typical *test_request_form* used in hospitals will have three sections: *test_information*, *patient_information* and *lab_information*. Within each section the data is grouped in a certain format. Figure 5.1 shows a typical form used in hospitals; Table 5.2 gives the grammar for the form. The grammar uses symbols from an alphabet, and predefined entities whose interpretations are as follows: the symbols $\langle L \rangle$, $\langle R \rangle$

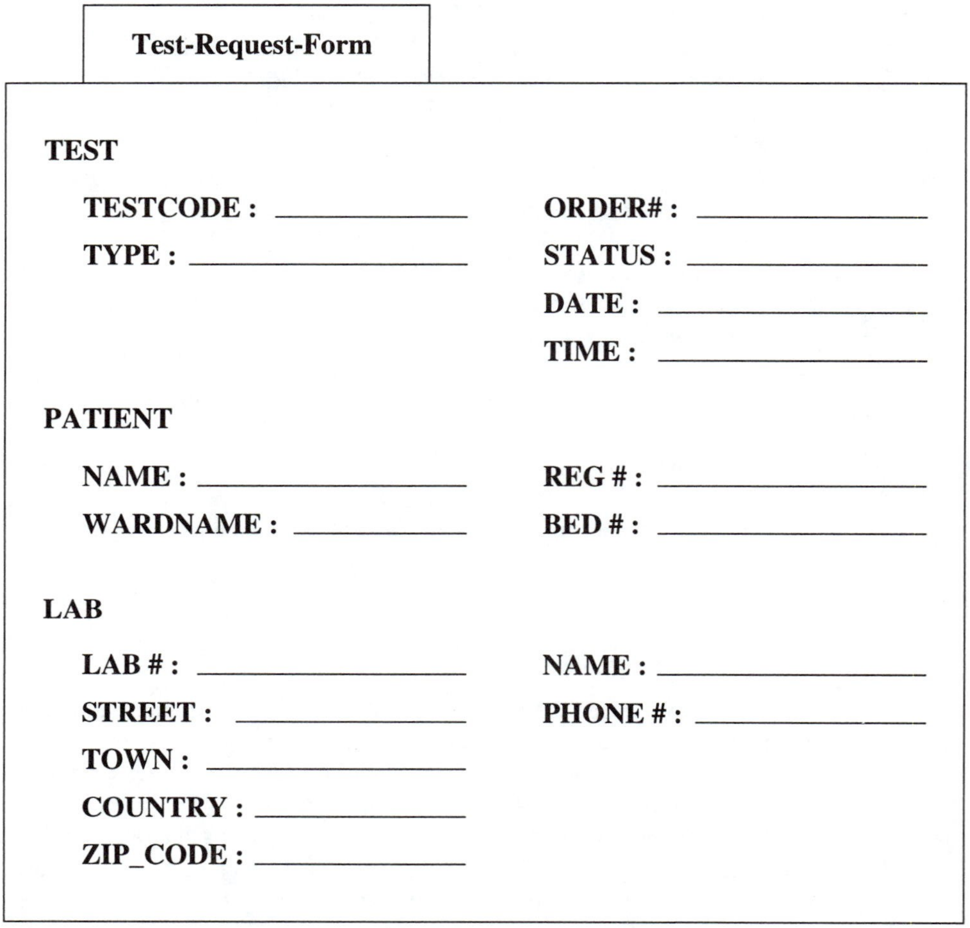

Test-Request-Form

TEST

    TESTCODE : _____   **ORDER# :** _____

    TYPE : _____   **STATUS :** _____

                                    DATE : _____

                                    TIME : _____

PATIENT

    NAME : _____   **REG # :** _____

    WARDNAME : _____   **BED # :** _____

LAB

    LAB # : _____   **NAME :** _____

    STREET : _____   **PHONE # :** _____

    TOWN : _____

    COUNTRY : _____

    ZIP_CODE : _____

FIGURE 5.1. Test_request_form as seen on the screen.

force the visual display of the entities to which they are bound to occur respectively left-justified or right-justified on the screen. The visual display of the entity *test_request_form* is characterized by a well-formed formula from this grammar. Some grammar rules involve the specification of actions. These correspond to the semantic interpretations for the rules. For instance, the semantic interpretation for *test_request_form* at the completion of expanding the rule for *lab* corresponds to the action *CREATE_LABLAYOUT* associated with *lab*. This action activates the procedures for displaying on the screen the part of the form corresponding to the layout for the lab information.

In this example, neither the grammar nor the actions indicate *how* the electronic form is to be used; it only defines the structure of the form. The formal model can be

test_request_form =	*test*, NL, *patient*, NL, *lab*;
	{action: CREATE_WINDOW}
test	= TEST, NL, *test_code*:⟨L⟩, *order#*:⟨R⟩, NL, *type*:⟨L⟩,
	status:⟨R⟩, NL, *date*:⟨R⟩, NL, *time_ordered*:⟨R⟩, NL;
	{action: CREATE_TESTLAYOUT}
patient	= PATIENT,NL,*name*:⟨L⟩,*reg#*:⟨R⟩, NL,*ward_name*:⟨L⟩,*bed#*:⟨R⟩,NL;
	{action: CREATE_PATIENTLAYOUT}
lab	= LAB, NL, *lab#*:⟨L⟩, *name*:⟨R⟩, NL, *address*:⟨L⟩, NL, *phone#*:⟨L⟩, NL;
	{action: CREATE_LABLAYOUT}
test_code	= TESTCODE, NAT(6);
order#	= ORDER#, NAT(20);
type	= TYPE, CHAR(15);
status	= STATUS, BITS;
date	= DATE, CHAR(8);
time	= TIME, CHAR(6);
name	= NAME, CHAR(20);
reg#	= REG#, NAT(8);
ward_name	= WARDNAME, CHAR(15);
bed#	= BED#, NAT(4);
lab#	= LAB#, NAT(3);
address	= *street, town, country, postal_code*;
street	= STREET, NAT(6), CHAR(20);
town	= TOWN, CHAR(10);
country	= COUNTRY, CHAR(10);
postal_code	= ZIP_CODE, CHAR(7);
phone#	= PHONE#, NAT(3), " ", NAT(3), " ", NAT(4);

TABLE 5.2. Grammar for test_request_form.

"executed" to mimick the ways in which the form can be used in real-life situations. In the next section, we construct a model to demonstrate the responsiveness of the *test_request_form* during user interaction. ∎

5.5.2 Extended Finite State Machine

A *test_request_form* has a *structure* and a *behavior*. The structure is defined by the grammar in Table 5.2. An infinite collection of test request forms can adopt this structure, each one corresponding to a well-formed formula of the grammar; however, they may differ in their behavior. Structurally identical forms may have been constructed in different ways with distinctive behavior. When a *test_request_form* is used, the various stages of completing the form and the different kinds of responses to user interaction characterize the behavior. Each stage represents a *state* of the form. The behavior is *observable* when the form changes its state due to an input. Such a change of state represents a *transition*. The states and transitions are conveniently expressed by a *state transition diagram*, the graphical representation of a finite state machine. Formally, a finite state machine is a 5-tuple (S, I, T, s_0, F), where

S is a finite nonempty set of states,

I is a finite nonempty set of inputs,

T is a function from $(S - F) \times I$ to S called the transition function,

$s_0 \in S$ is the initial state, and

F is the set of final states, $F \subset S$.

A state is an abstraction of the static condition symbolizing the event sequences leading to it. In general, when an object assumes a particular state, it can be receptive to only a selected set of events. The object changes its state only if one of these events occurs. The event that causes a state transition is called a *trigger* or a triggering event. An action is associated with each transition. When an action is being performed, the object is in a "non-observable" state. When the action is completed, the object enters a state determined by the trigger. The behavior of the object at any point is characterized by the history, sequence of alternating states, and actions. The state transition diagram gives all possible behaviors of the object modeled by it.

In a graphical representation, a state can be represented by a rectangle, and a transition by a directed arc from the source state to the destination state. A rectangle containing the asterix symbol inside denotes an initial state. A transition is labeled by an event name. Figure 5.2 shows the state transition diagram for a water level controller. The controller ensures that the water level is maintained between *[low, high]* in a tank. In its initial state, it may detect water flowing into the tank or flowing

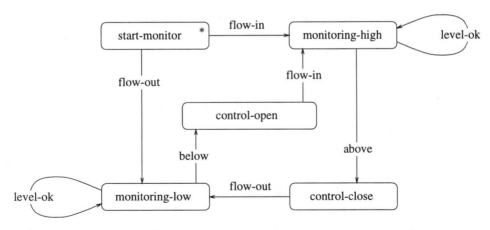

FIGURE 5.2. Finite state machine for a water level controller.

out of the tank. In the former case, it changes its state to *monitoring-high*, and in the later case, it changes its state to *monitoring-low*. It stays in the *monitoring-high* state as long as the level of water is in the range *[low, high]*. If the water level exceeds *high*, it changes its state to *control-close*, wherein it will close the valve of the water pipe and open the valve of the drain pipe. This triggers the event *flow-out*, which takes the controller to the state *monitoring-low*. The controller stays in this state as long as the water level is above *low*. When the water level goes below *low*, it transits to the state *control-open*, where it will ensure that the valve for drain pipe is closed and the valve for water pipe is open. This triggers the event *flow-in*, and the controller transits to the state of monitoring the water level at *monitoring-high*. Hence, the controller cycles through the activities of monitoring water levels and controlling the valves of the source and the drain.

The merit of the graphical notation is that it provides a full view of all possible behaviors of an object. However, this is also a weakness of the model. When the diagram has a large number of states and transitions, it is difficult to understand which components are relevant for the analysis of a specific problem. The "flat" nature makes state transition diagrams unsuitable for modeling complex objects. We discuss below some extensions to finite state machines that can be used to remedy this difficulty.

Combining States

We analyze the state space of domain objects to form subsets of states and select appropriate subsets for modeling a state transition system. This approach is illustrated in Figure 5.3 for a telephone example borrowed from Zave [20].

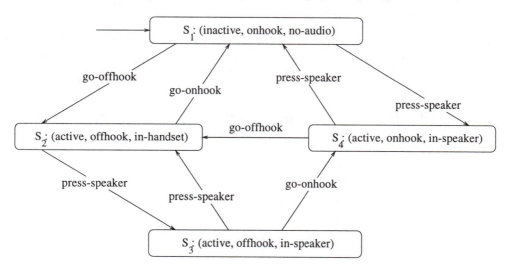

FIGURE 5.3. Partial specification of audio channels in a multiplexing telephone.

The goal is to have a partial specification of the behavior of multiplexing telephones that include built-in speakerphones. A multiplexing telephone has a predetermined limit to the degree of multiplexing. Each multiplexing opportunity requires a hardware resource. The operations include selecting any free multiplexing opportunity for placing a call, putting the currently active line on hold, and connecting the currently active line to a speaker. Multiplexing provides the ability to receive and place several calls simultaneously. To understand such a telephone, it should be specified when audio signals should be channeled through the speakerphone, and when they are to be channeled through the handset. Consequently, the state space of multiplexing telephone consists of sets of atomic states of the telephone and its speaker. To identify the states and triggers, we need to understand how the telephone is expected to work. Informally, the telephone is *inactive* when it is *onhook*. There is no audio signal when the telephone is inactive. Combining these three facts, a state labeled S_1 is created. A telephone becomes *active* when it is either *offhook* or when it is *onhook* and the audio signal is channeled through the *speaker*. When the telephone is *offhook*, the audio signal may be channeled through either the *handset* or the *speaker*. From this set of requirements, we can identify three other states: S_2, S_3, and S_4. When the telephone is in state S_1 and an event causing the telephone to go offhook occurs, then the state of the telephone changes to S_2. Since there could be any number of events that cause the telephone to go offhook, an abstraction should be applied here to define event types. It is appropriate to define an event-type T by a predicate $P(e)$; that is, $P(e)$ is true for all events e of type T. The types of events that cause transitions are *go-offhook(e)*, *go-onhook(e)*, and *press-speaker(e)*. The predicate *go-offhook(e)* is true for all events that cause the telephone to go offhook. Similar interpretations apply to the other predicates. Thus, by structuring the state space and abstracting event types, we have achieved precision and clarity in the state transition diagram.

A bottom-up approach to construct the finite state machine in Figure 5.3 is to construct the finite state machine for each object in the domain and combine them appropriately. The concept of product machines lead to the construction of complex machines from simple ones.

The product of the machines $M_1 = (S_1, I_1, T_1, s_1, F_1)$, and $M_2 = (S_2, I_2, T_2, s_2, F_2)$ is the machine $M = (S, I, T, s_0, F)$, where

$$S = S_1 \times S_2$$
$$I = I_1 \cup I_2$$
$$s_0 = s_1 \times S_2 \cup s_2 \times S_1$$
$$F = F_1 \times S_2 \cup F_2 \times S_1$$
$$T : (S - F) \times I \to S \text{ is defined as}$$

$$T((A, B), i) = \begin{cases} (T_1(A, i), B) & \text{if } i \in I_1 \\ (A, T_2(B, i)) & \text{if } i \in I_2 \end{cases} \quad \text{for all } A \in S_1, B \in S_2$$

Multiplexer Line

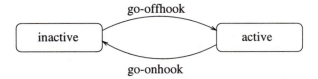

Telephone

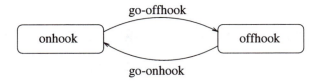

Audio

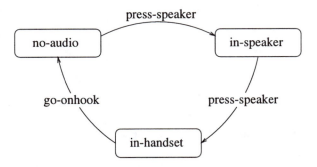

FIGURE 5.4. Finite state machines for the multiplexing telephone domain objects.

This definition can be generalized to construct a product of *n* machines, where $n \geq 2$.

The finite state machine in Figure 5.3 is a specialization of the product machine constructed from the three machines shown in Figure 5.4. Although there are twelve states in this product machine, not all states are meaningful. For example, the state *(inactive, offhook, no-audio)* is not a meaningful state, since the multiplexer line requires a telephone that is off the hook to be active. We retain those states in the product machine that are consistent with the requirements for a multiplexing telephone and ignore the rest. Not all events produced by the product machine construction may be meaningful to cause transitions among these retained states. For example, the telephone may be active when it is on the hook and the speaker is

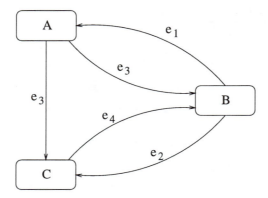

FIGURE 5.5. Finite state machine with partial states and multiple occurrences of events.

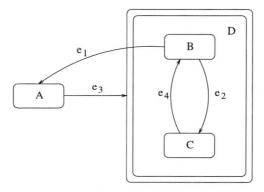

FIGURE 5.6. Finite state machine with a superstate equivalent to the machine in Figure 5.5.

on. Hence, the event *go-onhook* cannot cause a transition from state S_1 : *(inactive, onhook, no-audio)* to the state S_4 : *(active, onhook, in-speaker)*. So, the transition *go-onhook* from state S_1 to state S_4 in the product machine is ignored. The machine shown in Figure 5.3 is the result of removing the states and transitions that are not meaningful in the product machine.

Hierarchical States

In Figure 5.5, event e_3 causes a transition of the system from A to B or C. We can combine the simple states B and C into a new superstate D and replace the two transitions labeled e_3 by a single transition, as in Figure 5.6. The semantics of state D is analogous to the *exclusive-or* [8] abstraction. The system is in state D if it is either in state B or in state C, but not in both. That is, D is an abstraction of states B and C. The incoming transition to state D is then propagated to both B and C. The states of the superstate can be hidden or shown explicitly according to the level of abstraction required. Thus, the number of states and the number of transitions are substantially reduced. This abstraction leads to a bottom-up approach to system design. Another view of this methodology is top-down: Figure 5.6 is conceived first and subsequently *refined* into substates when more information becomes available, thus resulting in Figure 5.5. We consider two examples to illustrate these principles in designing *hierarchical state machines*. A state representing a root of a hierarchy of states is shown as a rectangle with two borders; all other states are shown as simple rectangles. A rectangle containing an asterix symbol denotes an initial state.

Example 5.9   A simplified version of the elevator-control problem, attributed to Davis [4], has the following requirements: There are n elevators to service a building with m floors. The problem is to develop a formal specification describing the movement of elevators between floors while satisfying the following constraints.

1. Each elevator has a set of buttons, one for each floor. The one pressed lights up and causes the elevator to visit the corresponding floor. The illumination is switched off when the corresponding floor is reached by the elevator.

2. Each floor, except the ground floor and top floor, has two buttons, one to request for an elevator to go up, and one to request for an elevator to go down. These buttons illuminate when pressed. The illumination is switched off when an elevator, which can move in the desired direction, visits the floor.

3. When there are no requests to service, an elevator remains at the floor where it has been with its doors closed.

An important assumption is that the internal mechanism of the elevators guarantees that in between two floors an elevator will keep moving without changing direction. We construct a hierarchical state machine for this elevator system, in a bottom-up style. There are three components to be modeled: elevator buttons, floor buttons, and elevator motion.

Elevator buttons   The language for specifying the buttons and their states and transitions is defined below:

- $eb_{i,j}$: the button for j-th floor in elevator i

- $ebon_{i,j}$: the state in which $eb_{i,j}$ lights up

- $eboff_{i,j}$: the state in which $eb_{i,j}$ is not illuminated

- $press\_eb_{i,j}$: the event-type that triggers the transition that occurs when $eb_{i,j}$ is pressed

- $arrives\_at_{i,j}$: the event-type that triggers the transition that occurs when elevator i arrives at floor j

The state transition diagram for elevator button $eb_{i,j}$ is shown in Figure 5.7.

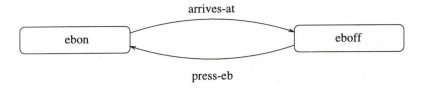

FIGURE 5.7. Finite state machine for the j-th floor button in elevator i.

Floor buttons   Each floor, except the ground floor and the top floor, has two buttons, one for calling an elevator to go up, and the other to call for an elevator to go down. The language elements required are

- $fb_{b,j}$: the button at floor j for direction b

- $fbon_{b,j}$: the button $fb_{b,j}$ lights up

- $fboff_{b,j}$: the button $fb_{b,j}$ is not illuminated

- $call\_fb_{b,j}$: the event-type that triggers the transition identifying that $fb_{b,j}$ is pressed

- $depart\_at_{b,j}$: the event-type that triggers the transition that occurs when an elevator going in direction b leaves floor j

The state transition diagram for floor button $fb_{b,j}$ is shown in Figure 5.8. The state transitions for the buttons at the ground floor and at the top floor are similar to each other and can be derived from the diagram in Figure 5.8.

Elevator motion   The observable scenarios for an elevator, with respect to a floor i, are illustrated in Figure 5.9, and enumerated here:

1. The elevator moves upwards without stopping.

2. The elevator moves downwards without stopping.

3. The elevator approaches from below, stops, and then continues upwards.

4. The elevator approaches from above, stops, and then continues downwards.

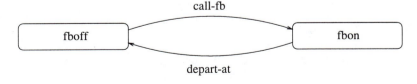

FIGURE 5.8. Finite state machine for the button at floor j for direction b.

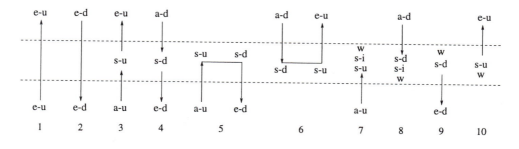

FIGURE 5.9. Scenarios for elevator motion observed at one floor.

5. The elevator approaches from below, stops, and then continues downwards.

6. The elevator approaches from above, stops, and then continues upwards.

7. The elevator approaches from below, stops, and then waits in the idle state.

8. The elevator approaches from above, stops, and then waits in the idle state.

9. From the idle state, the elevator moves downwards.

10. From the idle state, the elevator moves upwards.

For an observer at a floor, an elevator can be in one of the following states:

1. *wait:* waits at that floor with its doors closed.

2. *stop-idle:* stops at that floor; this happens when there is no outstanding request to process.

3. *stop-up:* stops at the floor during its upward motion.

4. *stop-down:* stops at the floor during its downward motion.

5. *approach-up:* approaches the floor during its upward motion.

6. *approach-down:* approaches the floor during its downward motion.

7. *exit-up:* leaves the floor in its upward motion.

8. *exit-down:* leaves the floor in its downward motion.

When an elevator stops at a floor and there is no request to process, its doors remain open. The model assumes that the internal mechanism has a built-in sensor that

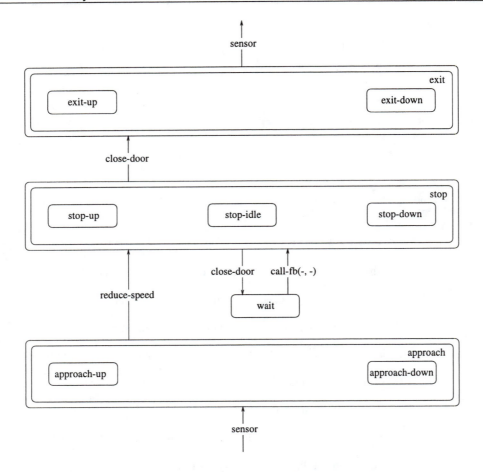

FIGURE 5.10. Generic state machine model for elevator observed at one floor.

slows (or accelerates) an elevator as required. In its upward motion, an elevator goes through the states *exit-up* and *approach-up* before entering one of the states *stop-up* or *stop-idle*. The transition labeled *reduce-speed* models this state change. The states *approach* and *exit* are observable when a button changes state.

The three states *stop-up, stop-down*, and *stop-idle* are combined to create the super-state *stop*; the two states *approach-up* and *approach-down* are combined into the super-state *approach*; the two states *exit-up* and *exit-down* are combined into the superstate *exit*. After stopping at a floor, an elevator leaves with its doors closed. The transition labeled *close-door* from the state *stop* to the state *exit* models this state change. Finally, when an elevator is called at a floor, and at that instant there is some elevator in the *wait* state, the elevator is made available. This is modeled by the transition labeled *call-fb(–,–)* from the state *wait* to the state *stop*. This generic model is shown in Figure 5.10.

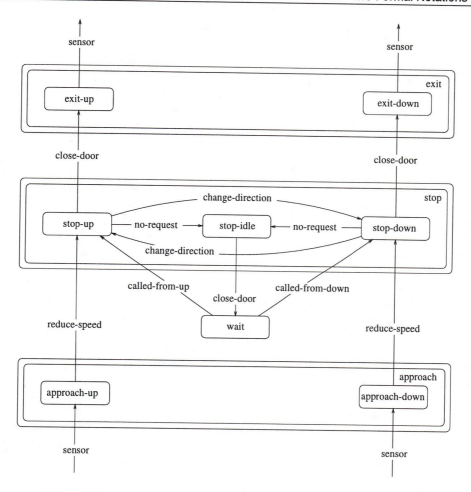

FIGURE 5.11. Generic state machine model for elevator observed at one floor.

However, this model is inaccurate because the semantics for a transition from a superstate S_1 to another superstate S_2 implies that the transition is from every substate of S_1 to every substate of S_2. This is remedied by showing the transitions relating all appropriate substates, as illustrated by Figure 5.11. Whenever there is a call for an elevator, and there is an elevator in the state *stop-idle* at that instant, its state changes to either *stop-up* or *stop-down*; when there is no such request, it goes into the *wait* state. This situation is captured by the transitions labeled *called-from-up*, *called-from-down*, *change-direction*, and *no-request*. Figure 5.11 shows several additional transitions relating the substates of the state *wait* and the state *stop*. Note that the states *stop-up* and *stop-down* can be modeled as complex states, and refined to capture the closing of the door of the elevator, as shown in Figure 5.12.

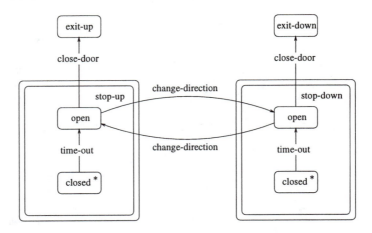

FIGURE 5.12. Refinement of the states *stop-up* and *stop-down*.

The state transition diagrams for the elevator as observed at different floors can be composed to obtain the state transition diagram for one elevator servicing a given number of floors. Let F_i denote the state machine for an elevator as observed at floor i. The transition from the state *exit-up* of F_i to the state *exit-up* of F_{i+1} corresponds to the case when the elevator is not stopping at the $(i + 1)$-th floor in its upward motion. The transition from the state *exit-up* of F_i to the state *approach-up* of F_{i+1} corresponds to the case when the elevator is stopping at the $(i + 1)$-th floor. Similar transitions exist between the state *exit-down* of F_i and the states *exit-down* and *approach-down* of F_{i-1}. The state machines corresponding to the ground and top floors are special cases; the states *exit-up* and *approach-down* do not exist in the machine corresponding to the top floor; the states *exit-down* and *approach-up* do not exist in the machine corresponding to the ground floor. Figure 5.13 illustrates the composed machine for an elevator servicing four floors. We show only the states and transitions involved in the composition.

For a building with several elevators with identical functionalities, the state machine specification for all the elevators is given by the product machine $E = E_1 \times E_2 \times \cdots \times E_k$, where E_i is the composed machine for elevator i. The elevator system needs to be managed by a controller so that all requests are serviced in a fair way. This can be accomplished by the controller maintaining a queue of requests, so as to coordinate the movement of the elevators efficiently. ∎

Example 5.10   This example illustrates the use of hierarchical state machines in a top-down development. Menu-driven user interfaces are implementations of hierarchical state machines. Denert [5] suggested the introduction of *user interaction points* in a state diagram. The purpose of user interaction points is to explicitly show the stages of user interaction, a prime concept in user interface design. A user interaction point is an *environmental* state, and must be distinguished from an object state. In state transition diagrams, a circle is used to denote user interaction points.

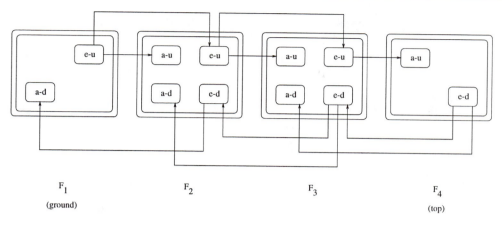

F₁

(ground)

F₂

F₃

F₄

(top)

e-u: exit-up
e-d: exit-down
a-u: approach-up
a-d: approach-down

FIGURE 5.13. State transition diagram for an elevator servicing four floors.

A *test_request_form* constructed according to the state transition diagram in Figure 5.14 conforms to the rules of the grammar described in Table 5.2. Corresponding to each nonterminal of the grammar, there exists a transition leading to a state in the state transition diagram. For example, the transition *test* leading into *test-layout* corresponds to the nonterminal *test*. Terminals are not included in the state transition diagram; they can be mapped to concrete representations at the time of user interaction. Additional states, such as *refresh and display*, and user interaction points such as *choose* are included in the state transition diagram to illustrate the steps in the design process.

When the event *enter_test_request_form* occurs in the initial state, the new state *refresh* and *display* is entered. The behavior in this state is the presentation of a refreshed window to the user. The transition from this state to the user interaction point *choose* occurs automatically, where a user has a choice of creating one of the three layouts in *test_request_form*. The action *CREATE_TESTLAYOUT* is performed in state S_3: *test-layout*; the action *CREATE_PATIENTLAYOUT* is performed in state S_4: *patient_layout*; and the action *CREATE_LABLAYOUT* is performed in state S_5: *lab_layout*. These three states are superstates, and can be refined. The states S_6: *close_form*, S_7: *check_form*, and S_8: *display_form* do not correspond to grammar rules. These states correspond to the design steps describing the actions performed on the *test_request_form* after exiting from the process of completing the components of the *test_request_form*.

The refinement of the complex state S_3 is shown in Figure 5.15. The terminal *TEST* in the grammar rule for *test* is mapped to the concrete textual representation "*TEST*" in the form. At the user interaction point entered from the intial state *create*

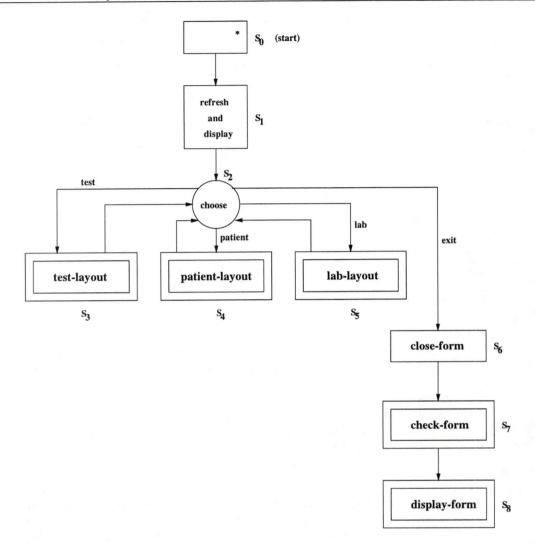

FIGURE 5.14. State transition diagram for test_request_form.

test layout, the user can choose one of several options for creating this part of the form. Choosing an option other than *exit* causes the object to enter one of the superstates - *3.3: code inf, 3.4: type inf, 3.5: order inf, 3.6: status inf, 3.7: date inf, 3.8: time inf*. These superstates are the states caused by transitions labeled by events corresponding to the nonterminals in the grammar rule for *test*. These superstates can be refined further using the grammar rules. The states *close text*, *check text*, and *display text* do not correspond to grammar rules; instead, they correspond to the design steps requiring further action on the completed form. Each superstate is further refined to a state transition diagram. This process continues until we arrive

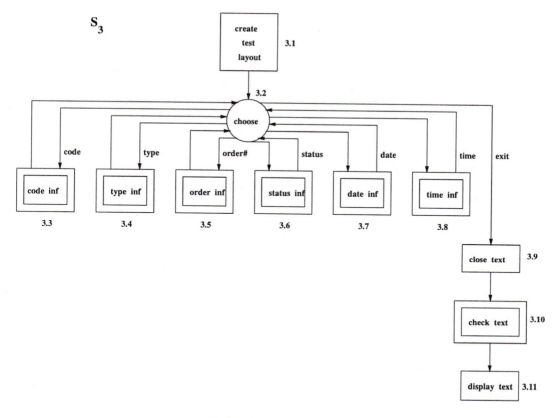

FIGURE 5.15. Refinement of superstate S_3.

at state transition diagrams containing only simple states. See Figure 5.16, which shows a refinement of the state *3.3: code inf.*   ∎

Adding More Details

As illustrated in Example 5.10, design brings in more information than what is contained in the specification. In principle, more details can be added to state transition diagrams, provided these details retain the specified behavior and do not violate the structure of the object defined by its grammar. For example, when semantically incorrect information or syntactically incorrect information is entered in the *test_request_form*, there needs to be a way of recovering from the error and continuing the activity from the latest valid state entered. This can be done by introducing a new state *abort*, and adding transitions from all other states to the *abort* state. Although the inclusion of this new state adds only little information to the model, the complexity of the model is significantly increased with the introduction of a large number of transitions. Once again, these can be resolved using hierarchical state structures, as shown in Figure 5.17. The highest level of

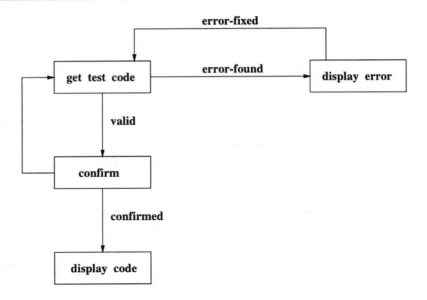

FIGURE 5.16. Refinement of superstate *code inf.*

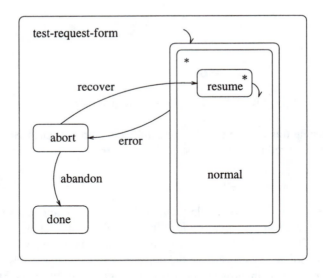

FIGURE 5.17. Error recovery using hierarchical states.

the machine has two states, a simple state *abort*, and a superstate *normal*. The superstate *normal* corresponds to the state machine shown in Figure 5.14, and is further refined in Figures 5.15 and 5.16. There are two initial transitions in Figure 5.17 showing that *normal* is the initial state at the top level, and it also contains an initial state among its substates. At every level of refinement there is an

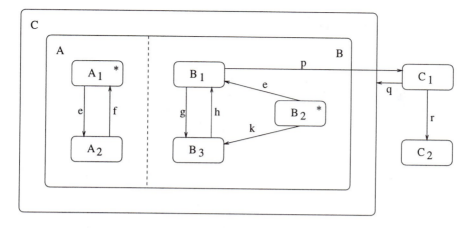

FIGURE 5.18. Orthogonal composition of two machines.

initial state. The transition labeled *error* is from the superstate *normal*, and hence from all its substates, to the state *abort*. The transition labeled *recover* is from the state *abort* to the initial state of the state *normal*. The transition labeled *abandon* is from the state *abort* to the terminal state *done*.

Composing State Machines

Denert [5] introduced the notion of superstates in state transition diagrams. Later, Harel [8] consolidated this notion in *statecharts*, a visual formalism for describing states and transitions in a modular fashion. This approach extends conventional state transition diagrams in two important ways: hierarchical states for clustering and deep descriptions, and composition of machines for concurrency.

A state transition system specifies the behavior of a set of sequentially ordered actions. The behavior of such a system is deduced by following the sequence of state transitions starting from an initial state to the state of interest. Such a sequence is called a *thread of control*. A concurrent system contains several threads of control that communicate among themselves to fulfill a certain task. The two primitive forms of interaction are *synchronization* and *communication*. One simple kind of synchronization is when a single event causes simultaneous transitions in several machines. Communication between machines can be achieved at the specification level in many different ways, including message passing, multicasting, and broadcasting. When synchronization and information exchange are combined, we obtain *synchronous communication*. In *asynchronous communication*, information exchange does not imply synchronization.

Example 5.11   The state transition diagram in Figure 5.18 shows a machine with a superstate C and two simple states C_1 and C_2. The dashed lines splitting the superstate C into two compartments is the statechart notation for capturing the orthogonal composition

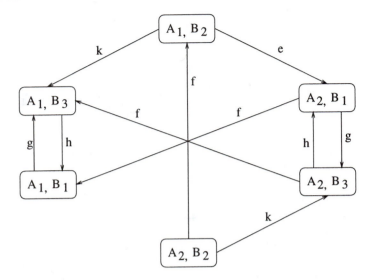

FIGURE 5.19. Full product machine of A and B.

of states A and B. Both A and B are machines with a single thread of control. They synchronously interact through their transitions labeled e. The outcome of this concurrent action can be understood from the full product machine of these two machines shown in Figure 5.19.

The notation illustrated in Figure 5.18 is a compact representation of this product machine, subject to the following semantics: A state of C is a pair (A_i, B_j), where A_i is a substate of A, and B_j is a substate of B. The initial state of C is (A_1, B_2). If event e occurs in the initial state, the transitions labeled e occur simultaneously in the two machines, causing the object to enter state (A_2, B_1). However, if event k occurs in the initial state, it causes a transition in the second machine only, changing its state from B_2 to B_3. That is, the effect of event k in the composed machine is to change its state from (A_1, B_2) to (A_1, B_3). No other event can effect a change on the composed machine when it is in its initial state. Notice that the product machine C in its flat representation has six states, which is the product of the number of states in A and the number of states in B. Composing two machines, each with a large number of states, leads to a product machine with a much larger number of states. The exponential explosion in the number of states is avoided in the representation shown in Figure 5.18.   ■

The state transition diagram in Figure 5.2, which models the behavior of a water-level controller, includes assumptions about the behavior of the source-valve and the drain-valve. Such assumptions violate the principle of *encapsulation*, a funda-mental concept in the design of *object-oriented* systems. Each finite state machine models the behavior of the object that it abstracts. Consequently, it should be independent of the behavior of any other object. This flaw in the specification of

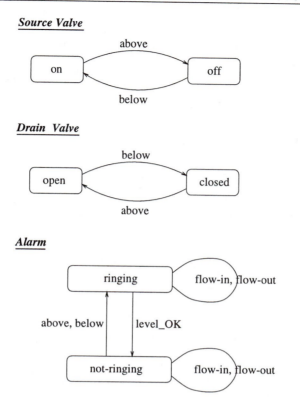

FIGURE 5.20. Finite state machines for source valve, drain valve, and alarm.

Figure 5.2 is remedied by specifying the behavior of the drain-valve and source-valve objects as distinct state machines, and composing them with the controller machine shown in Figure 5.2. We add an alarm subsystem in the water-level control system to demonstrate the expressiveness of the notation. The informal specification of the extended system is as follows: if the water level is too high, the source-valve is closed, the drain-valve is opened, and the alarm sounds. The system then starts monitoring the water level in the tank. If the water level is too low, the drain-valve is closed, the source-valve is opened, and the alarm sounds. The alarm stops sounding only when the water level is within the range *[low,high]*. The state transition diagrams for source-valve, drain-valve, and alarm are shown in Figure 5.20. The semantics of orthogonal composition clarifies the behavior of the composite machine whose components are the *controller, source-valve, drain-valve*, and *alarm*. When the water level is detected to be above *high*, the event *above* causes simultaneous transitions in four machines as follows: the controller machine changes state from *monitoring-high* to *control-close*; the *source-valve* changes state from *on* to *off*, signifying the closing of the water pipe; the *drain-valve* changes state from *closed* to *open*, to let the water flow out of the tank; the

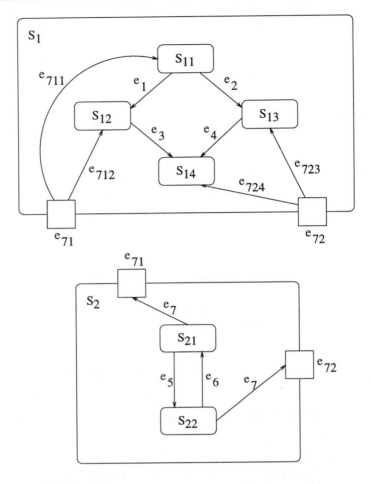

FIGURE 5.21. Message passing between finite state machines.

alarm changes state from *stop-ringing* to *start-ringing*. The system monitors the water level and the alarm is off while the water is flowing out. When the water level is detected to be below *low*, the event *below* causes simultaneous transitions in the four machines, causing the *alarm* to sound, the *drain-valve* to close, and the *source-valve* to open. The system returns to the state of monitoring the water level while the water flows in, and consequently, the alarm stops.

Transition Points

When a machine includes several superstates, modeling transitions between a sub-state of one superstate and a substate of another superstate requires a transition to cross state boundaries. To simplify the diagrammatic representation, *transition points* have been proposed by Selic, Gulleckson, and Ward [18]. This notation, illustrated in Figure 5.21, supports the creation of transition points at the boundaries of superstates, and use of appropriate naming conventions for events flowing across these points. The transition e_7 from state S_{21} stops at the transition point e_{71} in S_2. The two transitions e_{711} and e_{712} continue from the transition point e_{71} in S_1 to the states S_{11} and S_{12}. The semantics signifies that if the transition e_7 is triggered while S_2 is in state S_{21}, then either S_{11} or S_{12} will be the next state in the composed machine. The bonding between events e_7 and e_{711} (e_{712}) is established by the common transition point e_{71}. The semantics for transition e_7 at S_{22} is quite similar.

5.6 Formal Specification Methods—A Classification

In Chapter 2, we suggested that formal methods can be applied to several stages of software development with varying levels of rigor. When notations such as those discussed in the previous section or those from discrete mathematics are used to augment an existing development process with no emphasis on formal semantics and reasoning, we contend that only formal notations are used. The formal system is optimally used when specifications are developed with its formal specification language and are analyzed with its reasoning system. The proofs may not be done mechanically at this stage. The term *rigorous* is used to denote a proof style, wherein assumptions about proved results have been made. Because of potential gaps between proof steps, a rigorous proof cannot be mechanized and is more suitable for a manual development. The dividing line between formal systems and formal methods is the integrated support environment for specification development and mechanized proofs. The tools in the environment allow the specification to be developed with strict semantics and analyzed with a *proof checker*, checking those steps of the proof developed manually. A formal method should also provide a *theorem prover*, which attempts to develop proof steps with user assistance.

Formal methods are based on one or a combination of the following concepts: *algebra, logic, set theory,* and *relations.* In order to fully reap the benefits of formal methods, the specification languages based on these mathematical notions should also address software engineering concerns and allow specifications to be composable from simple structured units, to be generic and parametrized, and to have well-described interfaces. The specification languages corresponding to these mathematical notations and concepts are

1. logic-based languages such as temporal logic
2. Z, based on set theory
3. VDM, based on sets and relations
4. OBJ3, based on algebra
5. Larch, based on logic

Based on the work of Wing [19], we include a classification of specification methods. Formal specification languages are broadly categorized as *property-oriented*, *model-oriented*, and *state-machine-oriented*. Algebraic specification languages, first-order, and functional languages fall into the first category. Languages such as VDM and Z fall into the second category. Larch has two tiers: the first tier is property-oriented and the second tier uses the model from the first tier. Languages based on state-machines include statecharts and Petri nets.

Property-oriented specification methods   This category can be subdivided into two sub-groups, referred to as *axiomatic* and *algebraic*. In an axiomatic approach, objects are built from types, and operations on types are given as assertions in first-order predicate logic. Larch and Anna follow this style. In an algebraic approach, theory of objects and processes are defined as algebras. This method emphasizes the functionality of an object and not its representation. The object is specified as a set of *definitions*, and a set of *equations* defines the operations on the object. OBJ3, AFFIRM, and ACT ONE are algebraic specification languages.

Model-oriented specification techniques   The formal language consists of mathematical entities such as natural numbers and boolean; it includes their theories and the languages of sets, relations, and functions. A specifier builds a model of the system using these language elements. For example, a predefined data type representing a *sequence* may be used to specify a stack. Operations such as *push* and *pop* are written using the built-in operations on *sequence* data type. Usually, the behavior of such a system is specified in Hoare logic, using pre- and postconditions on the observable states of the entities. Z, VDM, and RAISE are model-oriented specification languages. We study OBJ3, VDM, Z, and Larch specification languages in later chapters.

Exercises

1. Give a specification of the "login" command using an extended state machine notation. The requirements for the command are as follows:

   - It prompts the user to enter the user name.
   - If the user name is not recognized by the system, it prompts the user to re-enter the user name until a valid user name is entered.
   - It prompts the user to enter a password.
   - If the password is incorrect, the user is given one more chance to enter a password; if both trials fail, the user must start the whole process again.
   - If the password is accepted, the user is prompted to enter the security level for the session.

- If the security level entered is higher than the security level assigned to the user, the system terminates the session with a warning message.

2. There are two commands, *send*, and *repl*, for a simple electronic mailing system. Assuming that each message has a unique name, give specifications in extended BNF for these commands. The requirements are

   - a message can be sent by a user to one or more users in the system;

   - a user can reply to only one mail at a time. The effect of *reply* is to compose a message, assign a unique name, assign a time-stamp, and send the message to the user from whom the original message was received.

3. A safe has a combination lock that can be in one of four positions 1, 2, 3, and 4. The dial can be turned clockwise (C) or anticlockwise (A). Assume that the correct combination to the lock is the sequence $\langle 1C, 4A, 3C, 2A \rangle$ and that any other combination will trigger an alarm. Devise a state transition diagram to specify the behavior of the lock.

4. Give a user-interface specification based on an extended state transition diagram notation for a small library system capable of performing the following transactions:

   - Books can be added, removed, and searched for.

   - Books can be loaned, renewed, and reserved.

   - Users can be added, removed, and traced for overdue books and unpaid fines.

5. An Automobile Registration System requires a visual user interface, similar to the electronic form discussed in Example 5.10. The requirements are as follows:

   - The form should have three sections: *Vehicle, Owner, Administration*.

   - The information in the *Vehicle* section should include the make, model, year, serial number, engine capacity, factory price, and color.

   - The *Owner* information should include the name, address, and phone numbers of the principal owner of the vehicle. It should also include the date of purchase and the purchase price of the vehicle.

   - The *Administration* section should include the status of the vehicle (pleasure or business), date and place of current registration, registration number of the vehicle, registration fee, and expiration date of registration.

   Design a form, give an extended BNF grammar for generating the form, and derive the corresponding extended state transition diagrams showing the user interaction points.

6. Specify the characteristics of a mouse for selecting, copying, and dragging items in a window-based editing environment.

7. Specify the behavior of a printer and its monitor that function synchronously: the printer is controlled by the monitor to print one job at a time; the printer

prints the header of a file and then prints its contents; while the printer is printing, all requests are received by the monitor, which maintains a queue of jobs; the monitor removes the first job in the queue when the printer is ready for printing.

8. A home-heating system consists of a furnace, a thermostat, and a fan for blowing air. Temperature control is distributed so that every room has a controller to maintain its temperature. When the temperature in a room goes below $t_r - 2$, where t_r is the desired room temperature, the furnace is turned on. When the temperature in the furnace reaches a certain limit T, the furnace is shut off and the fan starts blowing the hot air. The thermostat registers and monitors the room temperature. When the room temperature reaches $t_r + 2$, the furnace is shut off. The fan runs until the furnace temperature falls to $T - 5$. Assuming that $t_r + 2 \geq T$, give a statechart specification for the system.

9. Give a statechart diagram for the producer-consumer problem: there are two processes P and C. Process P produces items and puts them in a buffer, and process C consumes items from the buffer one at a time. The buffer can hold a maximum of two items. When the buffer is full, process P must wait until process C has consumed an item. If the buffer is empty, process C must wait until process P puts an item in the buffer.

Bibliographic Notes

Hopcroft and Ullman [14] present a comprehensive treatment of automata and formal language theory. The book includes a discussion on Turing machines, Church's thesis, and the halting problem. These works set limits on the nature of algorithmic solutions and suggest that there may be no satisfactory implementation for some of the algorithms. This limitation, combined with Gödel's result on incompleteness, has several implications on the theory of languages, and in particular on formal specification languages. Yet, formal languages are useful in practical applications such as development of compilers. See Aho, Sethi, and Ullman [1] for applications of formal languages to compiler design.

The formal notation used by Backus [2] to define the syntax of FORTRAN, and the notation used by Naur [15] to define the syntax of Algol60 have together come to be known as Backus Naur Form (BNF, for short). The Yacc parser generator [7] produces translators for programming languages based on BNF descriptions. An interesting use of formal grammars for prototyping has been suggested by Reisner [17] who used certain properties of the BNF notation to predict the complexity of a user interface. Jacob [6] uses both BNF and state transition diagrams to formally specify human-computer interfaces in the Military Message System project at the Naval Research Laboratory. This is one of the earliest papers to report problems and experiences in using formal methods for secure message systems.

The EPROL specification language designed by Hekmatpour and Ince [11] uses the extended state machine notation of Denert [5]. They illustrate the expressiveness of the notation for the user-interface specification of a library system. Harel [8] introduces several extensions for state diagrams in the statecharts formalism. These extended notations transform state diagrams into a compact and expressive notation for specifying complex computer systems, such as real-time systems, communication protocols, and telephony. A formal syntax and operational semantics for statecharts can be found in [9]. The Statemate tool is based on the statecharts formalism, and is now commercially available [10]. Selic et al.[18] have adapted statecharts to model real-time reactive systems in an object-oriented framework, and call their notation *Roomcharts*. The important extensions in *Roomcharts* are scoping rules for nested state machines, transition points for specifying transitions that span multiple layers of states, a mechanism for overriding group transitions, and evaluation methods of triggering rules.

Wing [19] reviews the features of several formal specification languages and compares their characteristics. The paper includes a number of examples. In his editorial article to two special volumes of *The Computer Journal* devoted to formal methods, Cooke [3] discusses the nature, features, limitations, and expectations of formal methods. Cooke states that

> ... formal methods (only) provide a framework in which programs can be developed in a justifiable way. It does not dictate, or even advise, on how manipulations should be applied.

References

[1] A.V. Aho, R. Sethi, and J.D. Ullman, *Compiler Design: Principles, Techniques, and Tools*, Addison-Wesley Publishing Company, Reading, MA, 1986.

[2] J.W. Backus, "The FORTRAN Automatic Coding System," *Proceedings of the AFIPS Western Joint Computer Conference*, 1957, pp. 188–198.

[3] J. Cooke, "Formal Methods - Mathematics, Theory, Recipes or What?," *The Computer Journal*, Vol. 35, No. 5, 1992, pp. 419–423.

[4] N. Davis, "Problem # 4: LIFT," *Fourth International Workshop on Software Specification and Design*, IEEE Computer Press, April 1987.

[5] E. Denert, "Specification and Design of Dialogue Systems with State Diagrams," *International Computing Symposium*, D. Ribbons (Ed.), North-Holland, 1977, pp. 417–424.

[6] R.J.K. Jacob, "Using Formal Specifications in the Design of a Human-Computer Interface," *Communications of the ACM*, Vol. 26, No. 4, 1983, pp. 259–264.

[7] S.C. Johnson, "Yacc: Yet Another Compiler Compiler," *Computer Science Technical Report* No. 32, Bell Labs, Murray Hills, NJ, 1975.

[8] D. Harel, "Statecharts: A Visual Formalism for Complex Systems," *Science of Computer Programming*, Vol. 8, 1987, pp. 231–274.

[9] D. Harel, A. Pnueli, J.P. Schmidt, and R. Sherman, "On the Formal Semantics of State-charts," *Proceedings of the Second IEEE Symposium on Logic in Computer Science*, IEEE Press, NY, 1987, pp. 54–64.

[10] D. Harel, H. Lachover, A. Naamad, A. Pnueli, M. Politi, R. Sherman, R. Shtull-Trauring, and M. Trakhtenbrot, "Statemate: A Working Environment for the Development of Complex Reactive Systems," *IEEE Transactions on Software Engineering*, Vol. 16, No. 4, April 1990, pp. 403–414.

[11] S. Hekmatpour and D. Ince, *Software Prototyping, Formal Methods and VDM*, Addison-Wesley Publishing Company, International Computer Science Series, 1988.

[12] P. Henderson, "Functional Programming, Formal Specification, and Rapid Prototyping," *IEEE Transactions on Software Engineering*, Vol. SE-12, No. 2, February 1986, pp. 241–250.

[13] W. Hershey, "Idea Processors," *Byte*, Vol. 10, No. 4, 1985.

[14] J. Hopcroft and J. Ullman, *Introduction to Automata Theory, Languages, and Computation*, Addison-Wesley Publishing Company, Reading, MA, 1979.

[15] P. Naur (ed.), "Revised Report on the Algorithmic Language Algol 60," *Communications of the ACM*, Vol. 6, No. 1, 1963, pp. 1–17.

[16] G. Peano, "The Principles of Arithmetic, Presented by a New Method," in J. van Heijenoort (Ed.), *From Frege to Gödel: A Sourcebook of Mathematical Logic*, Harvard University Press, Cambridge, MA, 1967.

[17] P. Reisner, "Formal Grammar and Human Factors Design of an Interactive Graphics System," *IEEE Transactions on Software Engineering* Vol. SE-7, No. 2, March 1981, pp. 229–240.

[18] B. Selic, G. Gulleckson, and P.T. Ward, *Real-Time Object-oriented Modeling*, John Wiley & Sons, New York, NY, 1994.

[19] J.M. Wing, "A Specifier's Introduction to Formal Methods," *IEEE Computer*, Vol. 23, No. 9, September 1990, pp. 8–24.

[20] P. Zave, "Feature Interactions and Formal Specifications in Telecommunications," *IEEE Computer*, Vol. 26, No. 8, August 1993, pp. 20–30.

6

Logic

Logic is a system for rational enquiry and is founded on axioms and inference rules for reasoning. Modern mathematical logic dates back to the works of Frege and Peano late in the 19th century. The first attempt to use computational power for proof procedures based on predicate calculus was made in the 1950s. Logic has influenced Artificial Intelligence, the design of programming languages, their semantics, program verification procedures, and the formal specification of software systems.

Examples of logic include classical propositional logic, first-order logic, modal and temporal logics. In this chapter, we investigate three of these: *propositional logic, first-order predicate logic,* and *temporal logic*. The focus is on how logic can be used as a tool in the analysis and presentation of system requirements. This requires an investigation of how assertions are formulated and combined, whether assertions imply intended conclusions, and how to mechanically prove certain results from the stated axioms without assigning truth values to the formulas.

We include in this chapter only brief and at times informal sketches of the language aspects of logic; however, we quote important results that are sufficient for the study of logic as a formal specification language.

6.1 Propositional Logic

A proposition is a statement that is either true or false, but not both. *Propositional logic*, the language of propositions, consists of well-formed formulas constructed from *atomic formulas* and the *logical connectives* $\wedge$ (*and*), $\vee$ (*or*), $\neg$ (*not*), $\Rightarrow$ (*if ... then*), $\Leftrightarrow$ (*if and only if*). The atomic formulas of propositional calculus are

$terminals = \{P, Q, R, \ldots, \wedge, \vee, \neg, \Rightarrow, \Leftrightarrow, (,)\};$
$nonterminals = \{ atomic\ formula,\ sentence\ \};$
$atomic\ formula = P \mid Q \mid R \mid \ldots;$
$sentence = atomic\ formula \mid$
$\qquad (,\ sentence\ ,) \mid \neg,\ sentence \mid$
$\qquad sentence\ ,\ \vee,\ sentence \mid$
$\qquad sentence\ ,\ \wedge,\ sentence \mid$
$\qquad sentence\ ,\ \Rightarrow,\ sentence \mid$
$\qquad sentence\ ,\ \Leftrightarrow,\ sentence;$

FIGURE 6.1. Formal language for propositional logic.

propositions such as "computer is intelligent," "program does not terminate," and "alarm rings forever." It is not the string of symbols in a proposition but the truth value of the assertion that gives meaning to the proposition. Thus, if P stands for "program does not terminate" and Q stands for "alarm rings forever," then $P \Rightarrow Q$ denotes the *compound proposition* "if program does not terminate then alarm rings forever," whose truth value is uniquely determined by the truth values of P and Q.

6.1.1   Syntax and Semantics

Figure 6.1 gives the syntax of the language for propositional logic. The grammar does not show all possible names for propositions; for example, subscripted symbols and strings from the application domain are members of the set of terminals. There is an infinite collection of symbols that can be used to denote propositions, although only a finite subset is used at any instant.

The semantics for propositional logic is obtained by assigning truth values, *true (T)* or *false (F)* to atomic propositions and evaluating the sentences according to the interpretation shown in Table 6.1. The language of propositional logic is composed of well-formed formulas. A sentence is *true* when under some specific truth assignment to the atomic propositions, it evaluates to true. The interpretations in Table 6.1 hold even when P and Q are replaced by any sentence in the language.

The logic operators observe precedence according to the following decreasing order: $\neg(highest)$, $\wedge$, $\vee$, $\Rightarrow$, $\Leftrightarrow$. $P \Rightarrow Q$ is sometimes written $Q \Leftarrow P$, and read "Q if P." Two well-formed formulas P and Q are *equivalent*, written $P \equiv Q$, if and only if they have the same truth values under every interpretation. Notice that $\equiv$ is a metasymbol and is not part of the language. For example, $(P \Rightarrow Q) \equiv (\neg P \vee Q)$ can be verified using a truth table. A number of equivalence rules exist that are useful in *simplifying* a well-formed formula. These include the distributive laws and De Morgan's laws [1]. A sentence F is *satisfiable* if there is an assignment of truth values to the atomic propositions in F for which F is true. A sentence that is not *satisfiable* is *contradictory*. If, for a list of sentences L, every assignment that makes the sentences in L true also makes the sentence P true, we say P is

P	Q	$\neg P$	$P \vee Q$	$P \wedge Q$	$P \Rightarrow Q$	$P \Leftrightarrow Q$
T	T	F	T	T	T	T
T	F	F	T	F	F	F
F	T	T	T	F	T	F
F	F	T	F	F	T	T

TABLE 6.1. Truth table defining semantics of propositional logic.

a *semantic consequence* of L, and write $L \models P$. The metasymbol $\models$ is termed *semantic turnstile*. If a sentence is true for every assignment F, it is termed a *tautology*, and we write $\models F$. For example, $P \vee false \Rightarrow P \wedge true$ is a tautology, and $P \vee true \Rightarrow P \wedge false$ is a contradiction. The statement $P \wedge true \Rightarrow P \wedge false$ is *contingent*; its truth value may be *true* or *false* depending on the truth values of its constituents.

6.1.2   Proofs

A proof is a mechanism for showing that a given claim Q is a logical consequence of some premises $P_1, \ldots, P_k$. In this view, the purpose of a proof is to make explicit what is already implicitly present. A proof is presented as a finite sequence of steps, each of which is either an axiom or the logical conclusion of a set of steps occurring earlier in the proof. The final step of the proof is the demonstration of the truth of the claim Q. A *formal proof* requires that all implicit assumptions are made explicit and the steps in the proof are shown with reference to the sources used in deriving each step. Mathematical proofs are rigorous but not formal because there may be large gaps in proof steps that make the proof unsuitable for automated reasoning.

There are two aspects in proving a result: proof construction, and proof presentation. The construction phase is often informal, and the presentation phase must be rigorous, if not fully formal. Although gaps may exist in a rigorous proof, they are usually easy to fill. Proof methods and their formal presentation in propositional logic framework are discussed below.

Reasoning Based on Adopting a Premise

Truth tables provide an exhaustive proof method for propositional calculus. To prove a claim Q from the premises $P_1, P_2, \ldots, P_k$, one constructs a truth table and determines whether or not there exists an assignment of truth values to the P_i's that makes Q true. The steps are as follows:

The relationship between premises $P_1, P_2, \ldots, P_k$ and Q is written as $P_1, P_2, \ldots, P_k \models Q$. This statement can be rewritten as $P_1 \wedge P_2 \wedge \ldots \wedge P_k \Rightarrow Q$, which is shown to be a tautology. The proof simplifies the expression $\neg(P_1 \wedge P_2 \wedge \ldots \wedge P_k) \vee Q$ and shows that it is true under all interpretations.

Inference Based on Natural Deduction

The natural deduction inference rules describe *valid* steps in a deduction process. A valid step is a pair (P, Q) of sentences such that Q logically follows from P. This is a purely syntactic method for deriving well-formed formulas from those that already exist. It is based on two sets of rules—one set introduces connectives and hence the rules are called *introduction rules*, and the other set eliminates connectives and hence the rules are called *elimination rules*.

Introduction Rules

$\vee$-Introduction $\qquad \dfrac{\alpha}{\alpha \vee \beta}$ and $\dfrac{\beta}{\beta \vee \alpha}$

$\wedge$-Introduction $\qquad \dfrac{\alpha, \beta}{\alpha \wedge \beta}$ and $\dfrac{\alpha, \beta}{\beta \wedge \alpha}$

$\neg$-Introduction $\qquad \dfrac{\alpha \vdash false}{\neg \alpha}$

$\Rightarrow$-Introduction $\qquad \dfrac{\alpha \vdash \beta}{\alpha \Rightarrow \beta}$

$\Leftrightarrow$-Introduction $\qquad \dfrac{\alpha \Rightarrow \beta, \beta \Rightarrow \alpha}{\alpha \Leftrightarrow \beta}$

Elimination Rules

$\vee$-Elimination $\qquad \dfrac{\alpha \vee \beta, \alpha \vdash \gamma, \beta \vdash \gamma}{\gamma}$

$\wedge$-Elimination $\qquad \dfrac{\alpha \wedge \beta}{\alpha}$ and $\dfrac{\alpha \wedge \beta}{\beta}$

$\neg$-Elimination $\qquad \dfrac{\neg\neg \alpha}{\alpha}, \dfrac{\alpha, \neg \alpha}{F}$

$\Rightarrow$-Elimination $\qquad \dfrac{\alpha, \alpha \Rightarrow \beta}{\beta}$

$\Leftrightarrow$-Elimination $\qquad \dfrac{\alpha \Leftrightarrow \beta}{\alpha \Rightarrow \beta}$ and $\dfrac{\alpha \Leftrightarrow \beta}{\beta \Rightarrow \alpha}$

Consider, for example, the first introduction rule for disjunction. This states that under the assumption that α has been proved, the disjunction of α with any other logical expression β is also proved. The validity of this inference rule comes from truth table interpretation: a disjunction is true in every interpretation where one of its disjuncts is true.

The introduction rules for conjunction and two-sided implication require individual proofs for their conjuncts. The conjunction elimination rules state that if $\alpha \wedge \beta$ has been proved, then both α and β are proved. Once again, the validity of this rule can be traced to truth table interpretation. To eliminate a disjunction, one has to have more information: the logical consequence of each disjunct. The implication elimination rule is also called the *law of excluded middle*.

Since these inference rules hold for arbitrary expressions α and β, whenever a proof step has expressions matching the pattern of the antecedent of a proof rule, that rule can be applied. For example, from $P \vee Q$, $\neg P$, and an application of conjunction introduction rule, infer $(P \vee Q) \wedge \neg P$. Apply the distribution law and simplify the consequence to $(P \wedge \neg P) \vee (\neg P \wedge Q)$. This expression reduces further to $\neg P \wedge Q$. An application of conjunction elimination rule proves $\neg P$ and Q. A more complex proof is shown in Example 6.1. Finding an appropriate proof strategy for proving results using these rules is not easy; it requires some expertise to choose the proper rule at each step.

Example 6.1   Show that

$$P \vee (Q \wedge R) \vdash (P \vee Q) \wedge (P \vee R)$$

Derivation steps:

1.	P	premise
2.	$P \vee Q$	$\vee$-Introduction
3.	$P \vee R$	$\vee$-Introduction
4.	$(P \vee Q) \wedge (P \vee R)$	$\wedge$-Introduction and from 2 and 3
5.	$Q \wedge R$	premise
6.	Q	$\wedge$-Elimination
7.	$P \vee Q$	$\vee$-Introduction
8.	R	$\wedge$-Elimination and 5
9.	$P \vee R$	$\vee$-Introduction
10.	$(P \vee Q) \wedge (P \vee R)$	$\wedge$-Introduction and from 7 and 9
11.	$P \vdash (P \vee Q) \wedge (P \vee R)$	from 1 to 4
12.	$Q \wedge R \vdash (P \vee Q) \wedge (P \vee R)$	from 5 to 10
13.	$P \vee (Q \wedge R) \vdash (P \vee Q) \wedge (P \vee R)$	$\vee$-Elimination and from 11, 12

The strategy of natural deduction proofs is bottom-up. In Example 6.1, we first recognize that $\beta = (P \vee Q) \wedge (P \vee R)$ is to be derived from $\alpha = P \vee (Q \wedge R)$, and so we start with α. Noticing the structure of α, we attempt $\vee$-elimination rule and attempt the proofs for $P \vdash \beta$ and $Q \wedge R \vdash \beta$. We then attempt the two subproofs. The difficult part of the proof process is to find the most appropriate elimination or introduction rule for an application. That is, a program that attempts to prove a theorem may have to exhaustively search through the rules and apply all those whose patterns match. This strategy inevitably generates all the relevant theorems. In principle, there can be an infinite number of theorems, and consequently bottom-up proofs cannot be efficiently automated. ∎

Proof by Resolution

A *literal* is an atomic formula or the negation of an atomic formula. In the former case the literal is *positive*, and in the latter case it is *negative*. If P_{ij}, for i = 1, ..., n; j = 1, ..., m, are literals, the disjunctions $C_i = P_{i1} \vee ... \vee P_{im}$, denoted by $\bigvee_{j=1}^{m} P_{ij}$, are clauses. The formula $F = C_1 \wedge ... \wedge C_n$, denoted by $\bigwedge_{i=1}^{n} C_i$, is in *conjunctive normal form* (CNF). For example, the sentence $(P \vee R) \wedge (Q \vee R) \wedge (P \vee S) \wedge (Q \vee S)$ is in CNF. For every formula F, there is an equivalent formula G that is in CNF.

Resolution is a simple syntactic transformation that can be applied to CNF formulas. For two clauses C_1 and C_2 of a formula F in CNF, the *resolvent* is defined as $R = (C_1 - \{L\}) \cup (C_2 - \{\bar{L}\})$, where

$$\bar{L} = \begin{cases} \neg P_i & \text{if } L = P_i \\ P_i, & \text{if } L = \neg P_i \end{cases}$$

The formulas F and $F \cup \{R\}$ are equivalent. The resolution inference rule consists of three parts:

resolution: $\dfrac{\alpha \vee P, \beta \vee \neg P}{\alpha \vee \beta}$ (eliminate P)

chain rule: $\dfrac{\neg \alpha \Rightarrow P, P \Rightarrow \beta}{\neg \alpha \Rightarrow \beta}$ (eliminate P)

modus ponens: $\dfrac{P, P \Rightarrow \alpha}{\alpha}$ (eliminate P)

The rules eliminate an atom P from two formulas. These rules are suitable for constructing a *proof by contradiction*. To establish

$$P_1, P_2, ..., P_n \vdash Q$$

the proof proceeds by negating the conclusion Q (that is, by assuming that Q is false) and assigning the value *true* to each premise and showing a contradiction as a consequence of these assumptions. The contradiction establishes that $P_1, P_2, ..., P_n, Q$ cannot all be true simultaneously. The proof steps are

1. Transform each premise and the negated conclusion (introduced as a new premise) into conjunctive normal form. Now each premise is a conjunction of one or more clauses and each clause is true.

2. Identify pairs of clauses that contain complementary literals; one contains an atom and the other contains its negation. Apply resolution to obtain the resolvent.

3. Apply repeatedly step 2 until P and $\neg P$ are derived, showing a contradiction. This completes the proof.

Example 6.2   Assuming that $P \Rightarrow Q$, and $R \vee P$ are axioms, show that $R \Rightarrow S \vdash S \vee Q$.

Proof

1. The premises are $P \Rightarrow Q, R \vee P, R \Rightarrow S$.

2. In conjunctive normal form the premises are $\neg P \vee Q, R \vee P, \neg R \vee S$.

3. The negation of the conclusion in conjunctive normal form is $\neg S, \neg Q$.

Clauses:

1.	$\neg P \vee Q$	premise
2.	$R \vee P$	premise
3.	$\neg R \vee S$	premise
4.	$\neg S \wedge \neg Q$	negation of conclusion
5.	$\neg S$	$\wedge$-elimination
6.	$\neg Q$	$\wedge$-elimination
7.	$R \vee Q$	(1), (2), resolution
8.	$\neg R$	(3), (5)
9.	Q	(7), (8)
10.	NIL	(6), (9)

Let us interpret the propositions in Example 6.2 as follows:

P	:	program does not terminate
Q	:	alarm rings forever
R	:	computer is not intelligent
S	:	computer runs forever

Now, the axioms are interpreted as follows:

1. If the program does not terminate, then the alarm rings forever.

2. Either the computer is not intelligent or the program does not terminate.

From this reasoning, we formulate a theorem: if "the computer runs forever" is implied by the fact that it is not intelligent, then either the computer runs forever, or the alarm rings forever. ∎

Consistency and Completeness

Propositional logic is both consistent and complete:

1. **Consistency or Soundness**— All provable statements are semantically true. That is, if a set of premises S syntactically entails a proposition P, then there is an interpretation in which P can be reasoned about from S. Formally, if $S \vdash P$, then $S \models P$. In particular, every theorem is a tautology.

2. **Completeness**— All semantically true statements are provable. That is, if a set of premises S semantically entails a proposition P, then P can be derived formally (syntactically) within the formalism. Formally, if $S \models P$, then $S \vdash P$.

There are two important consequences of completeness:

1. **Compactness**— If $S \models P$, then there is a finite subset S', $S' \subseteq S$ such that $S' \models P$.

2. **Decidability**— Given a finite set of propositions S and a proposition P, there is an algorithm that determines whether or not $S \models P$.

When a specification S is created within the propositional logic formalism, the decidability result confirms that S can be analyzed to demonstrate whether a property P holds in S or not. In Example 6.3, a set of requirements for checking out a book from a library is specified and analyzed for certain properties.

Example 6.3   The requirements for borrowing and returning a book from a school library are first stated informally and then formalized in propositional logic. A book can be in any one of the following four states: *on_stack*, *on_reserve*, *on_loan*, and *requested*. These are modeled by the propositions

- S—a book is on the stacks

- R—a book is on reserve

- L—a book is on loan

- Q—a book is requested

The constraints are

1. A book can be in only one of the three states S, R, L.

2. If a book is on the stacks or on reserve, then it can be requested.

The propositional logic formulas for the constraints are:

1. $S \Leftrightarrow \neg(R \vee L)$

2. $R \Leftrightarrow \neg(S \vee L)$

3. $L \Leftrightarrow \neg(S \lor R)$

4. $S \lor R \Rightarrow Q$

Transforming the above formulas into CNF, we get the following eight clauses:

1. $\neg S \lor \neg R$

2. $\neg S \lor \neg L$

3. $S \lor R$

4. $L \lor S$

5. $\neg R \lor \neg L$

6. $L \lor R$

7. $\neg S \lor Q$

8. $\neg R \lor Q$

It is easy to verify that the conjuncts enumerated above do not produce an empty clause. Hence, the requirements are consistent. We want to prove that the statement "if a book is on loan then it is not requested" is a consequence of the requirements. This is achieved by including the negation of the formula $L \Rightarrow \neg Q$ in the premises and applying the steps of the resolution principle to the clauses. Resolving $\neg L \lor \neg Q$ with the premise (7), we get $\neg S \lor \neg L$. Resolving $\neg L \lor \neg Q$ with premise (8), we get $\neg R \lor \neg L$. In the resolution steps below, the numbers refer to clauses enumerated above:

(I1)	$\neg S \lor \neg L$	resolvent
(I2)	$\neg R \lor \neg L$	resolvent
(I3)	*NIL*	from (1) and (3)
(I4)	*NIL*	from (2) and (4)
(I5)	*NIL*	from (5) and (6)
(I6)	*NIL*	from (4) and (I1)
(I7)	*NIL*	from (6) and (I2)

Propositional calculus cannot capture relationships among objects, for example, between books and borrowers of books, nor can assertions be made about a universe of objects. To generalize the assertions in Example 6.3 for all books in the library and all users who borrow books, we need more powerful formalisms. We study them in the next two sections.

6.2   Predicate Logic

Although assertions can be combined in propositional logic, an intrinsic relationship to the primitive propositions cannot be stated. In this section, we introduce the first-order predicate calculus with equality. The intrinsic relationship of objects and their attributes can be formalized in this formalism. Formulas are to be interpreted over structures rather than on simple values. Predicate logic, like propositional logic, uses symbols to represent knowledge. These symbols represent *constants, predicates, variables,* and *functions.*

Constants, such as *computer, mary,* and *temperature,* are used to represent objects or properties from the problem domain. Informally, the syntactic structure of a predicate is analogous to a parameterized procedure. It has a name and a set of arguments, which may be constants, variables, or functions. When the arguments are given values from certain domains, the predicate evaluates to true or false. For example, *mammal(x)* is a *unary* predicate. When the variable x is initialized to a *value* from the universe of mammals, the predicate *mammal(x)* evaluates to true; for all other values of x, the predicate evaluates to false. Predicates having n-arguments express a certain relationship among the n objects modeled by the arguments. For example, *lessthan* (a, b), *parent(x, y)*, *likes(a, b)*, and *ancestor(x, y)* express binary relations; the predicate *quotient* (a, b, c) defined by $c = a \, div \, b$ captures the ternary relation that c is the quotient when b divides a. The predicate *friends* (*father(x)*, *mother(y)*) states that the father of x and the mother of y are friends. Here, *father* and *mother* are function symbols. All propositions are predicates. The formal syntax, semantics, and inference mechanisms for predicate logic are introduced below.

6.2.1   Syntax and Semantics

The syntax of predicate logic contains variables, function symbols, predicate symbols, and quantifiers. The syntax shown in Figure 6.2 assumes the existence of predefined domains, IDENTIFIER, VARNAME, CONSTANT. Although some or all of the domains may be infinite, only a finite number of symbols from them will be used in constructing the predicate logic. First-order terms from these domains are constants denoted by uppercase letters, variables denoted by lowercase letters $x, y, \ldots$, and functions $f(t_1, \ldots, t_k)$, where f is a function symbol, and t_is are terms. An atomic formula is of the form $p(t_1, \ldots, t_n)$, where p is an n-ary predicate name. The grammar in Figure 6.2 defines the well-formed formulas in the language of predicate logic. These include

- atomic formulas
- $\neg F$, where F is a formula
- $F \wedge G, F \vee G, F \Rightarrow G, F \Leftrightarrow G$, where F and G are formulas, and
- $\forall x \bullet F, \exists x \bullet F$, where x is a variable and F is a formula

wff	= *proposition* | *predicate* | ¬ *wff* |
	quantified-wff |(, *wff*, *op*, *wff*,);
proposition	= *P* | *Q* | *R* | . . .;
predicate	= *predicate_name*, (, *term_list*,);
predicate_name	= IDENTIFIER;
term_list	= *term* | *term*, ",", *term_list*;
term	= *CONSTANT* | *variable* | *function*, (, *term_list*,);
variable	= *VARNAME*;
function	= IDENTIFIER;
quantified-wff	= *quantifier*, "•", *wff*;
quantifier	= ∃, *variable* | ∀, *variable*;
op	= ∨ | ∧ |⇒|⇔;

FIGURE 6.2. Formal syntax of predicate logic.

Some examples of well-formed formulas of predicate logic are

$\forall x \bullet \exists y \bullet (less(square(x), y))$
$\forall x \bullet \forall y \bullet (likes(x, y) \Rightarrow marry(x, y))$
$\exists x \bullet \exists y \bullet (airline(x) \land city(y) \land flies(x, y))$
$\forall x \bullet \exists y, z \bullet (airline(x) \land city(y) \land city(z) \land flies(x, y) \land flies(x, z) \Rightarrow (y = z))$

The last formula above asserts that every airline x flies to only one city. The meta symbol ∃! may be used as a shorthand to express uniqueness. That is, $\forall x \bullet \exists! y \bullet$ $(airline(x) \land city(y) \land flies(x, y))$ expresses the same fact as the last formula above.

Constants, which are simple proposition symbols, and connectives are interpreted as in propositional logic. Each n-ary predicate is a Boolean n-ary function, with the name of the predicate usually designating a real-world object. Predicates are always used with the exact number of arguments. The existential (∃) and universal (∀) quantifiers are used for contextual binding. The domain of interest for which a variable is bound can be made explicit. The occurrences of x, y in the predicate $\forall x : jobs \bullet \exists y : queues \bullet (\neg executing(x) \Rightarrow has(y, x))$ are *bound*. In the formula $\exists y \bullet on(x, y)$, the variable y is bound but x is "free." Formulas in which every variable is bound are called *closed* formulas. Every closed formula can be interpreted as a proposition.

The *meaning* to predicates and function symbols is assigned relative to a nonempty domain D. This domain is assumed to include all values that can be assigned to all variables in the language. The *interpretation* of an n-ary predicate p is a function that takes an assignment of values to the n arguments of p and returns *true* or *false*. An interpretation for a formula F assigns values to each free variable in F, and interprets each predicate in the formula as above. Thus, the meaning of a formula is an assignment of a truth value for each interpretation. The meaning of a formula is derived from the meanings of its subformulas:

1. If the formula is an atomic predicate $p(t_1, \ldots, t_n)$, the terms t_i's are constants or free variables, the chosen interpretation assigns values to the variables, and then evaluates the predicate to *true* or *false*.

2. If the formula involves functions, these are evaluated to reduce the arguments of the predicates to constants before the predicate is evaluated.

3. An expression $E = E_1 \; op \; E_2$, where E_1 and E_2 are unquantified, is *inductively* evaluated – E_1 and E_2 are evaluated under the chosen interpretation and the semantics of *op* is applied to their truth values.

4. In an expression E of the form $\forall x \bullet E_1$, E_1 is evaluated and if the truth value remains the same for every value in the domain of interpretation, then E is *true*; otherwise, E is *false*.

5. In an expression E of the form $\exists x \bullet E_1$, the domain of interpretation for E_1 is obtained by assigning a value from the domain of interpretation for E to x, and is used to evaluate E_1 inductively. If there exists at least one value of x for which this process evaluates E_1 to *true*, the formula E also evaluates to *true*; otherwise, E evaluates to *false*.

Example 6.4   Consider the following predicate logic formula:

$$G(x, y) \Rightarrow \exists z \bullet (G(x, z) \wedge G(z, y))$$

We discuss four different interpretations for the predicate G.

Interpretation I_1

1. The domain D is the set of integers.

2. $G(r, s)$ is *true* if $r > s$.

The interpretation assigns to G the infinite collection of ordered pairs on integers (r, s), such that $r > s$.

For this interpretation, the formula states that for any pair of integers x and y, if $x > y$, then there is some other integer z with the property $x > z$ and $z > y$. That is, z strictly lies between y and x. If $x = y$ or $y > x$, then $G(x, y)$ is *false*, and consequently, the formula is *true*. If $x = y + 1$, $G(x, y)$ is *true*; however, there is no integer z in between y and $x = y + 1$; hence, the formula has the value false. The formula is true for all interpretations, except when $x = y + 1$.

Interpretation I_2

1. The domain D is the set of positive integers.

2. The predicate $G(r, s)$ is true whenever r is a divisor of s.

For this interpretation, the formula states that for any pair of integers x and y, if x is a divisor of y, then there is some $z \in D$ with the property that x is a divisor of z, and

z is a divisor of y. For $x > y$, the predicate $G(x, y)$ is *false*, and consequently, the formula is *true*. For some pair of positive integers $x, y, x \leq y$, assume that $G(x, y)$ is *true*. The formula states that there is some positive integer z such that x divides z and z divides y. That is, z statisfies three properties:

1. $x \leq z \leq y$;

2. x divides z and y;

3. z divides y.

If $x = 8$, $y = 24$, $G(x, y)$ is *true*, but there is no z satisfying the above three conditions. However, if $x = 4$, $y = 24$, $G(x, y)$ is *true*, and there exists $z = 8$ for which $G(x, z)$ and $G(z, y)$ are both *true*, hence the formula is *true*. In general, the formula is *false* for some pairs (x, y), and is *true* for some other pairs (x, y). It is important to note that there are only a finite number of interpretations for the formula, because only finite number of values can be assumed by z in between x and y.

Interpretation I_3

1. The domain D is the set of real numbers.

2. $G(x, y)$ is true whenever $x \geq y$.

In between any two real numbers there are infinitely many real numbers. Hence, the formula is *true* for all pairs x, y of real numbers. That is, there are infinitely many interpretations for the formula based on any pair of values assigned to the variables x, y of predicate G.

Interpretation I_4   This interpretation is based on natural numbers and their cartesian products.

1. $D = N \cup E$, where N is a subset of natural numbers, and $E = N \times N$.

2. The predicate $G(x, y)$ is *true*, if $x \leq y \wedge (x, y) \in E$.

Under this interpretation the formula states that if $(x, y) \in E$, then for some $z \in N$ the pairs (x, z), $x \leq z$, and (z, y), $z \leq y$, also belong to E. If we choose

$$N = \{1, 2, 3\}, \text{ and } E = \{(1, 2), (1, 3), (2, 3)\}$$

then the formula is *true* for $x = 1$, $y = 3$, and $z = 2$. For several other assignments, such as $x = 2$, $y = 1$, and $z = 3$, the formula is *false*. In general, the formula is *true* if the free variables are assigned values from the domain $\{x, y : \mathbb{R} \mid x \leq y\}$.

∎

When requirements are translated from a natural language description into logic, the domain of interpretation is the environment in which the requirements are formulated. That is, the specifier does not go through the task of constructing a model for the formulas; the formulas are built from the requirements.

Equality and Equivalence

We introduce the binary infix predicate $=$ in the predicate logic. If s and t are terms, then $(s = t)$ is an atomic formula which may be true or false. This predicate satisfies the following equational axioms:

1. **Reflexive** $\forall x \bullet x = x$;
2. **Commutative** $\forall x, y \bullet (x = y) \Rightarrow (y = x)$;
3. **Transitive** $\forall x, y, z \bullet ((x = y) \wedge (y = z)) \Rightarrow (x = z)$;

The operation of substituting one variable for another is a common practice in mathematics. In predicate logic, this must be done with some care. Formally, if S is a formula, t a term and x a variable, we define $S[t/x]$ (read "S with t for x") to be the formula obtained from S on replacing every free occurrence of x by t, provided no free variable of t is bound in S. If some free variable of t is bound in S, then each bound variable must be renamed so that it is not bound in S.

Two formulas F and G are *equivalent*, written as $F \equiv G$, if they have the same truth value for all interpretations that are suitable for both F and G. If $F \equiv G$, and $x = y$, where x is a free variable in F and y is a free variable in G, then $F[t/x] \equiv G[t/y]$. That is, equivalent formulas remain equivalent when free terms in them that are equal are replaced by the same variable.

Example 6.5 We describe a predicate logic theory with equality for a projective plane in which lines and points satisfy the following properties: (1) two lines meet at a unique point, and (2) there is a unique line through any two points. The unary predicates *point*(x) (x is a point) and *line*(x) (x is a line) introduce points and lines. The binary predicate *lies_on*(x, y) relates the incidence property of point x to line y. The predicate logic formulas enforcing the properties are as follows:

1. *domain distinction*

   (a) $\forall x \bullet (point(x) \vee line(x))$;

   (b) $\forall x \bullet (\neg(point(x) \wedge line(x)))$;

2. *incidence*
   $\forall x, y \bullet (lies\_on(x, y) \Rightarrow (point(x) \wedge line(y)))$;

3. *equality for lines*
   $\exists x_1, x_2 \bullet (\neg(x_1 = x_2) \wedge lies\_on(x_1, y_1) \wedge lies\_on(x_1, y_2) \wedge lies\_on(x_2, y_1) \wedge lies\_on(x_2, y_2)) \Rightarrow y_1 = y_2$;

4. *unique line*
   $\forall x, y \bullet ((point(x) \land point(y) \land \neg(x = y)) \Rightarrow \exists!z \bullet (lies\_on(x, z)$
   $\land\ lies\_on(y, z)))$;

5. *unique intersection*
   $\forall x, y \bullet ((line(x) \land line(y) \land \neg(x = y)) \Rightarrow \exists!z \bullet (lies\_on(z, x) \land$
   $lies\_on(z, y)))$. ■

Example 6.6   This example specifies the sequence of discrete events affecting a light switch. A switch can be on or off at different times of a day. The status of the switch cannot be both on and off at the same time. Let *switch_on*(x) and *switch_off*(x) be predicates denoting that the status of the switch is on, and off, respectively, at time x. The domain of interpretation is discrete time, which is assumed to be the set of natural numbers. Consequently, in any finite interval, there can be only a finite number of state changes for the switch. A translation of the requirements into predicate logic is given below:

1. The switch is in only one state at any time.

   (a) $\forall x \bullet (switch\_on(x) \lor switch\_off(x))$;

   (b) $\forall x \bullet \neg(switch\_on(x) \land switch\_off(x))$;

2. The predicate $on(x, y)$ denotes the property that the switch is on at the time points $x, x + 1, \ldots, y - 1$. The predicate $off(x, y)$ denotes the property that the switch is off at the time points $x, x + 1, \ldots, y - 1$.

   (a) $on(x, y) \equiv switch\_on(x) \land \neg \exists z \bullet (lessthan(x, z) \land lessthan(z, y) \land switch\_off(z))$;

   (b) $off(x, y) \equiv switch\_off(x) \land \neg \exists z \bullet (lessthan(x, z) \land lessthan(z, y) \land switch\_on(z))$;

3. If the state of the switch is on (off) at time y and the previous time it was in the same state was at time x, then the switch stays off (on) throughout the interval (x, y).

   (a) $\forall x, y \bullet (switch\_on(x) \land switch\_on(y) \land lessthan(x, y)) \land \neg \exists z \bullet (switch\_on(z) \land lessthan(x, z) \land lessthan(z, y)) \Rightarrow off(x + 1, y)$;

   (b) $\forall x, y \bullet (switch\_off(x) \land switch\_off(y) \land lessthan(x, y)) \land \neg \exists z \bullet (switch\_off(z) \land lessthan(x, z) \land lessthan(z, y)) \Rightarrow on(x + 1, y)$;

4. The predicate $from\_off\_to\_on(u_1, v_2)$ denotes the property that the switch is off at time u_1, and on at time v_2, where $u_1 < v_2$, and either (1) the switch remained off for the time points $u_1, u_1 + 1, \ldots, v_2 - 1$, or (2) every

switch on is followed by a switch off in the interval (u_1, v_2). The predicate $from\_on\_to\_off(u_1, v_2)$ denotes the complementary property for the switch, when it is on at time u_1 and off at time v_2. We define the predicate $off\_on(u_1, v_2)$ to denote the property that every switch on is followed by a switch off, and the predicate $on\_off(u_1, v_2)$ to denote the property that every switch off is followed by a switch on and use them in defining the two predicates $from\_off\_to\_on$, and $from\_on\_to\_off$.

(a) $off\_on(u_1, v_2) \quad \equiv \quad \exists v_1, u_2 \bullet (lessthan(u_1, v_1) \wedge lessthan(v_1, u_2) \\ \wedge lessthan(u_2, v_2) \wedge off(u_1, v_1) \wedge off(u_2, v_2) \wedge on\_off(v_1, u_2));$

(b) $on\_off(v_1, u_3) \quad \equiv \quad \exists u_2, v_2 \bullet (lessthan(v_1, u_2) \wedge lessthan(u_2, v_2) \\ \wedge lessthan(v_2, u_3) \wedge on(v_1, u_2) \wedge on(v_2, u_3) \wedge off\_on(u_2, v_2));$

(c) $from\_off\_to\_on(x, y) \equiv switch\_on(y) \wedge (off(x, y) \vee off\_on(x, y));$

(d) $from\_on\_to\_off(x, y) \equiv switch\_off(y) \wedge (on(x, y) \vee on\_off(x, y));$

5. If the state of the switch is on (off) at times x and y, $x \geq y$, then either it is on (off) throughout $[x,y]$ or every switch off (on) is followed by a switch on (off) in the interval $[x,y]$. The predicates $on\_on(x, y)$, and $off\_off(x, y)$ denote these properties.

(a) $on\_on(x, y) \equiv on(x, y) \vee \exists z \bullet (on\_off(x, z) \wedge off\_on(z, y))$

(b) $off\_off(x, y) \equiv off(x, y) \vee \exists z \bullet (off\_on(x, z) \wedge on\_off(z, y))$ ∎

6.2.2   More on Quantified Expressions

In writing predicate logic expressions for requirements, multiple quantifiers are often necessary. For example, the requirement "all printing jobs are assigned to one printer queue" can be translated to

$\forall j : JOBS, \exists p : PRINTERQUEUE \bullet assign(j, p)$

To simplify the presentation of formulas, where the types of variables are obvious, the reference to types may be omitted. Thus,

$\forall j \exists p \bullet assign(j, p)$

is a shorthand for the formula above. Whenever all variables in a formula are universally quantified, the quantifiers may be dropped altogether from the presentation of the formula. For example, $\forall x, y \bullet P(x, y)$ is a closed formula, and can be written $P(x, y)$. Universal (existential) quantifier is a generalized conjunction (disjunction) operator. Consequently, negation can be moved in and out of quantified formulas by generalizing De Morgan's laws applicable to conjunction and disjunction. To enhance understandability, quantifiers can be interchanged or moved in front of a formula. Rules governing the movement of quantifiers are summarized below:

1. Moving negation out of quantifiers:

   (a) $\neg \forall x \bullet P(x) \equiv \exists x \bullet \neg P(x)$

   (b) $\neg \forall x \bullet \neg P(x) \equiv \exists x \bullet P(x)$

   (c) $\forall x \bullet \neg P(x) \equiv \neg \exists x \bullet P(x)$

   (d) $\forall x \bullet P(x) \equiv \neg \exists x \bullet \neg P(x)$

2. Driving quantifiers in front - If x does not occur free in Q, then the following equivalences hold:

   (a) $\forall x \bullet P \wedge Q \equiv \forall x \bullet (P \wedge Q)$

   (b) $\forall x \bullet P \vee Q \equiv \forall x \bullet (P \vee Q)$

   (c) $\exists x \bullet P \wedge Q \equiv \exists x \bullet (P \wedge Q)$

   (d) $\exists x \bullet P \vee Q \equiv \exists x \bullet (P \vee Q)$

3. Moving quantifiers out - The following equivalences hold when x is bound in both P and Q:

   (a) $(\forall x \bullet P \wedge \forall x \bullet Q) \equiv \forall x \bullet (P \wedge Q)$

   (b) $(\exists x \bullet P \vee \exists x \bullet Q) \equiv \exists x \bullet (P \vee Q)$

4. Interchanging the order of quantification:

   (a) $(\forall x \forall y \bullet P) \equiv (\forall y \forall x \bullet P)$

   (b) $(\exists x \exists y \bullet P) \equiv (\exists y \exists x \bullet P)$

Example 6.7   Informally, the equivalence below states that if $S(x) \Rightarrow S(y)$ is *true* (*false*) for any one specific value of x, then it has the same value for every x. To understand this, consider $S(x)$ as the *switch-on(x)* predicate in Example 6.6.

$$(\exists x \bullet (S(x) \Rightarrow S(y)) \equiv \forall x \bullet (S(x) \Rightarrow S(y))$$

The lefthand side expression is successively rewritten to get the result.

$\neg (\exists x \bullet S(x)) \vee S(y)$	$\Rightarrow$ *-elimination*
$\forall x \bullet \neg S(x) \vee S(y)$	*moving negation inside the quantifier scope*
$\forall x \bullet (\neg S(x) \vee S(y))$	*x is free in S(y)*
$\forall x \bullet (S(x) \Rightarrow S(y))$	$\Rightarrow$ *-introduction*

The quantifier rules can be used to put expressions with multiple quantifiers in *prenex* normal form, in which all quantifiers come first. As an example, the requirement "every procedure used by a program is stored in a reuse directory" has the predicate logic translation

$$\forall x \bullet ((procedure(x) \wedge \exists y \bullet (program(y) \wedge used\_by(x, y))) \Rightarrow$$
$$\exists y \bullet (reuse\_direc(y) \wedge stored\_in(x, y))).$$

When the quantifier rules are applied, the predicate logic expression is transformed to

$$\forall x \exists y \exists z \bullet ((procedure(x) \wedge program(y) \wedge used\_by(x, y)) \Rightarrow$$
$$(reuse\_direc(z) \wedge stored\_in(x, z))).\qquad\blacksquare$$

Predicate calculus embodies the language described above, propositional operators, interpretations, and quantified expressions. Example 6.8 illustrates the use of predicate logic to express the meaning of data and their constraints in a *data dictionary*.

Example 6.8   Structured system analysis is a graphical technique introduced in the 70s by DeMarco [2]. This method requires defining data dictionaries that include information on the meaning and representation of data to be used in the software development process. Predicate calculus formulas can be used to define data types, their integrity constraints, rules for using them, and relationships among the data. This example illustrates the application of constraints for a collection of data on *teams*, *players*, *coaches*, *games*, and *schedule* for a league. The predicates are

1. *memberof(x,y)*: x is a player, and y is a team

2. *coach(x,y)*: x is a coach, and y is a *team*;

3. *game(x,y,z,w)*: x, y are teams, z is a date, and w is a city

4. *schedule(x,y,z)*: x is a team, y is a date, and z is a city

5. *plays(x,y)*: x is a player, and y is a date.

The integrity constraints are

1. A player is a member of only one team in the league.
   $memberof(x, y) \wedge memberof(x, y') \Rightarrow y' = y.$

2. A coach coaches only one team; a team has only one coach.
   $coach(x, y) \wedge coach(x, y') \Rightarrow y = y'.$
   $coach(x, y) \wedge coach(x', y) \Rightarrow x = x'.$

3. A team plays at most one game a day.
   $schedule(x, y, z) \wedge schedule(x, y, z') \Rightarrow (z = z').$

4. No player of a team can be the coach of the team.
   $memberof(x, y) \wedge \neg coach(x, y).$

5. Every game played by a team should appear in the schedule.
   $game(x, y, z, w) \Rightarrow schedule(x, z, w) \wedge schedule(y, z, w).$

6. For every game, there are some players who do not play on the day of the game.
$game(x, y, z, w)$ $\Rightarrow$ $\exists p, q \bullet (memberof(p, x) \land memberof(q, y) \land \neg plays(p, z) \land \neg plays(q, z))$.

7. There are players on every team who do not play consecutively scheduled games.
$(schedule(x, y_1, z_1) \land schedule(x, y_2, z_2) \land \forall y \bullet ((y_1 < y) \land (y < y_2) \land \neg \exists z \bullet schedule(x, y, z))) \Rightarrow \exists p \bullet (member(p, x) \land \neg (plays(p, y_1) \land plays(p, y_2)))$. ∎

6.2.3 Proofs

To illustrate the generalization of the axiomatic deduction system of propositional calculus, let us revisit Example 6.5 and reason about the claims. Let a, b, c be three distinct points. That is, $point(a), point(b), point(c), \neg(a = b), \neg(a = c), \neg(b = c)$ are true. From the incidence assertion and the generalized inference rule "from p and $(p \Rightarrow q)$ infer q," we deduce that there exists unique lines z_1, z_2, z_3 such that the points a and b lie on z_1, the points a and c lie on z_2, and the points b and c lie on z_3. From the uniqueness property stated in the incidence assertion, $z_1 \neq z_2, z_1 \neq z_3, z_2 \neq z_3$. In addition to such proof rules of propositional logic, the predicate logic contains rules to deal with equality and quantifiers.

An essential step in a proof is syntactic substitution, which is described in section 6.2.1 under the heading *Equality and Equivalence*. When the substitution $[x/y]$ is applied to the formula $S : \forall x \bullet (x > 4) \land (y^2 = 4x) \Rightarrow (x > y)$, the bound variable x needs to be renamed, say to w, and then y is replaced by x in S. The expression $S[x/y]$ is $\forall w \bullet (w > 4) \land (x^2 = 4w) \Rightarrow (w > x)$.

We now discuss two proof methods: natural deduction, and resolution.

Natural Deduction Process

Natural deduction involves four inference rules that correspond to the elimination and introduction of quantifiers.

1. *Universal Generalization*

   ($\forall$-*Introduction*) $\dfrac{c \in X \vdash P(c)}{\forall x \bullet P(x)}$ where c is arbitrary.

   If we choose an arbitrary element c of the domain X and prove $P(c)$, then we can infer $\forall x \bullet P(x)$. For example, if for an arbitrary student from the domain of students it is proved that the student is registered in at least one course, then this property holds for every student in the domain.

2. *Universal Specification*

   ($\forall$-*Elimination*) $\dfrac{\forall x \in X \bullet P(x), c \in X}{P(c)}$ where c is arbitrary.

If P holds for all elements of the domain X, then it is true for any arbitrary element of the domain. The conclusion states that P can be treated as a proposition. For example, if X is the domain of prime numbers satisfying the property that every number from X can be written in the form $2^p - 1$, where p is a prime, then a prime number p can be found for any arbitrary element of X.

3. *Existential Generalization*

   ($\exists$-*Introduction*) $\dfrac{c \in X, P(c)}{\exists x \in X \bullet P(x)}$ where c is arbitrary.

   The rule establishes a disjunction over the elements of X, the domain of interest. The first hypothesis is that the set X is not empty, and the second hypothesis is that the property holds for some element of X. For example,

   $$pigeon \in \{dolphin, cat, pigeon\} \wedge bird(pigeon) \vdash$$
   $$\exists x \in \{dolphin, cat, pigeon\} \bullet bird(x).$$

4. *Existential Specification*

   ($\exists$-*Elimination*) $\dfrac{\exists x \in X \bullet P(x)}{P(c)}$ for some c in the domain of interest.

   In practice, it may be difficult to determine the particular value c from the domain for which $P(c)$ holds.

Example 6.9   This example models the behavior of a queue that always contains at least one item, and which is never full. The proof steps using universal elimination and existential generalization are shown. We will show that $\exists x \bullet (queued(x) \wedge next\_to(x, c))$ follows from the following three premises:

1. $\forall x \bullet (received(x) \Rightarrow queued(x))$: every message received is put in a queue.

2. $\forall x \bullet (queued(x) \Rightarrow next\_to(x, c))$: the received message is next to message c in the queue.

3. $received(m)$: message m is received.

The proof steps are the following:

1. Using universal elimination from the first two premises, derive

   (a) $received(m) \Rightarrow queued(m)$ premises (1) and (3).

   (b) $queued(m) \Rightarrow next\_to(m, c)$ premises (2) and (3).

2. Apply *modus ponens* to premise (3) and formula 1(a) to derive $queued(m)$.

3. Apply *modus ponens* to premise (2) and formula 1(b) to derive $next\_to(m, c)$

4. Apply $\wedge$-introduction rule to the results of steps (2) and (3) to derive $queued(m) \wedge next\_to(m, c)$.

5. Apply ∃-introduction rule to derive the conclusion
$\exists x \bullet (queued(x) \wedge next\_to(x, c))$. ∎

In Example 6.9, we can weaken the third premise to $\exists x \bullet received(x)$ and keep the other two premises. Still, we can obtain the same conclusion. The proof requires ∃-elimination and the third premise, in order to follow the proof steps shown above. In applying existential quantification, a name that is not already in use should be substituted for the quantified variable. Otherwise, the proof may conclude an irrelevant result. See exercise 3 of this chapter.

Example 6.10   From the premises

1. $\forall x \bullet (P(x) \Rightarrow Q(x))$

2. $\forall x \bullet \neg Q(x)$

prove that $\forall x \bullet \neg P(x)$.

Proof:
Let a stand for a new name denoting an arbitrary element from the domain of discourse. Applying ∀-elimination to each premise gives

1. $P(a) \Rightarrow Q(a)$

2. $\neg Q(a)$

Since the goal is to prove $\neg P(x)$, we must try to prove $\neg P(a)$ for an arbitrary a. This suggests negating the result in step (1) above, and using *modus ponens*. So, the proof steps are

$\neg Q(a) \Rightarrow \neg P(a)$	negation applied to step (1) above.
$\neg Q(a)$	from step (2) above.
$\neg P(a)$	modus ponens.
$\forall x \bullet \neg P(x)$	universal generalization. ∎

Resolution

The resolution principle for propositional logic is extended to deal with predicate logic by considering quantified expressions in *clausal forms* and using *unification*, a substitution method for variables to obtain resolvents.

Clausal Forms   Every clause expresses that a number (possibly zero) of joint conditions imply a number (possibly zero) of different conclusions. Both conditions and conclusions express relationships among objects in the problem domain. In the clausal form $P \Rightarrow Q$, also written $Q \Leftarrow P$, the *antecedent P* is a conjunction of its conditions, and the *consequent Q* is a disjunction of its conclusions. Each variable occurring in a clausal form is universally quantified with the whole formula as scope. A clause with no variables is called a *ground* clause. A clause with one or more conclusions is a *positive* clause, while a clause with no conclusion is a *negative* clause. Clauses with no condition represent *facts*; clauses with one or more conditions state rules and results. Thus, $Parents(x, y, z) \Leftarrow Mother(x, z), Father(y, z)$ is a positive conditional clause stating that x and y are parents of z if x is the mother of z and y is the father of z. Note the use of the symbol "," to denote "$\wedge$". It is possible to convert any predicate calculus expression to CNF; in particular, clausal forms can be converted to CNF.

Conjunctive Normal Form (CNF)   Reducing formulas of predicate logic to CNF is slightly more involved than in propositional logic. The steps are as follows:

1. Remove equivalences: replace $P \Leftrightarrow Q$ by $P \Rightarrow Q \wedge Q \Rightarrow P$.
2. Remove implications: replace $P \Rightarrow Q$ by $\neg P \vee Q$.
3. Move the negation signs: use De Morgan's laws to propagate negation signs in front of atoms from outside brackets.
4. Remove existential quantifiers: First reduce the expression to prenex normal form. A variable x quantified by $\exists x \bullet$ which is not itself within the scope of a universal quantifier, is replaced by a new constant (called *Skolem* constant) in the domain of interest. However, if $\exists x \bullet$ is within the scope of universal quantifiers, say $\forall y \, \forall z \bullet$, then x is replaced by $f(y, z)$ where the Skolem function f represents the existence of a unique x for every pair of y and z.
5. Remove universal quantifiers.
6. Apply the distributive law to separate out clauses.

Example 6.11   This example converts an expression to CNF.

The expression

$$(\neg(\forall x \bullet P(x, y) \vee \exists y \bullet Q(y, z)) \vee \forall z \bullet P(x, f(z)))$$

is rewritten using the equivalence axioms until its CNF is obtained:

$$((\neg(\forall x \bullet P(x, y)) \wedge \neg \exists y \bullet Q(y, z)) \vee \forall z \bullet P(x, f(z)))$$

$$\equiv$$

$$((\exists x \bullet \neg P(x, y) \wedge \forall y \bullet \neg Q(y, z)) \vee \forall z \bullet P(x, f(z)))$$

$$\equiv$$

$$\exists x \, \forall y \, \forall z \bullet (\neg P(x, y) \wedge \neg Q(y, z)) \vee P(x, f(z)),$$

Using Skolem constant c for x, we get

$$(\neg P(c, y) \vee P(c, f(z))) \wedge (\neg Q(y, z) \vee P(c, f(z))) \qquad \blacksquare$$

Unification   The resolution method requires that clauses be transformed so that two literals of opposite sign will have identical atoms. However, atoms may contain variable parameters. In this case, they can be made identical only when transformed by suitable substitutions. The process of finding a substitution and applying it to the clauses to be resolved so that the atoms in complementary literals are identical is called *unification*. For example, applying the substitution $[f(t)/x]$ to the clauses $\{P(x), \neg Q(x, y)\}$ and $\{\neg P(f(t))\}$ allow us to resolve them to obtain the resolvent $\neg Q(f(t), y)$. Suppose we have the clause $L(x, y), P(y, z), R(z, w) \Rightarrow S(x, w)$, and three known assertions $L(1, 3), P(3, 5), R(5, 7)$, then the substitution $[1/x, 3/y, 5/z]$ gives the new assertion $S(1, 7)$.

Example 6.12   The formula

$$C_1 \wedge C_2 \wedge C_3 \wedge C_4 \wedge C_5 \wedge C_6 \wedge C_7,$$

where

$$
\begin{aligned}
C_1 &= Q(w) \vee \neg T(a, w), \\
C_2 &= \neg Q(v) \vee \neg P(v), \\
C_3 &= \neg Q(u) \vee \neg S(u), \\
C_4 &= R(u) \vee S(u) \vee P(g(u)), \\
C_5 &= R(u) \vee S(u) \vee T(u, g(u)), \\
C_6 &= Q(a), \\
C_7 &= \neg R(a),
\end{aligned}
$$

is not satisfiable.

Proof:
Using resolution, the proof steps are as follows:

1. $Q(a)$ — clause C_6.
2. $\neg Q(u) \vee \neg S(u)$ — clause C_3.
3. $\neg S(a)$ — substitution [a/u] and applying resolution to steps 1 and 2.
4. $R(u) \vee S(u) \vee P(g(u))$ — clause C_4.
5. $R(a) \vee P(g(a))$ — substitution [a/u] and applying resolution to steps 3 and 4.
6. $\neg R(a)$ — clause C_7.
7. $P(g(a))$ — applying resolution to steps 5 and 6.
8. $R(u) \vee S(u) \vee T(u, g(u))$ — clause C_5.
9. $S(a) \vee T(a, g(a))$ — substitution [a/u] and applying resolution to steps 6 and 8.
10. $T(a, g(a))$ — applying resolution to steps 3 and 9.
11. $Q(w) \vee \neg T(a, w)$ — clause C_1.
12. $Q(g(a))$ — substitution [g(a)/w] and applying resolution to steps 10 and 11.

13. $\neg Q(v) \lor \neg P(v)$	clause C_2.
14. $\neg P(g(a))$	substitution $[g(a)/v]$ and applying resolution to steps 12 and 13.
15. *NIL*	applying resolution to steps 7 and 14.

Decidability

As in propositional logic, there is a distinction between what is *true* and what is *provable*. A statement that is true under all interpretations may or may not be provable using a certain proof method. Provability depends on the proof method used, such as natural deduction or resolution. However, predicate logic is both sound and complete with respect to interpretations:

> **the Soundness Theorem**   If $S \vdash p$, then $S \models p$. That is, if p is provable from S, then it is a true statement.

> **the Completeness Theorem**   If $S \models p$, then $S \vdash p$. Every statement that is true in all models is also provable from the rules and axioms of the proof method.

Whereas propositional logic is decidable, predicate logic is algorithmically *undecidable*. That is, showing the validity of expressions and proving the satisfiability of an arbitrary predicate logic formula are much harder, because one has to consider all possible meanings of terms from the underlying structure which may be infinite. There are predicate logic formulas that are satisfiable, but they do not have any model of finite size. This limits the extent to which proofs can be automated. In particular, mechanical theorem provers may not be able to derive proofs for certain complex programs. Strong heuristics to select proof strategies and methods to avoid complex predicate expressions that lead to undecidability are both essential in designing theorem provers.

6.2.4   More Specification Examples

In this section we discuss three specification examples using predicate logic. Example 6.13 illustrates the use of predicate logic for writing input and output assertions in the style of Hoare logic to describe the status of a system before and after execution of statements in a program fragment. An input assertion, also known as a *precondition*, is a predicate over the values in the state preceding execution of the statement, and it states the condition under which the program will have some effect. An output assertion, also known as *postcondition*, indicates how the variables are affected by the program when the precondition is true, and the statement is executed.

Example 6.13   A *file* is assumed to be a linear sequence of *records*, where the notion of record is primitive. The records of the file are sequentially numbered from zero. Thus $file_0$, $file_1, \ldots, file_{k-1}$ are the k records of a file at any instance. If $k < 1$, the file is empty. $file_j$, $0 \le j \le k - 1$ refers to the j-th record of the file. Editor commands *modify* the file by insertion, deletion, and replacement of records. Hence, in the postcondition, it is necessary to refer to the variables in the state prior to an operation, and to the variables in the state after the operation. We distinguish between the values of the variables prior to and after an operation by suffixing the variables with a prime to denote their values in the state after the operation. This is acceptable in the predicate logic formalism: a name refers to only one entity at any time, although more than one name may refer to the same entity. The substitution rule in predicate calculus supports the renaming of variables in assertions. If $S(x)$ is an invariant condition on x, and x' denotes the updated variable x after an operation, then $S(x')$ asserts the invariance in the state after the operation.

Let *position* denote the current position of a cursor that is considered to be between two adjacent records. There is a sequence of records, LP, to the left of *position*, and a sequence of records, RP, to the right of *position*. If *length* denotes the number of records in the file, the statement

$$S(position) : 0 \leq position \leq length$$

is an invariant assertion. That is, $S(position')$ is true after every operation affecting *position*.

EMPTY_FILE $position = 0 \land length = 0$

MOVE_LEFT   The cursor is moved to the left end of the previous record; if the file is empty the operation has no effect.

precondition   : $position > 0$
postcondition   : $(position' = position - 1) \land$
$(length' = length) \land (file' = file)$

MOVE_RIGHT   The cursor is moved to the right end of the following record; if the cursor is already at the right end of the last record in the file, the operation has no effect.

precondition   : $position < length$
postcondition   : $(position' = position + 1) \land$
$(length' = length) \land (file' = file)$

INSERT_RIGHT   Insert a new record r in the file so that the sequence of records to the left of the new position is {LP} and the sequence of records to the right of the new position is {r,RP}.

postcondition   : $(position' = position) \land (length' = length + 1) \land$
$\forall p \bullet ((0 \leq p < position) \Rightarrow file'_p = file_p \land$
$(p = position) \Rightarrow file'_p = r \land$
$(position \leq p < length) \Rightarrow file'_{p+1} = file_p)$

INSERT_LEFT   Insert a new record r in the file so that the sequence of records to the right of the new position is {RP} and the sequence of records to the left of the new position is {LP, r}.

The postcondition is similar to the previous operation except that $position' = position + 1$. The precondition is $position \geq 0$.

DELETE_LEFT   Delete the record r to the immediate left of the cursor. If the file is empty, or if the cursor is at the left end of the first record in the file, then the operation has no effect.

precondition   : $position \geq 1$
postcondition   : $(position' = position - 1) \land (length' = length - 1) \land$
    $\forall p \bullet ((0 \leq p < position') \Rightarrow file'_p = file_p \land$
    $(position' \leq p < length') \Rightarrow file'_p = file_{p+1})$

DELETE_RIGHT   Delete the record r to the immediate right of the cursor. If the cursor is at the right end of the last record in the file, or if the file is empty, then the operation has no effect.

precondition   : $0 \leq position < length$
postcondition   : $(position' = position) \land (length' = length - 1) \land$
    $\forall p \bullet ((0 \leq p < position') \Rightarrow file'_p = file_p \land$
    $(position' \leq p < length') \Rightarrow file'_p = file_{p+1})$ ■

The next example formalizes finite state machines as directed graphs and conduct reachability analysis.

Example 6.14   A directed graph is a 3-tuple (V, E, I), where V is a finite set of vertices, E is a finite set of edges, and I is a set of assertions denoting the incidence relationships between vertices and edges. For every vertex $v \in V$, the predicate $vertex(v)$ is true, and for every $e \in E$, the predicate $edge(e)$ is true. The predicates $first(x, e)$ and $second(y, e)$ denote the properties that the edge e is directed from vertex x to vertex y. The predicate $path(x, y)$ asserts that there is a path from vertex x to vertex y. The axioms are the following:

1. *vertices and edges*

    (a) $\forall x \bullet (vertex(x) \lor edge(x))$

    (b) $\forall x \bullet \neg(vertex(x) \land edges(x))$

    (c) $\forall e \bullet (edge(e) \Rightarrow \exists! x, y \bullet (vertex(x) \land vertex(y) \land first(x, e) \land second(y, e)))$

2. *path*

    (a) $\forall x, y \exists e \bullet (first(x, e) \land second(y, e) \Rightarrow path(x, y))$

    (b) $\forall x, y \bullet (path(x, z) \land path(z, y) \Rightarrow path(x, y))$

3. A point c is said to be a *cut point* if there exists a partition of V into V_1, V_2, and V_3 such that $V_1 \neq \varnothing$, $V_2 \neq \varnothing$, $V_3 = \{c\}$, $V_1 \cup V_2 \cup V_3 = V$, and every path between a member of V_1 and a member of V_2 passes through c. This can be specified as

$$\neg \exists a \in V_1, b \in V_2, e \in E \bullet ((first(a, e) \wedge second(b, e)) \vee (first(b, e) \wedge second(a, e)))$$

4. *reachability*

There are two kinds of connected graphs, namely strongly connected and weakly connected graphs. In a strongly connected graph, for any pair of vertices one vertex is reachable from the other. Formally,

$$\forall v_1, v_2 \in V \bullet (path(v_1, v_2) \wedge path(v_2, v_1))$$

A graph is weakly connected if for every pair of vertices v_1 and v_2, either v_1 is reachable from v_2 or v_2 is reachable from v_1. Formally,

$$\forall v_1, v_2 \in V \bullet (path(v_1, v_2) \vee path(v_2, v_1))$$

To informally reason about paths, consider the directed graph for which the following predicates are true:

$vertex(a), vertex(b), vertex(c), vertex(d)$;
$edge(e_1), edge(e_2), edge(e_3)$;
$first(a, e_1), second(b, e_1), first(b, e_2), second(c, e_2)$,
$first(b, e_3), second(d, e_3)$.

From the first path axiom, infer: $path(a, b)$, $path(b, c)$, $path(b, d)$. Exercise the second path axiom with the substitution $[a/x, b/z, c/y]$ to derive $path(a, c)$ and $path(a, d)$. This proves that every vertex is reachable from vertex a. Similar reasoning for the substituion $[b/x, a/y]$ does not result in $path(b, a)$, indicating that vertex a is not reachable from vertex b. Using appropriate substitutions and reasoning, the following conclusions can be reached: No vertex can be reached from vertex c; both vertices c and d can be reached from vertex b. ∎

An extended state machine defined in Chapter 5 can be further augmented with attributes, logical assertions on the attributes, and time constraints to model a reactive object. Assuming that the object has a single thread of control, it can communicate with its environment by synchronous message passing. A message involves an event and underscores an activity that takes an atomic interval of time. An event causes a computation that updates the state and the attributes. Associating time constraints to transitions allows a computation to cause the enabling of a reaction. An outstanding reaction may be fired in the form of a transition, thereby generating another event.

A transition is specified by an event, the source and destination states, an enabling condition, and a postcondition. The enabling condition and the postcondition are logical assertions on the attributes. The enabling condition specifies an assertion under which the transition is enabled, while the postcondition specifies the computation associated with the transition. A time constraint is associated with a transition; it constrains the occurrence of an event within a time interval from the time at which the computation associated with the transition takes place. When the transition occurs, the constrained event is enabled; it should be fired within the minimal and maximal delay of l and u time units from the occurrence of the transition. The constrained event signifies the response corresponding to the stimulus represented by the event labeling the transition. Once enabled, the event remains outstanding until fired or disabled.

The augmented state machine inherently expresses several forms of non-determinism, including

- Control nondeterminism, such that a number of choices concerning the transition to be fired may be available for a given state.
- Timing nondeterminism, such that the exact delay between trigger and response can be chosen from the interval specified by the minimum and maximum time delays.

Real-time features such as minimal and maximal delays, exact occurrences, and periodicity of event occurrences can be specified in this framework. This can be combined with temporal relations such as stimulus-response, response-response, stimulus-stimulus, and response-stimulus. We illustrate the formalism for a generalized version of the railroad crossing problem.

Example 6.15   In the railroad system considered here, more than one train can cross a gate simultaneously, through multiple parallel tracks; a train can independently choose the gate it will cross, probably based on its destination. The entities interacting in the system are trains, controllers, and gates. Each gate is controlled by one controller. Since several trains may simultaneously cross a gate, the controller for a gate monitors approaching trains and directs the gate to close. The safety property is that the controller is active and the gate remains closed until the train crossing it leaves the gate. Timing constraints include the maximum and minimum times required for a train to be in the gate from the instant it was observed by a controller, the maximum permitted time for a gate to open or close, and the time bounds for a train to cross a gate. The state diagrams shown in Figures 6.3, 6.4, and 6.5 show the behavior of train, controller, and gate. Each state diagram is annotated with a class specification, a textual description of the state machine diagram.

A train sends the message *Near* (*Exit*) to a controller indicating that it is approaching (exiting) the gate. The train triggers the internal event *In* within a window of 2 to 4 time units after sending the *Near* message, and sends the *Exit* message within 6 time units from sending the *Near* message. A controller sends the messages *Lower* (*Raise*) to the gate it is controlling, indicating that the gate has to be lowered (raised).

Class *Train*
  Events: *Near, Exit, In, Out*
  State: *∗S1, S2, S3, S4*
  Attributes:
  Attribute-function:
    $S1, S2, S3, S4 \mapsto \{\}$;
  Transition Spec:
    $R_1 : \langle S1, S2 \rangle$; *Near; true* $\implies$ *true*;
    $R_2 : \langle S2, S3 \rangle$; *In; true* $\implies$ *true*;
    $R_3 : \langle S3, S4 \rangle$; *Out; true* $\implies$ *true*;
    $R_4 : \langle S4, S1 \rangle$; *Exit; true* $\implies$ *true*;
  Time-constraints:
    $(R_1, In, [2, 4], \{\})$
    $(R_1, Exit, [0, 6], \{\})$
end

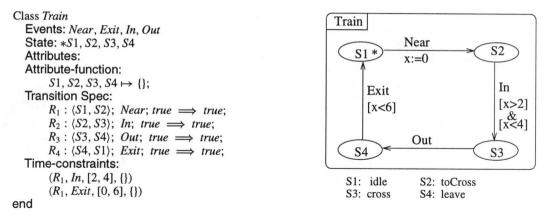

FIGURE 6.3. Class specifications for Train.

Class *Controller*
  Events: *Near, Exit, Lower, Raise*
  State: *∗C1, C2, C3, C4*
  Attributes:
  Attribute-function:
    $C1, C2, C3, C4 \mapsto \{\}$;
  Transition Spec:
    $R_1 : \langle C1, C2 \rangle$; *Near*;
        true $\implies$ *true*;
    $R_2 : \langle C2, C2 \rangle, \langle C3, C3 \rangle$; *Near*;
        true $\implies$ *true*;
    $R_3 : \langle C2, C3 \rangle$; *Lower; true* $\implies$ *true*;
    $R_4 : \langle C3, C3 \rangle$; *Exit*;
        true $\implies$ *true*;
    $R_5 : \langle C3, C4 \rangle$; *Exit*;
        true $\implies$ *true*;
    $R_6 : \langle C4, C1 \rangle$; *Raise; true* $\implies$ *true*;
  Time-constraints:
    $(R_1, Lower, [0, 1], \{\})$
    $(R_5, Raise, [0, 1], \{\})$
end

FIGURE 6.4. Class specifications for Controller.

The *Lower* message is sent by the controller within 1 time unit from receiving the *Near* message while in the *idle* state; the *Raise* message is sent within 1 time unit from receiving the *Exit* message from the last train leaving the crossing. The gate triggers the internal event *Down* within 1 time unit from receiving the *Lower* message from the controller, and triggers the internal event *Up* within a window of 1 to 2 time units after receiving the *Raise* message. The safety requirement is that whenever a train is crossing a gate, the gate must be closed. In addition, the controller must be monitoring the gate at that point. For the system to operate

Class *Gate*
    Events: *Lower, Raise, Down, Up*
    State: *$*G1, G2, G3, G4$*
    Transition Spec:
        R_1 : $\langle G1, G2 \rangle$; *Lower*; *true* $\Longrightarrow$ *true*;
        R_2 : $\langle G2, G3 \rangle$; *Down*; *true* $\Longrightarrow$ *true*;
        R_3 : $\langle G3, G4 \rangle$; *Raise*; *true* $\Longrightarrow$ *true*;
        R_4 : $\langle G4, G1 \rangle$; *Up*; *true* $\Longrightarrow$ *true*;
    Time-constraints:
        $(R_1, Down, [0, 1], \{\})$
        $(R_3, Up, [1, 2], \{\})$
end

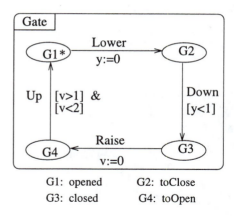

G1: opened	G2: toClose
G3: closed	G4: toOpen

FIGURE 6.5. Class specifications for Gate.

properly, the gate must eventually be raised, and must remain so for a certain period of time before it is lowered again.

We can specify the finite state machine behavior of the train, gate, controller objects using predicate logic. We use the predicate *was_at(s, t)* to specify that the object was in state *s* at time *t*, and the predicate *occur(e, t)* to specify that an event *e* was occurring at time *t*, thus including *time* explicitly in the logic. If the event *e* that labels the transition from state *S* to state *S'* occurs at time *t*, and the object is in state *S* at that time, then the state of the object changes to *S'* within a short interval of time ϵ. The formulas corresponding to the time constraints for the classes *Train*, *Gate*, and *Controller* are given below.

- *Train*

    1. $was\_at(S_2, t_1) \wedge \forall t \bullet ((t_1 < t < t_2) \wedge \neg was\_at(S_3, t)) \wedge$
       $was\_at(S_3, t_2) \wedge t_2 - t_1 > 2 \wedge t_2 - t_1 < 4$

    2. $was\_at(S_2, t_1) \wedge \forall t \bullet ((t_1 < t < t_2) \wedge \neg was\_at(S_1, t)) \wedge$
       $was\_at(S_1, t_2) \wedge t_2 - t_1 > 0 \wedge t_2 - t_1 < 6$

- *Gate*

    1. $was\_at(G_2, t_1) \wedge \forall t \bullet ((t_1 < t < t_2) \wedge \neg was\_at(G_3, t)) \wedge$
       $was\_at(G_3, t_2) \wedge t_2 - t_1 > 0 \wedge t_2 - t_1 < 1$

    2. $was\_at(G_4, t_1) \wedge \forall t \bullet ((t_1 < t < t_2) \wedge \neg was\_at(G_1, t)) \wedge$
       $was\_at(G_1, t_2) \wedge t_2 - t_1 > 1 \wedge t_2 - t_1 < 2$

- *Controller*

    1. $was\_at(C_2, t_1) \wedge \forall t \bullet ((t_1 < t < t_2) \wedge \neg was\_at(C_3, t)) \wedge$
       $was\_at(C_3, t_2) \wedge t_2 - t_1 > 0 \wedge t_2 - t_1 < 1$

2. $was\_at(C_4, t_1) \wedge \forall t \bullet ((t_1 < t < t_2) \wedge \neg was\_at(C_1, t)) \wedge$
$was\_at(C_1, t_2) \wedge t_2 - t_1 > 0 \wedge t_2 - t_1 < 1$

- *Synchronization between Train and Controller*

1. $was\_at(S_1, t) \wedge was\_at(C_1, t) \wedge occur(Near, t) \Rightarrow was\_at(S_2, t') \wedge$
$was\_at(C_2, t') \wedge (t' = t + \epsilon)$

2. $was\_at(S_1, t) \wedge was\_at(C_2, t) \wedge occur(Near, t) \Rightarrow was\_at(S_2, t') \wedge$
$was\_at(C_2, t') \wedge (t' = t + \epsilon)$

3. $was\_at(C_3, t) \wedge was\_at(S_1, t) \wedge occur(Near, t) \Rightarrow was\_at(C_3, t') \wedge$
$was\_at(S_2, t') \wedge (t' = t + \epsilon)$

4. $was\_at(C_3, t) \wedge was\_at(S_4, t) \wedge occur(Exit, t) \Rightarrow (u > 0 \wedge$
$was\_at(C_3, t') \wedge was\_at(S_1, t') \wedge (t' = t + \epsilon)) \vee (u = 0 \wedge was\_at(C_4, t') \wedge$
$was\_at(S_1, t') \wedge (t' = t + \epsilon))$

- *Synchronization between Controller and Gate*

1. $was\_at(C_2, t) \wedge was\_at(G_1, t) \wedge occur(Lower, t) \Rightarrow was\_at(C_3, t) \wedge$
$was\_at(G_2, t) \wedge (t' = t + \epsilon)$

2. $was\_at(C_4, t) \wedge was\_at(G_3, t) \wedge occur(Raise, t) \Rightarrow was\_at(C_1, t') \wedge$
$was\_at(G_4, t') \wedge (t' = t + \epsilon)$ ∎

6.3 Temporal Logic

In classical logic, the predicate P in "if $P \wedge (P \Rightarrow Q)$ then Q" retains its truth value even after Q has been derived. In other words, in classical logic the truth of a formula is *static*. However, real-life implications are *causal*. To handle causality, it must be possible to specify that "P and $P \Rightarrow Q$ was true," and now "P is not true and Q is true." This may also be stated as follows: We associate predicates with states on a 1-1 basis such that a predicate is true in some state S and false in all other states. Consider two predicates P and Q such that P is true in state S_1, and Q is true in state S_2. An event causes $P \Rightarrow Q$ to be true when the system is in state S_1. Consequently, Q becomes true; that is, the system is in state S_2, and P is no longer true. For example, the statements

P	the train is approaching the gate,
$P \Rightarrow Q$	if the train approaches the gate, the gate is lowered,
Q	the gate is lowered before the train is in the gate, and
R	the gate remains closed until the train crosses the gate

describe changes to the states of a reactive system. They cannot be formalized in classical logic. In order to formalize these statements, we need to provide semantics to terms such as *when, while, during, before, after, since,* and *until.* These terms can be used to express ordinal and causal relationships on events and state transitions, rather than the actual times at which they happen. Temporal logic was developed to describe such orderings.

Temporal logic supports specification and reasoning at different levels of abstractions. It provides one logical system in which behavior specification, design specification, and implementation level details can be expressed and related in an intuitive manner. Temporal logic is a suitable formalism for specifying and reasoning about the properties of concurrent and reactive system models.

6.3.1   Concurrent and Reactive Systems

A reactive program is one that continuously maintains an ongoing interaction with the environment controlled by it. The program and its environment taken together form a reactive system. The program controlling the train and the gate, according to the requirements stated above, is a reactive program. Reactive systems may be concurrent and may have to obey strict timing constraints. For example, "the train approaching the gate" and "the gate lowering" are concurrent activities. One can add the timing constraint that "the gate must be lowered within 3 seconds after receiving the message that the train is approaching." Although the temporal logic introduced in the following sections does not involve real-time measurements, it is possible to express real-time properties within the logic.

In the specification of concurrent or reactive systems, two important behavioral properties needs to be formally expressed. These properties were termed *safety* and *liveness* by Owiciki and Lamport [10]. Informally, a safety property implies that *something bad will not happen*, and a liveness property implies that *something good will eventually happen*. For example, *the gate will remain closed while a train crosses the gate* is a safety property; *whenever the gate is directed to raise, it will eventually do so* is a liveness property. Other examples of safety properties include

1. *partial correctness* - the program does not produce the wrong answer.

2. *mutual exclusion* - two processes are not simultaneously in the critical section.

3. *deadlock-freedom* - the program does not reach the state of deadlock.

Liveness properties include *program termination* and *starvation-freedom* where a process does not wait forever to be serviced. These properties can be described in temporal logic using temporal connectives to express *future, past,* and *eventuality.*

6.3.2   The Notion of Time

The behavior of a modeled object depends on the implicit notion of time, which orders the events affecting the modeled object. The underlying model of time in a temporal logic determines its suitability for modeling system requirements. In the logic discussed here there are no distinguished terms, as in mathematics or physics, to denote time—there are only operators which when associated with models convey the different notions of time, namely change, and ordering. This model of time can be structured by combining different notions of time as described below.

Discrete or Continuous

When certain computations or actions need to be described as continuously varying, a dense model of time is appropriate. In such a case, the topology of time is that of real numbers or a subset of real numbers. When a property is present over a sequence of intervals, and in each interval the property persists in every subinterval, then an interval and continuous model of time are used. When dealing with properties that are present only at certain time instants, a discrete model of time is chosen. In this case, the model of time is isomorphic to a subset of natural numbers.

Further specializations of the time model are possible: (1) A *bounded* time applies to dense (discrete) model when a finite subset of real numbers (natural numbers) is chosen to model time; (2) An interval time model has a discrete time structure, so that the next and previous intervals can be referred to. Within each interval, a property may hold in every subinterval or only at specific discrete points. In addition, time modeled as intervals may be bounded or unbounded.

Linear and Branching Models of Time

One may want to postulate that for any moment in time there is either exactly one future time or several possible future times. The former case is called the *linear model* of time, and the latter case is called the *branching model* of time. The branching model is useful to handle uncertainty, and hence possible alternative futures. Propositions such as "p is true *throughout every* possible future," "p is true *throughout in some possible* future," "p is true at the *next time in every possible* future," "p is true at the *next time in some possible* future," "p is true *eventually in every* possible future," and "p is true *eventually in some possible* future" can be stated and reasoned about in branching time temporal languages. We study linear time temporal logic in the following sections. Hereafter, by temporal logic we mean discrete linear temporal logic.

6.3.3 The Specification Hierarchy

Temporal logic can be used to specify requirements, design, and programs. At the requirements level, propositions and predicates are determined from the problem requirements, and temporal formulas are constructed to formalize the causal relationship among the predicates; this represents the behavioral specification. At the design level, the objects and their behavior are specified; this represents the design specification. For example, the behavior of an object can be characterized by a sequence of states, and the events triggering the successive state transitions. Nondeterminism and concurrency are captured by the set consisting of all such sequences. Temporal logic formulas for properties that hold over (1) all sequences of states, (2) some sequences of states, and (3) some future state in some sequence can then be asserted. A program state corresponds to an implementation of part or whole of a design state. So program states, as defined by data and control variables, are specializations of design specification states. The execution sequence of a program and a temporal formula specifying the sequence are related through a satisfaction relation. That is, a temporal formula f is said to be a specification of a program P, if every execution sequence of program P satisfies f. Verification of program properties can be done by stating each property as a temporal formula and then showing that the formula holds at the specified program steps.

In the following sections, we introduce the syntax and semantics of linear temporal logic and give several examples for specification and verification. We do not discuss any formal approach to program verification. The bibliographic notes include references to formal verification.

6.3.4 Temporal Logic—Syntax and Semantics

The vocabulary of temporal logic consists of a countable collection of names to denote constants, functions, propositions, states, and predicates. In addition, it also includes constant values (such as boolean constants, natural numbers, ϵ for the empty string (list), ϕ for the empty set), function symbols (such as $+$, $-$ for integers, $*$ for concatenation of strings, *head* and *tail* for lists, $\cup$, and $\cap$ for sets), and predicate symbols (such as $>$, and $\leq$ for integers, $\subset$, and $\in$ for sets, and *null* for strings). The equality symbol $=$ is assumed to operate on all typed variables and constants. A well-formed expression in temporal logic is a well-formed first-order logic formula. The formula $\forall x \bullet ((head(x) \geq y) \wedge tail(x) \neq null)$ is well-formed. The next step is to include *states*. A state is a function that assigns a value to each variable; this value is described as the value of the variable in that state. A linear time structure for the logic is a sequence $s_0, s_1, \ldots, s_n$ of states and a labeling function that assigns to each state a set of predicates that are *true* in that state. To complete the syntax of the language, a set of temporal operators that refer to the future, the past, and the next are included. The three basic operators are $\square$ (*always*), $\Diamond$ (*eventually*), and $\bigcirc$ (*next*).

All well-formed formulas from the predicate logic defined in Section 6.2 are also well-formed formulas in the temporal logic. The rule for constructing all well-formed formulas in the temporal logic is the following:

1. An atomic predicate is a well-formed formula.
2. If f is a well-formed formula, then so is $\mathcal{T}(f)$, where $\mathcal{T}$ is a temporal operator. The formulas $\neg(f)$, $\Box(f)$, $\Diamond(f)$ and $\bigcirc(f)$ are well-formed.
3. If f and g are well-formed formulas, then so are $(f \vee g)$, $(f \wedge g)$, $(f \Rightarrow g)$, and $(f \equiv g)$.

Some well-formed formulas are

1. $\Box(f \Rightarrow \bigcirc(g))$
2. $\exists q \bullet (head(s) = q) \wedge \Diamond(head(s) = q + 1)$
3. $\Box(p) \wedge \Diamond(q) \Rightarrow \Box\,(p \Rightarrow \bigcirc(r))$

By restricting to only propositions in the logic, we obtain *propositional linear temporal logic* (PLTL). With quantifiers and predicates in the logic, we obtain *first-order linear temporal logic* (FLTL).

Interpretation

An atomic action causes a state change. The history of state changes starting in state s_0 at time zero, as given by the sequence

$$\sigma : s_0, s_1, s_2, \ldots \tag{1}$$

represents the behavior of the object. The states in sequence (1) may correspond either to abstract object states in a design or to concrete states in a program. In order to verify whether the behavior includes a certain property as represented by a temporal logic formula f, the formula should be interpreted over the timeline σ. The formula can be interpreted by evaluating variables, expressions, and predicates of formula f over each state of σ. The value of a variable x (expression e, predicate p, formula f) in a state s is denoted by $s[x]$ ($s[e]$, $s[p]$, $s[f]$). The evaluation steps for formulas not involving temporal operators are described below:

1. Step 1—Evaluating Expressions
   An expression e is evaluated in a state s by assigning values to all free variables and associating meaning to basic constructs. The value of the expression $e = 2x - 3y$ in a state s is $s[e] = 2s[x] - 3s[y]$; the value of the expression $e = p * cons(head(q), r)$ is $s[e] = s[p] * cons(head(s[q]), s[r])$.

2. Step 2—Evaluating Predicates
   (a) For the predicate $P(t_1, \ldots, t_n)$, where $t_1, \ldots, t_n$ are terms, define $s[P(t_1, \ldots, t_n)] = P(s[t_1], \ldots, s[t_n])$.

(b) Predicate formulas

    i. $s[\neg p] = \neg s[p]$

    ii. $s[p \vee q] = s[p] \vee s[q]$

    iii. $s[p \wedge q] = s[p] \wedge s[q]$

    iv. $s[p \Rightarrow q] = s[p] \Rightarrow s[q]$

    v. $s[p \Leftrightarrow q] = s[p] \Leftrightarrow s[q]$

3. Step 3—Evaluating Quantified Formulas

    (a) $s[\forall x \bullet p] = \forall x \bullet s[p]$, where $s[p]$ is the evaluation of expression p in state s.

    (b) $s[\exists x \bullet p] = \exists x \bullet s[p]$.

For example, consider the state

$$s = \langle x = -1, y = 3, z = 1 \rangle.$$

The interpretation of the boolean formula

$$(x + y > z) \Rightarrow (y \leq 2 * z)$$

is

$$
\begin{aligned}
&s[(x + y > z) \Rightarrow (y \leq 2 * z)] \\
&= (s[x] + s[y] > s[z]) \Rightarrow (s[y] \leq 2 * s[z]) \\
&= (-1 + 3 > 1) \Rightarrow (3 \leq 2 * 1) \\
&= \textit{true} \Rightarrow \textit{false} \\
&= \textit{false}
\end{aligned}
$$

Semantics of Temporal Formulas

For any formula P, $\Box P$ means that P always holds, $\Diamond P$ means that P will hold sometimes, and $\bigcirc P$ means that P will hold at the next instant. $\Box P$ holds at the state s_j if and only if P holds at all states s_k, $k \geq j$; $\Diamond P$ holds at the state s_j if and only if P holds at some state s_k, $k \geq j$; $\bigcirc P$ holds at the state s_j if and only if P holds at the state s_{j+1}. The formula $\Box(lost(x) \Rightarrow \neg instacks(x))$ states that a lost book is not on the stacks. If the formula holds at a certain point, then it holds forever thereafter. The formula $\Box(inc(x) \Rightarrow \Box inc(x))$ states that once x is incremented, then it is incremented at every state thereafter. The formula $\bigcirc\Box(x = 1) \Rightarrow (\Diamond\Box(y = 0) \wedge \Diamond(z = 1))$ states that "if at the next step x becomes permanently 1, then either y eventually becomes permanently 0 or z eventually becomes 1." Below is a formal semantic interpretation for PLTL. Let $\sigma = s_0, s_1, \ldots$ denote an infinite sequence of system states. In each state s_i in σ, values are assigned to the atomic propositions of the temporal formulas. The semantics of a formula f for σ is defined inductively:

- $\sigma \models f$ iff $s_0 \models f$ and f is an atomic proposition.

- $\sigma \models \neg f$ iff $\neg(\sigma \models f)$.
- $\sigma \models f_1 \wedge f_2$ iff $\sigma \models f_1$ and $\sigma \models f_2$.
- $\sigma \models \bigcirc f$ iff $\sigma_1 \models f$ where σ_1 is the subsequence $s_1, s_2, \ldots$
- $\sigma \models \Box f$ iff $(\forall i \geq 0)(\sigma_i \models f)$ where σ_i is the subsequence $s_i, s_{i+1}, \ldots$
- $\sigma \models \Diamond f$ iff $(\exists i \geq 0)(\sigma_i \models f)$

The semantics for formulas in FLTL is given in a similar fashion by extending the semantics over the underlying structure used for interpreting the predicates. See Emerson [3] for details.

Example 6.16   Let g_1, g_2, g_3, g_4 denote the propositions:

g_1: the gate is lowered;
g_2: the gate is closed;
g_3: the gate is raised;
g_4: the gate is open;

Let tr_1, tr_2, tr_3 denote the propositions

tr_1: the train is approaching;
tr_2: the train is crossing the gate;
tr_3: the train has crossed the gate.

Assume that $\sigma = s_0, s_1, \ldots$ is a model for which the following hold:

at state s_0: $g_1 \wedge tr_1$ is *true*;
at state s_1: $g_2 \wedge tr_1$ is *true*;
at states s_2 and s_3: $g_2 \wedge tr_2$ is *true*;
at state s_4: $g_2 \wedge tr_3$ is *true*;
at state s_5: $g_3 \wedge tr_3$ is *true*;
at state s_6 and in all subsequent states: $g_4 \wedge tr_3$ is *true*.

From this model, we conclude the following:

1. $\Diamond(g_2)$ is *true* at states $s_j, j = 0, 1, 2, 3, 4$, and *false* for all other states.

2. $\bigcirc(g_2)$ is *true* for states $s_j, j = 0, 1, 2, 3$, and *false* for all other states.

3. $\Box(g_4)$ is *false* for states $s_j, j = 0, 1, 2, 3, 4, 5$, and *true* for all other states.

4. $\Box(tr_3)$ is *true* for all states $s_j, j \geq 4$.

5. $\Box(tr_3 \Rightarrow \Diamond g_4)$. This formula states the property that if a train has crossed the gate, the gate eventually will open. This formula is true in all states.

6. $\Box\Diamond(g_4)$. This formula states that there are infinitely many states in which the gate is open. That is, the gate is closed only in finitely many states, which correspond to the crossing of trains. This formula holds for all states.

7. $\Diamond\Box(\neg tr_1 \Rightarrow g_4)$. This formula states that there exists a state such that the formula $\neg tr_1 \Rightarrow g_4$ (the gate is open if the train is not approaching) holds at all later states. This formula is true because of state s_6.   ■

More Temporal Operators   We describe four other temporal operators below. Manna and Pnueli [8] include an exhaustive list of temporal operators.

The Until *Operator* $\mathcal{U}$

The formula $p\,\mathcal{U}\,q$ (read p until q) states that p occurs continuously at least until the first occurrence of q. That is, if the formula $p\,\mathcal{U}\,q$ holds at state s_k, then there exists a state $s_j, j \geq k$ at which q is true and p holds for all states $s_i, \forall i, k \leq i < j$. The truth of formula p from state s_j onwards cannot be determined from this formula. Hence, the formula $g_2\,\mathcal{U}\,tr_1 \vee tr_2 \vee tr_3$ is true for the specification in Example 6.16.

The Waiting-for *Operator* $\mathcal{W}$

The formula $p\,\mathcal{W}\,q$ (read p waiting-for q) states that p occurs forever or until the first occurrence of q. Hence, the formula $g_4\,\mathcal{W}\,tr_1$ states that the gate is open forever or until the train is approaching. This formula is true for all states $s_j, j \geq 6$, until the state s_0 reappears in the sequence σ.

The Since *Operator* $\mathcal{S}$

The formula $p\,\mathcal{S}\,q$ (read p since q) states that q has happened sometime in the past and p has continuously held since then. Thus, the formula $g_4\,\mathcal{S}\,tr_3$ states that the gate has remained open since the train crossed the gate.

The Once *Operator* $\diamondsuit\!\!\!\!-$

The formula $\diamondsuit\!\!\!\!-\,p$ (read sometimes in the past p) states that p has happened at sometime in the past. If $\diamondsuit\!\!\!\!-\,p$ holds at state s_j, then it holds at all states $s_k, k \geq j$. For example, $\diamondsuit\!\!\!\!-\,tr_3$ means that the train crossed the gate sometimes in the past; if this statement is true at state s_4, then it remains true for that train in all future states.

Not all operators are independent. The operators $\Box$ and $\Diamond$ are duals. The *Since* and *Once* operators are also related:

$$\Box P \equiv \neg\Diamond\neg P$$
$$\Diamond P \equiv \neg\Box\neg P$$
$$\diamondsuit\!\!\!\!-\,P \equiv true\,\mathcal{S}\,P$$

Below, we give some of the frequently used formulas and their interpretations.

1. $f \Rightarrow \Diamond g$

This formula states that if the model σ satisfies f, it also satisfies $\Diamond g$. A model σ satisfies f if f is true in s_0, and σ satisfies $\Diamond g$ if g holds at some state s_j, $j \geq 0$. Hence, the formula states the property of the model σ that if initially f, then eventually g. For example, $tr_1 \Rightarrow \Diamond g_2$ for the model in Example 6.16.

2. $\Box(f \Rightarrow \Diamond g)$

This formula expresses the property $f \Rightarrow \Diamond g$ of the model σ for all $j \geq 0$. For example, $\Box(tr_3 \Rightarrow \Diamond g_4)$ is true in all states for the model in Example 6.16.

3. $\Box(f \Rightarrow \bigcirc g)$

The subformula $f \Rightarrow \bigcirc g$ states that if f is true at s_j, then g is true at s_{j+1}. Consequently, the formula asserts the property for every state in σ where f is true.

4. $\Box(f \Rightarrow f \mathcal{U} g)$

In every state where f is true, f continues to remain true until g becomes true. For example, $\Box(g_2 \Rightarrow g_2 \mathcal{U} tr_3)$ is true for the model in Example 6.16.

5. $\Box(f \Rightarrow \diamondsuit g)$

The property expressed by this formula is that every state f in which it is true coincides with or is preceded by a state where g is true. For example, $\Box(tr_2 \Rightarrow \diamondsuit g_2)$ is true for the model in Example 6.16.

6.3.5 Specifications

We give specifications at three levels of abstraction to demonstrate that the temporal logic provides a single logical system for all three levels.

Behavioral Specification

A requirement is stated as a logical formula over predicates modeling events and actions. At this level of abstraction, an event corresponds to a high-level action, as opposed to a transition event. Interpretations for predicates and variables are given over the domain considered in the application. Quantifiers are omitted in the formulas.

Example 6.17 The following assertions represent requirements for borrowing and returning books in a library system. The corresponding temporal formula is given for each assertion.

The number of copies of a book with title x is non-negative and cannot exceed the maximum number of copies for that book:

$\Box\ (title(x) \land max\_copies(x, max(x)) \land has\_now(x, in(x)) \Rightarrow$
$(0 \leq in(x) \leq max(x)))$.

When a book has been borrowed, it is equivalent to stating that the book has not been returned since its last checkout:

$\Box\ (has\_borrowed(u, x) \equiv \neg returned(u, x))\ \mathcal{S}\ check\_out(u, x)$

The renewal of a book coincides with or follows the return of the book:

$\Box\ ((renew(u, x) \land returned(u, x) \lor (returned(u, x) \land \bigcirc renew(u, x))$

A book that has not been borrowed since it was last returned is in the stacks:

$$\neg has\_borrowed(u, x) \, S \, returned(u, x) \Rightarrow in\_stacks(x)$$

A book is in the stacks until it is borrowed or else it is not in the stacks and lost:

$$(in\_stacks(x) \, \mathcal{U} \, has\_borrowed(u, x)) \lor (\neg in\_stacks(x) \land lost(x)) \qquad \blacksquare$$

Example 6.18 Consider the problem of sending and receiving messages over a communication channel. Let $\{a, b\}$ denote the set of endpoints of a channel, and $e \in \{a, b\}$. Let

$$\bar{e} = \begin{cases} a & \text{if } e = a \\ b & \text{if } e = b \end{cases}$$

Let M denote the set of messages and $m \in M$ be any arbitrary message transmitted over the channel $\langle a, b \rangle$. The temporal logic formulas involve atomic formulas such as $accept(m, e)$ and $deliver(m, e)$ and temporal operators.

1. To state that a channel is operational, it is sufficient to state that both endpoints are accepting messages all the time.

   $$\Box \, (channel\_on(a, b) \Leftrightarrow accept(m, a) \land accept(m', b))$$

2. A channel cannot copy messages; if a message was delivered at some time, then it cannot be redelivered unless it was accepted again.

   $$(deliver(m, e) \land \neg \Diamond accept(m, e)) \Rightarrow \neg \bigcirc \Box \, deliver(m, e)$$

3. A channel cannot accept two different messages at the same endpoint at the same time:

   $$\Box \, (accept(m, e) \land accept(m', e) \Rightarrow m = m')$$

4. A message accepted at e will be delivered at $\bar{e}$ unless $\bar{e}$ has accepted a disconnect message at a preceding time.

   $$accept(m, e) \Rightarrow \Diamond(deliver(m, \bar{e}) \lor \, \Diamond \hspace{-0.6em}\text{-} \, accept(\text{DISCONNECT}, \bar{e}))$$

5. This axiom asserts the safety property that there can be no loss of messages in an active channel and that all messages accepted are eventually delivered. The messages are delivered at the endpoint $\bar{e}$ in the same order in which they were accepted at the endpoint e:

   $$(accept(m, e) \land \bigcirc \Diamond accept(m', e) \land m' \neq \text{DISCONNECT}) \Rightarrow$$
   $$\Box(deliver(m, \bar{e}) \Rightarrow \neg \, \Diamond \hspace{-0.6em}\text{-} \, deliver(m', \bar{e}))$$

6. When a "disconnect" message is accepted at one end, the channel stops functioning at that end. However, it continues to receive and deliver messages at

the other end until it receives and accepts a "disconnect" message, after which its operation stops.

$$(accept(\text{DISCONNECT}, e) \vee deliver(\text{DISCONNECT}, e)) \Rightarrow$$
$$\bigcirc \Box (\sim accept(m, e) \wedge \sim deliver(m, e))$$

7. An important liveness property of the action $deliver(m, e)$ is that the message at the front of $queue(\overline{e}, e)$, the queue of messages sent from $\overline{e}$ to e, must eventually be delivered.

$$(front(queue(\overline{e}, e)) = m) \Rightarrow \Diamond deliver(m, e) \qquad \blacksquare$$

Design and Program Specification

The software design phase involves the decomposition of the system into subsystems where each subsystem corresponds to one specific activity. Typically, a module implements an object; that is, abstract data types and operations are specified and implemented in a module. A module specification is a formal specification of the included data types and operations performed on them.

Design Specification   In Example 6.18, queue($\overline{e}$, e) denotes the sequence of messages transmitted from endpoint $\overline{e}$ to endpoint e. According to the requirements, the queue must operate on a FIFO (first-in-first-out) basis. Other subproblems at the design level may require the services of a queue. It is worthwhile to design a module that can fulfill the requirements of any subsystem requiring a queue.

A queue may be empty at some time and nonempty at other times. The state of the queue changes due to two operations: PUT, which inserts an element at the rear of the queue, and GET, which removes the element at the front of the queue. The behavior of a queue can be given by a sequence of *states* and the *actions* causing the transitions as follows:

$$s_0 \overset{a_1}{\Rightarrow} s_1 \overset{a_2}{\Rightarrow} s_2 \overset{a_3}{\Rightarrow} \ldots$$

where each action a_i is either a PUT or a GET. The state s_i describes the contents of the queue, the ordering and the number of elements, after successful completion of the preceding i operations. An action is a specific atomic operation and a snapshot of the state of the queue can be taken only after the completion of action.

The behavior of concurrent programs is modeled by the aggregation of all linearly ordered sequences of states and the actions causing the transitions. Thus, if a and b are concurrent actions in state s_i, we consider the behaviors

$$s_i \overset{a}{\Rightarrow} s_{i+1} \overset{b}{\Rightarrow} s_{i+2}$$
$$s_i \overset{b}{\Rightarrow} s'_{i+1} \overset{a}{\Rightarrow} s'_{i+2}$$

in discussing safety and liveness properties. The states obtained due to action *a* followed by *b*, and due to action *b* followed by *a*, are both part of acceptable execution sequences.

Example 6.19   This example illustrates temporal logic specification of a queue based on its states. The queue is a shared data type and hence PUT and GET operations may be initiated concurrently by more than one process. With the atomicity assumption and modeling concurrency as the interleaving of atomic operations, only one operation can occur on the queue at any specific time. Given the current contents of the queue, only one process can perform the PUT or GET operation on this state. A process uses GET to fetch a value at an instant; when the queue is empty, the process waits until another process puts a value in the queue. The functions characterizing the queue states are defined below, and the variables in the poststate are distinguished by suffixing them with a prime.

cur_queue:	the current state of the queue
putval:	argument to PUT. The precondition for PUT is *putval* $\neq$ *nil* and the postcondition is *putval'* = *nil*.
getval:	argument to GET. The precondition for GET is *getval* = *nil* and the postcondition is *getval'* $\neq$ *nil*.

enter(PUT), *enter*(GET), *exit*(GET), and *exit*(PUT) are Boolean-valued functions signaling the initiation and termination of the operations.

Liveness Properties

1. The liveness property for the PUT operation is that it terminates. The element *putval* is inserted only if it does not cause an overflow; the symbol '$*$' denotes insertion at the rear.

$$enter(\text{PUT}) \wedge (length(cur\_queue) < \text{max}) \Rightarrow$$
$$\Diamond(exit(\text{PUT}) \wedge (cur\_queue' = cur\_queue * putval))$$
$$enter(\text{PUT}) \wedge (length(cur\_queue) = \text{max}) \Rightarrow$$
$$\Diamond(exit(\text{PUT}) \wedge (cur\_queue' = cur\_queue))$$

2. The liveness property for the GET operation is that it terminates only when a value is fetched from the queue. That is, if the queue is empty the operation waits until a value is put in the queue and then fetches the value.

$$enter(\text{GET}) \wedge \neg empty(cur\_queue) \Rightarrow$$
$$\Diamond(exit(\text{GET}) \wedge (getval * cur\_queue' = cur\_queue))$$
$$enter(\text{GET}) \wedge empty(cur\_queue) \Rightarrow enter(\text{GET}) \; \mathcal{U} \; exit(\text{PUT})$$

3. When the queue is empty, some process will eventually put a value in the queue.

$$empty(cur\_queue) \Rightarrow \Diamond enter(\text{PUT})$$

Safety Properties

Safety properties assert what may or may not happen to the queue due to the actions PUT and GET. The state of the queue changes under the following situations:

1. *putval* $\neq$ *nil*, and PUT is invoked by some process on a queue that is not full.

2. GET is invoked by some process, and *cur_queue* is not empty.

Situation 1. Let (*enter*(PUT) $\wedge$ *putval* $\neq$ *nil*) hold for *cur_queue*. The next state is *cur_queue'* which is the same as *cur_queue* when the queue is full or *cur_queue'* = *cur_queue* * *putval*. So, the temporal logic formula is

$\Box$((*enter*(PUT) $\wedge$ *putval* $\neq$ *nil*) $\Rightarrow$
(((*length*(*cur_queue*) = max) $\wedge$ (*cur_queue'* = *cur_queue*))
$\vee$((*length*(*cur_queue*) < max) $\wedge$ (*cur_queue'* = *cur_queue* * *putval*)))).

Situation 2.   Let (*enter*(GET) $\wedge$ *getval* = *nil*) hold for *cur_queue*. The next state is *cur_queue'* which is the same as *cur_queue* when the queue is empty, or *cur_queue* = *getval* * *cur_queue'*. So, the temporal logic formula is

$\Box$((*enter*(GET) $\wedge$ *getval* = *nil*) $\Rightarrow$
((*empty*(*cur_queue*) $\wedge$ *empty*(*cur_queue'*))
$\vee$($\neg$*empty*(*cur_queue*) $\wedge$ (*cur_queue* = *getval* * *cur_queue'*)))).   ∎

Example 6.20 gives the hardware specification of an LSI circuit and analyzes the behavior of its design.

Example 6.20   Figure 6.6 shows a cell of an LSI dynamic register circuit. In the figure, T_1 and T_2 are path transistors, I_1 and I_2 are inverters, and X is the input signal, l is the load

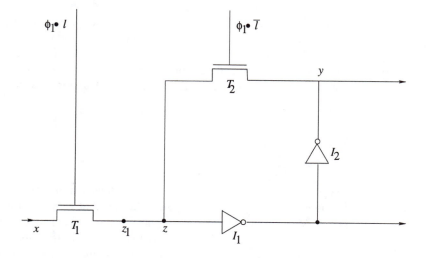

FIGURE 6.6. Circuit 1.

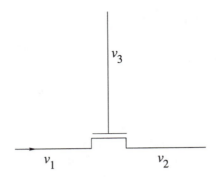

FIGURE 6.7. Circuit 2.

signal, and ϕ is the clock signal. The operation of the register is to store an input
data x into the cell if both the clock signal ϕ and load signal l are activated, and
to ensure that data x is not changed by path transistor T_2 during the period that no
fresh load signal is activated.

Specification of Elements
In order to describe the behavior of the circuit in Figure 6.6, we define operators
for transistor, inverter, and clock as follows:

- Specifying state change for potential:
  Define

  $$P \uparrow = \neg P \wedge \bigcirc P$$
  $$P \downarrow = P \wedge \bigcirc \neg P$$

  where P represents potential at point p in high level and $\neg P$ represents potential at point p in low level. $P \uparrow$ expresses the change of state of potential at
  point p from low level at this time to high level at the next time, and $P \downarrow$
  expresses the change from high level to low level. Besides, state change has
  the property that if potential at point p is in high (low) level, then the potential
  remains in high (low) level until the state gets changing. The corresponding
  temporal logic specification is

  $$\Box(P \Rightarrow (P \, \mathcal{U} \, P \downarrow))$$
  $$\Box(\neg P \Rightarrow (\neg P \, \mathcal{U} \, P \uparrow)).$$

- Specifying the path transistor:
  The path transistor can generally be represented as in Figure 6.7. Whenever
  the input signal at gate v_3 is activated, the signal at gate v_1 is transmitted to
  gate v_2. More specifically, when the potential at gate v_3 changes to high level,
  the potential at gate v_2 will also change to high level if the potential at gate v_1
  is in high level and at gate v_2 in low level; the potential at gate v_2 will decrease
  to low level if the potential at gate v_1 is in low level and the potential at gate

FIGURE 6.8. Circuit 3.

v_2 is in high level. This functionality is specified using the operator $\mathcal{PF}$:

$$\mathcal{PF}\,(v_1, v_2, v_3) =$$
$$\square(v_3 \uparrow \Rightarrow \bigcirc(v_1 \wedge \neg v_2 \Rightarrow v_2 \uparrow)) \wedge \square(v_3 \uparrow \Rightarrow \bigcirc(\neg v_1 \wedge v_2 \Rightarrow v_2 \downarrow))$$

- Specifying the inverter:
  The characteristic of the inverter shown in Figure 6.8 is that whenever the potential at gate v_1 is in high level, the potential at gate v_2 will also be in high level at the next instant, and whenever the potential at gate v_1 is in low level, the potential at gate v_2 will also be in low level at the next instant. This is specified as

  $$\square(v_1 \Rightarrow \bigcirc v_2)$$
  $$\square(\neg v_1 \Rightarrow \bigcirc \neg v_2)$$

- Specifying the clock:
  Operator $\mathcal{Y}$ is introduced to specify the cycle of clock ϕ. A four-cycle clock is specified as follows:

  $$\mathcal{Y}\phi = \phi \wedge \bigcirc\phi \wedge \bigcirc^2\phi \wedge \bigcirc^3\neg\phi \wedge \bigcirc^4\mathcal{Y}\phi,$$

  where $\bigcirc^2$ is the abbreviation for $\bigcirc\bigcirc$, $\bigcirc^3$ for $\bigcirc\bigcirc\bigcirc$, etc.

Specification of the Circuit

Using the operators defined above, the behavior of all elements of this circuit can be specified as follows:

- Path Transistor:

  $$T_1 : \square\mathcal{PF}\,(x, z, \phi \wedge l)$$
  $$T_2 : \square\mathcal{PF}\,(y, z, \phi \wedge \neg l)$$

- The combination of inverters:

  $$\square(z \Rightarrow \bigcirc y) \wedge \square(\neg z \Rightarrow \bigcirc \neg y)$$

- Statements about change of state of potential:

  $$\square(z \Rightarrow (z \,\mathcal{U}\, z \downarrow))$$
  $$\square(\neg z \Rightarrow (\neg z \,\mathcal{U}\, z \uparrow))$$
  $$\square(y \Rightarrow (y \,\mathcal{U}\, y \downarrow))$$
  $$\square(\neg y \Rightarrow (\neg y \,\mathcal{U}\, y \uparrow))$$

Reasoning about Performance of the Circuit

Generally speaking, the behaviors following from the specification can be described informally as

specification of behavior $\wedge$ input signal $\Rightarrow$ behavior.

There are four kinds of signals:

- Load Signal:
  Load signals are activated in the following order: low level, high level, high level, low level. This sequence is repeated forever, i.e.,

  $$\neg l \wedge \bigcirc l \wedge \bigcirc^2 l \wedge \bigcirc^3 \square \neg l$$

- Input Signal:
  Input signals are activated in the following order: low level, high level, high level, i.e.,

  $$\neg x \wedge \bigcirc x \wedge \bigcirc^2 x$$

- Clock Signal:
  Clock signals are generated as follows: initially low level, then in the sequence specified by $\mathcal{Y}\phi$, i.e.,

  $$\neg \phi \wedge \bigcirc \mathcal{Y}(\phi).$$

The input signal x, clock signal ϕ, load signal l, and potentials at point z and y can be described in Table 6.2:

Clearly, Y is true at each point after time point 3. This proves $\Diamond \square Y$.   ■

Program Specification   To describe the effect of a sequential program, it is sufficient to describe its initial state and the state when the program terminates. That is, a sequential program is a function that transforms an input to an output. However,

	Time Point	0	1	2	3	4	5	6	7	8
Input Signal	$\neg x$	x	x							
Clock Signal	$\neg \phi$	ϕ	ϕ	$\neg \phi$	$\neg \phi$	ϕ	ϕ	$\neg \phi$	$\neg \phi$	...
Load Signal	$\neg l$	l	l	$\neg l$	$\neg l$	$\neg l$	$\neg l$	$\neg l$	$\neg l$	...
$\phi \wedge l$	$\uparrow$		$\downarrow$							...
$\phi \wedge \neg l$					$\uparrow$		$\downarrow$		$\uparrow$	...
potential at z			z	z	z	z	z	z	z	...
potential at y				y	y	y	y	y	y	...

TABLE 6.2. Behavior of circuit.

this is not true for concurrent programs. To describe a concurrent program, it is necessary to describe what happens during its execution.

In the context of program specification, the safety properties to be verified are

1. *partial correctness*—the program produces the correct result although it is not guaranteed to terminate.
2. *mutual exclusion* —two active processes are not simultaneously accessing shared resources.
3. *deadlock-freedom* —processes do not wait indefinitely for each other to complete the task expected by the other.

The liveness properties to be verified are

1. *program termination* —the program eventually terminates.
2. *starvation-freedom* —every process eventually receives service.

In a program specification, variables, functions, and predicates occurring in a formula refer to program domain entities. For example, let x, y be program variables that take integer values, and P_1 and P_2 be two program fragments, as shown below:

$$
\begin{aligned}
&P_1 : \langle x := x + 2 \rangle \\
&P_2 : begin \\
&\qquad S_1 :: \quad \langle x := x - y + 1 \rangle; \\
&\qquad S_2 :: \quad \langle x := y + x + 1 \rangle; \\
&\qquad end
\end{aligned}
\tag{1}
$$

The angle brackets surrounding a statement indicate that the specified operation is *atomic*; that is, it is indivisible with respect to concurrently executed instructions. As sequential programs, the following programs

$$
\begin{aligned}
&begin \quad y := y + 2; \; P_1 \quad end; \\
&begin \quad y := y + 2; \; P_2 \quad end;
\end{aligned}
\tag{2}
$$

are equivalent; that is, they yield the same results. Using the predicate $becomes(x, e)$ to denote the assignment $x := e$, we can rewrite (1) as temporal formula assertions:

$$
\begin{aligned}
&\Box \, ((becomes(y, y + 2) \wedge terminate(P_1)) \vee (becomes(y, y + 2) \\
&\wedge terminate(P_2)) \Rightarrow becomes(y, y + 2) \wedge becomes(x, x + 2)).
\end{aligned}
\tag{3}
$$

Instead of considering sequential programs, consider the concurrent program

$$
Q : cobegin \langle y := y + 2 \rangle [] \; P \; coend
\tag{4}
$$

where [] indicates that $y := y + 2$ and P are to be executed in parallel, with atomic statements remaining indivisible. When P_1 is substituted for P in (4), it can be seen that the formula

$$\square \, (becomes(y, y + 2) \wedge becomes(x, x + 2)) \qquad\qquad (5)$$

holds after termination of program Q. However, when P_2 is substituted for P in (4), the final values of x and y depend upon whether or not S :: $\langle y := y + 2 \rangle$ is executed in between the atomic statements of P_2. The three possible interleaved execution sequences are

$$S_1 \, S_2 \, S$$
$$S_1 \, S \, S_2$$
$$S \, S_1 \, S_2$$

So, the behavior of the concurrent program is given by the assertion

$$\square \, (terminate(Q) \Rightarrow becomes(y, y + 2) \wedge$$
$$(becomes(x, x + 2) \vee becomes(x, x + 4) \vee becomes(x, x))). \qquad (6)$$

Mutual exclusion is an essential requirement in concurrent programs. If P_1 and P_2 are two parallel components of a program P, a block of statements s_1 in P_1 is considered critical relative to a block of statements s_2 in P_2, if P_1 and P_2 must not be in those sections at the same time. Example 6.21 illustrates how mutual exclusion can be achieved in a producer-consumer program.

Example 6.21   The concurrent program below has two processes C (consumer) and P (producer) sharing a common stack. The operations on the stack are PUT and GET. When a process makes a request to access the stack, it is eventually granted access to it. During its access, the other process cannot have access to the stack. A process accessing the stack eventually relinquishes the permission.

$$cur\_stack := nil; \; avail := n; \; now := 0; \; s := 1;$$

Process P (Producer)	*Process C* (Consumer)
loop	*loop*
produce(*putval*)	*request*(*now*)
request(*avail*)	*request*(*s*)
request(*s*)	*S2*: | GET(*getval*) *release*(*s*) |
S1: | PUT(*putval*) *release*(*s*) |	*release*(*avail*)
release(*now*)	*consume*(*getval*)
endloop	*endloop*

$S1$ in P and $S2$ in C are *critical sections*; that is, they may not be executed simultaneously by the two processes. Mutual exclusion requires that the formula

$$\square \neg (enter(S1) \wedge enter(S2)).$$

always holds. Because only one process can have access to the stack at any one time, either a PUT or a GET operation is executed at any time. When process C enters its critical section and $now > 0$ indicates the number of items in the stack is greater than 0, the top element of the stack is accessed for consumption. However, if $now = 0$, Process C cannot wait in its critical section for Process P to put an item on the stack, but must leave $S2$ and defer consumption to the next cycle when the stack becomes nonempty. So,

$$\Box((now = 0) \Rightarrow \neg enter(S_2))$$

holds for the consumer process. Similarly, for the producer process, the assertion is

$$\Box((avail = 0) \Rightarrow \neg enter(S1)). \qquad \blacksquare$$

Example 6.22 is a temporal logic specification for a sequence of actions to achieve a certain goal, and a proof for a given sequence of actions to satisfy the given specification.

Example 6.22   Planning problems require the construction of a series of actions such that the goal can be achieved by executing those actions. Temporal logic can be used to specify planning problems. The temporal logic specification can be refined to temporal logic programs and can be executed by following the techniques described in [9]. We consider the Tower of Hanoi problem to illustrate the methodology.

> Three pegs p_1, p_2, and p_3 and three disks A, B, and C are available. Initially the three disks are stacked on peg p_1, with the smallest disk, A, on top and largest one, C, at the bottom. It is required to plan a move of the disks from peg p_1 to peg p_3, using peg p_2 as a temporary storage area, such that after every single move, the disks are ordered with the largest one at the bottom.

The initial and final configurations are shown in Figure 6.9.

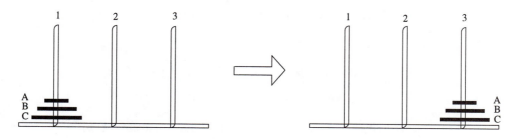

FIGURE 6.9. Towers of Hanoi.

Specification of Actions

1. Predicates:

$move(X, p)$: move disk X onto peg p;
$on(X, Y)$: disk X is on disk Y;
$smaller(X, Y)$: true if disk X is smaller than disk Y;
$top(X, p)$: disk X is the top disk on peg p;
$free(X)$: disk X can be moved.

2. Constraints:

- A disk can be moved if there is no other disk on it. That is,

$$free(X) \equiv \neg \exists Z \bullet on(X, Z).$$

- If disk X is at the top of peg p, then it is free to be moved. That is,

$$top(X, p) \Rightarrow free(X).$$

- The predicate comparing the sizes of disks satisfies the transitivity relation:

$$smaller(X, Y) \wedge smaller(Y, Z) \Rightarrow smaller(X, Z).$$

- A disk cannot be on two different disks at any one time:

$$\neg((Y_1 \neq Y_2) \wedge (on(X, Y_1) \wedge on(X, Y_2))).$$

3. Assumption:
An empty peg is assumed to have an *emptydisk*, which is larger than any of the given disks. Formally,

$$\forall p \bullet top(emptydisk, p) \Rightarrow \neg \exists X \bullet (top(X, p) \wedge on(X, emptydisk),$$
$$\forall X \bullet smaller(X, emptydisk).$$

4. Pre- and postconditions:

- Precondition $precond(X, p)$ for the action $move(X, p)$:

(a) Disk X is free.

(b) Disk X is smaller than the disk Y at the top of peg p.

$$precond(X, p) \equiv free(X) \wedge top(Y, p) \wedge smaller(X, Y)$$

- Postcondition $postcond(X, p)$ for the action $move(X, p)$:

(a) Disk X is on top of peg p.

(b) Disk Y, which was at the top of peg p, is not free and X is on Y;

(c) Disk Z, for which $on(X, Z)$ was true in the precondition, is free.

Hence, $postcond(X, p)$ is the conjunction of

$\bigcirc top(X, p)$,
$top(Y, p) \Rightarrow \bigcirc (on(X, Y) \wedge top(X, p)) \wedge \neg free(Y)$,
$on(X, Z) \wedge top(X, p') \Rightarrow \bigcirc (top(Z, p') \wedge \neg on(X, Z)) \wedge free(Z)$.

Note that the variable p denotes the destination peg for the move, and the variable p' denotes the originating peg.

5. Persistency:
Persistent axioms must be explicitly stated. There is no change in the status of the disks that are not affected by any postcondition:

(a) A free disk not affected by any postcondition will remain free.

(b) A disk that is on another disk will remain in the same state if unaffected by any postcondition.

The following formulas correspond to the above assertions.

$persistent\_free(X, p) \equiv$
$\forall X \bullet [free(X) \wedge \neg(postcond(X, p) \Rightarrow \exists Z \bullet on(Z, X)) \Rightarrow \bigcirc free(X)]$;
$\forall X \bullet persistent\_on(X, p) \equiv$
$\forall X, Y \bullet [on(X, Y) \wedge \neg(postcond(X, p) \Rightarrow \bigcirc \neg on(X, Y)) \Rightarrow \bigcirc on(X, Y)]$;

6. The Move axiom:
If the precondition for the action of moving a disk X onto peg p holds, and the move action is executed, then the postcondition as well as persistent axioms should hold:

$precond(X, p) \wedge move(X, p) \Rightarrow$
$\Diamond(postcond(X, p) \wedge persistent\_free(X, p) \wedge persistent\_on(Y, p))$

Initial State   Initially, disks A, B, and C are in peg p_1, with A at the top and C at the bottom. Disk A, peg p_2, and peg p_3 are free.

$\square(disk(A) \wedge disk(B) \wedge disk(C))$
$\square(smaller(A, B) \wedge smaller(B, C))$
$top(emptydisk, p_2) \wedge top(emptydisk, p_3) \wedge top(A, p_1) \wedge on(A, B)$
$\wedge\ on(B, C) \wedge on(C, emptydisk)$

Goal Specification   The goal is to have disks A, B, and C stacked on peg p_3 in the same order as in the inital state. The goal is specified as follows:

$\Diamond(on(C, emptydisk) \wedge on(B, C) \wedge on(A, B) \wedge top(A, p_3))$

Planning

There exists a sequence of actions consistent with the specification

$$Initial\ State \land Specification\ of\ Actions \Rightarrow (A\ series\ of\ Actions \Rightarrow Goal)$$

The claim is that a plan consisting of the following sequence of actions

$$move(A, p_3) \land \bigcirc move(B, p_2) \land \bigcirc^2 move(A, p_2) \land$$
$$\bigcirc^3 move(C, p_3) \land \bigcirc^4 move(A, p_1) \land \bigcirc^5 move(B, p_3) \land$$
$$\bigcirc^6 move(A, p_3)$$

satisfies the given specification and eventually generates the goal. To prove this claim we use Hoare's proof style. For each move in the plan, we prove that the precondition is satisfied and that the postcondition will leave the system in a state wherein the precondition for the next move holds.

Proof for first move:

1. Substitute $[A/X, emptydisk/Y, p_3/p]$ in the precondition precond(X,p):

   $$free(A) \land top(emptydisk, p_3) \land smaller(A, emptydisk)\ \text{is true.}$$

2. Move disk A to peg p_3, making $precond(A, p_3) \land move(A, p_3)$ true.

3. From the Move axiom, the postcondition for the move becomes true.

   (a) Substitute $[A/X, emptydisk/Y, B/Z, p_3/p, p_1/p]$ in $postcond(X, p)$

   (b) $\bigcirc top(A, p_3)$

   (c) $top(emptydisk, p_3) \Rightarrow \bigcirc(on(A, emptydisk) \land top(A, p_3))$

   (d) $on(A, B) \land top(A, p_1) \Rightarrow \bigcirc(top(B, p_1) \land \neg on(A, B))$

4. The postcondition modifies the initial state. By resolution, the modified state becomes

   $$disk(A) \land disk(B) \land disk(C)$$
   $$top(emptydisk, p_2) \land top(A, p_3) \land top(B, p_1) \land on(A, emptydisk) \land$$
   $$on(B, C) \land on(C, emptydisk)$$

Notice that following the persistent axioms, the predicates $top(emptydisk, p_2)$, $on(B, C)$, and $on(C, emptydisk)$ are unchanged. This situation is shown in Figure 6.10.

Proof for second move:

The second Move action is $move(B, p_2)$. This move is feasible only if $precond(B, p_2)$ is true. This can be verified by the substitution $[B/X, emptydisk/Y, p_2/p]$ in $precond(X, p)$, and resolving with the postcondition of the

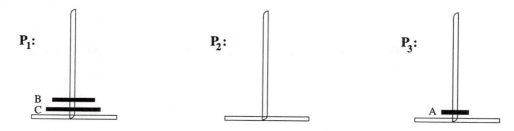

FIGURE 6.10. Tower 1.

first move. After moving disk B to peg p_2, the effect of the move is given by the postcondition and the persistent axioms. Evaluating the postcondition requires the following steps:

1. Substitute $[B/X, emptydisk/Y, C/Z, p_2/p, p_1/p']$ in $postcond(X, p)$ to obtain

   (a) $\bigcirc top(B, p_2)$

   (b) $top(emptydisk, p_2) \Rightarrow \bigcirc(on(B, emptydisk) \wedge top(B, p_2))$

   (c) $on(B, Z) \wedge top(B, p_1) \Rightarrow \bigcirc(top(C, p_1) \wedge \neg on(B, C))$

2. From the persistent axioms, infer that the rest of the disks are unaffected by this postcondition.

3. Resolving this postcondition with the current state of the system given above, we derive the next state:

   $disk(A) \wedge disk(B) \wedge disk(C)$
   $top(B, p_2) \wedge on(B, emptydisk) \wedge top(A, p_3) \wedge top(C, p_1) \wedge$
   $on(A, emptydisk) \wedge on(C, emptydisk)$

   This is shown in Figure 6.11.

Verifying that the other moves in the planning sequence satisfy the specification is included in the exercises. ∎

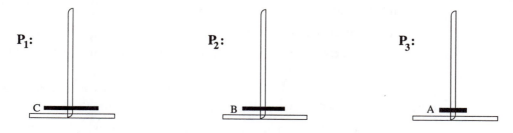

FIGURE 6.11. Tower 2.

Exercises

1. Give a proof based on natural deduction for each of the following claims:

   (a) $(P \wedge Q) \wedge R \vdash P \wedge (Q \wedge R)$

   (b) $(P \vee Q) \wedge (P \vee R) \vdash P \vee (Q \vee R)$

   (c) $P \wedge (Q \Leftrightarrow R) \vdash (P \wedge Q) \Leftrightarrow (P \wedge R)$

   (d) $\vdash (P \Rightarrow (Q \Rightarrow R)) \Leftrightarrow ((P \wedge Q) \Rightarrow R)$

   (e) $(\neg P \Rightarrow Q) \wedge (R \Rightarrow (S \vee T) \wedge (R \Rightarrow \neg S) \wedge (P \Rightarrow \neg S) \vdash R \Rightarrow Q$

2. Prove or disprove the claim below, using (1) natural deduction, and (2) proof by resolution.

   (a) The following premises are given:

      i. $\forall X \bullet (student(X) \vee teacher(X))$

      ii. $\forall X \bullet (student(X) \Rightarrow (tall(X) \wedge loves(c, X)))$

      iii. $\forall X \bullet (\neg small(X) \Rightarrow teacher(X))$

      iv. claim: $small(c)$

   (b) $\forall X \bullet P(X) \vdash \exists X \bullet \neg P(X)$

   (c) $\vdash \exists X \bullet (P(X) \Rightarrow \forall Y \bullet P(Y))$

   (d) $P(a, b) \wedge \forall X \bullet (\exists Y \bullet P(Y, X) \vee P(X, Y) \Rightarrow P(X, X)) \vdash P(X, a)$

3. Do Example 6.9 with the third premise weakened to $\exists x \bullet received(x)$. Hint: Choose a name different from the one already in use. If you choose the same name c in your proof to substitute for the quantified variable, what is the conclusion?

4. The statements given below relate to computer accounts for students. Translate each sentence into a predicate logic formula; then transform each formula into an equivalent prenex normal form; finally, give the equivalent CNF for each formula:

   (a) Every student has a unique user name and password.

   (b) Every student owns 200 MB of disk space.

   (c) No student can have two different disk spaces.

   (d) A student may erase the disk space he/she owns.

   (e) A student may give the disk space to some other student, but not to two students simultaneously.

   (f) A student who receives the disk space from another student cannot erase the contents of the disk space.

5. Write pre- and postconditions for the following operations on the file modeled in Example 6.13:

(a) *EXCHANGE*—The operation has no effect if *position* is either before the first record or after the last record in the file; otherwise, the records on either side of *position* are swapped.

(b) *COPY_LEFT(k)*—The operation has no effect if *position* is before the first record or $k \leq 0$; otherwise, the first k records to the left of *position* are copied to the right of *position* in the same order.

(c) *COPY_RIGHT(k)*—The operation has no effect if *position* is after the last record in the file or $k \geq 0$; otherwise, the first k records to the right of *position* are copied to the left of *position* in the same order.

6. In Example 6.15 the *controller* synchronously communicates with both the *train* and the *gate*. Introduce a state machine to specify the behavior of *signal*, which has three states *red, yellow, green*, and interacts with the gate and the controller in the following way:

(a) The controller informs the signal about the status of the gate through different messages.

(b) The state transitions for the signal correspond to the messages it received: for example, if it is in the state *red* and receives the message that the gate is open, it continues to stay in that state; when it receives the message that the gate is lowered, it transits to the state *yellow*; in the state *yellow*, if it receives the message "gate is closed," it transits to the state *green*; when it receives the message "gate is raised" in the state *green*, it transits to the state *yellow*; if the message "gate is open" is received in the state *yellow*, it transits to the state *red*; if it receives the message "gate is closed" in the state *red*, it transits to the state *green*; if it receives the message "gate is lowered" in the state *green*, it transits to the state *red*.

(c) The signals are conveyed by the controller to the *train*, which will assume one of the states *stop, slow*, and *resume_normal* upon receiving the signal. That is, the state machine for the train must be changed to include these new states and appropriate transitions.

Write predicate logic assertions translating the behavior of the state machines.

7. Consider program P with two parallel components P_1 and P_2 defined as follows:

(a) P_1: **while** $x > 0$ **do** $x := x - 1$ **od**; $y := y - 1$; **stop**

(b) P_2: **while** $y = 1$ **do** $z := z + 1$ **od**; **stop**

If the program starts with the initial condition $x \geq 0 \wedge y = 1 \wedge z = 0$, does it terminate? If it does, what are the values of x, y, and z after termination?

8. For the train-gate-controller problem in Example 6.15, assume that there is one train, one controller, and one gate. Using the predicate logic formulas for the state machine diagrams, give a proof that when the train is in state S_3, the controller is in state C_3, and the gate is in state G_3.

9. Complete the proof for the tower of Hanoi problem.

10. This exercise is concerned with specifying a plain old telephone system (POTS): a system consisting of a finite number of telephones, where communication between two telephones is possible. Each telephone has a unique number. The state of a telephone is determined by the truth values of the following set of predicates: *on-hook(x), off-hook(x), dial-tone(x), ringing(x), busy-tone(x)*. A user can perform the following actions: *lift-handset(x), replace-handset(x), dial-number(x,y)*. When a number *y* is dialed in a telephone *x*, either there is a busy tone at the telephone *y*, or the telephone *y* rings. In the latter case, either the phone is eventually picked up or it is not picked up. If the telephone is picked up, the telephone is said to be connected, and if the telephone is not picked up, there is no connection. In such an operation no other telephone is affected.

    (a) Give temporal logic expressions for the following:
        i. all basic predicates
        ii. user interactions
        iii. constraints on state predicates
            Example:
            (1) A telephone is either on-hook or off-hook, but not both.
            (2) A phone cannot have a busy tone and not be connected to some number.

    (b) Give temporal logic specifications for the following:
        i. constraints on actions
        ii. pre- and postconditions for actions
        iii. persistency conditions

    (c) Specify a sequence of actions for placing a phone call that results in a connection. Give a proof that it satisfies the specification.

Bibliographic Notes

Different kinds of logic, their history, evolution, and their impact on computing are surveyed by Robinson [11]. Mechanical theorem provers and proof assistants are based on the principles of deduction in logic. Grant and Minker [4] have surveyed the influence of logic on the design of Prolog, a logic programming language, and have provided a solid theoretical foundation for databases. Logic databases, also known as deductive databases, are useful in the design of expert systems and knowledge-based systems.

The concept of a proof, different proof techniques, informal development of proofs, and formal presentation of proofs are discussed from first principles by Bairwise and Etchemendy [1]. Jones [5] gives a number of rules for logic, proof obligations that arise in specification development, and properties of data in axiomatic style.

Lamport [7] is a major source of inspiration in developing the section on temporal logic. Different kinds of temporal logic and modal logic are discussed and compared by Emerson [3]. Manna and Pnueli [8] study temporal logic specifications for reactive systems. Kröger [6] gives the formal semantics of linear time temporal logic and formally presents logical verification of concurrent program properties.

References

[1] J. Bairwise and J. Etchemendy, *The Language of First-Order Logic* (third edition), Center for the Study of Language and Information, Stanford, CA, 1995.

[2] T. DeMarco, *Structured Analysis and System Specification*, Yourdon Press, New York, NY, 1978.

[3] E.A. Emerson, "Temporal and Modal Logic," in J. van Leeuwen (Ed.), *Handbook of Theoretical Computer Science*, North-Holland, Amsterdam, 1989, pp. 995–1072.

[4] J. Grant and J. Minker, "The Impact of Logic Programming and Databases," *Communications of the ACM*, Vol. 35, No. 3, 1992, pp. 67–81.

[5] C.B. Jones, *Systematic Software Development using VDM* (second edition), Prentice-Hall International (UK), 1990.

[6] F. Kröger, *Temporal Logic of Programs*, EATCS Monographs on Theoretical Computer Science, Springer-Verlag, Berlin/Heidelberg, 1986.

[7] L. Lamport, "What Good is Temporal Logic?" Invited Paper, *Proceedings of IFIP'83 Congress – Information Processing*, North-Holland, Amsterdam, 1983, pp. 657–668.

[8] Z. Manna and A. Pnueli, *The Temporal Logic of Reactive and Concurrent Systems: Specifications*, Springer-Verlag, New York, NY, 1992.

[9] B. Moszkowski, *Executing Temporal Logic Programs*, Cambridge University Press, Cambridge, England, 1986.

[10] S. Owiciki and L. Lamport, "Proving Liveness Properties of Concurrent Programs," *ACM Transactions on Programming Languages and Systems*, Vol. 4, No. 3, 1982, pp. 455–495.

[11] J.A. Robinson, "Logic and Logic Programming," *Communications of the ACM*, Vol. 35, No. 3, 1992, pp. 41–65.

7

Set Theory and Relations

The main goal of this chapter is to demonstrate the usefulness of mathematical abstractions such as sets, relations, functions, and sequences in software development. In particular, the chapter lays the foundation for the specification languages presented in the next four chapters.

Software systems deal with real-world objects, their attributes, and their interactions. Collections of such objects are abstracted as *sets* or *sequences*, and the interactions between pairs of objects are abstracted as *relations* or *functions*. When such abstractions are not created and used in software development, the modeling of real-world objects may be influenced by implementation details.

Sets correspond to structures for providing truth values to propositions and predicates. Each n-ary predicate $P(x_1, x_2, \ldots, x_n)$ is interpreted over a structure $R \subseteq U^n$, where U is the universal set, such that the predicate is true for tuples in R. The domain R consists of all relations $r(x_1, x_2, \ldots, x_n)$ for which $P(x_1, x_2, \ldots, x_n)$ is true. For a unary predicate $p(x)$, the domain is the set of values of the argument x for which $p(x)$ is true. This view of sets of objects and relations, implicitly defined by predicates over the objects, is useful for introducing the notion of *type* and defining *type invariants* in the specification of software systems.

7.1 Formal Specification Based on Set Theory

The vocabulary, the syntax, and the semantics of the formalism are borrowed from set theory. The syntax includes the notation for set presentation, set membership, and set extension. The semantics conduces to reasoning about specifications based on the notation.

7.1.1   Set Notation

A set may be presented by enumerating its elements. Thus,

$status = \{idle, \ on, \ off\}$

introduces the set *status* whose elements describe the three possible states of a process. To introduce a set that cannot be enumerated but whose membership criterion can be asserted, we use the "let" construct. For instance, we describe sets using the following statements: "Let *Person* denote the set of all persons registered in an employment registration bureau" and " Let *P* denote the set of printers." Such definitions may be used in defining other sets. We also use standard mathematical notations such as $\mathbb{N}$ to denote the set of natural numbers.

The set comprehension notation is used to introduce sets obtained by specializing nonempty sets that have already been defined. For example, the set

$\{x : \mathbb{N} \mid 1 < x < 1000 \land prime(x)\}$

introduces the finite set of prime numbers in the range 1..1000. The set

$retired = \{e : \text{Person} \mid age(e) \geq 65\}$

refers to the set of persons who have reached the age of 65.

In this chapter, we adopt the notion that a *type* is a *maximal set* of values. In general, specification languages have built-in types; some provide facilities to construct complex types. An object is associated with a type, and an identifier is used to denote the object. When a type denotes a *maximal* set of values, an object can belong to only one type. Within this framework there is no notion of subtyping. The set constructors, $\cup$, $\cap$, $-$ are also used as type constructors. The expression $x : retired \cap male$ introduces a variable denoting a male retired person. The two expressions $x \in retired$, and $x : retired$ have the same meaning.

The *powerset* of a set S, denoted by $\mathbb{P} \, S$, represents the set of all subsets of S. It serves as the type for collections of objects. To formalize statements such as " let X and Y denote two sets of retired people," it is sufficient to write $X, Y : \mathbb{P} \, retired$. The set membership operation $\in$ may be used to determine subset relationships. For instance, $(\forall e : X \bullet e \in Y) \Rightarrow X \subset Y$. If T is a type and $S \subset T$, we assert that $P(x)$ is true for some $x \in S$, by writing

$\exists x : T \bullet x \in S \land P(x)$, or
$\exists x : S \bullet P(x)$

The declaration $e : X - Y$ introduces a variable of type $X - Y$, that is, a variable whose values belong to the set X, but not to the set Y.

A set cannot represent an ordered collection of objects. Information that requires some ordering is represented using n-tuples. If x and y are elements of sets X and Y, then the ordered pair (x, y) is an element of the *Cartesian Product type* $X \times Y$.

The cartesian product notion can be generalized:

$$X_1 \times X_2 \times \ldots \times X_n$$

is the set of all n-tuples $\{x_1, x_2, \ldots, x_n\}$, where $x_i \in X_i$. Two n-tuples $\{x_1, x_2, \ldots, x_n\}$, and $\{y_1, y_2, \ldots, y_n,\}$ are *equal* if $(x_1 = y_1 \wedge x_2 = y_2 \wedge \ldots \wedge x_n = y_n)$. The ordering of components in a cartesian product is meaningful. The cartesian products $T \times T \times T$, $T \times (T \times T)$, $(T \times T) \times T$ correspond to different sets. Set equality is extended to cartesian products. Two tuples are equal if and only if their corresponding components are equal. If $S, T \subset X \times Y$, then $S = T$ if and only if they have the same tuples. The data type *date* can be modeled using cartesian product as follows:

> *date* = *Year* × *Month* × *Days*, where
> *Year* = $\{x : \mathbb{N} \mid 2000 \leq x \leq 4000\}$,
> *Month* = $\{Jan, Feb, Mar, Apr, May, Jun, Jul, Aug, Sep, Oct, Nov, Dec\}$,
> *Days* = $\{x : \mathbb{N} \mid 1 \leq x \leq 31\}$.

This type includes some invalid tuples such as (2000, *Feb*, 30). To exclude invalid values for a type, we need *type invariant*. These are described in detail in Chapter 9.

7.1.2 Reasoning with Sets

Proofs about sets are constructed from the semantics of set operators introduced in the previous section. Natural deduction is the frequently used proof technique. It uses the following axioms for set operations.

1. *empty set*
   A basic axiom of set theory is that the empty set, denoted as $\emptyset$, exists and has no elements:

   $$\frac{\emptyset}{\forall x : S \bullet x \notin \emptyset}$$

   This axiom uses the set membership operator $\in$, which is axiomatized next.

2. *membership*

   $$\frac{e \in S}{S \neq \emptyset}$$
   $$\frac{e = x_1 \vee \ldots \vee e = x_k}{e \in \{x_1, \ldots, x_k\}}$$
   $$\frac{\exists x : S \mid P(x) \bullet a[x] = e}{e \in \{x : S \mid P(x) \bullet a[x]\}}$$

   The first axiom states that if there exists an element in a set, then the set is not empty. The second axiom is applicable for set enumeration. The third axiom applies for set comprehension.

3. *subset*

$$\overline{\varnothing \subseteq S}$$

$$\frac{\forall x : S \bullet x \in T}{S \subseteq T}$$

$$\frac{S \subseteq T \land T \subseteq U}{S \subseteq U}$$

4. *equality*

$$\frac{S \subseteq T \land T \subseteq S}{S = T}$$

5. *membership in powerset*

$$\frac{S = \varnothing}{\mathbb{P} S = \varnothing}$$

$$\frac{T \subseteq S}{T \in \mathbb{P} S}$$

6. *membership in cartesian product*

$$\frac{e_1 \in X_1 \land \ldots \land e_n \in X_n}{(e_1, \ldots, e_n) \in X_1 \times \ldots \times X_n}$$

7. *equality of tuples*

$$\frac{x_1 = y_1 \land \ldots \land x_n = y_n}{(x_1, \ldots, x_n) = (y_1, \ldots, y_n)}$$

8. *union, intersection, difference*

[*union*]— $$\frac{x \in (S \cup T)}{x \in S \lor x \in T}$$

[*distributed union*]— $$\frac{x \in \bigcup S}{\exists X : S \bullet x \in X}$$

[*intersection*]— $$\frac{x \in S \cap T}{x \in S \land x \in T}$$

[*distributed intersection*]— $$\frac{x \in \bigcap S}{\forall X : S \bullet x \in X}$$

[*difference*]— $$\frac{x \in S - T}{x \in S \land x \notin T}$$

Example 7.1   Prove (i) $S \subset S \cup \{e\}$, and (ii) if $e \in S$, $S = S \cup \{e\}$.
Proof of (i):

1. $S = \varnothing$. From the first axiom for empty set, infer $\varnothing \subset \varnothing \cup \{e\}$.

2. $S \neq \emptyset$.

   - From $x \in S$, infer $x \in S \vee x \in \{e\}$ ($\vee-introduction$)

   - From the union axiom and the previous step, infer $x \in S \cup \{e\}$

3. From 1 and 2, infer $S \subset S \cup \{e\}$.

Proof of (ii):

1. $S \subset S \cup \{e\} \ldots$ proved in (i).

2. From $x \in S \cup \{e\}$ and the union axiom, infer $x \in S \vee x \in \{e\}$.

3. If $x = e$, from the premises and from the second subset axiom infer $S \cup \{e\} \subset S$.

4. If $x \neq e$ and $x \in S \cup \{e\}$, from the second axiom for set membership infer $S \cup \{e\} \subset S$.

5. From set equality axiom, and steps 3 and 4, infer $S = S \cup \{e\}$.

From Example 7.1 it follows that sets $X = \{3, 7, 3, 5, 8, 5\}$ and $Y = \{3, 5, 8, 7\}$ are equal. Reordering or introducing duplicate elements in a set will not create a different set.   ■

7.1.3 A Specification Example

A Computer-Assisted Education Tool (CAET) is a multiuser environment for distance learning. A simplified version of CAET is specified in the following example. The focus is on abstracting application domain objects such as users, access rights, files, and user commands.

Example 7.2   Some of the requirements of CAET are stated informally and formalized using set notation.

1. *User Categories*—There are four classes of users: *author, teacher, student,* and *administrator*. An author, who can be a teacher but not a student, prepares lessons. A teacher can be an author but not a student or an administrator. An administrator has special privileges for managing accounts of students registered for courses offered by CAET and hence cannot be an author, teacher, or student. The categories of users are modeled by sets.

   Let u denote the set of all user names, and *curusers* denote the set of all current users; *author, teacher, student,* and *administrator* denote the sets of all authors, teachers, students, and administrators in CAET.

> $(curusers \subseteq u) \wedge$
> $(curusers = author \cup teacher \cup student \cup administrator) \wedge$
> $(author \cap student = \varnothing) \wedge (teacher \cap student = \varnothing) \wedge$
> $(teacher \cap administrator = \varnothing) \wedge$
> $(student \cap administrator = \varnothing) \wedge$
> $(author \cap administrator = \varnothing)$

2. *File categories*—There are three categories of system files: 1) lessons and quizzes; 2) class list and grade list for students; 3) author list and teacher list. Authors, teachers, and students can access files in the first category; teachers and administrators can access files in the second category, and only administrators can access files in the third category. The specification models the structure of the *file store*, and not the structure of the files in the file stores.

Let *file_store_a* denote the type of file store exclusively owned by administrators. All administrators have the same set of privileges for files in *file_store_a*. The store is a collection of ordered pairs:

> $file\_store\_a = \mathbb{P}(administrator \times ad\_files),$

where *ad_files* is the type of file names owned by the administrators.

Let *file_store_b* denote the type of file store jointly owned by teachers and administrators, containing the set of class lists and grade lists. A class list is created by an administrator who authorizes the teacher of the section to read or copy the list. A teacher can access only the class list of his/her section, and cannot modify the list. The grade list for the class can be created and modified by the teacher of the section only; an administrator can only view the grades. File access privileges are asymmetrical with respect to the class of users. The type of *file_store_b* corresponds to the union type of two sets of ordered pairs:

> $file\_store\_b = \mathbb{P}(administrator \times (teacher \times class\_files)) \cup$
> $\mathbb{P}(teacher \times (administrator \times grade\_files))$

where *class_files* and *grade_files* are file names for class and grade lists, respectively.

Let *file_store_c* denote the type of file store that may be jointly accessed by administrators, teachers, and students. The files in this store are exclusively created by authors, and hence may be modified only by the authors. Students and teachers can read the files or copy the files into another file store. The file store has the type

> $file\_store\_c = \mathbb{P}(author \times course\_no \times lesson) \cup$
> $\mathbb{P}(author \times course\_no \times quiz),$

where *course_no* is the type defining the set of courses, and *lesson* and *quiz* denote types of file names containing lessons and quizzes. The implication of this model is that several lesson files and several quiz files may be created by several authors for one course. In addition, the authors may own other auxiliary files. The type of auxiliary files is modeled as collections of ordered pairs (*user*, *file*):

$$aux\_file\_store = \mathbb{P}(curusers \times file\_names),$$

where *file_names* = *quiz* ∪ *lesson* ∪ *class_files* ∪ *grade_files* ∪ *ad_files*.

3. *File store access rights*—Each file category can be accessed by a designated set of users. This requirement is described by the type

$$fsar = \mathbb{P}(file\_store \times \mathbb{P}(curusers)),$$

where

$$file\_store = file\_store\_a \cup file\_store\_b \cup file\_store\_c \cup aux\_file\_store$$

4. *Access rights*—The set

$$privileges = \{read, write, edit, copy, execute, nil\}$$

defines all possible access rights in the system. A user can have one or more of these rights for a file. Thus, access rights for files are described as a collection of triples (*u*, *f*, *A*), such that user *u* has the rights enumerated in set $A \subseteq$ *privileges* for the file with name *f*:

$$ufar = \mathbb{P}(curusers \times file\_names \times \mathbb{P}(privileges))$$

5. *Access rights invariants*—

   (a) It is a requirement that the access rights granted to users for certain files remain compatible with the file store rights granted to user categories.

$$\forall x : ufar \bullet ((u, f, A) \in x \Leftrightarrow$$
$$((f \in file\_store\_a \wedge u \in administrator) \vee$$
$$(f \in file\_store\_b \wedge (u \in administrator \vee u \in teacher)) \vee$$
$$(f \in file\_store\_c \wedge u \in authors) \vee$$
$$(f \in aux\_file\_store \wedge u \in curusers)))$$

   (b) Files containing lessons and quizzes must remain accessible to users of CAET. The author of a lesson or quiz must be able to read, write, edit, and copy the files containing the material.

$$\forall x : file\_store\_c \bullet ((a, c, l) \in x \Rightarrow$$
$$\exists y : ufar \bullet (a, l, A) \in y \wedge$$
$$\forall z : curusers \exists w : ufar \bullet ((z, l, B) \in w \wedge B \subseteq \{read, copy\}))$$

A similar assertion can be made for a quiz file in *file_store_c*.

6. *Transferring access rights*—For every file in *aux_file_store*, the owner of the file has all the privileges on the file. Any user who is not an owner of a file can have the same privileges if granted by the owner. A user u_1 can grant to another user u_2 certain privileges $B \subseteq privileges$ on a file f such that (u_1, f) exists in *aux_file_store*. To describe accesses granted by users, we introduce the type

$$grant\_access = \mathbb{P}(curusers \times curusers \times file\_names \times \mathbb{P}(privileges))$$

such that

$$\forall g : granted\_access \bullet (g = (u_1, u_2, f, B) \Leftrightarrow$$
$$B \subseteq privileges \land \exists x : aux\_file\_store \bullet (u_1, f) \in x)$$

7. *State invariants*—The *state* of CAET at an instant is characterized by a set of users, a collection of files in the file stores, and access rights of users on the files in the stores. Both *file_store_c* and *aux_file_store* may keep different versions of the same file. However, versioning of files in other file stores is permitted subject to certain constraints. For example, a lesson prepared by an author may be revised by another author. A revision is an ordered pair $((a, c, l), (a', c, l'))$. Versioning is described by the following types:

$$\mathbb{P}(L \times L), \quad L = \mathbb{P}(author \times course\_no \times lesson)$$
$$\mathbb{P}(Q \times Q), \quad Q = \mathbb{P}(author \times course\_no \times quiz)$$
$$\mathbb{P}(A \times A), \quad A = \mathbb{P}(curusers \times file\_names)$$

These types are constrained by the following invariants:

$$sucl : \mathbb{P}(L \times L); \; sucq : \mathbb{P}(Q \times Q); \; suca : \mathbb{P}(A \times A);$$
$$sucl \subseteq file\_store\_c \times file\_store\_c \land$$
$$sucq \subseteq file\_store\_c \times file\_store\_c \land$$
$$suca \subseteq aux\_file\_store \times aux\_file\_store$$

8. *Operations*—We specify only two operations, namely file creation and file deletion. Other operations are included in the exercises at the end of the chapter. We use unprimed and primed variables to denote respectively the state before and after an operation.

   (a) *File creation* - Let
   $$storea : file\_store\_a,$$
   $$storeb : file\_store\_b,$$
   $$storec : file\_store\_c,$$
   $$auxstore : aux\_file\_store, \text{ and}$$
   $$ur : ufar$$

denote the status of the stores. Files may be created by any user. For example, an administrator can create a new file in three different ways:

i. A file to be used exclusively by administrators is protected from all other user categories, and is maintained in *storea*. The other file stores are unchanged. Assuming that the syntax of *create* command is *create userid, file, status*, it has the following effect:

$$(command = create) \wedge (userid \in administrator) \wedge$$
$$(status = ad\_protect) \Rightarrow$$
$$(storea' = storea \cup \{(userid, file)\} \wedge (storeb' = storeb) \wedge$$
$$(storec' = storec) \wedge (auxstore' = auxstore) \wedge$$
$$(ur' = ur \cup \{(userid, file, privileges)\})$$

ii. An administrator may create a file to be shared with some teacher and hence the file is added to *storeb*. Assuming that the syntax of *create* command is

$$create\ userid_1,\ userid_2,\ file,$$

its effect is specified as follows:

$$(command = create) \Rightarrow ((userid_1 \in administrator) \wedge$$
$$(userid_2 = teacher) \Rightarrow ((storea' = storea) \wedge$$
$$(storeb' = storeb \cup \{(userid_1, (userid_2, file))\}) \wedge$$
$$(storec' = storec) \wedge (auxstore' = auxstore) \wedge$$
$$(ur' = ur \cup \{(userid_1, file, \{read, copy\}),$$
$$(userid_2, file, \{read, copy\})\})))$$

iii. An administrator may create a file in *auxstore* for general usage. Assuming that the syntax of *create* command is

$$create\ userid, file,$$

its effect is

$$(command = create) \Rightarrow$$
$$(auxstore' = auxstore \cup \{(userid, file)\}) \wedge$$
$$(storea' = storea) \wedge (storeb' = storeb) \wedge (storec' = storec)$$

(b) The *delete* command is used to remove an existing file from a filestore. Deleting the file *filename* requires annulling access rights on the file for user *userid* and annulling the granted rights on the file. We use variables *storeu* and *storeg* in the following formulas, where

    storeu: *ufar*
    storeg: *granted_access*

Let *remove_privilege(userid,filename)* be the predicate

$\exists B : \mathbb{P}\, privileges\bullet$
$\quad \{userid, filename, B\} \in storeu \Rightarrow$
$\qquad (storeu' = storeu - \{(userid, filename, B)\}) \wedge$
$\exists u : curusers, \exists C : \mathbb{P}\, privileges\bullet$
$\quad (\{userid, u, filename, C\} \in storeg \wedge C \subseteq B) \Rightarrow$
$\qquad (storeg' = storeg - \{(userid, u, filename, C)\})$

i. The effect of the *delete* command on student files is

$(command = delete) \wedge (userid \in student) \Rightarrow$
$((auxstore' = auxstore - \{(userid, filename)\}) \wedge$
$(storea' = storea) \wedge (storeb' = storeb) \wedge$
$remove\_privilege(userid, filename)$

ii. An author may delete files from *storec* or from *auxstore*:

$(command = delete) \wedge (userid \in author) \Rightarrow$
$((\exists c : course\_no \bullet (storec' = storec - \{(userid, c, filename)\})) \oplus$
$(auxstore' = auxstore - \{(userid, filename)\}) \wedge$
$(storea' = storea) \wedge (storeb' = storeb) \wedge$
$(storec' = storec)) \wedge remove\_privilege(userid, filename)$

where the operator $\oplus$ denotes the exclusive-or operation, which enforces that only one of the two deletions occurs. The effect of the *delete* command for other categories of users and files can be described in a similar fashion.   ∎

7.2   Formal Specification Based on Relations and Functions

A direct way to express a relationship between two objects is to construct the ordered pair of the two objects. When the relationship is specialized, as in the case when only one object is related to another object, a function is more appropriate to express the relationship. Relationships among several objects can be expressed as ordered tuples. Symbol tables, dictionaries, and database information are all instances of relations.

7.2.1   Relations and Functions

Binary relations model objects that relate members of two sets. If X and Y are sets, then $X \leftrightarrow Y$ denotes the set of all relations from X to Y:

$$X \leftrightarrow Y = \mathbb{P}(X \times Y)$$

We use the notation $r : X \leftrightarrow Y$ to denote a relation r from X to Y. Binary relations can express one-one, one-many, and many-many dependencies between members of the two sets. For instance, "an account-holder holds only one current account" is a one-one relationship between *account_holders* and *current_accounts*, "a student takes several courses" is a one-many relationship between *student* and *course*, and "patients are allocated to different labs for tests" is a many-many relationship between *patient* and *lab*.

All set operations, except union, can be meaningfully applied to the relations $r, s : (X \leftrightarrow Y)$. The two other operations are

1. *inverse*—The inverse relation $s = inverse(r)$ of relation r can be computed by the rule:

   $$(x, y) \in r \Leftrightarrow (y, x) \in s$$

2. *composition*—The composition rule constructs a new relation from two given relations. The composite relation $w = r \circ u$ can be constructed by the rule

   $$r : (X \leftrightarrow Y); u : (Y \leftrightarrow Z)$$
   $$w : (X \leftrightarrow Z)$$
   $$(x, z) \in w \leftrightarrow \exists y \in Y \bullet (x, y) \in r \wedge (y, z) \in u$$

The composition rule plays a significant role in specifications, especially when relations defined on a set are applied repeatedly to the set. Let r^n be defined as the composition of r^{n-1} with r, where r^0 is the *identity relation*. The relation $r^{re} = r \cup r^0$ is *reflexive*; the relation $r^{sy} = r \cup inverse(r)$ is *symmetric*; the relation $r^+ = \bigcup r^n$ is the *transitive closure* of r. In fact, r^+ is the smallest transitive relation containing r. For instance, if *flies* : $(city \times city)$ is a relation describing the property that $(x, y) \in flies$ if there is a direct flight from city x to city y, then the transitive closure relation *flies*$^+$ contains all ordered pairs such that there is a flight (direct or indirect) between each pair of cities. The relation *flies*^{sy} contains the tuples (x, y), such that a direct flight from x to y and from y to x exists.

A *total function f* from X to Y, written $f : X \rightarrow Y$, maps every element of X to exactly one element of Y. When f is defined on only a proper subset of X, f is called a *partial function*. The set of all total functions from X to Y is denoted by $X \rightarrow Y$, and the set of all partial functions from X to Y is denoted by $X \nrightarrow Y$. Functions can be defined recursively, take functions as arguments, and return other functions.

A function specification may either be *implicit* or *direct*. An implicit specification defines *what* is to be computed, whereas a direct specification defines explicitly *how* the result may be computed. Implicit specifications are more abstract and shorter in description than direct specifications. Another compelling argument for implicit specification is that the computational model and algorithms for arriving at the result can be postponed to later stages of the design process. Implicitly defined function must include preconditions and postconditions. When the function is applied to arguments satisfying the precondition, its results should satisfy the postcondition. The function cannot be applied to arguments not satisfying the precondition. We do not consider the consequences of partial functions for which certain terms in the precondition are undefined. The appropriate logic dealing with partial functions is discussed in Jones [2].

The syntax for implicit and direct function specifications varies from one specification language to another. However, the semantics confirms to the pattern described above. Example 7.3 illustrates the difference in the respective specification styles.

Example 7.3   The greatest common divisor (*gcd*) of two positive integers x, y is the largest integer among the common divisors of x and y. A formal specification for *gcd* is

$gcd : \mathbb{N} \times \mathbb{N} \to \mathbb{N}$
pre $x > 0 \wedge y \geq 0$
post $d > 0 \wedge ((d \text{ div } x) \wedge (d \text{ div } y) \wedge \neg \exists s \bullet ((s \text{ div } x) \wedge (s \text{ div } y) \wedge d < s))$

An implicit definition of the *gcd* function is constructed from three other function definitions. The predicate *divides*(x, y) is a truth-valued function, the function *common_divisors* maps a pair of non-negative integers to the set of their common divisors, and *max* maps a set of positive integers to their maximum:

$divides : \mathbb{N} \times \mathbb{N} \to Bool$
$divides(x, y) == y \bmod x = 0$
$common\_divisors : \mathbb{N} \times \mathbb{N} \to \mathbb{P}\,\mathbb{N}$
$common\_divisor(x, y) == S$
post $\forall r \in S \bullet (divides(r, x) \wedge divides(r, y))$
$max : \mathbb{P}\,\mathbb{N} \to \mathbb{N}$
$max(S) == r$
post $r \in S \wedge \neg \exists y \bullet (y \in S \wedge r < y)$
$gcd : \mathbb{N} \times \mathbb{N} \to \mathbb{N}$
$gcd(x, y) == r$
pre $x > 0 \wedge y \geq 0$
post $r = max(common\_divisors(x, y))$

A direct function specification for *gcd* is given below. A proof that the function specification satisfies its requirements (definition) is given in section 7.2.4.

$$gcd(x, y) = \begin{cases} x, & \text{if } y = 0, x > y \\ gcd(y, x \bmod y), & \text{if } x \geq y > 0 \\ gcd(y \bmod x, x), & \text{if } 0 \leq x < y \end{cases} \qquad \blacksquare$$

7.2.2   Functions on Relations

The *domain* of a relation $R : X \leftrightarrow Y$, written as *dom R*, is the subset $A \subseteq X$ defined by

$$A = \{x : X \mid \exists y : Y \bullet (x, y) \in R\}$$

Hence, the domain of a relation can be defined as a function:

$$dom : (X \leftrightarrow Y) \to \mathbb{P} X$$

In particular, when the relation R is a function, the argument of the function *dom* is R, a function, and the image of *dom* is a *set*. Functions such as *dom* that take functions as arguments are called *higher-order functions*.

The *range* of a relation $R : X \leftrightarrow Y$, written as *ran R*, is defined similarly as the subset $B \subseteq Y$,

$$B = \{y : Y \mid \exists x : X \bullet (x, y) \in R\}$$

That is, $ran : (X \leftrightarrow Y) \to \mathbb{P} Y$ is also a higher-order function. Example 7.4 uses higher-order functions in specifying time-dependent events in a reactive system.

Example 7.4   Let E denote the set of all event *names* used in describing a computer system. An event $e \in E$ is said to *occur* if there is a time interval during which the effect of e is realized. Assigning values to variables, ringing a bell, and activating a print operation are examples of events.

1. *Event occurrence*—An event occurs continuously during an interval of time. Moreover, an event can occur several times during system execution. To model these requirements, we need a continuous model of time, as discussed in Chapter 6. Let $\mathbb{R}$ denote the time domain. Since occurrence implies *discrete instances*, the k-th occurrence of an event is associated with a beginning time and an ending time. We conceive the event occurrences as higher order-functions:

   $$\text{TIME}_1, \text{TIME}_2 : E \to (\mathbb{N} \to \mathbb{R})$$

   so that

   $$\forall e : E \bullet \text{TIME}_1(e), \text{TIME}_2(e) : \mathbb{N} \to \mathbb{R} \text{ and}$$
   $$\forall n : \mathbb{N} \bullet \text{TIME}_1(e)(n) = t_n, \text{TIME}_2(e)(n) = t'_n \text{ with } t'_n \geq t_n$$

   The initiation time of the n-th occurrence of event e is t_n, and its completion time is t'_n. By including the constraint that $t'_n \geq t_n$ as part of the specification, we satisfy the safety requirement that terminations can be observed only for initiated events.

2. *History of variables*—Variables assume different values at different points in time. For each variable $v \in V$, the function *ASSIGN* produces the event *ASSIGN(v)*. The event *ASSIGN(v)* assigns a value from the domain *DOM*

to the variable v. Since $ASSIGN(v)$ is an event, it may occur any number of times; for each occurrence, it takes a certain amount of time to complete assigning a value to v. $TIME_1(ASSIGN(v))(k)$ and $TIME_2(ASSIGN(v))(k)$ denote the start and completion times of the k-th assignment to v.

$$ASSIGN : V \to E,$$
$$VALUE : V \to (\mathbb{N} \to DOM),$$
$$\forall v : V \bullet (VALUE(v) : \mathbb{N} \to DOM),$$
$$\forall v : V \bullet (\forall k : \mathbb{N} \bullet (VALUE(v)(k) \in DOM))$$

The value $v_k \equiv VALUE(v)(k)$ is the value assigned to variable v during the interval

$$[TIME_1(ASSIGN)(k), \ TIME_2(ASSIGN)(k)]$$

The value v_k remains unchanged in the interval

$$[TIME_2(ASSIGN)(k), \ TIME_1(ASSIGN)(k+1)]$$

The diagram in Figure 7.1 shows the relationship among VALUE, ASSIGN, and TIME functions.

3. *Measure of events*—The functions $COUNT_1$, $COUNT_2$ are higher-order functions producing counting functions for each event $e \in E$. For $t : \mathbb{R}$, $COUNT_1(e)(t)$ is the number of initiations of e *strictly before* time t, and $COUNT_2(e)(t)$ is the number of observed completions of e *strictly before* time t.

$$COUNT_1, COUNT_2 : E \to (\mathbb{R} \to \mathbb{N})$$

$$\forall e : E \bullet (COUNT_1(e), COUNT_2(e) : \mathbb{R} \to \mathbb{N}) \Rightarrow$$
$$\forall e : E \bullet (\forall t : \mathbb{R} \bullet (COUNT_1(e)(t), COUNT_2(e)(t) \in \mathbb{N}))$$

where $COUNT_2(e)(t) \leq COUNT_1(e)(t)$.

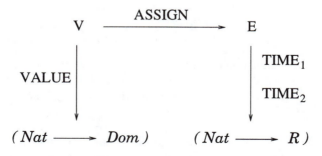

FIGURE 7.1. Relationship among VALUE, ASSIGN, and TIME functions.

The higher-order functions $LAST_1$ and $LAST_2$ are defined as follows:

$$LAST_1, LAST_2 : E \rightarrow (\mathbb{R} \rightarrow \mathbb{R}).$$

$$\forall e : E \bullet (\forall t : \mathbb{R} \bullet (LAST_1(e)(t), LAST_2(e)(t) \in \mathbb{R})$$

$LAST_1(e)(t) = t_1$ if $t_1 < t$ and event e was last initiated at time t_1. Similarly, $LAST_2(e)(t) = t_2$ if $t_2 < t$ and event e was last completed at time t_2. An interesting relationship among these six functions is that

$$LAST_1(e) = TIME_1(e) \circ COUNT_1(e), LAST_2(e) = TIME_2(e) \circ COUNT_2(e) \quad \blacksquare$$

In database applications, it is sometimes required to construct sets of objects satisfying a given property and to redefine attributes on subsets of objects. These operations may be specified using the restriction and overriding operators.

The operator $\lhd$ restricts the domain, and the operator $\rhd$ restricts the range of relations. The operators are defined as functions:

$$\lhd : \mathbb{P}X \times (X \leftrightarrow Y) \rightarrow (X \leftrightarrow Y)$$

$$\forall S : \mathbb{P}X, R : X \leftrightarrow Y \bullet$$
$$S \lhd R = \{(a, b) \mid a \in S \wedge (a, b) \in R\}$$

$$\rhd : (X \leftrightarrow Y) \times \mathbb{P}Y \rightarrow (X \leftrightarrow Y)$$

$$\forall T : \mathbb{P}Y, R : X \leftrightarrow Y \bullet$$
$$R \rhd T = \{(a, b) \mid b \in T \wedge (a, b) \in R\}$$

$S \lhd R$ filters tuples $(a, b) \in R$ for which $a \in S$ and produces the result relation. $R \rhd T$ filters $(c, d) \in R$ for which $d \in T$ and produces the result relation.

Given

$$rel = \{(1, x_3), (4, x_2), (5, x_6), (7, x_6), (9, x_8)\}$$
$$S = \{4, 7, 9\}$$
$$T = \{x_3, x_6\}$$

the expression $S \lhd rel$ corresponds to the relation

$$\{(4, x_2), (7, x_6), (9, x_8)\}$$

and the expression $rel \rhd T$ corresponds to the relation

$$\{(1, x_3), (5, x_6)\}$$

Two other useful derived operators are $\ntriangleleft$ and $\ntriangleright$, the subtraction operators for the domain and range of a relation, respectively. $S \ntriangleleft R$ filters tuples (a, b) of R for which $a \notin S$. $R \ntriangleright T$ filters tuples (c, d) of R for which $d \notin T$. The following relationships are observed on the operators:

$$S \triangleleft R = (X - S) \triangleleft R$$
$$R \triangleright T = R \triangleright (Y - T)$$

It follows from these definitions that $S \triangleleft R$ and $S \triangleleft R$ are complementary and partition the relation R. That is,

$$R = (S \triangleleft R) \cup (S \triangleleft R),$$
$$(S \triangleleft R) \cap (S \triangleleft R) = \varnothing$$

Similarly,

$$R = (R \triangleright T) \cup (R \triangleright T),$$
$$(R \triangleleft T) \cap (R \triangleleft T) = \varnothing$$

The *union* ($\cup$), *intersection* ($\cap$), and *difference* ($-$) operators are functions:

$$\cup, \cap, - \ : \mathbb{P}(X) \times \mathbb{P}(X) \to \mathbb{P}(X)$$

Union and intersection are *commutative* and *associative*; but difference is neither commutative nor associative. Commutativity and associativity allow any number of sets to be combined in any order; that is, both union and intersection can be applied to more than two sets. Although the meaning for intersection and difference applied to relations can be carried over from set theory, the meaning for union should be given in such a way that it will ensure that the result is a relation. When $dom \, f \cap dom \, g = \varnothing$, the union of the two relations $f, g : X \leftrightarrow Y$ is the set union $f \cup g$. In particular, if f and g are functions, then $h = f \cup g : X \to Y$ is also a function:

$$h(x) = \begin{cases} f(x), & x \in dom \, f \\ g(x), & x \in dom \, g \end{cases}$$

When $dom \, f \cap dom \, g \neq \varnothing$ and f and g yield different results for some values in their common domain, "f overrides g" or "g overrides f." The relational overriding $f \oplus g$ defines a relation that agrees with f outside the domain of g, and agrees with g in the domain of g. For functions f and g, the overriding of f with g is the function $h = f \oplus g$, such that

$$h(x) = \begin{cases} g(x), & x \in dom \, g \\ f(x), & x \in dom \, f - dom \, g \end{cases}$$

$$\forall f, g : X \to Y \bullet (f \oplus g = (dom \, g \triangleleft f) \cup g)$$

7.2.3 Reasoning

Functions can be analyzed for various properties: *total* or *partial*, *injective*, *surjective*, or *bijective*, and more importantly, for satisfaction of their specifications. In this section, we focus on the latter aspect and discuss two methods for reasoning.

Proof by cases

When conditional expressions are used in an explicit function definition, a case-by-case analysis is required. This proof technique is used when two functions have to be compared or composed over their common domain.

Example 7.5   Prove that neither $f(n) > g(n)$, nor $f(n) < g(n)$, holds for all values of $n \geq 0$, where $f, g : \mathbb{N} \to \mathbb{N}$,

$$f(n) = \begin{cases} n^2, & \text{if } 0 \leq n \leq 4 \\ n, & \text{if } n > 4 \end{cases}$$

and

$$g(n) = 2n + 3.$$

Proof: To compare the functions in their full domain, it is necessary to compare their definitions case by case:

Case 1: $0 \leq n \leq 4$.

$$f(n) - g(n) = n^2 - 2n - 3 = (n - 3)(n + 1).$$

Hence, for $n \geq 3, f(n) \geq g(n)$, and for $0 \leq n < 3, f(n) < g(n)$.

Case 2: $n > 4$.

$$f(n) - g(n) = -(n + 3) < 0. \text{ So}, f(n) < g(n).$$

A case-by-case proof is useful in showing the satisfaction of a direct function definition to its specification. Example 7.6 shows one such proof.   ∎

Example 7.6   Prove that the specification

$$abs : \mathbb{Z} \to \mathbb{N}$$
$$v = abs(m)$$
$$\textbf{post } v \geq 0 \land (v = m \lor v = -m)$$

is satisfied by the direct function definition

$$abs(m) == \textit{if } m < 0 \textit{ then } -m \textit{ else } m$$

Proof:

1. $m \in \mathbb{Z}$.

2. $m < 0 \lor m \geq 0$.

3. from $m < 0$ and the function definition,

   (a) $abs(m) = -m$.

   (b) infer $m < 0 \land abs(m) = -m$.

(c) from the postcondition of the *abs* function and the previous step, infer $v = -m \wedge v \geq 0$.

4. from $m \geq 0$ and the function definition,

(a) $abs(m) = m$

(b) infer $m \geq 0 \wedge abs(m) = m$.

(c) from the postcondition of the *abs* function and the previous step, infer $v = m \wedge v \geq 0$.

5. $m \in \mathbb{Z} \Rightarrow (abs(m) \in \mathbb{N} \wedge$
$((abs(m) = -m \wedge m < 0) \vee (abs(m) = m \wedge m \geq 0))$ ∎

Proof by Induction

Mathematical induction is founded on *the well-ordering property*, which states that every nonempty set of non-negative integers has a least element. Induction is applied to prove propositions of the form $\forall n \bullet P(n)$, where the universe of discourse is the set of non-negative integers. We consider two versions of the induction principle below, and a third version in section 7.3.3.

Induction—version I

An inductive hypothesis $P(n)$ expresses a property to be proved for every non-negative integer. The basis step consists of proving $P(0)$, while the inductive step is to prove that $\forall n \bullet P(n) \Rightarrow P(n+1)$. From these two steps, we conclude that $P(n)$ is proved for all $n \geq 0$. We express the proof steps as an inference rule:

$$[\mathit{first-ind}] - \frac{P(0); \quad m \in \mathbb{N}, P(m) \vdash P(m+1)}{\forall n : \mathbb{N} \vdash P(n)}$$

Example 7.7   Prove that the function $f(n) = n! - 2^n$ is positive for $n \geq 4$.

Proof:

1. $n \in \mathbb{N}$ and $P(n) : n! - 2^n > 0$.

2. $P(4) : 4! - 2^4 > 0$ is *true*.

3. $P(m)$ is *true*, $m \geq 4$.

4. $m! - 2^m > 0$, from step (3).

5. $(m+1)! - 2^{m+1} = (m+1).m! - 2.2^m$.

6. $m + 1 > 2$, from step (3).

7. $(m + 1)(m! - 2^m) > m! - 2^m$, from steps 4 and 5.

8. $P(m + 1)$ is *true*, from steps 4 and 6.

9. $P(m) \Rightarrow P(m + 1)$.

10. From steps 2 and 9, infer $P(n)$ is *true*.   ■

Induction—version II

This version of induction is more powerful than the first version. When it is required to prove $P(m)$, the inductive hypothesis $P(n)$ is permitted to hold for all predecessors of m. That is, the inductive proof requires the proof for $(P(1) \wedge \ldots \wedge P(m)) \Rightarrow P(m + 1)$ for every positive integer m. The rule is

$$[second-ind] - \frac{P(0); \quad m \in \mathbb{N}, (\forall m, m < n \Rightarrow P(m) \vdash P(n))}{\forall n \in \mathbb{N} \vdash P(n)}$$

Although these two versions of induction are equivalent, the second one is more powerful and simpler to apply. Let us consider the specification for the greatest common divisor (gcd) function and its direct function definition given in Section 7.2.2. The postcondition in the specification can be rewritten as

$gcd(x, y) = d$
post $divides(d, x) \wedge divides(d, y) \wedge \neg \exists s \bullet ((divides(s, x) \wedge divides(s, y) \wedge d < s)$

A proof that the direct definition for gcd satisfies its specification is shown in Example 7.8. This example also illustrates the use of induction for recursively defined functions.

Example 7.8   The two basic results that we use are

1. P1: Every nonzero integer is its own divisor and divides 0.

2. P2: For non-negative integers a and b, where $b \leq a$, there are integers q and r such that $a = b.q + r, 0 \leq r < b$.

The proof uses these results and the second version of induction, and proceeds by case analysis based on the constraints introduced in the function definition.

1. Let $P(m, n), m > n$ be the proposition that the direct function definition for gcd(m,n) satisfies the postcondition in the specification.

2. Basis: $P(m, 0), m \geq 1$

   (a) from the first case, $y = 0$ in the function definition, $gcd(m, 0) = m$.

   (b) To prove that m satisfies the postcondition:

i. $S = commondivisor(m, 0) = \{m\}$ from P1.

ii. $\neg \exists s \bullet (s \in S \wedge m < s)$ is *true*.

iii. infer m satisfies the postcondition.

$P(m, 0)$ is proved.

(c) Inductive step: $P(m, n)$ is true. That is, the direct function definition for gcd(m,k) satisfies the postcondition of the specification for $0 \leq k \leq n < m$. We must prove $P(m, n + 1)$.

i. Rewriting the inductive step

$$g = gcd(m, n) \wedge divides(g, m) \wedge divides(g, n) \wedge$$
$$\neg \exists s \bullet (s \in S \wedge divides(s, m) \wedge divides(s, n) \wedge g < s).$$

ii. From the inductive hypothesis, infer $n + 1 \leq m$.

iii. From P2, if $m = (n + 1).q + r$, then $0 \leq r < n + 1$.

iv. Infer from the previous step that if d divides m and $n + 1$, then d divides r. Hence, $gcd(m, n + 1) = gcd(n + 1, r), 0 \leq r < n + 1$.

v. By the inductive hypothesis, $P(n + 1, r)$ is true. That is, $gcd(n + 1, r)$ satisfies the postcondition of the specification.

vi. Infer that $gcd(m, n + 1)$ satisfies the specification. That is, $P(m, n + 1)$ is true.

vii. The inductive step is proved.

viii. Infer $P(m, n)$ for all $n, m > n$.   ∎

7.2.4   A Specification Example

Functions are mathematical objects and consequently have the important property of substitutivity. After a function has been defined, it can be used in any context where it is appropriate. Function composition, overriding, and the possibility of defining functions with functions as arguments make the functional approach to specification both elegant and expressive. Example 7.9 is a simplified and adapted version of the security model discussed by McLean [3]. The specification below formally explicates security by constructing formal models of objects and security policies using relations and functions.

Example 7.9   A computing environment consists of a set of *objects O* such as programs, files and system utilities, and a set of *subjects S* such as users and programs that access and manipulate the objects. Security involves the enforcement of rules governing the accessibility of objects by subjects. Subjects and objects are usually hierarchically classified and the security level is determined by the position of subject(object) in the hierarchy. Below, the model and security requirements are stated informally and then specified.

1. *Type*—A subject is assigned certain rights against an object in the system. So, there is a ternary relationship to be captured here: the tuple $(s, x, a), s \in S, x \in O, a \in A$ denotes that s has access a on object o. Hence, $M = \mathbb{P}(S \times O \times A)$ models all access right combinations.

2. *Security functions*—Every object has a unique *security level classification* and every subject has a unique *security level clearance*. These may be modeled by functions: there exist security level functions $f : S \rightarrow \mathbb{N}$, $g : O \rightarrow \mathbb{N}$, where $f(s)$ gives the *security level clearance* for the subject $s \in S$, and $g(o)$ gives the *security level classification* for the object $o \in O$.

3. *Information flow*—Information flows from *lower security levels* to *higher security levels*. If $f(s) > f(t)$, then the subject t can transfer its information knowledge, including its access rights, to the subject s.

4. *System state security*—The state of system M is minimally secure only if subjects that are allowed to access an object have a higher clearance level than the object. Formally, this security requirement translates to

$$\forall m : M \bullet ((s, x, read) \in m) \Rightarrow f(s) > g(x).$$

A stronger security condition for state M is that every subject s having *read* access to an object x, and having *write* access to an object y, must satisfy the constraint $g(y) > g(x)$. That is, information can be passed from a lower level object x to a higher level object y. Formally,

$$\forall m, n : M \bullet ((s, x, read) \in m) \wedge ((s, y, write) \in n) \Rightarrow g(y) > g(x)$$

In particular, an object from a lower security level can be copied into an object from a higher security level by a subject who has *read* access to the former object. Formally,

$$\forall m : M \bullet ((s, x, read) \in m) \wedge \exists y : O \bullet ((g(y) > g(x)) \Rightarrow copy(s, x, y))$$

5. *Constraints on access rights*—We define the following higher-order function to specify constraints on access rights assigned to subjects.

$$F : S \rightarrow (O \rightarrow A)$$
$$\forall s \in S, F_s : O \rightarrow A$$

There is a function F_s for each subject $s \in S$, and $F_s(o)$ gives the access rights assigned to s for object o. The constraint that two subjects s_1 and s_2 have the same rights for an object o_1 is specified as

$$F_{s_1}(o_1) = F_{s_2}(o_1)$$

The set of objects for which a given subject s has only "write" access is given by

$$\{s : S, o : O \mid (F_s(o) = \{write\}) \bullet o\}$$

Specifying the operation of cancelling all access rights assigned to a subject s on the objects in the set X, $X \subset O$, requires the overriding function. Define the function

$$G_s(o) = \begin{cases} \emptyset, & o \in X \\ F_s(o), & o \notin X \wedge o \in A \end{cases}$$

The function

$$H : S \to (O \to A), \text{ such that}$$
$$H_s = F_s \oplus G_s$$

defines the modified access rights.

6. *Secure flow of information*—Let *flows* $: S \leftrightarrow S$ be a relation on S with the interpretation that $(a, b) \in flows$ or $flows(a, b)$ if $f(a) < f(b)$. That is, information may flow from a subject of lower security clearance to a subject of higher security clearance. The relation is reflexive and transitive. The reflexive closure relation *flows** contains all tuples (a, b) such that information flows from subject a to subject b either directly or through a sequence of subjects. The set $B = ran(A \lhd flows)$, such that $A \subset S$, gives the set of subjects whose information is reachable from members of A. Similarly, the set $C = dom(flows \rhd A)$ is the set of subjects from whom information can reach members of A. Information from members of A cannot reach the set of subjects $D = ran(A \ntriangleleft flows)$. The set $E = dom(flows \rhd A)$ is the set of subjects whose information can flow to members of A. Two subjects s, t belong to the same security level if $(s, t) \in flows^*$ and $(t, s) \in flows^*$. It is easy to prove that

$$\forall A, A' : \mathbb{P}(S) \bullet (ran(A \lhd flows) \cap ran(A' \lhd flows) = \emptyset \leftrightarrow A \cap A' = \emptyset).$$

7. *Secure object transfer*—The content of information flow is an object (file or program), and it is characterized by a sequence of *read* and *write*. If $(a, b) \in flows$ and subject a owns an object y, then the actual flow of y from a to b can be formalized as

$$\forall(a, b) : flows \bullet (\exists m, n : M \bullet (m = (a, y, write) \wedge$$
$$n = (b, z, read) \wedge g(z) > g(y)))$$

Since a owns y, $f(a) > g(y)$ and $n \in M$ implies $f(b) > g(z)$. Hence the constraint $g(z) > g(y)$ enables the copying of y into z without violating the security constraint $f(b) > f(a)$.   ■

7.3   Formal Specification Based on Sequences

Sets, relations, and functions do not imply any *ordering* on the objects modeled. Sequences are ordered collections of objects. A sequence is appropriate for modeling container entities, such as queues, for which the ordering of items is meaningful.

7.3.1   Notation

A sequence is characterized by a function $f : \mathbb{N} \rightarrow X$. The elements of the sequence can be enumerated as $f(1), f(2), \ldots, f(n)$; it is usual to write f_n for $f(n)$. The element f_n is the n-th element of the sequence defined by f. Since the images $f(i)$ and $f(j)$ may be equal, a sequence may include the same element more than once. For instance, let $X = \{a, b\}$, and $f(i) = a$ if i is odd, and $f(i) = b$ if i is even. The infinite sequence is composed of alternate a's and b's.

The set of all functions of type $\mathbb{N}_1 \rightarrow X$ characterizes the set of all sequences over X:

$$seq[X] \quad \triangleq \quad f : \mathbb{N}_1 \rightarrow X$$

A finite sequence is a function f whose domain is a finite initial segment of $\mathbb{N}_1$.

$$f : \{1, 2, \ldots, n\} \rightarrow X$$

The notation $seq[X]$ also denotes the type of sequences defined on a finite set X. When $X = \varnothing$, $seq[X]$ is the empty sequence. If $|X| = k(> 0)$ and the initial segment of $\mathbb{N}$ is $\{1, \ldots, n\}$, $seq[X]$ consists of all sequences of length n, where each sequence has elements from the k-element set X. There are k^n sequences in $seq[X]$.

One important consequence of the above definitions is that every element of a sequence $s : seq[X]$ is of type X. A finite sequence can be described by an orderly enumeration of the elements:

$$\langle s_1, s_2, \ldots, s_i \rangle, i \leq |X|$$

The number of elements in a finite sequence s is denoted by $\# s$. We also use the notation $s_i, 1 \leq i \leq \# s$ to denote the i-th element of the sequence s.

7.3.2   Sequence Operators

Two sequences of the same element type can be composed to form a single sequence in such a way that the order of each sequence is maintained, and the elements of one sequence follow the elements of the other. The composition operator $\frown$, representing *concatenation*, is defined as

$$\frown: seq[X] \times seq[X] \to seq[X]$$
$$\forall s, t : seq[X]$$
$$\forall i : 1 \le i \le \# s \, (s \frown t)_i = s_i$$
$$\forall i : 1 \le i \le \# t \, (s \frown t)_{i+\# s} = t_i$$

The function #, which assigns to each sequence its number of elements, is *additive*; that is,

$$\# (s \frown t) = \# s + \# t$$

A *subsequence* of $f : \{1, 2, \ldots, n\} \to X$ is described by $f \circ r$, where $r : \{1, 2, \ldots, n\} \twoheadrightarrow \{1, 2, \ldots, n\}$ is an increasing injective partial function. For example, $s_1 = \langle x_3, x_4, x_5, x_6 \rangle$, $s_2 = \langle x_2, x_5 \rangle$, and $s_3 = \langle x_1, x_6, x_8 \rangle$ are subsequences of $s = \langle x_1, x_2, x_3, x_4, x_5, x_6, x_7, x_8 \rangle$; however, $s_4 = \langle x_6, x_3, x_7 \rangle$ is not a subsequence of s. The sequence s_2 is obtained by composing the function $f(i) = x_i$, $1 \le i \le 8$ with $r(1) = 2, r(2) = 5$. There is no function r that can be composed with f to obtain the sequence s_3. If $r_1, r_2, \ldots, r_k$ are subsequence functions with disjoint ranges, then the subsequences $f \circ r_1, f \circ r_2, \ldots, f \circ r_k$ are disjoint. The ranges of the functions r_1 and r_2 defined by $r_1(1) = 2, r_1(2) = 5, r_2(1) = 1, r_2(2) = 6, r_2(3) = 8$ are disjoint. Notice that $s = f \circ r_1$, and $s' = f \circ r_2$ are disjoint sequences.

To compare sequences we must define an *order* on X and then extend this definition for sequences of any length. Let $(\le, X)$ be a *totally (linearly)* ordered set. Using the symbol $\preceq$ to denote ordering on sequences, we define $\langle x_i \rangle \preceq \langle x_j \rangle$ if $x_i \le x_j$ in X. Sequences having only one element are comparable and can be sequentially enumerated. For $s, t : seq[X]$, if $s = \langle x_1, x_2, \ldots, x_k \rangle$ and $t = \langle y_1, y_2, \ldots, y_k \rangle$, we define $s \preceq t$ if $x_1 \le y_1$ and $\langle x_2, \ldots, x_k \rangle \preceq \langle y_2, \ldots, y_k \rangle$. A strict inequality can be defined:

$$s \prec t \quad \triangleq \quad (\# s < \# t) \vee (\# s = \# t) \wedge (s \preceq t)$$

Thus, $\langle 1, 3, 5 \rangle \preceq \langle 1, 3, 7 \rangle \prec \langle 1, 3, 7, 9 \rangle$.

Another operation is to rearrange a sequence. If two sequences $s, t : seq[X]$ of length k have the same elements, there is a permutation $p : \{1, 2, \ldots, k\} \to \{1, 2, \ldots, k\}$ such that $s_i = t_{p(i)}, i \in \{1, 2, \ldots, \# s\}$. For example, for sequences $s = \langle 1, 3, 5, 3, 7 \rangle$ and $t = \langle 3, 5, 7, 3, 1 \rangle$, there are two permutations; one of them is defined by $p(1) = 5, p(2) = 4, p(3) = 3, p(4) = 1, p(5) = 3$. The problem of finding the permutation for a linear ordering on the elements of a sequence is analogous to sorting. We define below several functions on sequences. Other functions are defined in the exercises. We denote the nonempty sequence type by $seq_1[X]$.

1. The function *first* returns the first element of a nonempty sequence.

$$first : seq_1[X] \to X$$
$$first(s) \quad \triangleq \quad s_1$$

2. The function *next* accepts a nonempty sequence and returns the sequence following its first element.

$$next : seq_1[X] \rightarrow seq[X]$$
$$(next(s))_i = s_{i+1}, 1 \le i \le \# s - 1$$

That is, $next(s)$ is the sequence $\langle s_2, s_3, \ldots, s_k \rangle$. Notice that $next(s) = \langle \rangle$ if $\# s = 1$.

3. The function *locate* returns true if a given element is an element of the sequence; otherwise it returns false. Recursive definitions such as the one given below can be shown to define a unique function.

$$locate : seq_1[X] \times X \rightarrow \text{Boolean}$$
$$\text{if } \# (s) = 1 \text{ then } locate(s, a) \quad \triangleq \quad s_1 = a$$
$$\text{if } \# (s) > 1 \text{ then } locate(s, a) \quad \triangleq \quad (first(s) = a) \vee (locate(next(s), a))$$

4. The function *find* returns the smallest index at which a given object is located in the sequence; if the object is not found, the function returns 0.
$find : seq_1[X] \times X \rightarrow \{0, 1, \ldots N\}$, where N denotes the length of the longest sequence in $seq_1[X]$.

$$find(s, a) \quad \triangleq \quad \begin{cases} 0, & s_i \ne a, i \in 1, 2, \ldots, \# s \\ k, & s_i \ne a, i \in 1, 2, \ldots, k - 1, s_k = a, k \le \# s \end{cases}$$

5. Given a sequence s and an element a, the function *find_all* returns the sequence of indices at which a occurs in s.

$$find\_all : seq[X] \times X \rightarrow seq[\mathbb{N}_1]$$

where $\mathbb{N}_1 = dom(seq[X])$.

$$find\_all(s, a) \quad \triangleq \quad \langle j_1, \ldots, j_k \rangle$$

which describes the sequence of locations in sequence s at which there is a match for a.

Example 7.10 shows that the function *find_all* can be recursively defined using the other functions defined above.

Example 7.10 The goal is to define *find_all*(s, a) using functions defined on sequences. Since an empty sequence contains no element, *find_all* returns an empty sequence if s is empty. When s is nonempty, either the given element a is not in s or it is found in one or more locations. In the former case, the result returned is an empty sequence. In the latter case, there is a first match at a location k, which is found by the function *find*(s, a). It is necessary to construct the result as a sequence. We construct an intermediate result sequence t in which k is inserted. The sequence s is now split at location k, the elements $s_1, \ldots, s_k$ are discarded, and the sequence $s^{(1)}$ is constructed with the remaining elements of s. The sequence obtained recursively from *find_all*$(s^{(1)}, a)$, is concatenated to t. This is not the final answer; to understand why, we illustrate the steps of the function *find_all* with an example:

For $s = \langle 1, 3, 7, 1, 8, 11, 3, 4, 1, 15 \rangle$, and $a = 1$ *find_all*(s, a) should produce the sequence $r = \langle 1, 4, 9 \rangle$.

The steps for constructing r are as follows:

1. *locate*$(s, a) = true$; *find*$(s, a) = 1$; *split*$(s, find(s, a)) = s^{(1)} = \langle 3, 7, 1, 8, 11, 3, 4, 1, 15 \rangle$

2. *locate*$(s^{(1)}, a) = true$; *find*$(s^{(1)}, a) = 3$; *split*$(s^{(1)}, a) = s^{(2)} = \langle 8, 11, 3, 4, 1, 15 \rangle$

3. *locate*$(s^{(2)}, a) = true$; *find*$(s^{(2)}, a) = 5$; *split*$(s^{(2)}, a) = s^{(3)} = \langle 15 \rangle$

4. *locate*$(s^{(3)}, a) = false$; $\langle \rangle$ is returned

5. The temporary sequence t is $\langle 1, 3, 5 \rangle$

6. The sequence r is the sequence of partial sums of the sequence t.

A definition for sequence t is

$temp : seq[X] \times X \rightarrow seq[N_1]$
$temp(s, a) = t,$
where
$t \quad \triangleq \quad if\ locate(s, a)\ then$
$\quad \langle find(s, a) \rangle \frown find\_all(split(s, find(s, a)), a)$
$\quad else \langle \rangle$

The definition for *split* is

$split : seq[X] \times \{1, \ldots, N\} \rightarrow seq[X]$
$split(s, k) = s^{(1)},$
where
$s_i^{(1)} = s_{i+k}, 1 \leq i \leq \#(s) - k$

The definition for the sequence of partial sums is

$part\_sum : seq[N_1] \rightarrow seq[N_1]$
$part\_sum(t) = if\ t = \langle \rangle\ then\ \langle \rangle\ else$
$if\ next(t) \neq \langle \rangle\ then\ \langle head(t) \rangle \frown part\_sum(\langle head(next(t)) + head(t) \rangle \frown$
$(next(t)))\ else\ \langle head(t) \rangle$

Finally, the function *find_all*(s, a) is defined as the composite function *part_sum* $\circ$ *temp*. ∎

7.3.3 Proofs

The definition of sequences imposes an ordering on the elements of a sequence. We can thus refer to the first element of a sequence, and to the rest of the sequence.

The first element of the rest of a sequence is the second element of the sequence. The successive elements of a sequence are indexed by terms of the form $succ^k(0)$. This suggests the applicability of induction to structures constructed using a finite number of generators.

The induction rules discussed in section 7.2.3 are based on the generators *zero* and *succ* for natural numbers. A finite sequence may be viewed as generated by $\langle \rangle$ and $\frown$. These two generators are sufficient for generating all finite sequences. For example, the sequence $\langle 1, 5, 3 \rangle$ may be generated by the successive concatenations

$$\langle \rangle; \langle 3 \rangle \frown \langle \rangle; \langle 5 \rangle \frown \langle 3 \rangle \langle \rangle; \langle 1 \rangle \frown \langle 5 \rangle \langle 3 \rangle \langle \rangle$$

The empty sequence $\langle \rangle$ is analogous to *zero*, and the operator $\frown$ is analogous to *succ*. We consider *zero* as the index for an empty sequence, and for a sequence of *oldindex* elements, we consider *succ(oldindex)* as the new index concatenated to the sequence. We reformulate the induction rule *first_ind* for sequences.

$$[seq\_ind] - \frac{P(\langle \rangle);}{} \frac{e \in X, s \in seq[X], P(s) \vdash P(\langle e \rangle \frown s)}{s \in seq[X] \vdash P(s)}$$

A sequence allows multiple occurrences of an element to be distinguised by their ordering. A set neither allows multiplicity nor imposes an ordering on its elements. A *bag* or a *multiset* allows multiplicity, but no ordering. When only multiplicities, but not ordering, are required to be recorded, the *bag* type should be chosen. In the following discussion, we develop a simple theory for bags and show its relationship to the theory of finite sets and sequences.

For a finite set X, the type $Bag[X]$ is the set of all bags defined on X. The definition $b : Bag[X]$ introduces a bag b, which records ordered pairs of elements from X and their occurrence counts.

$$b = \{(x_1, n_1), \ldots, (x_k, n_k)\},$$
where $x_i \in X, n_i > 0.$

We use the set notation $\in$ for bag membership, and $\perp$ to denote an empty bag. The following functions are defined on bags:

1. *Add a member*—This function adds an entry (e, k) to a given bag. If a tuple of the kind (e, n) exists in the bag, the multiplicity of e is incremented by k; otherwise, the given pair is included in the bag.

   $add : Bag[X] \times (X \times \mathbb{N}) \rightarrow Bag[X]$
   $add(\perp, (e, k)) = \{(e, k)\}$
   $add(b, (e, k)) = b'$
   post $\neg(\exists(a, n) \in b \bullet a = e) \rightarrow b' = b \cup \{(e, k)\}$
   $\vee (\exists(a, n) \in b \bullet a = e) \rightarrow b' = b - \{(e, n)\} \cup \{(e, n + k)\}$

2. *Test for membership*—Given an element $e \in X$, this function returns true if an ordered pair for e is included in the given bag; otherwise, the function returns false.

$locate : B[X] \times X \rightarrow \mathbb{B}$
$locate(b, e) = \exists (a, n) \in b \bullet e = a$

3. *Extract elements from the base domain*—This function extracts the elements of the basic domain from a bag, constructing a set of the elements while ignoring their occurrence counts.

$elemb : Bag[X] \rightarrow \mathbb{P}X$
$elemb(\bot) = \emptyset$
$elemb(add(b, (e, k))) = if \ locate(b, e) \ then \ elemb(b) \ else \ elemb(b) \cup \{e\}$

4. *Multiplicity of a base element*—The multiplicity of a base element e in a bag b is 0 if e is not in $elemb(b)$; otherwise, it is determined by a unique entry in b.

$count : Bag[X] \times X \rightarrow \mathbb{N}$
$count(\bot) = 0$
$count(add(b, (e, k)), a) = (e \neq a \Rightarrow count(b, a)) \vee$
$(e = a \Rightarrow (k + count(b, a)))$

5. *Bag construction from a sequence*—Given a sequence, this function records the elements and their occurrence counts as ordered pairs, ignoring the ordering on the elements of the sequence.

$consb : seq[X] \rightarrow Bag[X]$
$consb(\langle \rangle) = \bot$
$consb(e \frown s) = add(consb(s), \langle e, 1 \rangle)$

The *elems* function constructs a set containing all the elements of a sequence, ignoring the ordering on the elements and their occurrence counts.

$elems : seq[X] \rightarrow \mathbb{P}X$
post $Y \in \mathbb{P}X \wedge \forall i \bullet (1 \leq i \leq \# s \wedge s[i] \in Y)$

We claim that the three functions *elems*, *elemb*, *consb* are related by the commutative diagram shown in Figure 7.2. We consider a simple example before giving a proof by induction for this claim.

$X = \{a, b, c, d\}; s : seq[X]; t : Bag[X]$
$s = \langle b, c, b, a, b, a \rangle$
$t = \{ (a, 2), (b, 3), (c, 1)\}$
$elems(s) = \{a, b, c\} \subset X$
$consb(s) = t$
$elemb(b) = \{a, b, c\} \subset X$
$elems(s) = elemb(consb(s)) = (elemb \circ consb)(s)$

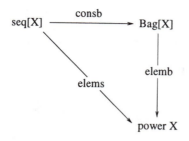

FIGURE 7.2. Setseqbag.

Proof:
The proof is by the induction rule *[seq_ind]* stated previously in this section.

1. *Basis step.*

$$elems(\langle\rangle) = \varnothing \ldots \text{ definition of elements}$$
$$consb(\langle\rangle) = \bot \ldots \text{ definition of } consb$$
$$elemb(\bot) = \varnothing \ldots \text{ definition of } elemb$$
$$infer \; elems(\langle\rangle) = (elemb \circ consb)(\langle\rangle)$$

2. *Inductive step.*
   Assume that for $s : seq[X], s \neq \langle\rangle$

   $$elems(s) = (elemb \circ consb)(s)$$

   To complete the inductive step, it must be shown that

   $$\forall e \in X \bullet elems(e \frown s) = (elemb \circ consb)(e \frown s)$$

   There are two cases to consider: $e \notin consb(s)$ and $e \in consb(s)$.

3. *Case 1: $e \notin consb(s)$*
   The right-hand side in step 2 is rewritten using the definition for *consb*:

   $$elemb(consb(e \frown s)) = elemb(add(consb(s), \langle e, 1 \rangle))$$

   Using the definition of *elemb*, rewrite the right-hand side as

   $$elemb(consb(s)) \cup \{e\} = (elemb \circ consb)(s) \cup \{e\}.$$

   By inductive hypothesis, rewrite the right-hand side as

   $$elems(s) \cup \{e\} = elems(s) \cup elems(\{e\}) = elems(e \frown s).$$

4. Case 2: $e \in consb(s)$
   Since $locate(consb(s), e)$ is *true*, we rewrite the right-hand side in step 2 as $elemb(consb(s))$, using the definition of *elemb*. By the inductive hypothesis, we rewrite this as $(elemb \circ consb)(s) = elems(s)$. Using the equality property of sets, we infer that $elems(s) = elems(e \frown s)$.

5. The proof for the inductive step is now complete. By the *[seq_ind]* principle of induction, the proof of the claim follows.

7.3.4   A Specification Example

In Chapter 5, we introduced formal definitions for the data types involved in an *Idea Processor*. In this section, we define several functions on these data types.

Let *word* be a basic type denoting the set of all words to be included in a dictionary. A finite sequence of words is a basic unit of ideas, called *note*. The type of this basic unit is defined as *note* = *seq*[*word*]. We define the ordering on the words as in a dictionary, such that two words $w_1, w_2 \in$ *word* can be compared; $w_1 < w_2$ if w_1 precedes w_2 in the dictionary. This represents a *total order* on *word*. The ordering can be extended to sequences of words, as explained in section 7.3.1. The functions *first, next, locate, find,* and *find_all* defined in section 7.3.2 apply to this sequence. An *idea* is recorded as a set of notes; that is, *idea* : $\mathbb{P} X$, where $X = \{n : note \bullet n\}$ is a collection of *note*. Based on these data types, we define functions for manipulating ideas.

$$
\begin{array}{lll}
create & : & \rightarrow idea \\
add & : & idea \times note \quad \rightarrow idea \\
remove & : & idea \times note \quad \rightarrow idea
\end{array}
$$

create is a null-ary function producing an empty database of type *idea*. The other functions are

$$
\begin{array}{lll}
add(t, n) & \triangleq & t \cup \{n\} \\
remove(t, n) & \triangleq & t - \{n\}
\end{array}
$$

Since *t* is a set type, adding a note that already exists in *t*, or removing a note that does not exist in *t*, produces acceptable behavior. Since the elements of *t* are of type sequence, explicit methods can be given for testing membership in *t*. We introduce these primitives, *empty* and *is_member*, to operate on ideas.

$$
\begin{array}{lll}
empty & : & idea \quad\quad\quad \rightarrow Boolean \\
is\_member & : & idea \times note \quad \rightarrow Boolean
\end{array}
$$

Since *create* produces an empty set of ideas, *empty*(*create*) is *true*; however, *empty*(*add*(*t, n*)) is *false*. Applying *is_member* on an empty set of notes has the following result:

$$
is\_member(create, n) = (n = \langle \rangle)
$$

Using these functions, the definitions of *remove* and *add* may be rewritten:

$$
\begin{array}{lll}
remove(t, n) & \triangleq & if\ is\_member(t, n)\ then\ t - \{n\}\ else\ t \\
add(t, n) & \triangleq & if\ is\_member(t, n)\ then\ t\ else\ t \cup \{n\}
\end{array}
$$

To define *is_member*(*t, n*) for any nonempty set of notes, we need an equality relation for sequences. We can either use the ordering $\preceq$ defined on sequences or the function *find_all*. In the later case, the function *is_member*(*t, n*) can be specified as follows:

$equal : note \times note \rightarrow Boolean$

$equal(m, n) \quad \triangleq \quad elems(m) = elems(n) \land$
$\qquad\qquad\qquad (\forall w : word \bullet find\_all(n, w) = find\_all(m, w))$

$is\_member(t, n) \quad \triangleq \quad \exists m : note \bullet (m \in t \land equal(m, n))$

From the above functions, we can prove the following properties:

1. $add(remove(t, n), n) = t = remove(add(t, n), n)$
2. $add(add(t, n), n) = t$
3. $add(add(t, n_1), n_2) = add(add(t, n_2), n_1)$

Exercises

1. Using the set axioms given in section 7.1.2, give a formal proof for the following or disprove by giving a counter example:

   (a) $\dfrac{A \times B = A \times C}{B = C}$

   (b) $\dfrac{\mathbb{P}\,X = \mathbb{P}\,Y}{X = Y}$

   (c) $(A - B) - C = (A - C) - (B - C)$

2. Let $S \in \mathbb{P}\,X$. Define the function:

   $put : X \times S \rightarrow S$
   $put(e, s) = \{e\} \cup s$

   Prove the following properties on the function put:

   (a) S is generated by $\varnothing$ and put.

   (b) $e_1 \in put(e, s) = (e_1 = e) \lor e_1 \in s$.

   (c) $put(e_1, put(e, s)) = put(e, put(e_1, s))$.

3. Specify the following constraints and operations for Example 7.2:

   (a) A student can own a maximum of 20 files. The author of a lesson can own a maximum of 50 files. An administrator can own a maximum of 100 files.

   (b) A student is able to read and copy a quiz file. The author of the quiz is able to read, write, edit, and copy the quiz file.

   (c) When the *view* command is invoked by a user, only the file store for which the user has access rights can be seen. Moreover, the status of the file store remains unchanged.

   (d) Specify the access rights invariant for quiz files in *file_store_c*.

(e) Specify an operation to be invoked by a teacher that modifies the contents of a grade file.

(f) Specify an operation to be invoked by students to copy a lesson file into a student auxilary file.

4. Let *courses* denote the set of courses offered in a department. Registering for a course may require prerequisite courses. Write a specification that produces *seq_courses*, a sequence of courses from the set *courses* satisfying the following properties: (1) every course in *courses* occurs in the sequence *seq_courses*; and (2) if $c_1 = seq\_courses[i]$, and $c_2 = seq\_courses[j]$, and $i < j$, then course c_1 is a prerequisite for course c_2.

5. Let S denote the set of students in a residential college. The college has k dormitories $d_1, \ldots, d_k$. Every student lives in some dormitory, and no student can live in more than one dormitory. A collection $P = \{S_1, \ldots, S_j\}$, where $j \leq k$, $S_i \subset S$, the set of students living in dormitory d_i, and $1 \leq i \leq j$, is an instance of a model for students and the dormitories where they live. Do the following:

(a) Give the type definition for P.

(b) State formally the following constraints: (1) every student lives in some dormitory; (2) no student lives in more than one dormitory.

(c) Give the specification of a function to remove a student from the dormitory.

(d) Given two students $a, b \in S$, determine the dormitories to which they belong. If they belong to two different dormitories, then merge the two dormitories into one dormitory.

6. Prove the following claim made in Example 7.9:

$$\forall A, A' : \mathbb{P}(S) \bullet (ran(A \lhd flows) \cap ran(A' \lhd flows) = \emptyset \leftrightarrow A \cap A' = \emptyset).$$

7. For any finite set X and for some $n > 0$, prove or disprove the claim that

$$\emptyset \cup X \cup X^2, \ldots, X^n$$

defines all sequences of length not exceeding n on X.

8. For a finite sequence type, define the following functions:

(a) *min* that finds a minimum among the elements of the sequence.

(b) *swap* that exchanges the elements in two given locations of the sequence.

(c) *rotate* that cyclically shifts the elements in the sequence right.

(d) *reverse* that uses *rotate* to reverse the ordering of elements in the sequence.

(e) Prove $reverse(s_1 \frown s_2) = reverse(s_2) \frown reverse(s_1)$.

Bibliographic Notes

We included a preliminary mathematical review of sets and relations to clarify the specification notation. For a more detailed review of the fundamental concepts of discrete mathematics, the reader is referred to Alagar [1] and Rosen [4].

Specifications based on sets and relations are model-based, while implicit functional specifications are property-oriented. The Z notation [5] is based on set theory and the semantics for Z specifications are assigned from set operations. VDM specifications [2] can be written in a pure functional style, with or without sets and relations. These formal notations are discussed in chapters 9 and 10.

References

[1] V.S. Alagar, *Fundamentals of Computing - Theory and Practice*, Prentice-Hall, Englewood Cliffs, NJ, 1989.

[2] C.B. Jones, *Systematic Software Development using VDM* (second edition), Prentice Hall International (UK), 1990.

[3] J. McLean, "The Specification and Modeling of Computer Security," *IEEE Computer*, Vol. 23, No. 1, January 1990, pp. 9–16.

[4] K.H. Rosen, *Discrete Mathematics and its Applications* (second edition), McGraw-Hill, New York, NY, 1990.

[5] J.M. Spivey, *Understanding Z: A Specification Language and its Formal Semantics*, Cambridge University Press, Cambridge, England, 1988.

8

Algebraic Specification

Algebraic specification emerged in the 70s as a formal technique for specifying data structures in an implementation-independent style. This approach has given rise to several specification methods providing techniques for *data abstraction*, *theory formulation*, *specification property analysis*, *modular development*, and *hierarchical composition*. Algebraic specification is founded on equational logic, and the underlying semantics is derived from algebra, where different mathematical structures such as groups, rings, and fields are studied. In this chapter we look at how to construct algebras for specifying various software artifacts.

8.1 Algebra and Specification

An *algebra* can be considered as a collection of sets, together with operations on the sets. If we regard sorts (types) as sets, we get the equation *Algebra = Sorts (Types) + Operations*. If we represent a system as a collection of sets and describe the functionality of the system by equations on operations defined on the sets, we obtain an algebra. The resulting algebra may be viewed as an *algebraic specification* of the system. For instance, we may view a system as a collection of objects $O_1, O_2, \cdots, O_n$, where each O_i is modeled as a set. We describe the functionality of object O_j by a set f_j of functions. The algebraic specification of a software system expresses the collective behavior of the objects through a set of equations on the functions.

The justifications for viewing a system specification as an algebra include the following:

- An abstract axiomatic specification of a program is given by its algebra. To understand this paradigm, let us consider the conventional view of programs put forth by Wirth [13] : *Algorithms + DataStructures = Programs*. An abstraction of data structures in a program is obtained by composing *sorts*, types based on set-theoretic constructs. The resulting abstractions are termed *Abstract Data Types* (ADT). We abstract algorithmic details by disregarding *how* operations are performed, and emphasizing *what* they perform. This abstraction corresponds to the operations on sorts. We thus obtain the abstraction *Sorts+Operations* corresponding to *DataStructures+Algorithms*. Having defined *Algebra* as *Sorts + Operations*, it follows that *Algebra* is an abstraction of *Programs*. In other words, a program can be specified as an algebra.

- The terms of an algebra are free of representation constraints. The effect of operations on the terms of an algebra is expressed by axioms. Axiomatic definitions are more abstract than model-based definitions.

- An algebraic specification is an abstract model of a program. It can be refined into a concrete representation which is another algebraic specification or a program. Using an algebraic specification, we can describe programming tasks and reason about them.

- In general, we can derive several concrete representations for an algebra. Consequently, programs describing *dissimilar* objects and sharing a common *structure* correspond to an algebra.

Example 8.1 introduces an abstract algebra and three other algebras that are its concrete representations.

Example 8.1   Let S denote a set with four operations *right*, *left*, *below*, *above* defined on it. The axioms constraining these operations are

1. $left(right(x)) = x = right(left(x))$

2. $above(below(x)) = x = below(above(x))$

3. $right(above(x)) = above(right(x))$

4. $left(above(x)) = above(left(x))$

5. $right(below(x)) = below(right(x))$

6. $left(below(x)) = below(left(x))$

The set S, together with the operations and the axioms, defines an algebra $\mathcal{U}$. We describe three different concrete structures that are modeled by $\mathcal{U}$; i.e., $\mathcal{U}$ is a specification of the structures. ∎

1. Lattice points—Algebra $\mathcal{L}$

Let $L = \{x, y \mid x, y \in \mathbb{Z}\}$ with four operations *rightnext*, *leftnext*, *abovenext*, and *belownext* defined on it:

$\forall p \in L$
$\quad rightnext(p) = (x + 1, y)$
$\quad leftnext(p) = (x - 1, y)$
$\quad abovenext(p) = (x, y + 1)$
$\quad belownext(p) = (x, y - 1)$

It is easy to verify that the axioms of algebra $\mathcal{U}$ are true for this interpretation. The elements of set L have a representation, and consequently the algebra $\mathcal{L}$ is more concrete than algebra $\mathcal{U}$.

2. Linear Transformations—Algebra $\mathcal{T}$

Let us consider the integer matrix A:

$$A = \begin{pmatrix} 1 & 2 & 4 \\ 3 & 5 & 7 \\ 6 & 8 & 9 \end{pmatrix}$$

Let CRS be the cyclical right-shift operation on columns (elements of column 1 are moved to column 2; elements of column 2 are moved to column 3; elements of column 3 are moved to column 1).

$$CRS(A) = \begin{pmatrix} 4 & 1 & 2 \\ 7 & 3 & 5 \\ 9 & 6 & 8 \end{pmatrix}$$

Let CBS be the cyclical counter-clockwise shift operation on rows (elements of row 1 are moved to row 2 and so on). Let CLS denote the cyclical left-shift operation on columns, and CAS be the cyclical clockwise-shift operation on rows.

$$CLS(A) = \begin{pmatrix} 2 & 4 & 1 \\ 5 & 7 & 3 \\ 8 & 9 & 6 \end{pmatrix}$$

$$CAS(A) = \begin{pmatrix} 3 & 5 & 7 \\ 6 & 8 & 9 \\ 1 & 2 & 4 \end{pmatrix}$$

$$CBS(A) = \begin{pmatrix} 6 & 8 & 9 \\ 1 & 2 & 4 \\ 3 & 5 & 7 \end{pmatrix}$$

The axioms of the algebra $\mathcal{U}$ can be verified for these operations applied to matrix A. The axioms hold when these operations are applied to any $n \times n$ matrix. Algebra $\mathcal{T}$, for $n \times n$ matrices with these four operations, is a concrete model of algebra $\mathcal{U}$.

3. Strings—Algebra S

Consider a set S of strings over an alphabet. Define CROT and CLOT to be the cyclical right shift and cyclical left shift of characters in a string. For instance, $CROT(abac) = (caba)$, and $CLOT(abac) = (baca)$. The two other operations on set S are identities LID and RID. It is straightforward to verify the axioms of algebra $\mathcal{U}$ for algebra S under this interpretation.

The mathematical machinery of algebras and the generality achievable in this framework allow algebraic specifications be written as mathematical objects in an accurate, unambiguous, and implementation-independent manner. The fundamental concepts of algebras are introduced in the next section through their mathematical foundations. We include an informal introduction to the concepts, avoiding mathematical details, and illustrate the concepts with several examples.

8.2   Algebras—A Brief Introduction

A *many-sorted algebra* is an abstract structure consisting of a family S of sets and a family $\Omega = \{\Omega_1, \Omega_2, \ldots, \Omega_k\}$, $\Omega_i \cap \Omega_j = \varnothing$, where Ω_i is a set of operations with arguments and results belonging to the sets in S. The sets in S correspond to sorts, and Ω corresponds to a family of operator names. The pair $\langle S, \Omega \rangle$ forms a *signature*. Each operation in Ω_i has the same type; this type represents the *scheme* of the operator.

Example 8.2   In Example 8.1, algebra $\mathcal{U}$ is one-sorted or homogeneous. The signature of $\mathcal{U}$ is $\langle T, \Omega \rangle$, where

$$T = \{S\}$$
$$\Omega = \{right, \; left, \; above, \; below\} : S \rightarrow S$$

There is only one sort and one scheme.   ■

In order to handle ADT's rigorously in software engineering contexts, we need to consider many-sorted or heterogeneous algebras. For example, the stack structure can be adequately described by considering the set of stacks, the set of element type it holds, for example integers or strings, and the set of Booleans to describe equality relationship on items. Notice that algebra S in Example 8.1 is an inadequate description of strings because many useful operations on strings could not be described in that homogeneous algebra.

Example 8.3   In this example, we consider a file of records storing some database information. The three concepts to be abstracted are *file*, *record*, and *information*. We choose the three sorts *file*, *record*, and *infor*, each corresponding to one database concept. Some of the operations that we consider are

- *insert*: to add a record in a file

- *delete*: to remove a record from a file

- *trash*: to purge a file

- *update*: to revise information in a record

A signature for the algebra of transactions is $\langle S, \Omega \rangle$, where

$$S = \{file, record, infor\}$$
$$\Omega = \{\{insert, delete\}: file \times record \rightarrow file$$
$$\{update\}: file \times record \times infor \rightarrow file$$
$$\{trash\}: file \rightarrow file\}$$

The four operators in this example are grouped into three schemes. ■

8.2.1 Homomorphisms

A *homomorphism* is a structure-preserving map between two algebras. We first deal with homomorphisms of homogeneous algebras and then introduce homomorphisms of heterogeneous algebras.

Homogeneous Algebras   A *homomorphism* is a map between two algebras preserving various algebraic properties. For example, if an operation $*$ is defined on two sets X and Y, then the map $f : X \rightarrow Y$ is a homomorphism if, for all $x, y \in X$, $f(x*y) = f(x)*f(y)$. If X has an *identity* element e, satisfying the property $x*e = x$ for all $x \in X$, then $f(e)$ is an identity for Y. The proof follows from the definition of homomorphism. If X contains an identity element e, an element $x \in X$ may have an *inverse* $x^{-1} \in X$ satisfying the property $x * x^{-1} = e$. If e' is the identity in Y that is the image of e in X, then

$$e' = f(e) = f(x * x^{-1}) = f(x) * f(x^{-1})$$

Hence, $f(x^{-1}) \in Y$ and is the inverse of $f(x) \in Y$. Moreover, if the operation $*$ is commutative (associative), then f preserves the commutative (associative) property in Y. The following theorem summarizes these results.

Theorem   If $f : \langle X, * \rangle \rightarrow \langle Y, * \rangle$ is a homomorphism and e is an identity for X, then $f(e)$ is an identity for Y. If for all $x \in X$ for which an inverse $x^{-1} \in X$ exists, $f(x^{-1}) \in Y$ is an inverse of $f(x) \in Y$. The map f preserves commutative and associative properties, if any.

Example 8.4   Consider the set of two-dimensional vectors on real numbers $\mathbb{R}$, with the operation $+$ (vector addition) defined as

$$\langle x, y \rangle + \langle a, b \rangle = \langle x + a, y + b \rangle.$$

The operation $+$ is both commutative and associative. The vector $\langle 0, 0 \rangle$ is the identity element and $\langle -x, -y \rangle$ is the inverse of vector $\langle x, y \rangle$. Define $f : \mathbb{R} \to \mathbb{R}$ by

$$f(\langle x, y \rangle) = \langle Ax + By, Cx + Dy \rangle,$$

where A, B, C, D are constants. The map f is a homomorphism. To prove it, show that $f(\langle x, y \rangle + \langle x', y' \rangle) = f(\langle x, y \rangle) + f(\langle x', y' \rangle)$. Since $f(\langle 0, 0 \rangle) = \langle 0, 0 \rangle$, the identity is mapped onto itself. Since $f(\langle -x, -y \rangle) = \langle -Ax - By, -Cx - Dy \rangle = -(\langle Ax + By, Cx + Dy \rangle) = -f(\langle x, y \rangle)$, f maps the inverse of $\langle x, y \rangle$ to the inverse of $f(\langle x, y \rangle)$. The homomorphism preserves commutative and associative properties. Notice that f is a linear transformation defined on 2×2 matrices.   ■

If a homomorphism $f : X \to Y$ is an onto mapping from X to Y, f is called an *epimorphism*. For example, consider $(\mathbb{N}, +)$, the algebra of integers under addition and $(\mathbb{N}_n, +)$, the algebra of integers under addition modulo n. Define the map $f : \mathbb{N} \to \mathbb{N}_n$, $f(a) = a \bmod n$. The map is onto; that is, for every $k \in \{0, 1, \ldots, n-1\}$, there is a $j \in \mathbb{N}$ such that $j \bmod n = k$. For $a, b \in \mathbb{N}$, since $(a + b) \bmod n = (a \bmod n) + (b \bmod n)$, the map f is a homomorphism. Hence f is an epimorphism.

If a homomorphism $f : X \to Y$ is one-to-one, it is called a *monomorphism*. A homomorphism that is both an epimorphism and a monomorphism is called an *isomorphism*. Isomorphic algebras have essentially the same structure—only their names are different.

Example 8.5   Consider the set $X = \{0, 1, \ldots, 2^k - 1\}$ with addition modulo 2^k and the set Y of k-bit binary digits with addition modulo 2. Define the map $f : Y \to X$, where f maps a binary digit to the natural number it represents. For two binary digits $b_1 \neq b_2$, $f(b_1) \neq f(b_2)$. For every number in X, there exists only one binary digit. Hence f is an isomorphism.   ■

Example 8.6   Consider algebra $\mathcal{U}$ with operators *right*, *left*, *above*, *below*, and algebra $\mathcal{T}$ with operators CRS, CLS, CAS, CBS defined in Example 8.1. Define a homomorphism $f : \mathcal{U} \to \mathcal{T}$, which maps an element of algebra $\mathcal{U}$ to an $n \times n$ matrix of algebra $\mathcal{T}$, and maps operators as follows:

$$f(right) = \text{CRS}; \quad f(left) = \text{CLS};$$
$$f(above) = \text{CAS}; \quad f(below) = \text{CBS}.$$

A term of the form $above(x)$ in $\mathcal{U}$ will be mapped by f to the term $f(above)(f(x)) = \text{CAS}(m)$ in algebra $\mathcal{T}$. The axioms are mapped accordingly. For example, the axiom $above(below(x)) = x = below(above(x))$ will be mapped to CAS(CBS $(m)) = m = \text{CBS}(\text{CAS}(m))$. Similarly, we can define homomorphisms from $\mathcal{U}$ to $\mathcal{L}$ and from $\mathcal{U}$ to $\mathcal{T}$.   ■

Heterogeneous Algebras   The software development process involves designing complex data types composed from basic data types such as integer, Boolean, array, and record. For instance, a database file may be composed from set and record data types. In such a case, a file operation should preserve the operations on sets and records. This situation charaterizes a heterogeneous homomorphism. Informally, a homomorphism F, from an algebra A with signature $\Sigma_A = \langle S_A, \Omega_A \rangle$ to an algebra B with signature $\Sigma_B = \langle S_B, \Omega_B \rangle$, maps each sort $s \in S_A$ to a sort $F(s) \in S_B$, and each operator $h \in \Omega_A$ to an operator $F(h) \in \Omega_B$, such that each scheme θ of Ω_A is mapped to a scheme $F(\theta)$ of Ω_B, in which the arity of scheme θ is preserved. For example, if the domain of scheme θ is

$$S_1 \times S_2 \times \ldots \times S_k,$$

then

$$\forall x_1 \in S_1, x_2 \in S_2, \ldots, x_k \in S_k,$$
$$F(h(x_1, x_2, \ldots, x_k)) = F(h)(F(x_1), F(x_2), \ldots, F(x_k))$$

F preserves the arity and the types of the operators.

Example 8.7   Consider algebra S with signature $\langle S_1, \Omega_1 \rangle$, and algebra C with signature $\langle S_2, \Omega_2 \rangle$, where

$$S_1 = \{Stack, Elm\}$$
$$\Omega_1 = \{\{push\}: Stack \times Elm \rightarrow Stack$$
$$\{pop\}: Stack \rightarrow Stack$$
$$\{top\}: Stack \rightarrow Elm$$
$$\{newstack\}: \rightarrow Stack\}$$
$$S_2 = \{Container, Item\}$$
$$\Omega_2 = \{\{put\}: Container \times Item \rightarrow Container$$
$$\{get\}: Container \rightarrow Item$$
$$\{newc\}: \rightarrow Container\}$$

Define a map $F : S_2 \rightarrow S_1$, such that $F(Container) = Stack$, $F(Item) = Elm$, $F(put) = push$, $F(newc) = newstack$, and $F(get) = top$. It is easy to verify that F is a homomorphism from C to S. For example, F maps the term $put(newc, i)$ to $push(newstack, e)$. ∎

8.3   Abstract Data Types

Informally, an abstract data type D is a set S of data structures and a collection Ω of services provided by them. The abstract data type D is modeled by an algebra A over the signature $\langle S, \Omega \rangle$. The set S consists of the sorts needed to construct D. The operations in Ω correspond to abstract algorithmic procedures manipulating the modeled data.

The syntactic structure of data type D is determined by the signature of algebra A, and the semantics is derived from the notion of *computation structure*. The computation structure is a many-sorted algebra in which all elements of set S

can be denoted by *ground terms*. A term of a sort may refer to nullary functions, functions defined in the algebra, and free variables. Every such term must be reduced to a ground term. The conjoint interpretation of all the ground terms gives the computation structure of the data type modeled by algebra $\mathcal{A}$.

Assuming that *Elm* corresponds to *Nat*, the sort of natural numbers, some of the ground terms of algebra $\mathcal{S}$ modeling a stack data type in Example 8.7 are

1. *newstack*—an empty stack.

2. *push(push(newstack, zero), succ(zero))*—a stack with two elements, *succ (zero)* on top of *zero*.

3. *top(pop(push(push(newstack, zero), succ(succ(zero)))))*—the top element of a stack containing *zero*.

8.3.1 Presentation

A *presentation* of an abstract data type is a signature together with a set of *axioms*. The axioms characterize the properties of the data type within a many-sorted logical formalism. Usually, this formalism is restricted to a first-order logic with equality. Frequently, properties characterized by choices may be written as conditional equations using *if-then-else* expressions. The example in Figure 8.1 is a presentation of the data type of natural numbers; it is a one-sorted specification. A presentation for the stack algebra discussed in Example 8.7 is shown in Figure 8.2. This presentation includes the sort *Nat*; it is a two-sorted specification.

In a presentation, information is organized in the following sequence:

Spec: *Natural*;
Sorts: *Nat*;
Operations:
  $zero : \rightarrow Nat$;
  $succ : Nat \rightarrow Nat$;
  $add : Nat \times Nat \rightarrow Nat$;
  $mult : Nat \times Nat \rightarrow Nat$;
Variables:
  $a, x : Nat$;
Axioms:
  $add(zero, a) = a$;
  $add(succ(x), a) = add(x, succ(a))$;
  $mult(zero, a) = zero$;
  $mult(succ(x), a) = add(mult(x, a), a)$;

FIGURE 8.1. The data type *Nat*.

Spec: *Stack*;
Sorts: *Stack*, *Nat*;
Operations:
  zero : $\rightarrow$ *Nat*;
  succ : *Nat* $\rightarrow$ *Nat*;
  newstack : $\rightarrow$ *Stack*;
  push : *Stack* $\times$ *Nat* $\rightarrow$ *Stack*;
  pop : *Stack* $\rightarrow$ *Stack*;
  top : *Stack* $\rightarrow$ *Nat*;
Variables:
  s : *Stack*; *n* : *Nat*;
Axioms:
  pop(*newstack*) = *newstack*;
  top(*newstack*) = *zero*;
  pop(*push*(*s*, *n*)) = *s*;
  top(*push*(*s*, *n*)) = *n*;

FIGURE 8.2. The data type *Stack*.

- The name of the presentation, which may include the name of a generic parameter of some sort, is given in **Spec** clause.

- The **extend by** clause is optional; it enumerates the names of presentations introducing sorts that are required in defining this presentation.

- The **Sorts** clause introduces the names of sorts defined in the presentation.

- The **Operations** clause introduces the operations on the sorts. The order of listing the operations is not important.

- The **Variables** clause introduces variables of sorts introduced earlier for writing axioms. The order of listing the variables is not important.

- The **Axioms** clause lists the axioms constraining the operations. The order of their listing is not important.

The name of the presentation must be unique. The sort names associated with formal parameters, if any, must be specified. The name space for sorts and presentations are not distinct; that is, a sort defined in a presentation may have the same name as the presentation. For instance, the name of the presentation in Figure 8.2 is *Stack*, which is also the name of a sort introduced in the presentation. It is more convenient to name the sort differently from the presentation defining it. The **extend by** clause is essentially the import list that includes all presentations of which reference is made in this presentation. The sorts and operators introduced in these included presentations can be used freely in defining new sorts. The operator names, introduced as functions, can only refer to the distinguished sorts defined in the presentation and those that have been introduced in the presentations mentioned in the **extend by** clause. The functions may be partial or total. The axioms define the operations in terms of their relationships and are universally quantified over the sorts introduced in the **variables** clause. An algebra denoted by a presentation *satisfies* the axioms in the presentation if for each axiom $t_1 = t_2$, the two terms t_1 and t_2 denote the same element of the algebra for each possible assignment of values to the variables in the terms. Hence, the two terms

$push(newstack, succ(zero))$

and

$push(pop(push(newstack, zero)), succ(zero))$

are equal. The equality symbol "=" is often *overloaded*; in the context of "*if a = b then x else y*," "=" is a relational operator. When a and b are terms of the same sort, the axiom $a = b$ means that a and b are *congruent (equivalent, have the same value)*. A term a occurring in an expression e can be substituted by a term b to give an expression e' equivalent to e. This substitution rule allows *rewriting* of equations. The axiom $a = b$ may be viewed as the rewrite rule $a \Rightarrow b$, meaning that the right-hand side b is substituted wherever the left-hand side a occurs in expressions. Rewriting can be used to reduce equations to *ground terms*, that is, terms with no variables. An expression containing no variable can be evaluated to a term in the algebra; this term can be associated to a unique sort. In order to obtain expressions containing only ground terms that cannot be reduced any further, the specification should have *constructors*. We discuss such specifications in the next section.

8.3.2 Semantics

For a given signature there exists a collection of algebras and several possible homomorphisms among them. An algebra $\mathcal{I}$ of this collection is an *initial* algebra if for every other algebra $\mathcal{A}$ in this collection, there exists a unique homomorphism from $\mathcal{I}$ to $\mathcal{A}$. If an initial algebra exists in the collection, it is unique up to an isomorphism. That is, if there exists more than one initial algebra in the collection, then there exists an isomorphism between each pair of initial algebras. See Goguen [6]. The initial algebra can also be understood through equality of terms in the algebra: in the semantics of the initial algebra, two variable-free terms denote different objects unless it can be proved from the stated axioms that they denote the same object.

Another frequently used semantic model is the *final (terminal) algebra*. The final algebra is the term algebra satisfying the stated axioms of the presentation and having the smallest number of terms. There is a unique homomorphism from any other algebra satisfying the axioms to the final algebra. The final algebra can also be understood through the inequality of terms: in the semantics of the final algebra, two variable-free terms of the same sort denote the same object unless it can be proved from the stated axioms that they denote different objects. The difference between

Spec: *Simpleset*;
extend Boolean **by**
Sorts: *S*;
Operations:
    empty : $\rightarrow S$;
    insert : $Nat \times S \rightarrow S$;
    member : $Nat \times S \rightarrow Bool$;
Variables:
    s : *S*; *n*, *m* : *Nat*;
Axioms:
    member(*n*, *empty*) = *false*;
    member(*n*, *insert*(*m*, *S*)) = (*m* = *n*) $\vee$ *member*(*n*, *S*);
    insert(*n*, *insert*(*m*, *S*)) = *insert*(*m*, *insert*(*n*, *S*));

FIGURE 8.3. Specification for a simple set.

these two semantics is illustrated in Figure 8.3, which extends the presentation
Boolean in section 8.4.

The initial algebra semantics for the presentation in Figure 8.3 is the *bag* of natural
numbers. The terms *insert*(2, *S*) and *insert*(2, *insert*(2, *S*)) yield different values
and correspond to the semantics of initial algebra. The final algebra semantics
for this presentation is the *set* of natural numbers. Two sets are different if the
function *member* gives different results on the sets for at least one member. Since
member(2, *insert*(2, *empty*)) and *member*(2, *insert*(2, *insert*(2, *empty*))) are both
true, and *member*(*n*, *insert*(2, *empty*)) and *member*(*n*, *insert*(2, *insert*(2, *empty*)))
are both false for $n \neq 2$, the terms *insert*(2, *empty*) and *insert*(2, *insert*(2, *empty*))
denote the same object, namely the set with only one member, the number 2.

In this book, the initial algebra semantics is considered in defining algebraic specifications.

8.4 Properties of Algebraic Specifications

In this section we study reasoning by term rewriting, extension of many-sorted
specifications, classification of operations, and the adequacy of algebraic specifications.

8.4.1 Reasoning

Presentations can be analyzed to establish a property that holds for all objects of
a sort defined in the presentation, as well as to identify inconsistent requirements.
Equational reasoning and *induction* are the techniques frequently used in such

Spec: *Boolean*;
Sorts: *Bool*;
Operations:
$$true, false : \rightarrow Bool;$$
$$not : Bool \rightarrow Bool;$$
$$\_and\_: Bool \times Bool \rightarrow Bool;$$
$$\_or\_: Bool \times Bool \rightarrow Bool;$$
$$\_impl\_: Bool \times Bool \rightarrow Bool;$$
$$\_==\_: Bool \times Bool \rightarrow Bool;$$
Variables:
$$x, y : Bool;$$
Axioms:
$$false = not(true);$$
$$true = not(false);$$
$$false = false \ and \ x;$$
$$x = true \ and \ x;$$
$$true = true \ or \ x;$$
$$x = false \ or \ x;$$
$$x \ or \ y \ = y \ or \ x;$$
$$x \ and \ y \ = not(not(x) \ or \ not(y));$$
$$x \ impl \ y \ = (not \ x) \ or \ y;$$
$$x \ == \ y \ = (x \ impl \ y) \ and \ (y \ impl \ x);$$

FIGURE 8.4. The datatype *Bool*.

analysis. The first-order axioms serve the role of a verifier for the properties of the data type. The induction method is quite similar to the structural induction technique discussed in Chapter 7. We briefly outline equational reasoning based on term rewriting for the data types *Nat* and *Bool*. The presentation for *Bool* is shown in Figure 8.4. The two constant functions *true* and *false* are the values of the sort *Bool*.

Example 8.8 illustrates the reduction of algebraic equations to some canonical form using axioms as rewrite rules.

Example 8.8   An expression with variables is reduced to a variable-free expression by using the axioms as rewrite rules. In rewriting an expression e, a subexpression f of e is matched against the left-hand side t_1 of an axiom $t_1 = t_2$, and if it matches then f is replaced by the right-hand side t_2.

1. To simplify the expression

$$add(succ(succ(zero)), succ(succ(a))),$$

the following steps are done:

(a) Identify the axiom in the presentation *Natural* that is appropriate for application. In this case, we choose the axiom $add(succ(u), v) = add(u, succ(v))$. The term $succ(zero)$ is matched with u, and the term $succ(succ(a))$ is matched with v in the left-hand side of this axiom. When substituted for u and v, the right-hand side of the axiom when substituted gives the rewritten expression

$$add(succ(succ(zero)), succ(succ(a))) \Rightarrow$$
$$add(succ(zero), succ(succ(succ(a))))$$

(b) One more application of the same axiom, with u matched to $zero$, and v matched to $succ(succ(succ(a)))$, rewrites the above expression to

$$add(zero, succ(succ(succ(succ(a)))))$$

(c) We then use the first axiom $add(zero, a) = a$ to get the equivalent expression

$$succ(succ(succ(succ(a))))$$

This expression is variable-free and cannot be reduced further.

2. It can be verified from the axioms in the presentation *Natural* that the expressions

$$mult(succ(succ(0)), a) \text{ and}$$
$$add(add(0, a), a)$$

are equivalent.

3. From the first two axioms of the *Boolean* presentation given in Figure 8.4, it can be proved that

$$x = not(not(x)),$$
$$not(x \text{ or } y) = not(x) \text{ and } not(y).$$

The proof consists of two steps:

(a) substitute $not(x)$ for x, $not(y)$ for y in the axiom $x \text{ and } y = not(not(x) \text{ or } not(y))$:

$$not(x) \text{ and } not(y) = not(not(not(x)) \text{ or } not(not(y)))$$

(b) The result $x = not(not(x))$ is used in the right-hand side:

$$not(x) \text{ and } not(y) = not(x \text{ or } y) \qquad \blacksquare$$

8.4.2   Extending Many-Sorted Specifications

It is sometimes convenient to reuse an existing specification by incrementally adding more functions and axioms. Larger presentations can be constructed by reusing already defined sorts. The **extend by** clause is used to construct a larger specification with or without the introduction of new sorts. The extended version inherits the sorts, operations, and axioms defined in the original presentation. If $SP_1 = \langle\langle S_1, \Omega_1 \rangle, E_1 \rangle$, then the expression

Spec SP $=$ **extend** SP_1 **by sorts** S **Operations** Ω **Axioms** E

denotes the specification $\langle \Sigma, E_1 \cup E \rangle$, where $\Sigma = \langle S_1 \cup S, \Omega_1 \cup \Omega \rangle$.

The specification given in Figure 8.5 extends *Natural*, defined in Figure 8.1. The new sort *Ternary* is a subsort of *Nat*. The operators *zero, succ, add,* and *mult* are also defined for the new sort *ternary*. There is no new operator defined. The new axiom enforces that every multiple of 3 is reduced to *zero*. Instead of the axiom written in Figure 8.5, we could have included any one of the following axioms:

$$succ(succ(succ(zero))) = zero$$
$$add(x, add(succ(x), succ(succ(x)))) = zero$$

An extension of the many-sorted specification *Stack* given in Figure 8.2 is shown in Figure 8.6. The specification extends the sort *Stack* with operations *size* and *push*1. For the objects of the sort *Bstack*, all the operations of *Stack* are available. In the extended specification, a new element can be pushed onto the stack only if the number of elements on the stack does not exceed the maximum size M. It would be appropriate to hide the *push* operation from the users of the *Boundedstack* specification.

8.4.3   Classification of Operations

The operations for an abstract data type may be divided into *constructors* and *non-constructor operations*. Informally, constructors are operations that generate objects of the abstract data type, whereas non-constructor operations describe the

> **Spec:** *Mod3_enrich_natural*;
> **extend** *Natural* **by**
> **Sorts:** *Ternary*;
> **Variables:**
> $x : Ternary$;
> **Axioms:**
> $succ(succ(succ(x))) = x$;

FIGURE 8.5. Data type *Ternary* enriches *Natural*.

Spec: *Boundedstack*;
extend *Stack* **by**
Sort: *Bstack*;
Operations:
$\qquad M :\to Nat$;
$\qquad size : Bstack \to Nat$;
$\qquad push1 : Bstack \times Nat \to Bstack$;
Variables:
$\qquad s : Bstack$; $n : Nat$;
Axioms:
$\qquad size(newstack) = 0$;
$\qquad push1(s, n) = if\ size(s) < M\ then\ push(s, n)\ else\ s$;
$\qquad size(push1(s, n)) = if\ size(s) < M\ then\ 1 + size(s)\ else\ M$;

FIGURE 8.6. Specification for a bounded stack.

functionality of the objects of the data type. Another way to view this is that constructors provide data abstraction, while non-constructors provide procedural abstraction. The operations may be classified as follows:

1. *Primitive constructors:*   These operations take no input and create objects of their abstract date type. Examples are *zero* of *Natural*, *empty* of *Simpleset*, *true* and *false* of *Boolean*, and *newstack* of *Stack*.

2. *Constructors:*   These operations take objects of their abstract date type as input and create other objects of their corresponding abstract data type. For example, *succ*, *add*, and *mult* are constructors for *Natural*, and *and*, *or*, *impl*, and == are constructors for *Boolean*.

3. *Mutators:*   These operations modify objects of their abstract data type. For example, *push* and *pop* are mutators for *Stack*, and *insert* is a mutator for *Simpleset*.

4. *Observers:*   These operations take objects of their abstract data type and zero or more objects of other abstract data types and return results of other abstract data types. For example, *member* is an observer operation for the objects of the sort *Simpleset*, and *size* is an observer operation for the objects of the sort *Bstack*.

Primitive constructors create only objects of their type. For example, *empty* of *Simpleset* produces an empty bag. The other objects are produced by constructors and mutators. For instance, *insert* of *Simpleset* produces different objects of the sort *Simpleset* depending on the natural numbers inserted in the object. All constructors are assumed to be total functions.

8.4.4 Adequacy

Adequacy is a context-dependent notion. To satisfy the requirements imposed by a context of usage, a sufficient set of operations for a data type should be provided. For example, we have not provided operations for comparing natural numbers in *Natural*. When we include these operations, sufficient axioms to characterize the properties of the additional operations should be included. From such an enriched specification, it is possible to infer more information about natural numbers. Still, there are other operations such as integer division producing quotient and remainder that cannot be performed in this extended specification. In general, we decide whether a specification is adequate by identifying the operations that are mandated in the user requirements. We then provide

- a sufficient number of operations for describing the objects and their modifications in the context of their usage; and
- a sufficient number of axioms to capture the behavior of objects.

A rule to achieve a reasonable degree of adequacy, given by Liskov and Guttag [11], is to include operations from at least three of the four classes discussed in the preceding section. An abstract data type specification should include primitive constructors, observers, and either constructors or mutators. Notice that immutable types such as *Natural* have only constructors, whereas mutable types such as *Stack* have mutators. The axiom part should include axioms describing the effect of each observer operation over each constructor/mutator. We illustrate these concepts in the specification *Orderednatural* shown in Figure 8.7, and in the specification *NatTree* shown in Figure 8.8.

The data type *Orderednatural* extends *Natural* with three observer operations. The effect of an observer operation on constructor pairs is shown in Figure 8.7. For the data type *NatTree*, the primitive constructor is *empty*, *node* is a constructor, the operations *left*, *right* are mutators, and *content*, *isempty*, *isfound* are observers. The effect of the observer operations on the constructor is described in three axioms. We could include additional axioms such as $content(left(node(x, n, y))) = content(x)$, but such axioms are implied by the stated ones. Operations such as *content*, *left*, *right* are not meaningful for an empty binary tree. Hence, although terms of the form $content(empty)$, $content(left(empty))$, $content(right(empty))$, $content(left(right(empty)))$ are in the initial algebra of *NatTree*, they do not correspond to any element in *Nat*. That is, this algebra does not represent the computation structure of naturals. Informally, terms of the form $content(empty)$, $left(empty)$, $content(right(empty))$ denote incorrect function applications. This can be handled by adding one axiom for each kind of erroneous term. The set of axioms in Figure 8.8 is therefore not adequate. An alternative way of remedying this inadequacy is to restrict the algebra to contain only terms that are determined by axioms to be valid. We look at this alternative in section 8.6.

Spec: *Orderednatural*;
extend *Natural* **by**
Operations:

   $eq : Nat \times Nat \to Bool$;
   $lt : Nat \times Nat \to Bool$;
   $le : Nat \times Nat \to Bool$;

Variables:

   $x, y, z : Nat$;

Axioms:

   $eq(zero, zero) = true$;
   $eq(zero, succ(x)) = false$;
   $eq(succ(x), zero) = false$;
   $eq(succ(x), succ(y)) = eq(x, y)$;
   $lt(zero, zero) = false$;
   $lt(zero, succ(x)) = true$;
   $lt(succ(x), succ(y)) = lt(x, y)$;
   $le(x, y) = eq(x, y) \vee lt(x, y)$;

FIGURE 8.7. Specification for ordered natural.

Spec: *NatTree*;
extend *Orderednatural* **by**
Sorts: *Tree*;
Operations:

   $empty : \to Tree$;
   $node : Tree \times Nat \times Tree \to Tree$;
   $left, right : Tree \to Tree$;
   $content : Tree \to Nat$;
   $isempty : Tree \to Bool$;
   $isfound : Tree \times Nat \to Bool$;

Variables:

   $x, y : Tree$; $n, m : Nat$;

Axioms:

   $isempty(empty)$;
   $\neg isempty(node(x, n, y))$;
   $left(node(x, n, y)) = x$;
   $right(node(x, n, y)) = y$;
   $content(node(x, n, y)) = n$;
   $\neg isfound(empty, m)$;
   $isfound(node(x, n, y), m) = (m = n) \vee isfound(x, m) \vee isfound(y, m)$;

FIGURE 8.8. Specification for a binary tree.

8.5   Structured Specifications

It is convenient to design specifications in a structured fashion by refining and composing existing modules of specifications. The **extend by** clause may be used for the incremental development of complex specifications. We select a subset of requirements from the *Idea Processor* example discussed by Henderson [10] to illustrate the incremental specification process.

The primary purpose of an Idea Processing System (IPS) is to support users in organizing and sharing ideas on different subjects, providing facilities for editing and retrieving items of cognitive content. An IPS provides editing operations such as *add, modify, delete*, and *merge*, storage and retrieval operations, and a display operation for a selected group of ideas. Chapter 5 includes a formal grammar for defining the structure of objects in an IPS. In Chapter 7, we have given a functional specification for some of the operations in IPS. Neither of these formalisms specified all the data types in an IPS. In the following discussion, we specify all the abstract data types for an IPS; however, we include specifications for editing functions only.

Requirements and model   An IPS is a database of *ideas*, where each *idea* is associated with one topic of interest. An idea is a collection of major ideas pertaining to that topic, and each major idea is referred to as a *group*. We model an idea, which is a collection of groups, as a *list*. A group may be composed of other major ideas. In order to distinguish between the major ideas within a group, each group is required to have a *heading*. The *body* of a group may include other major ideas and/or a *note*, a description of the major idea under the chosen heading. A note is a subidea modeled by a sequence of words. Subideas are identified by unique *keywords*. Subideas can be moved around within a group and one or more subideas can be merged within a group. An IPS allows the creation and manipulation of ideas towards composing them into a major text.

Primitive sort   The primitive data type *Word* defined in Figure 8.9 captures the notion of words. We define two observer operations "=="(equality) and "$\leq$" (less than or equal). We interpret $w_1 \leq w_2$ to mean that word w_1 precedes w_2 in alphabetical order.

Presentation of note   We define *note* as a sequence of words. We follow the abstraction from Chapter 7 for data type sequence. Figure 8.10 shows the specification of the sort *Note*. We have chosen the representation 0 for *zero*, 1 for *succ(zero)*, and + for *add* for the functions in sort *Nat*. The operations *length, eq*, and *head* are observer operations. The operations *addf, tail, cat* are mutators, and *empty* is the only constructor. Writing one axiom for each observer operation over each mutator and constructor, we obtain a collection of twelve axioms. Notice

Spec: *Primitivesort*;
extend Boolean **by**
Sorts: *Word*;
Operations:

$\_==\_$: *Word* × *Word* → *Bool*;
$\_\leq\_$: *Word* × *Word* → *Bool*;

FIGURE 8.9. The data type *Word*.

Spec: *Sequence*;
extend *Natural*, *Primitivesort* **by**
Sorts: *Note*;
Operations:

empty : → *Note*;
addf : *Word* × *Note* → *Note*;
tail : *Note* → *Note*;
head : *Note* → *Word*;
cat : *Note* × *Note* → *Note*;
length : *Note* → *Nat*;
eq : *Note* × *Note* → *Bool*;

Variables:

u, *v* : *Note*;
x, *y* : *Word*;

Axioms:

$length(empty) = 0$;
$length(addf(x, u)) = 1 + length(u)$;
$eq(empty, empty) = true$;
$eq(empty, addf(x, u)) = false$;
$eq(addf(x, u), empty) = false$;
$eq(u, v) = (head(u) == head(v)) \wedge eq(tail(u), tail(v))$;
$head(addf(x, u)) = x$;
$tail(empty) = empty$;
$tail(addf(x, u)) = u$;
$cat(empty, u) = u$;
$cat(u, empty) = u$;
$cat(addf(x, u), v) = addf(x, cat(u, v))$;

FIGURE 8.10. The data type *Note*.

Spec: *Orderedpair*;
extend Sequence **by**
Sorts: *Ordpair*;
Operations:
    pair : *Word* × *Note* → *Ordpair*;
    first : *Ordpair* → *Word*;
    second : *Ordpair* → *Note*;
    eqp : *Ordpair* × *Ordpair* → *Bool*;
Variables:
    s : *Word*; *t* : *Note*; *p*, *q* : *Ordpair*;
Axioms:
    first(*pair*(*s*, *t*)) = *s*;
    second(*pair*(*s*, *t*)) = *t*;
    eqp(*p*, *q*) = (*first*(*p*) == *first*(*q*)) ∧
                                    eq(*second*(*p*), *second*(*q*));

FIGURE 8.11. Specification of ordered-pair ⟨ word, note ⟩.

that the effect of the operation *tail* on an empty sequence is to produce an empty sequence, and the effect of the operation *head* on an empty sequence is undefined.

In Chapter 7, we defined the precedence relation for sequences so as to establish a partial ordering on all sequences. The following signature and axioms may be added to the presentation in Figure 8.10.

pred : *Note* × *Note* → *Bool*;

pred(*u*, *u*) = *false*;
pred(*empty*, *addf*(*x*, *u*)) = *true*;
pred(*addf*(*x*, *u*), *empty*) = *false*;
pred(*u*, *v*) = (*head*(*u*) ≤ *head*(*v*)) ∨
    ((*head*(*u*) == *head*(*v*)) ∧ *pred*(*tail*(*u*), *tail*(*v*)));

Presentation of subideas: (keyword, note)   Each note is associated with a unique keyword of type *word*. We focus on specifying the sort (*keyword*, *note*) shown in Figure 8.11. It has one constructor *pair*, and three observers *eqp*, *first*, and *second*. The function *first* extracts the keyword from a pair (*keyword*, *note*), and the function *second* extracts *note* from a pair (*keyword*, *note*). The equality operator *eqp* uses the equality operator "==" defined for the sort *word*, and the observer operator *eq* defined for the sort *note*.

Presentation of a set of (keyword, note)   There are several design options for storing and manipulating elements of the sort *note*. One option is to form classes of elements of the sort *note* so that elements in the same class are equivalent in having the same keyword. Another alternative is to merge the elements of sort *note* having

Spec : *Setofpairs*;
extend *Ordpair* **by**
Sort : *Setp*;
Operations:

   emptyset : → *Setp*;
   insert : *Ordpair* × *Setp* → *Setp*;
   delete : *Ordpair* × *Setp* → *Setp*;
   member : *Ordpair* × *Setp* → *Bool*;
   size : *Setp* → *Nat*;
   merge : *Ordpair* × *Ordpair* × *Setp* → *Setp*;
   match : *Ordpair* × *Ordpair* → *Bool*;

Variables:

   s : *Setp*; *x*, *y* : *Ordpair*; *n* : *Nat*;

Axioms:

   member(*x*, *emptyset*) = *false*;
   member(*x*, *insert*(*y*, *s*)) = *eqp*(*x*, *y*) ∨ *member*(*x*, *s*);
   match(*x*, *y*) = (*first*(*x*) = *first*(*y*)) ∧ (*second*(*x*) ≠ *second*(*y*));
   merge(*x*, *y*, *s*) = *if member*(*x*, *s*) ∧ *member*(*y*, *s*) ∧ *match*(*x*, *y*) *then*
        insert(*ordpair*(*first*(*x*), *cat*(*second*(*x*), *second*(*y*))),
        delete(*y*, *delete*(*x*, *s*)));
   size(*empty*) = 0;
   size(*insert*(*x*, *s*)) = *if member*(*x*, *s*) *then*
        size(*s*) *else* 1 + *size*(*s*);
   size(*delete*(*x*, *s*)) = *if member*(*x*, *s*) *then*
        size(*s*) − 1 *else size*(*s*);
   delete(*x*, *emptyset*) = *emptyset*;
   delete(*x*, *insert*(*y*, *s*)) = *if* (*x* == *y*) *then s*
        else insert(*y*, *delete*(*x*, *s*));

FIGURE 8.12. Specification of a set of subideas.

the same keywords into a single note. We follow this option and specify a set of subideas as a set of ordered pairs (*word*, *note*). Figure 8.12 shows the presentation for such a set. The operations include

- the familiar set operations *insert*, *delete*, *membership*
- an operation *match* to determine whether or not two subideas have the same keyword
- an operation *merge* to put together by concatenation those subideas that are related by a common keyword

Notice the disadvantage of the merge operation (a mutator)—the two subideas do not exist anymore as separate entities. To remedy this situation, one can create new sets using the *copy* constructor.

Spec : *Nordpair*;
extend : *Setofpairs* **by**
Sorts: *Group*;
Operations:

  headline : *Group* → *Note*;
  body : *Group* → *Item*;
  makeg : *Note* × *Item* → *Group*;
  is_note : *Item* → *Bool*;
  is_group : *Item* → *Bool*;

Variables:

  n : *Note*; *t* : *Item*; *p* : *Group*;

Axioms:

  headline(*makeg*(*n, t*)) = *n*;
  body(*makeg*(*n, t*)) = *t*;
  is_note(*headline*(*p*)) = *true*;
  is_group(*body*(*p*)) = ¬*is_note*(*body*(*p*));

FIGURE 8.13. The data type *Group*.

Presentation of a group A *group* is an ordered pair (*note, item*), where an *item* is modeled as a discriminated union of *note* and *group*. The *Orderedpair* presentation in Figure 8.11 needs to be modified for the new sorts that make up the *group*. The operations *headline* and *body* for a group in Figure 8.13 are similar to the operations *first* and *second* defined for the sort *Orderedpair*. The two observer operations *is_note* and *is_group* distinguish between the different types of objects within a group.

Finally, the database of ideas is modeled as a list of groups in Figure 8.14. Each element in the list is an idea, which can be accessed through the *head* operation. An idea can be inserted using the *insert* operation; an idea can be deleted using the *delete* operation.

Several other operations for an idea processor have been discussed by Henderson [10]; some of them are mentioned in the exercises.

8.6 OBJ3—An Algebraic Specification Language

In the preceding section, we discussed algebraic specifications without restriction to any specification language. In this section we introduce OBJ3, an algebraic specification language described by Goguen and Winkler [7], and illustrate the features of the language with several examples.

Spec: *List*;
extend *Nordpair* **by**
Sorts: *Idealist*;
Operations:
     null : $\rightarrow$ *Idealist*;
     insert : *Group* $\times$ *Idealist* $\rightarrow$ *Idealist*;
     head : *Idealist* $\rightarrow$ *Group*;
     tail : *Idealist* $\rightarrow$ *Idealist*;
     delete : *Group* $\times$ *Idealist* $\rightarrow$ *Idealist*;
     isin : *Group* $\times$ *Idealist* $\rightarrow$ *Bool*;
Variables:
     f, g, h : *Idealist*; *a, b, c* : *Group*;
Axioms:
     head(*insert*(*a, null*)) = *a*;
     head(*insert*(*a, insert*(*b, null*))) = *head*(*insert*(*a, null*));
     tail(*insert*(*a, null*)) = *null*;
     tail(*insert*(*b, insert*(*a, null*))) = *insert*(*a, tail*(*insert*(*b, null*)));
     delete(*a, null*) = *null*;
     delete(*a, insert*(*b, f*)) = **if** *a* == *b* **then** *f* **else** *insert*(*b, delete*(*a, f*));
     isin(*a, null*) = *false*;
     isin(*a, insert*(*b, f*)) = **if** *a* == *b* **then** *true* **else** *isin*(*a, f*);

FIGURE 8.14. Specification for a list of ideas.

OBJ3 is a wide spectrum functional programming language that is rigorously based upon order-sorted equational logic. The OBJ3 system consists of the OBJ3 specification language, an interpreter, and an environment for executing specifications. The philosophy underlying the design of OBJ3 is incremental and modular development of specifications that are executable, reusable, and composable. This goal is achieved by providing three kinds of entities in the language: *object, theory*, and *view*. An object encapsulates executable code. A theory defines properties that may be satisfied by another theory or object. The *module* concept refers to an object or a theory. A view is a binding (mapping) between a theory and a module. For specification execution, OBJ3 system uses the *term rewriting*, a reduction process to evaluate expressions with respect to a defined object.

An OBJ3 specification is an *algebra*, and functionalities of the system are algebraic expressions, such that every expression is valid in this algebra. OBJ3 follows the initial algebra semantics. To determine whether the system under development conforms to a certain behavior, we write an algebraic expression characterizing that behavior and use the interpreter to check whether this expression is reducible to *true*. This procedure is performed in the OBJ3 system in two steps:

```
obj FLAVOURS is sort Flavour .
   op first : Flavour Flavour -> Flavour .
   op _second_ : Flavour Flavour -> Flavour .
   ops Chocolate Vanilla Strawberry : -> Flavour .
   vars X Y : Flavour .
   eq first(X,Y) = X .
   eq X second Y = Y .
endo
```

FIGURE 8.15. Definition of the object FLAVOURS.

1. *Creation of rewrite rules or equations*
   An interpreter constructs the rewrite rules from the axioms and introduces them to the system database.

2. *Reduction*
   A program then extracts the rewrite rules from the database and applies them to the given expression.

The result of reducing an expression is either an atomic value (*true*, *false*, etc.) or a term that is irreducible in the algebra.

8.6.1   Basic Syntax

The fundamental unit of OBJ3 is the *object*, which encapsulates executable code. Syntactically, the definition of an object starts with the keyword obj, and ends with the keyword endo. The identifier of the object appears immediately after the keyword obj. The keyword is follows the name; thereafter appears the body of the object.

An example of an unparameterized *sort* is shown in Figure 8.15. The specification of an object consists of the following five components:

1. *Defining sorts*
   The object (*module*) name FLAVOURS, and the sort (type) name Flavour are introduced in the first line of Figure 8.15. By convention, object names are written in upper case letters and sort names start with an upper case letter. A sort in OBJ3 is similar to a type in Pascal or Ada. The object declaration

   ```
   obj NUMBER is sorts Nat Rat .
   ```

   introduces the object NUMBER and two sorts with sort names Nat and Rat. Blank spaces are a requisite.

2. *Defining operations*
   Operations can be defined in three different styles:

- *functions* (standard form)

    ```
    op first : Flavour Flavour -> Flavour .
    ```

- *mixfix operations*

    This kind of definition uses place-holders, indicated by an "underscore" character, to show where arguments should appear. For example, the following is a mixfix definition:

    ```
    op _second_ : Flavour Flavour ->
    Flavour .
    ```

    The operation can be used in an expression like X second Y. As another example, the definition

    ```
    op _ _ : Bit Bits -> Bits .
    ```

    can be used to create a bit string. A typical expression using this syntax is 1 011, whose result is 1011.

- *constants*

    A constant is an operation with arity 0. For example,

    ```
    ops Chocolate Vanilla Strawberry : ->
    Flavour .
    ```

    The keyword ops is used for introducing more than one operation. It is more convenient to use parentheses to separate operations in complex cases as in

    ```
    ops (_+_) (_-_) : IntExp IntExp -> IntExp .
    ```

3. *Declaring variables*

    A variable is declared using the keyword var. More than one variable of the same sort can be introduced using the keyword vars, as in

    ```
    vars X Y : Flavour .
    ```

    By convention, variable names start with an upper-case letter.

4. *Defining axioms*

    Axioms are referred to as *equations*; the following are examples of axioms:

    ```
    eq first (X, Y) = X .
    eq X second Y = Y .
    ```

5. *End of specification*

    The keyword endo marks the end of the specifications for the object. There is NO period after endo!

The OBJ3 interpreter accepts the specification of the object FLAVOURS line by line, parses it, creates the set of rewrite rules, and introduces into the system database under the name FLAVOURS. We have now defined a module FLAVOURS. We may define other object modules with their own respective algebraic specifications. All objects are sequentially introduced into the OBJ3 database.

8.6.2 Built-in Sorts and Subsorts

OBJ3 is based on strong sorting—every symbol has a sort or can be associated to a sort. Sorts are introduced in OBJ3 with the syntax

    sorts ⟨Sortids⟩,

as in

    sorts Nat Int .

Built-in sorts

The OBJ3 system includes a library comprising of several built-in sorts. These represent frequently used abstract data types and include the following predefined modules:

- TRUTH-VALUE provides the constant truth values true and false.
- TRUTH enriches TRUTH-VALUE with the operations ==, =/=, and if _ then _ else _ fi.
- BOOL provides the Boolean logic operators and, or, xor, prefix not, and infix implies.
- IDENTICAL, which can be used instead of BOOL checks for literal identity of terms without evaluating them.
- NAT provides natural numbers.
- NZNAT provides nonzero naturals.
- INT provides integers.
- RAT provides rational numbers.
- FLOAT provides floating point numbers.
- ID provides identifiers; it includes lexicographic ordering, and all the operations available in BOOL.
- QID is similar to ID, except that the identifiers start with an apostrophe symbol; for example, 'a, 'b, '1300, and 'anyidentifier. It has no built-in operation.
- QIDL provides identifiers with apostrophes and includes all the operations available in BOOL; in addition, it includes lexicographic ordering.

These predefined sorts may be imported in the specification of a user-defined module.

Order-sorted algebra

One of the main features of OBJ3 is the introduction of subsorts. This supports the treatment of partial operations, multiple inheritance, and error handling. The OBJ3 language can be used to formally specify a hierarchy of object-oriented software components.

A sort s ' is a subsort of the sort s, written s ' < s, if the value of the domain s includes that of s ', and the operations of s are available to s '. The basic syntax for a subsort declaration in OBJ3 is

```
subsort s' < s .
```

The subset partial ordering can be established among locally defined and imported sorts. For example,

```
subsort MyRat < MyInt < MyReal .
```

where MyInt is a subset of MyReal, and MyRat is a subset of MyInt. Thus, any operation defined for the sort MyReal is available to variables of the sorts Myint and MyRat. The following examples illustrate the subsort relation:

1. The sort Nznat defining positive integers is a subsort of the sort Nat defining natural numbers.

   ```
   subsort NzNat < Nat .
   ```

2. A nonempty list is a subsort of a list.

   ```
   subsort NeList < List .
   ```

3. A bounded stack is a subsort of a stack.

   ```
   subsort BStack < Stack .
   ```

4. A nonempty tree of naturals is a subsort of a tree of naturals.

   ```
   subsort NeNatTree < NatTree .
   ```

Subsorting ensures correct function application to variables of appropriate subsorts and induces the reasoning process to handle exceptional situations properly:

- The division operator is defined only for NzNat; we thus avoid division by 0.
- The *head* operation defined for *Idealist* in Figure 8.14 can be restricted to a nonempty list.
- The *size* operation is meaningful only for a bounded stack Bstack, a subsort of the Stack sort.
- The operations *left, right, content*, and *isfound* defined for the sort *NatTree* in Figure 8.8 can be redefined to be restricted to *NeNatTree*, the sort characterizing nonempty trees of natural numbers.

The order-sorted algebra also supports multiple inheritance such that a subsort may have more than one distinct supersort.

Import clause

An OBJ3 module can be divided into smaller units so that each unit can be understood, analyzed, and reused independently. A hierarchical relationship is explicitly introduced to bring out the dependency of a module on other modules. Whenever module A has to use the sorts and operations declared in module B, module B must be explicitly imported in module A. Since a module in OBJ3 can import several other modules, OBJ3 supports *multiple inheritance*, an important feature of object-oriented programming. Notice that in this hierarchy higher level modules *include* lower level modules.

The OBJ3 language incorporates four modes for importing modules, protecting, extending, including, and using. The abbreviations pr, ex, inc, and us can be used to denote the corresponding modes of importation. By convention, if a module X imports a module Y that imports a module Z, then module Z is also imported into module X; that is, the *imports* relation is a transitive relation. The meaning of the import modes is related to the initial algebra semantics. The semantics for the four modes are as follows:

```
obj X is
   protecting Y .
      . . .
endo
```

- protecting (no junk, no confusion)
  Module X imports module Y, and module Y is protected. No new data item of sorts from module Y can be defined in this module. The signature of module Y cannot be changed; that is, no new operation with sorts of module Y as domain can be introduced. Moreover, a function already defined in module Y cannot be redefined. However, the signature of module Y can be used in defining operations in module X. That is, there is neither junk data nor confusion introduced in the imported clause. The module NATTREE in Figure 8.16 protects the imported modules NAT and BOOL. The subsort relation asserts that Nat (naturals) is a subsort of Nebtree (nonempty binary tree), which in turn is a subsort of Btree (binary tree).

```
obj X is
   extending Y .
      . . .
endo
```

- extending (no confusion)
  If module X imports module Y, and module Y is extended, then new data items of sorts from Y may be defined in module X. However, the operations in module X do not redefine any function already defined in module Y. This implies that new operations can be added to extend the behavior of module Y in module X. This is illustrated in the module ORDLIST.

```
obj ORDLIST is sort List .
  extending LIST .
  op insert : List Nat -> List .
  vars I J : Nat . var L : List .
  eq insert(null, I) = (I null) .
  cq insert(I L, J) = if I > J then (J I L)
                              else (I insert(L, J)) .
endo
```

```
obj X is
  using Y .
    . . .
endo
```

- using

  If module X imports module Y in the using mode, then there is no guarantee
  in the sense that new data items of sorts from module Y may be created, as
  well as old data items of sorts from module Y may be redefined. This import
  mode is analogous to code reuse in object-oriented paradigm. The OBJ3
  interpreter implements using by copying the imported module's top-level
  structure, sharing all of the modules that it imports. Hence, the sorts defined
  within a given module are required to have distinct names, and that all copied
  operations are uniquely identified by their name and rank.

```
obj X is
  including Y .
    . . .
endo
```

- including

  If module X includes module Y, then module Y is incorporated in module
  X without copying. This is the only difference between the using and
  including modes.

Note that the OBJ3 interpreter does not check whether the user's import declarations
are correct. The consequences of an incorrect import declaration can be serious,
leading to incomplete reductions in some cases, and insufficient reductions in
others.

Declaration of attributes

It is convenient to consider certain properties of an operation as attributes
and declare them within the syntax of the operation. These properties include
axioms like associativity, commutativity, and identity. Declaring the attributes of an
operation influences the order of evaluation and parsing.

Associativity and commutativity

The following example illustrates the declaration of associative operations:

```
op _or_ : Bool Bool -> Bool [assoc] .
op _ _ : NeList List -> NeList [assoc] .
```

Expressions involving an associative operator do not require parentheses; for example, we can write

```
(x or y or z)
```

instead of

```
(x or (y or z))
```

Binary infix operations can be declared as *commutative* with the attribute comm, which is semantically a commutativity axiom, implemented by commutative rewriting. Axioms such as

```
eq x + y = y + x
```

lead to non-terminating rewrite rules. Care must be exerted to avoid such axioms, and include the commutativity property as an attribute for the operation eq. A binary operation can bear both commutative and associative attributes.

Identity

The identity attribute can be declared for a binary operation; for example, in

```
op _or_ : Bool Bool -> Bool [assoc id: false] .
```

the attribute

```
id: false
```

gives the effect of the identity equations

```
(B or false = B)
```
and
```
(false or B = B).
```

Identity attributes can be constants such as 0 for + and 1 for ∗, as well as ground terms such as *nil* for list addition, and *emptyset* for set union.

8.7 Signature and Equations

An OBJ3 module or theory is constructed following the syntactic conventions explained in the previous section. The signature includes the definition of subsorts and the modes for imported modules. The syntax for expressions should be consistent with the signature of operations as defined in the module and in the imported modules.

Signature of a module

The signature of an object consists of the sorts, the subsort relations (optional), the import list of modules (optional), and the operations available on the object. The signature of module NATTREE in Figure 8.16 introduces two sorts Nebtree and Btree, representing a nonempty tree of natural numbers, and a tree of natural numbers. The module NATTREE imports the built-in modules NAT and BOOL. With the introduction of subsort Nebtree, the functions left, right, content, and isfound become total functions defined only for Nebtree. However, all the operations defined for Btree remain available for Nebtree as well. All the operations defined for Nebtree remain available for its subsort Nat; however, they are not meaningful for Nat.

Every term in the algebra generated by NATTREE is either a natural number, or a nonempty tree, or a tree. This ensures the closure property for the algebra. A comparison of this specification with the specification *NatTree* shown in Figure 8.8 reveals that the terms content(empty), left(empty), right(empty) do not form part of this new algebra.

Equations

The ability to write equations (axioms) requires an understanding of the operators used. Similar to the classification of operations discussed in Section 8.4.3, OBJ3 operations can also be broadly divided into two groups: Constructors and Observers. Notice that no axioms are defined for basic constructors. An observer cannot modify the values of an object. The operational semantics corresponds to *reduction* by term rewriting. The reduction of an expression is carried out by matching the expression or a subexpression of the expression with the left-hand side of an equation, and then replacing the matched subexpression with the corresponding right-hand side of the equation. An expression that already contains only basic constructors cannot be reduced any further. Any other expression can be reduced to an expression containing only the basic constructors. For example, the expression

> content (left (node (node (empty, 1, empty), 3,
>   node (node (empty, 5, empty), 7, node (empty, 9, empty)))))

```
obj NATTREE is sorts Nebtree Btree .
  protecting NAT .
  protecting BOOL .
  subsorts Nat < Nebtree < Btree .
  op empty : -> Btree .
  op node : Btree Nat Btree -> Nebtree .
  op left : Nebtree -> Btree .
  op right : Nebtree -> Btree .
  op content : Nebtree -> Nat .
  op isempty : Btree -> Bool .
  op isfound : Btree Nat -> Bool .
  vars X Y : Btree . vars N M : List .
  eq isempty(empty) = true .
  eq not isempty(node(X,N,Y)) .
  eq left(node(X,N,Y)) = X .
  eq right(node(X,N,Y)) = Y .
  eq content(node(X,N,Y)) = N .
  eq not isfound(empty,N) .
  eq isfound(node(X,N,Y),M) = (M == N)
     or isfound(X,M) or isfound(Y,M) .
endo
```

FIGURE 8.16. Definition of the binary tree object.

is rewritten using the equation

```
eq left(node(X,N,Y)) = X .
```

to

$$content(node(empty,1,empty)) = 1$$

and then further reduced to 1 by using the equation

```
content(node(X,N,Y)) = N .
```

A conditional equation may be created using cq instead of eq when declaring the equation. For example,

```
cq min(X,Y) = X if X < Y else Y fi .
cq isTriangle(A,B,C) = true if A < B + C and
   B < A + C and C < A + B .
```

The operational semantics for rewriting conditional equations is as follows: first, a match for the left-hand side of the expression is found; next, the conditional equation is evaluated by substituting the bindings obtained from the match; if it evaluates to *true*, then the rewriting is done as described above for the right-hand side of equations. The evaluation strategy in the OBJ3 system is guided by the declaration of attributes, which in fact, can affect both efficiency and termination.

8.8 Parameterized Programming

In Section 8.5, we constructed a specification for the *Idea Processor* example using data type specifications that are specific to the needs of that application. To maximize the potential for reuse, data type specifications must remain as self-contained and general as possible. In this section we discuss how OBJ3 specifications can be constructed to have such properties.

Abstract data types such as set and sequence arise as basic building blocks of more complex data types in various applications. Sets of integers, sets of reals, and sets of sequences, for instance, do not require separate specifications. The set operations can be abstracted independently of the element type. It would be convenient to be able to specify a set of elements of type E by using a parametrized specification module *SET*[T], where T is a formal parameter that can be mapped to sort E. The OBJ3 language provides a parametric specification mechanism: types(sorts) are used to parameterize types (sorts), in a way analogous to the use of types to parameterize functions and procedures in programming languages. The intent of parameterized programming is to decompose the code into parameterized components. At the specification level, objects, theories, views, and module expressions provide formal support for writing parametric specifications. A theory can be used to define the interface and properties of a parameterized module. A view expresses that a certain module satisfies a certain theory in a certain way by binding actual parameters of a module to a theory. Instantiating a parameterized module, using a particular view as an actual parameter, yields a new module. Module expressions involving interacting modules can be formally evaluated with no side-effect.

8.8.1 Theories

Theories express the properties of a module or an object; they provide a means for describing entities that cannot be defined in terms of objects. Theories in OBJ3 have the same structure as objects; they describe sorts, operations, variables, and equations. Theories can import other theories and objects and can also be parameterized. The difference between objects and theories is that objects are executable, while theories only define properties. Figure 8.17 shows the simple theory TRIV, which is predefined in OBJ3; TRIV introduces a new sort Elt.

A theory of a pre-ordered set is shown in Figure 8.18.

```
th TRIV is
   sort Elt .
endth
```

FIGURE 8.17. A simple theory.

```
th PREORDERED is
  sort Elt .
  op _<=_ : Elt Elt -> Bool .
  vars E1 E2 E3 : Elt .
  eq E1 <= E1 = true .
  cq E1 <= E3 = true if E1 <= E2 and E2 <= E3 .
endth
```

FIGURE 8.18. The preordering theory.

```
view TRIV-TO-FLAVOURS from TRIV to FLAVOURS is
  sort Elt to Flavour .
  op newop to first .
endv
```

FIGURE 8.19. Mapping from theory TRIV to object FLAVOURS.

```
view NATORD from PREORDERED to NAT is
  sort Elt to Nat .
  vars X Y : Elt .
  op X <= Y to X < Y or X == Y .
endv
```

FIGURE 8.20. Mapping from theory PREORDERED to NAT.

8.8.2 Views

A *view* describes the association between a *theory* and an *object*, such that the sorts of the theory are mapped onto the sorts of the object, while preserving the subsort relation. The operations of the theory are mapped onto the operations of the object. A view is a homomorphism from the algebra described by the theory to the algebra described by the object. In Figure 8.19, TRIV-TO-FLAVOURS is the name of the mapping, TRIV is the theory, and FLAVOURS is the object. The view NATORD in Figure 8.20 describes the *less-than or equal-to* ordering on *NAT*.

8.8.3 Parameterized Modules

Parameterized modules are declared as follows:

```
  obj NAME[X ::THEORY1]
or
  th NAME[X ::THEORY1]
```

```
obj POSET[X :: TRIV] is protecting BOOL .
   op _<=_ : Elt Elt -> Bool .
   op _=P=_ : Elt Elt -> Bool .
   vars X Y Z : Elt .
   eq X <= X = true .
   eq X =P= X = true .
   eq (X <= Y) and (Y <= X) = X =P= Y .
   eq (X <= Y) and (Y <= Z) = X <= Z .
endo
```

FIGURE 8.21. The partially ordered parametric object POSET.

The theory THEORY1 must have been defined before the declaration of NAME in an OBJ3 specification. With such a declaration the sorts, operations, and equations of THEORY1 become visible to the module NAME. An example of a parameterized module defining a partial order is shown in Figure 8.21. This module imports the object BOOL in protecting mode, and hence the sort Bool is visible within the module. The two operations introduced in the module define the partial order and the equality relation on sort Elt belonging to the theory TRIV. The specification in Figure 8.14 can be adapted to a parameterized module LIST[X::TRIV].

Modules can have more than one parameter; a two-parameter module has the following signature:

```
obj NAME[X :: THEORY1, Y :: THEORY2]
```

If the two theories are the same, we can write:

```
obj NAME[X Y :: THEORY1]
```

The parameterized module in Figure 8.22 has two parameters S and T satisfying the theory TRIV. Notice that this module imports POSET[S], and POSET[T] in protecting mode. Hence all the properties of partial ordering are available without any change in the module ORD-PAIR. This module generalizes the *Orderedpair* specification shown in Figure 8.11; it allows the components of the ordered pair to belong to two different sorts.

8.8.4   Instantiation

Instantiation of a parameterized module replaces its formal parameters by the actual parameters. Each theory is replaced by the corresponding actual module, using the views to bind the actual parameters to the formal parameters. Instantiation avoids multiple copies of imported modules. Instantiating the module BAR, with the formal parameter X mapped to the object FLAVOURS, can be carried out using one of the following constructs:

```
obj ORD-PAIR[S :: TRIV, T :: TRIV] is sort OrdPair .
  protecting POSET[S] .
  protecting POSET[T] .
  protecting BOOL .
  op pair : Elt.S Elt.T -> OrdPair .
  op first : OrdPair -> Elt.S .
  op second : OrdPair -> Elt.T .
  op eqp : OrdPair OrdPair -> Bool [comm] .
  var Et : Elt.T . var Es : Elt.S . vars P Q : OrdPair .
  eq first(pair(Es, Et)) = Es .
  eq second(pair(Es, Et)) = Et .
  eq eqp(P, Q) = (first(P) =P= first(Q)) and
     (second(P) =P= second(Q)) .
endo
```

FIGURE 8.22. A parameterized module for ordered-pair.

```
obj BAR[X :: TRIV] is sort Flavour .
```

by the object FLAVOURS, one of the forms given below can be used:

- The view is used as actual parameter:

  ```
  BAR[TRIV-TO-FLAVOURS] .
  ```

- An unnamed view is used as actual parameter:

  ```
  BAR[view from TRIV to FLAVOURS is endv] .
  ```

- The default view from TRIV to FLAVOURS is used as actual parameter:

  ```
  BAR[FLAVOURS] .
  ```

When an instantiated algebra is used in several contexts and in reduction, it is convenient to name the algebra using the *make* command; for example,

```
make BAR-FLAVOURS is BAR[TRIV-TO-FLAVOURS] endm .
```

where BAR-FLAVOURS is the name given to the instantiated object BAR[TRIV-TO-FLAVOURS]. The make command allows us to instantiate a module only once, and simplifies *module expressions*.

Using the default view from TRIV to NAT, the parameterized module ORD-PAIR may be instantiated with NAT as actual parameter to get a module expression for the object POINT:

```
make POINT is ORD-PAIR[NAT,NAT] endm .
```

```
obj SEQUENCE[X :: ELEMS] is sort Seq .
  protecting POSET[X] .
  protecting NAT .
  protecting BOOL .
  subsort Elems < Seq .
  op empty : -> Seq .
  op _ _ : Seq Seq -> Seq [assoc id: empty] .
  op tail : Seq -> Seq .
  op head : Seq -> Elems .
  op length : Seq -> Nat .
  op equ : Seq Seq -> Bool [comm] .
  vars U V : Seq . vars X Y : Elems .
  eq length(empty) = zero .
  eq length(X U) = succ(length(U)) .
  eq head(X U) = X .
  eq tail(empty) = empty .
  eq tail(X U) = U .
  eq equ(empty, empty) = true .
  cq equ(U, empty) = false if U =/= empty .
  cq equ(U, V) = equ(tail(U), tail(V))
    if U =/= empty and V =/= empty and head(U) == head(V) .
  cq equ(U, V) = false
    if U =/= empty and V =/= empty and head(U) =/= head(V) .
endo
```

FIGURE 8.23. A parameterized module for sequence.

Using different default views, from TRIV to NAT, and from TRIV to BOOL, the parameterized module ORD-PAIR can be instantiated with the actual parameters NAT and BOOL to obtain the module expression:

```
make PAIR-NATBOOL is ORD-PAIR[NAT,BOOL] endm .
```

Using the default view from TRIV to POINT, we can obtain the module expression:

```
make LINE-SEGMENT is ORD-PAIR[POINT,POINT] endm .
```

In Figure 8.23, we define the parametric module SEQUENCE, which can be instantiated to obtain different sequences; for example,

- A sequence of natural numbers is defined by the module:
  ```
  make SEQUENCE-OF-NAT is SEQUENCE[NAT] endm .
  ```
- The *word* entity in the *Idea Processor* example can be modeled using the built-in sort QID for identifiers. We can then define the data type *note* as a sequence of words, with the module:

```
make SEQUENCE-OF-WORDS is SEQUENCE[QID] endm .
```

- The ordered pairs (*key*, *note*) in the *Idea Processor* example can be characterized by the module:

```
make ORD-PAIR[QID, SEQUENCE[QID]] endm .
```

8.8.5 Module Expression

A *module expression* is an expression of an OBJ3 specification that may consist of a homogeneous or a heterogeneous algebra. Evaluating a module expression involves only functions applied to arguments; there is no variable, no assignment, and no side-effect. Module expressions form a formal basis for software reuse. They allow the definition, construction, and instantiation of modules, as well as various forms of module modification. Thus, a given module can be reused in various contexts. The three major combination modes for modules are *Instantiation*, *Renaming*, and *Sum*.

- *Instantiation* is discussed in the previous section.
- *Renaming* is used to create a new module by renaming the sorts and operations of an existing one. In Figure 8.24, the sort *Element* is renamed to Newelement. In Figure 8.25, the sort Flavour is renamed to Vegetable, the operation first is renamed to newfirst, and the operation second to newsecond. Renaming is applied to a module expression postfix after the symbol "*", creating a new module with the specifications of the preceding module.
- *Sum* constructs a union of objects; it creates a new module by composing the specifications of all the components of the sum. The expression A + B creates a module that incorporates the union of axioms, variables, operations, and sorts of both modules A and B.

```
th NEWELEMENT is
   using ELEMENT * (sort Element to Newelement) .
endth
```

FIGURE 8.24. Renaming sorts.

```
FLAVOURS * (sort Flavour to Vegetable .
   op first to newfirst .
   op _second_ to _newsecond_ .)
```

FIGURE 8.25. Renaming sorts and operations.

8.9   Case Study—A Multiple Window Environment

We develop an OBJ3 specification for managing a screen with multiple windows, where each window is associated with a set of geometrical shapes. For the sake of simplicity, the requirements are restricted to windows associated with squares.

Requirements

A screen is a rectangular area that contains a collection of windows. Each window in the screen is a rectangle with its sides parallel to the axes of the screen. A window is associated with the collection of square shapes drawn within it. When the window is moved to a different location within the screen, the square shapes associated with it are also moved without any change to their relative positions inside the window. It is required to provide the following functionalities for window objects and square shapes:

1. Create a window.
2. Determine whether the cursor is within a given window.
3. Select a window identified by the cursor.
4. Move a window to a specified location within the screen.
5. Determine whether two windows overlap.
6. Add a window to the collection of windows.
7. Associate a list of squares with a given window.
8. Add a square to the list of squares associated with a window.
9. Translate a square horizontally within a window.
10. Translate a square vertically within a window.

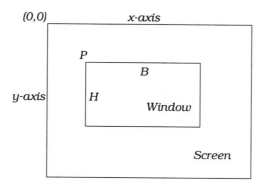

FIGURE 8.26. Coordinate axes for window environment.

Modeling

We define the coordinates of a point in the screen as a pair of natural numbers. We model the cursor as a point. A rectangle is constructed from a point indicating its top-left corner, and two natural numbers denoting its breadth and height. We specialize the rectangle object by extending it with new operations and axioms to obtain a square object. Similarly, we specialize the rectangle object to model a window.

We define a parametric object that takes one parameter to model a list of elements of some sort. This object can be instantiated to obtain lists of squares and lists of windows. We model a screen as a list of windows, where each window is associated with a list of squares.

The position of a point on the screen is given with respect to coordinate axes, where the origin is at the top-left corner of the screen, the x-axis as the horizontal axis, and the y-axis as the vertical axis, as shown in Figure 8.26.

Formal Specifications

```
***  ********************************************************
***                  SIMPLE   WINDOW   SYSTEM             ***
***                     OBJ SPECIFICATION                 ***
***  ********************************************************

*** an object representing the two coordinates of a point.

obj POINT is sort Point .
  protecting NAT .

  op point : Nat Nat -> Point .
  op x     : Point -> Nat .
  op y     : Point -> Nat .

  vars A B : Nat .

  eq x(point(A,B)) = A .
  eq y(point(A,B)) = B .

endo

***  _____  ***

*** defining an object representing the click at a point.

obj CURSOR is sort Cursor .
  protecting NAT .
  protecting POINT .

  op cursor : Point -> Cursor .
  op move   : Cursor Nat Nat -> Cursor .
  op x      : Cursor -> Nat .
  op y      : Cursor -> Nat .

  vars X Y : Nat . var P : Point .

  eq x(cursor(P)) = x(P) .
```

```
    eq y(cursor(P)) = y(P) .
    eq move(cursor(P),X,Y) = cursor(point(X,Y)) .

endo

*** ————————————— ***

*** defining an object representing a rectangle.

obj RECTANGLE is sort Rectangle .
  protecting NAT .
  protecting POINT .

  op rectangle : Point Nat Nat -> Rectangle .
  op locate    : Rectangle -> Point .
  op breadth   : Rectangle -> Nat .
  op height    : Rectangle -> Nat .

  op topleft   : Rectangle -> Point .
  op topright  : Rectangle -> Point .
  op downleft  : Rectangle -> Point .
  op downright : Rectangle -> Point .

  var P : Point . vars B H : Nat .

  eq locate(rectangle(P,B,H)) = P .
  eq breadth(rectangle(P,B,H)) = B .
  eq height(rectangle(P,B,H)) = H .

  eq topleft(rectangle(P,B,H))  = P .
  eq topright(rectangle(P,B,H)) = point(x(P) + B, y(P)) .
  eq downleft(rectangle(P,B,H)) = point(x(P), y(P) + H) .
  eq downright(rectangle(P,B,H))= point(x(P) + B, y(P) + H) .

endo

*** ————————————— ***

*** defining an object representing a square.

obj SQUARE is
  extending RECTANGLE * ( sort Rectangle to Square ,
                          op rectangle to square ) .
  protecting NAT .
  protecting POINT .

  op square : Point Nat -> Square .
  op side   : Square -> Nat .

  var P : Point . vars B H S : Nat .

  cq locate(square(P,B,H)) = P if B == H .
  cq side(square(P,B,H))   = B if B == H .
  eq locate(square(P,S))   = P .
  eq side(square(P,S))     = S .
  cq square(P,B,H) = square(P,B) if B == H .

endo

*** ————————————— ***

*** defining an object representing a window.

obj WINDOW is
  extending RECTANGLE * ( sort Rectangle to Window ,
```

```
                                      op rectangle to window ) .
    protecting NAT .
    protecting BOOL .
    protecting POINT .
    protecting CURSOR .

    op move      : Window Point  -> Window .
    op contains : Window Cursor -> Bool .
    op cross     : Window Window -> Bool .

    vars B H : Nat . vars P : Point . var C : Cursor .
    vars W W1 W2 : Window .

    *** move window to a specified location.

    eq move(W,P) = window(P, breadth(W), height(W)) .

    *** true if the window contains the location of the cursor

    eq contains(window(P,B,H),C) = x(C) >= x(P) and
                                   x(C) <= (x(P) + B) and
                                   y(C) >= y(P) and
                                   y(C) <= (y(P) + H) .

    *** two windows cross each other if one of them has a
    *** corner which is contained in the other window.

    eq cross(W1,W2) = contains(W1,cursor(topleft(W2))) or
                      contains(W1,cursor(topright(W2))) or
                      contains(W1,cursor(downleft(W2))) or
                      contains(W1,cursor(downright(W2))) .

endo

*** _____ ***

*** a parameterized object LIST which takes one parameter.

obj LIST[X :: TRIV] is sort NeList List .
    protecting NAT .
    protecting BOOL .
    subsorts Elt < NeList < List .

    op null     : -> List .
    op _ _      : List List -> List [assoc id: null] .
    op _ _      : NeList List -> NeList .
    op tail _   : List -> List .
    op head _   : NeList -> Elt .
    op empty? _ : List -> Bool .
    op length _ : List -> Nat .
    op copy     : List List -> List .

    var X : Elt . vars L L1 : List .

    eq empty? null = true .
    eq empty? L = L == null .
    eq length null = 0 .
    eq length(X L) = length(L) + 1 .
    eq head(X L) = X .
    eq tail(null) = null .
    eq tail(X L) = L .
    eq empty?(copy(null,L)) = true .
    eq tail(copy((X L),L1)) = L .

endo
```

```
*** _____ ***

*** defining a view from the predefined theory TRIV
*** to the object WINDOW.

view WIN from TRIV to WINDOW is
  sort Elt to Window .
endv

*** creating an object representing a list of windows.
*** instantiating the parameterized object LIST.

make WINLIST is
  LIST[WIN] * ( sort List to Winlist ) .
endm

*** _____ ***

*** defining an object representing a screen.

obj SCREEN is sort Screen .
  protecting BOOL .
  protecting CURSOR .
  protecting WINDOW .
  protecting WINLIST .

  op screen  : Winlist -> Screen .
  op winlist : Screen -> Winlist .
  op addwin  : Screen Window -> Screen .
  op overlap : Screen Window -> Bool .
  op select  : Screen Cursor -> Window .

  var B : Cursor . var W : Window .
  var WL : Winlist . var S : Screen .

  eq winlist(screen(WL))  = WL .
  eq winlist(addwin(S,W)) = W winlist(S) .

  eq overlap(screen(null),W) = false .
  eq overlap(S,W) = cross(head(winlist(S)),W) or
                    overlap(screen(tail(winlist(S))),W) .

  eq select(screen(WL),B) = if contains(head(WL),B)
                            then head(WL)
                            else select(screen(tail(WL)),B)
                            fi .

endo

*** _____ ***

*** defining a view from the predefined theory TRIV
*** to the object SQUARE.

view SQUAR from TRIV to SQUARE is
  sort Elt to Square .
endv

*** creating an object representing a list of squares.
*** instantiating the parameterized object LIST.

make SQUARELIST is
  LIST[SQUAR] * ( sort List to Squarelist ) .
endm
```

```
*** _____- ***

*** defining an object representing the shapes in a window.
*** the object associates a window with a list of squares.

obj WINDOWSHAPES is sort Windowshapes
  protecting NAT .
  protecting BOOL .
  protecting POINT .
  protecting CURSOR .
  protecting WINDOW .
  protecting SQUARELIST .

  op windowshapes       : Window Squarelist -> Windowshapes .
  op win                : Windowshapes -> Window .
  op squarelist         : Windowshapes -> Squarelist .
  op squarewithin       : Square Window -> Bool .
  op addsquare          : Square Windowshapes -> Windowshapes .
  op htranslatesquare   : Square Window Nat -> Square .
  op vtranslatesquare   : Square Window Nat -> Square .

  var W : Window . var SL : Squarelist .
  var WS : Windowshapes . var S : Square .
  var P : Point . vars L X Y : Nat .

  eq win(windowshapes(W,SL)) = W .
  eq squarelist(windowshapes(W,SL)) = SL .

  *** determine if a square fits within a window.

  eq squarewithin(square(P,L),W) =
       contains(W,cursor(topleft(square(P,L)))) and
       contains(W,cursor(topright(square(P,L)))) and
       contains(W,cursor(downleft(square(P,L)))) and
       contains(W,cursor(downright(square(P,L)))) .

  *** add square to list of squares if within the window.

  eq addsquare(S,WS) =
       if squarewithin(S,win(WS))
       then windowshapes(win(WS), (S squarelist(WS)))
       else WS fi .

  *** translate square horizontally if it fits in window
  *** at new location.

  eq htranslatesquare(square(P,L),W,X) =
       if squarewithin(square(point(x(P) + X, y(P)), L), W)
       then square(point(x(P) + X, y(P)), L)
       else square(P,L) fi .

  *** translate square vertically if it fits in window
  *** at new location.

  eq vtranslatesquare(square(P,L),W,Y) =
       if squarewithin(square(point(x(P), y(P) + Y), L), W)
       then square(point(x(P), y(P) + Y), L)
       else square(P,L) fi .

endo

*** _____- ***
```

Exercises

1. Define a homomorphism on the set of n-dimensional vectors of real numbers. Hint: See Example 8.4.

2. Give an algebra for representing a queue of elements. Identify the different schemas needed. Hint: See Example 8.7.

3. Define a presentation for the algebra characterizing a queue, as requested in Exercise 2, including a set of axioms.

4. Define the operation *position* for the data type *note* shown in Figure 8.10; the operation determines the position of a given word in a note. Use the already defined operations in your definition of *position*.

5. A collection of subideas is specified as a set in Figure 8.12. What property is violated if a *copy* function, which makes copies of subideas, is introduced? What data type is appropriate if two subideas having the same key are required and must be considered together to form a single subidea? Rewrite the complete specification for the collection of subideas with the proposed changes.

6. Use the signature of the specification in Figure 8.10 to write a function *mentionsall*, which takes two arguments n, n' of type *note* and returns a sequence composed of *words* occurring in note n as well as in note n'.

7. Use the signature of the specification in Figure 8.10 to write a function *replaceall*, which takes three arguments w, w' of type *word*, and n of type *note*, and replaces all occurrences of the word w by the word w' in the note n.

8. Give a parametric specification for a binary tree. Define (1) a view for constructing a binary tree of natural numbers, and (2) a view for constructing a binary tree of identifiers. Give reductions for printing the contents of the tree in preorder and postorder traversals.

9. Extend the specification discussed in the case study for a multiple window environment, as follows:

   (a) Give a specification for constructing ordered pairs of points. Include operations to determine whether or not the second component of the pair is (1) above, (2) below, (3) to the left, (4) to the right, (5) above and left, (6) above and right, (7) below and right, and (8) below and left of the first component. Give sufficient equations for the axioms.

   (b) Give specifications for a *line segment* object. A line segment is a straight line of finite length. Include operations for translating a line segment parallel to the coordinate axes.

   (c) Use the ORD-PAIR[S::TRIV, T::TRIV] parametric specification given in the text to derive modules for constructing (1) points, and (2) line segments. Hint: Construct appropriate views and use the renaming mechanism.

(d) Include the following operations for the WINDOW object: (1) *fulltop* to extend the height of the window up to the top of the screen, (2) *fullright* to extend the breadth of the window to the right up to the screen boundary, (3) *fulldown* to extend the height of the window up to the bottom of the screen, (4) *fullleft* to extend the breadth of the window to the left up to the screen boundary, (5) *fullscreen* to resize a window so as to fill the entire screen. Include sufficient axioms.

(e) The rectangles considered in the case study have their sides parallel to the coordinate axes. Consequently, the intersection of two rectangles forms a rectangle. The parameters P, B, H of the rectangle, formed by the intersection of any two rectangles $R = rectangle(P_1, B_1, H_1)$, and $R' = rectangle(P_2, B_2, H_2)$, is determined by the dimensions and the relative positions of rectangles R and R'. Introduce operations and axioms for determining the intersection of two rectangles.

(f) Introduce one more sort for the rectangle object to denote its color. Assume that a window may be white or blue. The color of a window W_1 is white when the window is created. It changes to blue when another window W_2 hides part of window W_1. Introduce the notion of hiding and write axioms that are to be satisfied by windows on a screen.

(g) Use the OBJ3 interpreter to verify that the horizontal and vertical translation axioms in WINDOSHAPES are commutative and transitive. In addition, verify that vertical and horizontal translations commute.

(h) Introduce sorts for triangle and circle objects. Make a list of triangle objects, and a list of circle objects. Associate these lists with window objects.

Bibliographic Notes

Data abstraction was first discussed within the *class* concept of the SIMULA programming language [4]. The algebraic approach to specification of data types can be traced back to several papers published in mid 70s, including Goguen, Thatcher, Wagner, and Wright [6], Guttag [8], and Guttag and Horning [9]. A formalization of abstract data types within a many-sorted algebra based on initial algebra semantics was done by the ADJ-group, and reported in Goguen, Thatcher, and Wagner [5]. Since then, several algebraic specification languages have been designed, and several books [1, 11] and papers have been written on the theoretical as well as the practical aspects of algebraic methodology for software specification. Wirsing [12] gives a comprehensive survey of algebraic specification theory and methods.

The specification language CLEAR, developed by Burstall and Goguen [3] was the first language designed for constructing structured algebraic specifications. The seminal paper of Burstall and Goguen [2] on *"putting theories together"* has influenced the design of several other algebraic specification languages, in particular the OBJ family. The design of OBJ, initiated by Goguen, was carried through by several researchers [7]. The parameterization concept introduced in the design of OBJ3 was influenced by CLEAR.

References

[1] J.A. Bergstra, J. Heering, and P. Klint, *Algebraic Specification*, ACM Press, New York, NY, 1989.

[2] R. Burstall and J. Goguen, "Putting Theories to Make Specifications," *Proceedings Fifth International Joint Conference on Artificial Intelligence*, 1977, pp. 1045–1058.

[3] R. Burstall and J. Goguen, "An Informal Introduction to Specifications using CLEAR," in R. Boyer and J. Moore (Eds.), *The Correctness Problem in Computer Science*, Academic Press, New York, NY, 1981, pp. 185–213.

[4] O.J. Dhal, B. Myhrhang, and K. Nygaard, *Common Base Language*, Norsk Reguesentral, Oslo, 1970.

[5] J. Goguen, J. Thatcher, and E. Wagner, "An Initial Algebra Approach to the Specification, Correctness and Implementation of Abstract Data Types," in R.T. Yeh (Ed.), *Current Trends in Programming Methodology, Vol. IV*, Prentice-Hall, Englewood Cliffs, NJ, 1976, pp. 80–149.

[6] J.A. Goguen, J.W. Thatcher, E.G. Wagner, and J.B. Wright, "Initial Algebra Semantics and Continuous Algebras", *Journal of the ACM*, Vol. 24, 1977, pp. 68–95.

[7] J. Goguen and T. Winkler, *Introducing OBJ3*, Technical Report SRI-CSL-88-9, SRI International, Menlo Park, CA, August 1988.

[8] J. Guttag, *The Specification and Application to Programming of Abstract Data Types*, Ph.D. Thesis, Department of Computer Science, University of Toronto, Toronto, Canada, 1975.

[9] J.V. Guttag and J.J. Horning, "The Algebraic Specification of Abstract Data Types," *Acta Informatica*, Vol. 10, 1978, pp. 27–52.

[10] P. Henderson, "Functional Programming, Formal Specification, and Rapid Prototyping," *IEEE Transactions on Software Engineering*, Vol. SE-12, No. 2, February 1986, pp. 241–250.

[11] B. Liskov and J. Guttag, *Abstraction and Specification in Program Development*, The MIT Press, Cambridge, MA, 1989.

[12] M. Wirsing, "Algebraic Specification," in J. van Leeuwen (Ed.), *Handbook of Theoretical Computer Science*, North-Holland, Amsterdam, 1990.

[13] N. Wirth, *Algorithms + Data Structures = Programs*, Prentice-Hall, Englewood Cliffs, NJ, 1976.

9

Vienna Development Method

The *Vienna Development Method* (VDM) is an environment for the modeling and development of sequential software systems. The specification language of VDM has evolved from Meta-IV, the language used at IBM's Vienna development laboratory for specifying the semantics of the PL/I programming language in the early 70s. The current version of the VDM specification language, VDM-SL, has been standardized by the International Standards Organization (ISO). It supports the modeling and analysis of software systems at different levels of abstraction. Using VDM-SL constructs, both data and algorithmic abstractions expressed in one level can be refined to a lower level to derive a concrete model that is closer to the final implementation of the system.

In this chapter, we present a tutorial of VDM-SL, explain refinement techniques, and discuss proof rules. Mathematical proofs are used to demonstrate the consistency of models and also to show that a refined concrete model faithfully conforms to its abstract model. However, we put less emphasis in proof techniques and focus on the use of abstraction to construct precise models. We introduce several examples to illustrate the effective use of VDM-SL features for modeling software systems of reasonable complexity.

9.1   Structure of a VDM Specification

VDM supports two kinds of abstractions—*representational abstraction* and *operational abstraction*. In representational abstraction, the data is abstracted from the representational details of data structures to be used in the final implementation of the system. Operational abstraction describes the abstract algorithmic manipulations of the data introduced in the representational abstraction as first-order predicate logic formulas. These constraints are expressed as functions and operations in the specification.

A VDM specification is structured into various blocks, where each block is identified by a distinct keyword:

types
          <type definitions>
values
          <value definitions>
functions
          <function definitions>
operations
          <operation definitions>
state <state name> **of**
          <state definition>
end

There is no explicit ordering among these blocks. Moreover, not all of them are required to be present in a specification. To illustrate, a portion of the VDM specification for a hotel reservation system is given in Example 9.1.

Example 9.1   *Specification for a hotel reservation system.*

types
    RoomNumber = {*1,· · ·,100*};
    RoomStatus = *Available* | *Occupied*
state *Reservation* **of**
    rooms: RoomNumber $\xrightarrow{m}$ *RoomStatus*
    init mk-*Reservation (rooms)* $\triangleq$
        $\forall$ *rn* $\in$ **dom** *rooms* • *rooms(rn)* = *Available*
end
operations
    book-room (roomno: RoomNumber)
    ext wr *rooms: RoomNumber* $\xrightarrow{m}$ *RoomStatus*
    pre *roomno* $\in$ **dom** *rooms*
    post
        let *st: RoomStatus* = *Occupied* **in**
        rooms = $\overleftarrow{rooms}$ † {*roomno* $\mapsto$ *st*};

In Example 9.1, *RoomNumber* denotes the type of room numbers, numbers ranging from 1 to 100. The status of a room is either available or occupied. The state of the system consists of the rooms and the status of each room in the hotel. The only operation specified in this example is *book-room*. The precondition of the operation checks the validity of the room number. The postcondition ensures that the status of the selected room is occupied.   ∎

9.2   Representational Abstraction

Representational abstraction describes the modeling primitives necessary to specify a software. A model of the software is constructed from the data types built into the language and from those data types that can be constructed by composing the already defined types. There are five mathematical structures—*set, sequence, map, record,* and *tuple*. These structures help us to build composite types.

9.2.1   Identifiers

Identifiers in VDM-SL are formed using alphanumeric characters and Greek letters. The language does not restrict the length of identifiers. Hyphens and primes are permitted within identifiers but they should not appear at the beginning of an identifier. The identifiers in VDM-SL are case sensitive. Thus, the two identifiers *student* and *Student* are different.

Table 9.1 describes conventional font selection followed in this book for various syntactic structures. In addition, we also use subscripts as part of identifiers.

Comments and Separators   Comments in VDM-SL are written with '–' preceding the comment. Any text preceding '–' is part of the specification:

– This is a comment in VDM-SL.

$x \notin S$ – x is not a member of the given set

If comments extend to several lines, it is necessary to start each line of comment with '–'. Each line in VDM-SL corresponds to a line in printed output of the specification.

Convention	Synopsis	Used for
lowercase bold roman	**nil**	keywords
lowercase italics	*student*	variables
lowercase italics with first letter in uppercase italics	*Faculty*	types
uppercase roman	ORANGE	quote type, state variables
lowercase bold	**mk-** . . .	make function
– lowercase roman	– comments	comments

TABLE 9.1. Conventions for identifiers.

Within a block of a VDM specification, such as a type definition and an operation definition, individual statements or expressions are separated by semicolons. However, there is no semicolon at the end of the block; instead, the keyword such as **types** and **functions** itself acts as the separator.

9.2.2 Simple Types

Simple types in VDM-SL can be classified into two categories: *primitive types* defined in the language, and *quote types* introduced by the user. These types are called simple because they are treated as basic elements of the current specification. Consequently, these types are not further elaborated in the current specification. Representation of these types is left to the implementation level. The operations that can be performed on simple types include testing for equality, inequality, and membership.

Primitive Types   The primitive types in VDM-SL are given in Table 9.2. Types other than the **token** type resemble those in a programming language. The **token** type contains a countable collection of distinct values, called *tokens*. There is no internal representation for a token. It is generally used to define a type whose definition is deferred until the later stages of the development process. For example, the type definition

Person = **token**

introduces the type *Person*, which is left unspecified in the current specification.

Arithmetic and Logical Operators   In addition to the standard set of arithmetic operators such as '+', '−', '∗', '/' and logical operators '<', '>', '≤' and '≥', operators enumerated in Table 9.3 are also available in VDM-SL.

The sign of "a **rem** b" is the same as that of "a"; the sign of "a **mod** b" is the same as that of "b". Other operators in Table 9.3 have their usual meanings.

Symbol	Type
$\mathbb{Z}$	Integer
$\mathbb{N}$	Natural number
$\mathbb{N}_1$	Natural number excluding zero
$\mathbb{R}$	Real number
$\mathbb{Q}$	Rational number
$\mathbb{B}$	Boolean
char	Character
token	Token type

TABLE 9.2. Primitive types in VDM-SL.

Operator	Synopsis	Meaning
↑	a ↑ b	exponentiation
div	a **div** b	integer division
rem	a **rem** b	remainder after integer division
mod	a **mod** b	modulus operator
abs	**abs** a	returns the absolute value
floor	**floor** (a/b)	floor operator

TABLE 9.3. Arithmetic operators in VDM-SL.

Quote Types   A quote type, unlike a token, has an internal representation defined by a string of distinguished letters. In this book, we use upper case alphabets in Roman fonts to represent quote types. The string representing a quote type denotes both the type and its value. For example, ORANGE is a quote type whose value is ORANGE.

9.2.3   Composite Types

Composite types are constructed from the types already introduced in the specification (simple or composite) using type constructors. In general, a composite type is defined along with its type invariant which constrains the set of elements of the type.

Union type

A *union* type allows us to combine two or more types into one composite type. The syntax is as follows:

$$T = T_1 \mid T_2 \mid \ldots \mid T_n$$

where T is a union type and $T_1, T_2, \ldots, T_n$ are component types; the symbol '|' is part of the syntax. The semantics of a union type is that an instance of type T can be substituted by an instance of any one of its component types. For example, if the type *User* in a library environment is defined as

$$User = Faculty \mid Student$$

then members of the type *User* are the union of the members of the types *Faculty* and *Student*.

Union and quote types can be composed as in

$$Message = SUCCESS \mid INPUT\text{-}ERROR \mid MISSING\text{-}PARAMETER$$

where *Message* can be used, for example, to denote the return values of a function.

Union type is associative and commutative. The following definitions are equivalent.

> *User = (Faculty | Student) | Staff*
> *User = Faculty | (Student | Staff)*
> *User = Staff | (Faculty | Student)*

VDM-SL uses a special keyword **nil** to denote a null type. As the name implies, **nil** stands for a type having no value. However, **nil** cannot be used by itself. It can only be combined with other types composing a *union* type. For example,

> *B* = **nil**

is illegal, and

> *B* = $\mathbb{N}$ | **nil**

denotes a type *B* whose instances include natural numbers and null value.

An optional type, represented by [*T*], consists of the union of some type *T* and **nil** type; i.e.,

> [*T*] ≡ *T* | **nil**

Set

VDM-SL deals with only finite sets [9]. Countable sets, although not finite, are treated as if they are finite. This seems to simplify some proof obligations. VDM-SL uses the notion for set enumeration and set comprehension as discussed in Chapter 7.

The syntax for a declarative definition of a set in VDM-SL is

> *P*–**set**

which denotes the set of elements of type P; the symbol "–" and the keyword **set** are part of the syntax. Some examples for set type definition are given below:

> *Digits* = {*0, 1, 2, 3, 4, 5, 6, 7, 8, 9*}
> *Even* = {*n* ∈ $\mathbb{N}$ | *n* **mod** *2 = 0*}
> – no predicate part
> *Even* = {*n* | *n* ∈ $\mathbb{N}$ ∧ *n* **mod** *2 = 0*}
> – type inferred from declaration; no predicate part
> *Even* = {*n* | *n* ∈ $\mathbb{N}$ • *n* **mod** *2 = 0*}
> *Person* = **token**
> *Employee* = *Person*-**set**

Operator	Synopsis	Meaning
card	**card** S	cardinality of the set S
$\in$	$x \in S$	x is a member of the set S
$\cup$	$S_1 \cup S_2$	set union
$\cap$	$S_1 \cap S_2$	set intersection
$\backslash$	$S_1 \backslash S_2$	set difference
$\subseteq$	$S_1 \subseteq S_2$	subset
$\subset$	$S_1 \subset S_2$	proper subset
$=$	$S_1 = S_2$	set equality
$\neq$	$S_1 \neq S_2$	set inequality
$\bigcup$	$\bigcup SS$	distributed union of the sets SS
$\bigcap$	$\bigcap SS$	distributed intersection of the sets SS
$\{i,\ldots,j\}$	$\{i,\ldots,j\}$	subset of integers from i to j, both inclusive

TABLE 9.4. Set operators.

Empty set is denoted by {}.

Table 9.4 enumerates the VDM-SL operators on sets. The semantics for these operators is derived from set theory.

Notice that there is no symbol in VDM-SL for superset and proper superset; instead, they can be specified using the symbols for subset and proper subset.

Sequence

A sequence type can be defined using the declarative syntax, as a type or using the constructive style as enumeration and comprehension. The two forms of declarative syntax for sequences are T^* and T^+ in which T denotes the type of elements of the sequence. The declaration T^+ defines a nonempty sequence type, whereas the declaration T^* introduces a general sequence type that includes an empty sequence with no value.

The syntax for sequence enumeration is similar to that for sets, except the parentheses "{" and "}" in sets are replaced by the square brackets "[" and "]", respectively. For example,

$Vowels = [\text{'a', 'e', 'i', 'o', 'u'}]$

introduces the sequence *Vowels* having five members.

Sequence comprehension uses the syntax that is similar to that of set comprehension in which the curly parentheses are replaced by square brackets. Thus,

$Cubes = [\, n \uparrow 3 \mid n \in \{1,2,3\} \,]$

refers to the sequence [1,8,27]. This sequence can also be written as

$$Cubes = [\, m \in \mathbb{N} \mid m = n \uparrow 3 \wedge n \in \{1,2,3\} \,]$$

The ordering of the elements in the sequence *Cubes* depends on the natural order of elements in the set {1, 2, 3}. Thus, the following definitions denote the same sequence.

$$Cubes_1 = [\, m \in \mathbb{N} \mid m = n \uparrow 3 \wedge n \in \{1,2,3\} \,]$$
$$Cubes_2 = [\, m \in \mathbb{N} \mid m = n \uparrow 3 \wedge n \in \{1,\ldots,3\} \,]$$
$$Cubes_3 = [\, m \in \mathbb{N} \mid m = n \uparrow 3 \wedge n \in \{3,2,1\} \,]$$

Empty sequence is represented by [ ].

Individual elements of a sequence can be accessed by subscripts as in *d(5)*, *d(i)*, and *d(i + j − k)*. The parentheses are part of the syntax. In the second and third cases, the variable "i" and the expression "i + j − k" must be of type $\mathbb{N}_1$. By convention, VDM-SL sequences always start at the index position 1.

Operators on sequences are listed in Table 9.5. The semantics of most of the operators on sequences are given in Chapter 7; this is reinforced in the following example.

Example 9.2   *Operations on a sequence.*

Let $S_1 = [a,b,c,d,e]$, $S_2 = [b,c,d,e,a]$, $S_3 = [f,g,h]$ and $SS = [S_1\ S_2\ S_3]$

Operator	Synopsis	Meaning
len	**len** S	length of the sequence S
⁀	$S_1 \frown S_2$	sequence concatenation
conc	**conc** SS	distributed concatenation of the sequence of sequences SS
hd	**hd** S	head of the sequence S
tl	**tl** S	tail of the sequence S
inds	**inds** S	indices of the sequence S; returned as a set of positive integers
elems	**elems** S	set of elements comprising the sequence S
(i,...,j)	S(i,...,j)	subsequence of S from the ith element to the jth element, both inclusive.
=	$S_1 = S_2$	sequence equality
≠	$S_1 \neq S_2$	sequence inequality

TABLE 9.5. Sequence operators.

$$S_1 \frown S_2 = [a,b,c,d,e,b,c,d,e,a]$$
$$\textbf{conc } SS = [a,b,c,d,e,b,c,d,e,a,f,g,h]$$
$$\textbf{inds } S_1 = \{1,2,3,4,5\}$$
$$\textbf{inds } S_2 = \{1,2,3,4,5\}$$
$$\textbf{inds } S_3 = \{1,2,3\}$$
$$\textbf{elems } S_1 = \{a,b,c,d,e\}$$
$$\textbf{elems } S_2 = \{a,b,c,d,e\}$$
$$\textbf{elems } S_3 = \{f,g,h\}$$
$$S_1 \ (1,\ldots,3) = [a,b,c]$$
$$S_3 \ (2,\ldots,2) = [g]$$
$$S_2 \ (3,\ldots,2) = \textbf{undefined} \text{ since } j < i \qquad\qquad \blacksquare$$

Map

A map in VDM-SL is an abstraction of a finite function. As with functions, a map also has a *domain* and a *range*. A map associates each element from the domain to at most one element in the range. It is convenient to think of a map as a finite table of pairs where each domain element appears at most once. A map can be defined declaratively as a type or can be constructively defined by enumeration or comprehension. The VDM-SL syntax for map is

$$D \xrightarrow{m} R$$

where D is the domain of the map and R is its range. The symbol $\xrightarrow{m}$ is part of the syntax. In the following example, M denotes a map type from X to Y:

$$X = \{1, 2, 3, 4, 5\}$$
$$Y = \{1, 8, 27, 64, 125\}$$
$$M = X \xrightarrow{m} Y$$

Individual elements of a map can be enumerated as

$$M_1 = \{1 \mapsto 1, 2 \mapsto 8, 3 \mapsto 27, 4 \mapsto 64, 5 \mapsto 125\}$$

The symbols "{", "$\mapsto$" and "}" are part of the syntax. The empty map is represented as $\{\mapsto\}$.

The syntax for map comprehension closely resembles that of set comprehension:

$$M_2 = \{n \mapsto m \mid n \in X \wedge m \in Y \bullet m = n \uparrow 3\}$$

Notice that maps in VDM-SL are finite. It is possible to define a map type T in which the domain type is infinite (e.g., $\mathbb{N}$). However, when a variable v is declared to be of type T, the domain of v must be constrained to a finite set. This can be achieved by specifying a condition on v. See the following example:

Operator	Synopsis	Meaning
dom	**dom** M	domain of the map M
rng	**rng** M	range of the map M
M^{-1}	M^{-1}	inverse of the map M; M should be an injective map; $M^{-1} = \{b \mapsto a \mid a \mapsto b \in M\}$
$\cup$	$M_1 \cup M_2$	map union
$\dagger$	$M_1 \dagger M_2$	map overriding
$\circ$	$M_1 \circ M_2$	map composition
( )	M(a)	map application
$\triangleleft$	$D \triangleleft M$	domain restriction
$\triangleleft\!\!\!-$	$D \triangleleft\!\!\!- M$	domain subtraction
$\triangleright$	$M \triangleright R$	range restriction
$\triangleright\!\!\!-$	$M \triangleright\!\!\!- R$	range subtraction

TABLE 9.6. Map operators.

$$M_3 = \mathbb{N}_1 \xrightarrow{m} \mathbb{N}_1$$
$$Cubes : M_3 = \{n \mapsto m \mid n \leq 5 \bullet m = n \uparrow 3\}$$

Table 9.6 summarizes map operators in VDM-SL. The semantics for many of these operators have been discussed in Chapter 7. The following example reinforces the semantics:

Example 9.3   *Operations on a map.*

Let $M_1 = \{1 \mapsto a, 2 \mapsto b, 3 \mapsto c\}$, $M_2 = \{1 \mapsto a, 3 \mapsto a\}$,
    $M_3 = \{a \mapsto \theta, b \mapsto \phi, c \mapsto \psi\}$ and $M_4 = \{1 \mapsto a, 4 \mapsto d\}$.

$$M_1^{-1} = \{a \mapsto 1, b \mapsto 2, c \mapsto 3\}$$

Notice that the inverse of a map M need not be a map; however, if M is bijective, the inverse M^{-1} of M is bijective. Note that M_2^{-1} is not a map.

The union of two maps is defined only if they have consistent maplets. $M_1 \cup M_2$ cannot be determined because the maplets $3 \mapsto c$ in M_1 and $3 \mapsto a$ in M_2 are inconsistent. The union of M_1 and M_4 exists and is given by:

$$M_1 \cup M_4 = \{1 \mapsto a, 2 \mapsto b, 3 \mapsto c, 4 \mapsto d\}$$

$$M_1 \dagger M_2 = \{1 \mapsto a, 2 \mapsto b, 3 \mapsto a\}$$

Two maps can be composed only if the range of the first map is a subset of the domain of the second map.

$$M_1 \circ M_3 = \{1 \mapsto \theta, 2 \mapsto \phi, 3 \mapsto \psi\}$$

The map composition operator $\circ$ is right-associative. The semantics of domain and range restriction operators are carried over from Chapter 7.

$$\{1\} \lhd M_1 = \{1 \mapsto a\}$$
$$\{1\} \ntriangleleft M_1 = \{2 \mapsto b, 3 \mapsto c\}$$
$$M_2 \rhd \{a\} = \{1 \mapsto a, 3 \mapsto a\}$$
$$M_2 \ntriangleright \{a\} = \{ \mapsto \}$$
$$M_1(1) = a, M_2(3) = a, M_4(4) = d \qquad \blacksquare$$

Record

While set and sequence types are constructed from the same type of elements, a composite type with different component types can be represented by a *record* type. VDM-SL syntax for a record is

$$T :: v_1 : T_1$$
$$ v_2 : T_2$$
$$ \dots$$
$$ v_n : T_n$$

where T is a record type and $T_1, T_2, \dots, T_n$ represent the types of components of T. These components, called *fields*, are identified by the variables $v_1, v_2, \dots, v_n$. The symbol "::" is part of the syntax. The record type given below defines a collection of books:

$$Book :: title : String$$
$$ author : String$$
$$ year : \mathbb{N}$$

Individual fields of a composite type can be extracted using the selection operator "." as in *Book.author* and *Book.year*. An object of the composite type can be constructed using the "**mk-**" (make) function on the values of the individual fields. For example, if *tit, aut*, and *y* are the values of the individual fields of a book, the book object can be constructed as

mk-*Book (tit, aut, y)*

The arguments for the **mk-** function can be constants, variables, or expressions:

mk-*Book (tit, "John", 1984)*

While constructing an object of a record type, the values of the individual fields in the **mk-** function should be given to match the order and types of the components in the definition of the record type. For example, the **mk-** function

mk-*Book (aut, tit, y)*

is type correct; however, it does not represent the same object as the book

mk-*Book (tit, aut, y)*

Two records r_1 and r_2 of type T are equal if the values of their corresponding fields are equal.

The values of the individual fields of a record can be modified using the μ operator; the syntax for μ operator is

$$\mu \ (<record>, \ <field_1 > \mapsto <value_1 >, \ <field_2 > \mapsto <value_2 >, \ldots,$$
$$<field_n > \mapsto <value_n >)$$

The expression

$\mu \ (Book, \ title \mapsto \text{``Set Theory''}, \ author \mapsto \text{``Shaw''}, \ year \mapsto 1945)$ denotes the book "Set Theory" written by "Shaw" with its date of publication "1945."

Cartesian product

A *Cartesian product* type is an ordered collection of types grouped together by a single name. VDM-SL syntax for Cartesian product type is

$$T = T_1 \times T_2 \times \ldots \times T_n$$

where T is the name of the product type and $T_1, T_2, \ldots, T_n$ are the component types. The symbol "$\times$" is part of the syntax. Cartesian product types are not associative. They can be compared for equality. Two product types T_1 and T_2 are equal if and only if the order and the types of individual components in both product types are the same. For example, if the types *Book, Monograph, Collection,* and *Lecture_notes* are defined as

$Book = String \times String \times \mathbb{N}$
$Collection = String \times String \times \mathbb{N}$
$Monograph = \mathbb{N} \times String \times String$
$Lecture\_notes = String \times (String \times \mathbb{N})$

then

Book = Collection
Book ≠ Monograph   – ordering different
Book ≠ Lecture_notes   – types mismatch

The elements of a Cartesian product type are called *tuples*. A tuple belonging to a Cartesian product type can be constructed using **mk-** function. As an example, a tuple of type *Book* can be constructed as follows:

mk-*("Set Theory", "Shaw", 1945)*

Notice that the **mk-** function for tuples does not involve any name, which is in contrast to the **mk-** function for records. As a result, one cannot infer the product type of a tuple from the **mk-** function. For example, the tuple

mk-*("Set Theory", "Shaw", 1945)*

may belong to either *Book* or *Collection* or both.

Function types

A function type has a domain and a range, and its elements are functions having the same domain and range. Thus, in

$F = \mathbb{N} \to \mathbb{N}$

F is a function type that defines the set of all functions from natural numbers to natural numbers. The values of a function type can be given using a lambda expression or using a function definition. Following are some instances of the function type F:

$(\lambda\, n : \mathbb{N} \bullet n + 2) \in F$
    – *accepts n, returns n* + 2
$(\lambda\, n : \mathbb{N} \bullet n^2) \in F$
    – *accepts n, returns n*^{2}
$(\lambda\, n : \mathbb{N} \bullet n \textbf{ mod } 2) \in F$
    – *accepts n, returns n* **mod** 2

Flat types

Function types in VDM-SL are treated separately and are called *non-flat types*. Correspondingly, the values of a non-flat type are called *non-flat values*. Non-flat types and non-flat values can be used just like their flat counterparts such as set, sequence, map, and Cartesian product, except in the following situations:

1. Non-flat types can neither be passed as parameters to operations nor be returned as results from operations; however, they can be passed as parameters or results of a function.

2. Values of set and map types should not contain non-flat values. For example, in

$$Square = (\lambda\, n : \mathbb{N} \bullet n^2)$$
$$Squares\text{-}set = Square\text{-}\mathbf{set}$$

the type *Squares-set* is not valid since elements of this set are non-flat values. Constructors of set and map types cannot be applied to non-flat types.

3. State and local variable declarations should not contain non-flat types.

4. Equality and inequality are not defined for non-flat values.

9.2.4   Patterns, Bindings, and Values

A pattern in VDM-SL is a template consisting of a nonempty collection of identifiers, symbols, and values. The purpose of a pattern is to match the entities in the template to a set of values of appropriate types. Table 9.7 lists some patterns, the types for the identifiers in the patterns, and their matching values. When an identifier in a pattern matches a value, a binding occurs between them. For example, if a pattern (x, y) matches the value (2, 3), then the binding "x to 2 and y to 3" occurs. Pattern matching and binding are tightly coupled in the sense that they always occur together. VDM-SL supports tuple patterns, set patterns, sequence patterns, and record patterns. Table 9.7 lists several tuple patterns. While defining a set or a sequence pattern, the set or the sequence cannot be defined using comprehension. Record patterns match with values of records with the same record tag. Record patterns are generally used in defining type invariants, state invariants, and initial state conditions. The initial state definition

$$\mathbf{init}\ \mathbf{mk\text{-}}\mathit{Reservation\ (rooms)}\quad \triangleq$$
$$\forall\ rn \in dom\ rooms \bullet rooms(rn) = \mathit{Available}$$

in Example 9.1 involves a record pattern matching the record *Reservation*. Patterns may sometimes include *don't care identifiers* as in (x, -, y). In such a case, the pattern denotes a tuple with three components that match with any 3-tuple value as long as the types of *x* and that of the first component are the same and the types of *y* and that of the third component are the same. The matching of the second component is ignored. For example, if x and y are both natural numbers, then both tuples (0, {1,2,3}, 10) and (15, [3,4,7], 32) will match the pattern (x, -, y).

Table 9.8 illustrates the values that match some set and sequence patterns:

Pattern	Type Information	Some Possible Matching Values	Comment
x	$x : \mathbb{Z}$	-15 2478 0 . . .	any integer value
(x, y)	$x : \mathbb{N}, y : \mathbb{N}$	(0,0) (1,2) (10,12) . . .	pair of natural numbers
(4, n, b)	$n : \mathbb{Z}, b : \mathbb{R}$	(4,0,1.6) (4,-7,-3.68) (4,17,0.0) . . .	The first value must be the integer constant "4"
(x, –, y)	$x : \mathbb{Z}, y : \mathbb{Z}$	0, {1,2,3}, 10 15, [3,4,7], 32 1, 2, 3 . . .	triple with second element as "don't care"

TABLE 9.7. Simple patterns.

Pattern	Type Information	Some Possible Matching Values	Comment
{a,b,c}	$a,b,c : \mathbb{Z}$	{1,2,3} {-100,0,100} . . .	set of three integers
$s_1 \cup s_2$	$s_1, s_2 : \mathbb{Z}\text{-}\mathbf{set}$	{1,8} ∪ {7,8} {} ∪ {3,7} . . .	union of two integer sets
$s_1 \setminus \{5\}$	$s_1 : \mathbb{Z}\text{-}\mathbf{set}$	{} \ {5} {1,5,7} \ {5} . . .	difference between two integer sets; the second set must be a singleton with its only element as "5"
[a,b,c]	$a,b,c : \mathbb{Z}\text{-}\mathbf{set}$	[{1,2}, {5}, {2, 0, -17}] [{}, {}, {}] . . .	sequence of three integer sets
$t_1 \frown t_2$	$t_1, t_2 : \mathbf{char}^*$	['a'] ⌢ ['b'] ['a','b','c'] ⌢ [ ] . . .	concatenation of two character sequences

TABLE 9.8. Set and sequence patterns.

9.2.5   State Representation

A model of the software system under development can be constructed using the VDM-SL type definitions and structures introduced in the previous sections. A VDM specification for a problem consists of a *state*, which includes data type representations for problem domain objects, and *operations*, which express the changes to the state variables consistent with the requirements of the problem. In other words, the state is a model of the problem and operations on the state bring out the behavior of the model. The following example illustrates the construction of a model from the requirements.

Example 9.4   *Course registration system.*

This example constructs a model of a course registration system based on the following set of requirements:

A course registration software system maintains information on the courses offered by a department in one semester. Each course has only one section of offering. Information on the courses completed and the courses currently taken by the students in the department, the times of course offerings, the days on which a course is offered, and the faculty members who teach these courses are to be recorded. A course has a unique name and a unique number. A course may have a finite number of prerequisite courses. A teacher teaches a finite number of courses.

The model

Every course has a name, a number, a place and time of offering, and has a set of prerequisite courses. So, it can be modeled as a record type consisting of the fields: course-name, course-number, classroom, days, start-time, end-time, pre-requisites:

> *Course :: course-name : String*
> *course-number : String*
> *classroom : Room*
> *days : WeekDays–***set**
> *start-time : Time*
> *ending-time : Time*
> *pre-requisites : String–***set**   *– course names*

The type *String* is assumed to be a basic type for this level of specification and will not be defined further. Therefore, it can be defined using the **token** type.

> *String* = **token**

Every room has a unique room number, possibly prefixed by the building where the room is situated. Based on this domain knowledge, we may define the type

Room to be a union of subsets of natural numbers where each number uniquely identifies one classroom.

$$Room = \{100,\ldots,120\} \cup \{200,\ldots,220\} \cup \{300,\ldots,320\}$$

The type *WeekDays* defines the days in a week and is modeled as a quote type.

$$WeekDays = \text{MONDAY} \mid \text{TUESDAY} \mid \text{WEDNESDAY} \mid \text{THURSDAY} \mid \\ \text{FRIDAY}$$

Time can be modeled as an ordered pair of integers, representing hours and minutes. This could be modeled either as record type or as cartesian product type. The latter representation is used here.

$$Time = \{0,\ldots,23\} \times \{0,\ldots,59\}$$

The record types *Student* and *Teacher* model students and teachers, respectively. A student has a name and an identification number. Information on courses completed and courses currently taken are modeled as sets of courses. This information is held as part of a student record to show the association between a student and courses taken by a student. A teacher has a name and teaches a finite set of courses. From these requirements, the record types for student and teacher entities are constructed.

> *Student* :: *name* : *String*
>   *idnumber* : *String*
>   *courses-finished* : *Course*–**set**
>   *courses-taken* : *Course*–**set**

> *Teacher* :: *name* : *String*
>   *courses-teaching* : *Course*–**set**

The state of the course registration system is modeled using the three types *Course, Student*, and *Teacher*.

> **state** *Department* **of**
>   *courses* : *Course*–**set**
>   *students* : *Student*–**set**
>   *teachers* : *Teacher*–**set**
> **end**

The model that we have constructed reflects the requirements and no more. It inherits some domain knowledge, in this case from a University environment, in defining the state to consist of the entities that are relevant to course registration.

The three state variables are *courses*, *students*, and *teachers*; the identifiers *String*, *Course*, *Room*, *WeekDays*, *Time*, *Student*, and *Teacher* are type names. The identifier *Department* is the name of the state.   ■

9.2.6 Invariants

An invariant of an entity is an assertion constraining the behavior of that entity. The properties implied by the invariant must be preserved before and after every operation performed on that entity in order to ensure the correct behavior of that entity. There are two types of invariants in VDM—*type invariant* and *state invariant*. A type invariant, as the name implies, is associated with a type. A type invariant constrains type construction. All built-in types have well-defined constructors. For each user-defined composite type, constraints if any, should be stated as an invariant. Type invariant in VDM is quite similar to integrity constraints in databases. A state invariant, associated with a state space definition, constrains the behavior of the system when it is subject to modifications by the operations specified on the state.

Type Invariant   The invariants for types and the state in course registration problem are as follows: The type invariant for *Course* can be expressed as a conjunction of two predicates: (1) the starting time of a course should be earlier than its ending time, and (2) the set of prerequisites for a course should not include the course itself:

$$\textbf{inv mk-}\textit{Course (cn, c\#, rm, d, st, et, pr)} \quad \triangleq \quad \textit{earlier (st, et)} \land cn \notin pr$$

The expression

$$\textbf{mk-}\textit{Course (cn, c\#, rm, d, st, et, pr)}$$

constructs an instance of the type *Course*. The invariant asserts that for every instance, the conjunction

$$\textit{earlier (st, et)} \land cn \notin pr$$

holds. The boolean function *earlier (st, et)* is not yet defined; its intended meaning is that the function will return the value *true* if *st* precedes *et* in a 24-hour clock time. A type invariant for *Student* is that a student is not permitted to repeat a completed course. That is, the set of courses completed by a student and the set of courses currently taken by the student should be distinct:

$$\textbf{inv mk-}\textit{Student (n, id, cf, ct)} \quad \triangleq \quad cf \cap ct = \{\}$$

State Invariant   The state invariant for *Department* is a conjunction of the following constraints: (1) all prerequisite courses for a course should be offered by the same department; (2) the courses completed and the courses currently taken by each student in the department must be offered by the same department; and (3) the courses taught by every teacher are offered by the same department.

inv mk_Department *(cs, sts, ts)* $\triangleq$
   $\forall\ c \in cs \bullet c.pre\text{-}requisites \subset cs \land$
   $\forall\ st \in sts \bullet (st.courses\text{-}finished \subseteq cs \land st.courses\text{-}taken \subseteq cs) \land$
   $\forall\ t \in ts \bullet t.courses\text{-}teaching \subseteq cs$

A type invariant constrains the values that an object of the type can assume. If the type is composite, it cannot relate a component to another variable or constant outside the definition of a composite type. A state invariant asserts the relationships among the state variables. It can also relate the state variables with other type declarations and global constants. For example, if the type of a state variable is a union type, any assertion involving this state variable will require the definitions of all component types of the union type.

9.3   Operational Abstraction

While representational abstraction describes the objects in the domain of a software system, the observable behavior of the model is captured through operational abstraction. In VDM-SL, operational abstraction is defined by functions and operations. The behavior of the model is defined by describing the effects of functions and operations on the model. The major difference between functions and operations is that functions do not access global variables, while operations not only access global variables, but may change them.

The syntax for an operation definition in VDM-SL has a separate clause that identifies all global variables accessed in that operation, thereby making the difference between functions and operations explicit. An operation may be defined either implicity or explicitly in VDM-SL. In the implicit style, a function or an operation is specified by two sets of assertions, called *precondition* and *postcondition*. Explicit style uses constructive methods for operation definitions.

The precondition of a function is a boolean expression that is true only on those input values to which the function may be applied. The postcondition of a function is another boolean expression that states how the result of the function is related to its input. The precondition of an operation is an assertion on the state of the system that must be true before the operation is invoked in that state. The postcondition of an operation is an assertion that states the relationship among the state variables after a successful termination of the operation. If the function or the operation does not terminate, the postcondition is not valid. If the precondition of a function or an operation fails, the status of the corresponding postcondition is undefined.

9.3.1 **Let** Expression

When a complex expression is repeatedly used in a specification, it is convenient to assign a name for it and use the name instead of the full expression. This naming convention is only a syntactic sugar that simplifies typing and improves readability of the specification. VDM-SL provides such a syntactic sugar through the **let** expression. A **let** expression has the following syntax:

> **let** <*definition*> **in** <*expression*>

The <*definition*> clause is of the form

> <*variable*> : <*type*> = <*expression*$_1$ >   or
> <*variable*> = <*expression*$_1$ >

The term <*expression*> uses <*definition*> given in the **let** expression and hence defines the scope of the **let** expression. Multiple <expression> definitions can be given, provided they are separated by commas. See the examples below:

> **let** *student : Student* = **mk-***Student* (*"John Major"*, *"12345"*, {}, *SoftEng*) **in**
>   *validate_student (student)*
>   . . .
> **let** *origin* = **mk-***Point (0.0, 0.0)*, *p* = **mk-***Point (x, y)* **in**
>   *distance (p, origin)* = . . .
>   . . .
> **let** *axis* = **mk-***LineSegment* (**mk-***Point (x,y)*, **mk-***Point(p,q)*) **in**
>   . . .

9.3.2 Function Definitions

There are four kinds of function definitions in VDM-SL.

Implicit Function

An implicit function in VDM-SL characterizes the result by stating the properties. The syntax is

> *fun* $(p_1 : t_1, p_2 : t_2, \ldots, p_n : t_n)$ *p : t*
> **pre** *B*
> **post** *B'*

where *func* is the name of the function, $p_1, p_2, \ldots, p_n$ are input parameters of types $t_1, t_2, \ldots, t_n$, respectively, p is the output parameter of type t, and B, and B' are boolean expressions.

The function *find* given below is an example of an implicit function. If a given element is found in the sequence, the function returns its index. If the element is not a member of the sequence, the function returns zero. The sequence in this example is defined as a nonempty and non-duplicating sequence.

> *find (S : X⁺, x : X) result :* $\mathbb{N}$
> **pre card elems** *S =* **len** *S*   *– non-duplicating*
> **post**
>   *(*∃ *i* ∈ *{1,...,***len** *S}* • *S(i) = x)* ⇒ *result = i* ∧
>   ¬ *(*∃ *i* ∈ *{1,...,***len** *S}* • *S(i) = x)* ⇒ *result = 0*

Sometimes one may want to introduce only the signature of an implicit function without giving its definition. The signatures of all the functions used in the specification must be stated. Where the definition is not given, the signature of the function is augmented with the phrase **is not yet defined**, as in

> *fun-one (p₁ : t₁, p₂ : t₂, ..., pₖ : tₖ) p : t* **is not yet defined**

An implicit function may have an empty set of input parameters, in which case the function is treated as a constant. Implicit functions may be recursively defined; however, recursion can occur only in the postcondition.

Explicit Function

The explicit style of a function specification has two components—function declaration and function definition. The declaration of a function includes only its signature.

> *fun-two :* $t_1 \times t_2 \times \ldots \times t_n \to t$

The syntax for the definition of an explicit function is

> *fun-two (p₁, p₂, ..., pₙ)* $\triangleq$ *E*
> **pre** *B*

where E denotes an expression of type t and the parameters $p_1, p_2, \ldots, p_n$ are of types $t_1, t_2, \ldots, t_n$, respectively. The precondition is optional.

The function *max* given below is written using the explicit style:

$$max : \mathbb{Z} \times \mathbb{Z} \to \mathbb{Z}$$
$$max\ (x, y) \quad \triangleq \quad \textbf{if}\ x > y\ \textbf{then}\ x\ \textbf{else}\ y$$
$$\textbf{pre}\ x \neq y$$

An explicit function may be recursive and can be defined with or without input parameters. The result of an explicit function can be an undefined value, in which case the keyword **undefined** is used to denote the result.

Higher-Order Function

VDM-SL also permits the definition of higher-order functions, known as *curried functions*. A function is a curried function if its output is another function, instead of a value. Curried functions can be defined only explicitly. The exponentiation function for integer arguments can be defined as a curried function:

$$power : \mathbb{N}_1 \to \mathbb{N} \to \mathbb{N}_1$$
$$power\ (n)(x) \quad \triangleq \quad n \uparrow x$$

The function takes a positive number n as input and returns a function $f = power(n)$, which can compute $n \uparrow x$ for any argument x.

Polymorphic Function

A function is polymorphic, or *generic*, if its definition can be given as a template that can be instantiated with appropriate parameters. For example, the function $f[T]$ is a generic function whose definition does not depend on the type of the formal parameter T. Later, when we instantiate f with some element, say a set, the complete definition of f will be available. The built-in function **elems** for sequence types is polymorphic:

$$elems\ [@S] : @S^* \to @S\text{-}\textbf{set}$$
$$elems\ (s) \quad \triangleq \quad \textbf{if}\ s = [\ ]\ \textbf{then}\ \{\}$$
$$\textbf{else hd}\ s \cup \textbf{elems}\ (\textbf{tl}\ s)$$

Notice that $@S$ in the above function may be of any type and the definition of **elems** does not depend on the type $@S$. The square bracket surrounding $@S$ is part of VDM-SL syntax for defining generic functions.

The function *subsequence* defined below is also generic, which asserts whether or not a given sequence *small* is a subsequence of another sequence *large*:

$$subsequence[@X] : @X^* \times @X^* \to \mathbb{B}$$
$$subsequence\ (small, large) \quad \triangleq$$
$$\exists\ i,j \in \textbf{inds}\ large \mid j > i \wedge \textbf{len}\ small = j - i + 1\ \bullet$$
$$\exists\ m : (\textbf{inds}\ small) \xrightarrow{m} i \ldots j\ \bullet$$
$$\forall\ k \in \textbf{inds}\ small \bullet small(k) = large(m(k))$$

9.3.3 Operation Definitions

There are two styles of operation definitions in VDM-SL.

Implicit Operation

The syntax for implicit operation is given below:

$$oper\ (p_1 : t_{11},\ p_2 : t_{12},\ \ldots,\ p_n : t_{1n})\ p\mathord{:}\ t$$
$$\textbf{ext } \textit{<mode>}\ g_1 : t_{21}$$
$$\textit{<mode>}\ g_2 : t_{22}$$
$$\ldots$$
$$\textit{<mode>}\ g_k : t_{2k}$$
$$\textbf{pre } B$$
$$\textbf{post } B\text{'}$$
$$\textbf{err } e_1 : B_1 \to B_1^{'}$$
$$e_2 : B_2 \to B_2^{'}$$
$$\ldots$$
$$e_m : B_m \to B_m^{'}$$

The syntax of an implicit operation is similar to the syntax of an implicit function; however, it includes the two additional clauses: *external clause* **ext** and *error block* **err**. The external clause lists all the global variables that are accessed in this operation. The declaration of each global variable is preceded by <mode>, which is either **rd** or **wr** indicating "read" and "write" attributes, respectively, of the global variable within the scope of that operation. If the mode is **wr** for a variable, the value of that variable might have been changed when the operation successfully terminates.

The error block contains a list of named error conditions labelled by the identifiers denoted as e_i's. An error condition has its own precondition B_i and a postcondition $B_i^{'}$. If one or more of the error preconditions hold, then the effect of the operation is the conjunction of the corresponding postconditions.

Let us consider the state space definition of the course registration system. An operation that adds a new student to this system can be written in implicit style as follows:

$$Message = \text{SUCCESS} \mid \text{ERROR} - \text{add these to } \textbf{types}$$
$$add\text{-}student\ (n : String,\ id : String)\ report : Message$$
$$\textbf{ext wr } students : Student\text{–}\textbf{set}$$
$$\textbf{pre } \forall\ s \in students \bullet s.idnumber \neq id$$
$$\textbf{post}$$
$$students = \overleftarrow{students} \cup \{\textbf{mk-}Student\ (n,\ id,\ \{\},\ \{\})\} \wedge$$
$$report = SUCCESS$$

err *already-exists :*
$(\exists \; s \in students \bullet s.idnumber = id) \rightarrow report = ERROR;$

The hook notation $\overleftarrow{students}$ denotes the value of the global variable *students* in the prestate of the operation. The value of the same variable after the operation is written without the hook. The postcondition asserts the inclusion of a new student record in *students* and reports the success of the operation. The hook notation is applicable only to global variables, thus indicating state changes. Consequently, it should appear only in postconditions.

The definition of an implicit operation can also be left incomplete by adding the phrase "**is not yet defined**". VDM-SL does not permit recursive operation definitions.

Explicit Operation

The signature of an explicit operation in VDM-SL is

$$oper\text{-}two : t_1 \times t_2 \times \ldots \times t_n \xrightarrow{o} t$$

The symbol $\xrightarrow{o}$ makes the syntactic difference between the signature of an explicit function and that of an explicit operation. The definition of an explicit operation is given as follows:

$$oper\text{-}two \; (p_1, p_2, \ldots, p_n)$$
$$\triangleq \quad St$$
$$\textbf{pre} \; B$$

where $p_1, p_2, \ldots, p_n$ are, respectively, the parameters of type $t_1, t_2, \ldots, t_n$, and *St* refers to a statement. We discuss statements in detail in the next section. The operation returns a result of type *t* through a **return** statement.

The following explicit operation adds a new teacher to the course registration system:

$$add\text{-}teacher: String \times Course\text{-}\mathbf{set} \xrightarrow{o} Message$$
$$add\text{-}teacher \; (n, ct) \quad \triangleq$$
$$teachers := teachers \cup \{\mathbf{mk\text{-}}Teacher \; (n, ct)\};$$
$$\mathbf{return} \; SUCCESS$$
$$\mathbf{pre} \; \forall \; t \in teachers \bullet t.name \neq n;$$

The definition for *add-teacher* consists of two statements: an assignment statement (indicated by :=), and a return statement. The semicolon between the two statements indicates sequential composition of statements. Unlike implicit operations, there is no **ext** clause in the definition of an explicit operation. It is assumed that an explicit operation can modify all the variables in the state in which the operation is defined. Thus, the operation *add-teacher* modifies the state variable *teachers*.

9.4 Statements

VDM-SL also supports statements, quite similar to those found in programming languages such as Pascal and C. Statements are generally used during refinement of VDM specifications. A specification written in assertional style can be refined into another specification written using statements. The refined specification resembles a program except that execution control is not present. Therefore, it seems easier to map the refined specification into a program in one of the block structured languages. Because of these advantages, VDM is considered as a software development environment or framework rather than a simple specification language.

Table 9.9 gives a partial list of statements supported by VDM-SL; see [27] for a complete list. Below, we discuss some of the distinguishing features of these statements.

Let statement   The semantics of **let** statement is similar to that of the **let** expression in VDM-SL, except that the <definition> in **let** statement is applied to a statement rather than to an expression.

Assignment statement   The <designator> in assignment statement is an identifier whose type is the same as that of <expression> in the assignment statement. This identifier must have been declared before the assignment statement. The semantics of the assignment statement is to overwrite the value previously held by <designator>. Therefore, the assignment statement does not use the hook notation (e.g., $\overset{\frown}{previous}$) for a variable in <expression>. A major advantage of the assignment statement is that it can be used to modify only a portion of a state variable when the variable is of composite type.

Declare statement   A declare statement is used to introduce local variables to a block of statements. The block of statements is enclosed in parantheses that also define the scope of variables introduced through the declare statement.

For statement   VDM-SL supports five kinds of **for** statements. The first two of these statements are similar to those found in programming languages. The statement

for all <pattern> ∈ <expression> **do** <statement>

Statement	Syntax
let statement	**let** \<definition\> **in** \<statement\>
assignment statement	\<designator\> := \<expression\>
conditional statement	**if** \<expression\> **then** \<statement\> **else** \<statement\>

case statement	**cases** \<expression\>:
	    \<pattern$_1$ \> $\rightarrow$ \<statement$_1$ \>,
	    \<pattern$_2$ \> $\rightarrow$ \<statement$_2$ \>,
	    . . .
	    \<pattern$_n$ \> $\rightarrow$ \<statement$_n$ \>,
	    others $\rightarrow$ \<statement$_k$ \>
	end

declare statement	**dcl** \<name\> : \<type\>
	dcl \<name\> : \<type\> := \<initial value\>
block statement	(\<statement\>; . . . ;\<statement\>)
for statement	**for** \<name\> = \<expression\> **to** \<expression\> **do** statement
	for \<name\> = \<expression\> **by** \<expression\> **to** \<expression\> **do** statement
	for all \<pattern\> $\in$ \<expression\> **do** \<statement\>
	for \<pattern\> $\in$ \<expression\> **in** \<expression\> **do** statement
	for \<pattern\> : \<type\> **in** \<expression\> **do** statement
while statement	**while** \<expression\> **do** \<expression\>
return statement	**return** \<expression\>
exit statement	**exit** \<expression\>
error statement	**error**

TABLE 9.9. Statements in VDM-SL.

is used to iterate over all elements of a given set. Generally, this kind of **for** statement is used while refining a universally quantified expression. The last two kinds of **for** statements in Table 9.9 are used to iterate over sequences.

Cases statement   The semantics of a **cases** statement is similar to the `case` statement in Pascal or `switch` statement in C. The <expression> is the key or selector that identifies the choice among the several alternatives. For a given <expression>, one of the patterns may match the key, in which case the corresponding statement will be considered. The statement corresponding to **others** will be considered when none of the listed patterns can match the key. The **others** clause is optional; it can be omitted if the listed alternatives cover all possible patterns. The scope of the **cases** statement ends with the **end** keyword.

The following example illustrates the use of some of these statements:

types
    Mark = {0,...,100};
    IDNumber = **token**;
    Grade = A | B | C | D | F
values
    maxtermwork : $\mathbb{N}$:= 5;
state *Grading* **of**
    termwork : *IDNumber* $\xrightarrow{m}$ *Mark*$^+$
    total : *IDNumber* $\xrightarrow{m}$ *Mark*
    grades : *IDNumber* $\xrightarrow{m}$ *Grade*

    inv mk-*Grading (tw, tt, gr)* $\triangleq$
       dom *tw* = **dom** *tt* = **dom** *gr* $\wedge$
       $\forall$ *id* $\in$ **dom** *tw* • **len** *tw(id)* $\leq$ *maxtermwork*

    init mk-*Grading (–, tt, –)* $\triangleq$
       $\forall$ *id* $\in$ **dom** *tt* • *tt(id)* = 0
end
operations
    compute-grade () $\xrightarrow{o}$ *()* $\triangleq$
       for all *id* $\in$ **dom** *termwork* **do**
          (**dcl** *i* : $\mathbb{N}$:= 1; *sum* : $\mathbb{N}$:= 0;
          while *(i* $\leq$ **len** *termwork(id))* **do**
             (sum := sum + termwork(id)(i);
             i := i + 1;
             );
          if *sum* > *100* **then** *total(id)* := *100* **else** *total(id)* := *sum*;
          let *excellent* = {85,...,100},
            good = {70,...,84},
            fair = {60,...,69},
            pass = {50,...,59} **in**
            cases *true* :

$$total(id) \in excellent \rightarrow grades(id) := A,$$
$$total(id) \in good \rightarrow grades(id) := B,$$
$$total(id) \in fair \rightarrow grades(id) := C,$$
$$total(id) \in pass \rightarrow grades(id) := D,$$
$$\textbf{others} \rightarrow grades(id) := F$$
end
);

The above example specifies the computation of grades for students in a course. The term work for a student is represented by a sequence of marks. The state invariant asserts that the domains of the three maps representing the term work, total, and the grades are the same. The operation *compute-grade* is given in explicit style. The **for** statement iterates over all the elements of the three maps. For each entry, the sum of term work is computed using the **while** loop. This while loop uses a local variable *i* declared using the **dcl** statement. The **if** ... **then** ... **else** statement ensures that the total mark does not exceed 100. The **let** statement introduces four local variables that are used to classify the marks in various grading categories. Finally, the **cases** statement assigns the grade to each student according to the category to which the total mark belongs.

9.5 Specification Examples

VDM-SL specifications consist of type defintions, state space definitions, invariants, functions and operations. Comments are permitted in between the specification text. In this section, we discuss three examples emphasizing the choice of the various structures and type definitions that are appropriate for their modeling. Each example in this section is given in the following format: problem description, additional requirements, assumptions, the model, VDM-SL specification, and comments on the specification.

Example 9.5   *Employment exchange.*

Problem description

An employment exchange collects and manages information on two sets of people—*unemployed*, representing the set of people who have registered with the exchange but not yet employed by any employer, and *employed*, representing the set of people who are employed after registering with the exchange. A person cannot be both in *employed* and in *unemployed* at the same time. Operations for registration and changing status of persons must be made available.

Assumptions

1. Personal details of individuals are not stated in the problem description and consequently will not be included in the employment exchange registry.

2. People, once registered, will not be deleted from the exchange.

The model

Since personal details of individuals are not required to be included in the specification, each person registered with the employment exchange can be modeled as the type *Person*, which is defined to be a **token** type. The state space can be modeled with two collections *employed* and *unemployed*, both of which are of type *Person*-**set**. We choose sets to model the two collections since the problem description does not require an ordering on the registration process.

The state invariant asserts that no person should be in both the sets simultaneously. The initial state of the employment exchange asserts that in the beginning there are no registered members.

The two operations *register* and *change-status* are specified. The operation *register* accepts a person as input, ensures that the person has not been registered with the exchange, and modifies the set *unemployed* to include this person. The operation *change-status* changes the status of the given person from *unemployed* to *employed*.

VDM-SL specification

> **types**
>   *Person* = **token**
> **state** *Emp-Exch* **of**
>   *employed : Person*–**set**
>   *unemployed : Person*–**set**
>   **inv mk-***Emp-Exch (em, unem)* $\triangleq$ *em* ∩ *unem* = {}
>   **init mk-***Emp-Exch (em, unem)* $\triangleq$ *em* = {} ∧ *unem* = {}
> **end**
> **operations**
>   *register (p : Person)*
>   **ext**
>   **wr** *unemployed : Person*–**set**
>   **rd** *employed : Person*–**set**
>   **pre** $p \notin unemployed \land p \notin employed$
>   **post** $unemployed = \overleftarrow{unemployed} \cup \{p\}$;
>
>   *change-status (p : Person)*
>   **ext**

$$\textbf{wr } unemployed : Person\text{–}\textbf{set}$$
$$\textbf{wr } employed : Person\text{–}\textbf{set}$$
$$\textbf{pre } p \in unemployed$$
$$\textbf{post}$$
$$unemployed = \overset{\frown}{unemployed} \setminus \{p\}$$
$$employed = \overset{\frown}{employed} \cup \{p\};$$

Comments

The initialization of the state asserts that none is registered with the exchange initially. Since the operations that modify the state do not have any result parameter, the result of each operation is the truth value of the postcondition of that operation. If the requirements of the employment exchange change, more operations may become necessary. For example, if it is required to re-register a person after the person loses the job, an operation to delete a person from the set of employed persons must be included to the system specification.   ∎

Example 9.6   *Automated transaction machine (ATM).*

Problem description

An automated transaction machine provides fast banking services for depositing and withdrawing cash. Each user of the ATM has a card that is coded with a unique password of the user. To initiate a transaction, the machine is accessed with a card and password. If the password coded in the card matches the password entered by the user, the user is permitted to execute the transaction; otherwise, the transaction is terminated.

It is assumed that only one account can be accessed with one card. The machine allows only two types of transactions—*withdraw* and *deposit*.

Additional requirements

1. Each account in the bank is uniquely identified by an account number.

2. A user can have several accounts with the bank; however, the user needs one card for each account.

3. Several users can share an account; however, every user must have a separate card.

4. The machine has a reserve that can hold a fixed amount of cash.

5. If there is a request to withdraw an amount exceeding the balance in that account or in the machine's reserve, the withdrawl request will not be completed. No partial withdrawal is permitted.

6. The machine's reserve can be modified only by an employee of the bank. Each employee of the bank has a distinct card to access a special account. An employee can update the reserve of the machine using the distinct card.

7. Error messages should be given to user stating why a certain operation is not successful.

Assumptions

1. All account holders have equal privileges.

2. Sufficient funds are deposited into the machine's reserve on a regular basis.

The model

Since no personal details, such as name and address, are mandated by the requirements, it is assumed that users themselves need not be modeled. The cards will be the representatives of the users.

Cards and accounts are modeled as record types. A *card* contains a *card number* and a *password*. An *account* contains an *account number, balance* and *holders*, a set of card numbers associated with this account. The cardinality of the set *holders* is the number of cards associated with the account.

Since each card accesses only one account, the relationship between cards and accounts is modeled as a map. ATM's reserve is modeled as a global variable of type $\mathbb{N}$. Since only an employee can update the bank's reserve, the employee has a distinct card that is mapped to a particular account number. The state of ATM system is modeled by the database of card holders (*dbase*), the bank's reserve (*reserve*), and the special account for updating the reserve (*special-account*).

We provide four operations—*validate-card, withdraw, deposit*, and *update-reserve*. The *validate-card* operation is *internal* to the system and is not accessible to any user of ATM. This operation validates the given card before allowing access to an account. The operation *update-reserve* is restricted to a bank employee who is authorized to access it. The other two operations are accessible to all card holders of ATM.

VDM-SL specification

types
   Card :: card-number : $\mathbb{N}$
           code : $\mathbb{N}$*;*

   Account :: account-number : $\mathbb{N}$
              balance : $\mathbb{N}$
              holders : $\mathbb{N}$**-set***; – set of card numbers*

$$Message = VALID\text{-}CARD \mid INVALID\text{-}CARD \mid UPDATED \mid$$
$$INSUFFICIENT\text{-}BALANCE \mid NO\text{-}MONEY\text{-}IN\text{-}RESERVE;$$

state *ATM* **of**

    dbase : *Card* $\xrightarrow{m}$ *Account*

    reserve : $\mathbb{N}$

    special-account : *Account*   – *Account# for employee's card.*

    inv mk-*ATM* *(db,–, sa)* $\triangleq$

        $(\forall\, ac_1,\, ac_2 \in \mathbf{rng}\; db \bullet ac_1.account\text{-}number = ac_2.account\text{-}number \Leftrightarrow$

        $ac_1 = ac_2) \land$

        $(\forall\, c \in \mathbf{dom}\; db \bullet db(c).holders \neq \{\} \land$

            $\forall\, h \in db(c).holders \bullet$

                $\exists\, ca \in \mathbf{dom}\; db \bullet ca.card\text{-}number = h \land db(ca) = db(c)) \land$

        $(\forall\, h \in sa.holders \bullet \exists\, ca \in \mathbf{dom}\; db \bullet ca.card\text{-}number = h \land$

           $db(ca) = sa) \land$

        $sa.holders \neq \{\}$

    init mk-*ATM* *(–, re, –)* $\triangleq$ *re > 0*

end

operations

    validate-card : *Card* $\times\; \mathbb{N} \xrightarrow{o}$ *Message*

    validate-card (c, n) $\triangleq$

        if *c.code = n* **then return** *VALID-CARD*

                else return *INVALID-CARD*

        pre *c* $\in$ **dom** *dbase;*

    update-reserve : *Card* $\times\; \mathbb{N} \times \mathbb{N} \xrightarrow{o}$ *Message*

    update-reserve (sc, code, amount) $\triangleq$

        reserve := reserve + amount;

        return *UPDATED*

        pre

            validate-card (sc, code) = VALID-CARD $\land$

            dbase(sc) = special-account;

    withdraw : *Card* $\times\; \mathbb{N} \times \mathbb{N} \xrightarrow{o}$ *Message*

    withdraw (c, code, amount) $\triangleq$

        if *dbase(c).balance* $\geq$ *amount* **then**

            if *reserve* $\geq$ *amount* **then**

                (dbase(c).balance := dbase(c).balance − amount;

                reserve := reserve − amount;

                return *UPDATED)*

            else return *NO-MONEY-IN-RESERVE*

        else return *INSUFFICIENT-BALANCE*

        pre *validate-card (c, code) = VALID-CARD;*

$$deposit : Card \times \mathbb{N} \times \mathbb{N} \xrightarrow{o} Message$$
$$deposit\ (c,\ code,\ amount) \quad \triangleq$$
$$\quad dbase(c).balance := dbase(c).balance + amount;$$
$$\quad reserve := reserve + amount;$$
return *UPDATED*
pre *validate-card (c, code) = VALID-CARD;*

Comments

The state invariant asserts that (1) each account has a unique account number; (2) each account is accessible by at least one card; (3) each account that can be accessed by a card should include the corresponding card number in the account; and (4) the number of the card that is used to access the special account must have been recorded in the special account itself. The state invariant in this case is an assertion on the users of the card and not on the reserve of the machine. Consequently, the second parameter to the **mk-** function for the state invariant is not specified. The initial state asserts that there should be some money deposited into the machine's reserve. All operations in this example are given in explicit style. The explicit style enables us to use statements in VDM-SL. In particular, the assignment statement

$$dbase(c).balance := dbase(c).balance - amount;$$

in operation *withdraw* and the assignment statement

$$dbase(c).balance := dbase(c).balance + amount;$$

in operation *deposit* indicate that only part of the record *dbase(c)* is modified without modifying the rest of the record. This is permissible only in explicit operations. ■

Example 9.7   *Home heating system.*

Problem description

A home heating system controls and maintains temperature in each room of the home according to a predefined pattern corresponding to that room. An entry for a room in the pattern consists of an interval of time in a 24-hour clock and the desired temperature during that interval. The control system maintains the temperature in each room at its stable level as defined in the pattern; however, it can also change the temperature in each room dynamically depending on the occupancy of the room. Occupancy is true when there is at least one person in the room and is false when there is nobody in the room. A sensor in each room detects the occupancy.

Additional requirements

1. The home has a finite number of rooms.

2. The three levels of temperature to be maintained in a room are normal, below normal, and above normal.

3. The system permits the temperature in a room to be maintained at one of the three levels during a certain interval of time. Temperature pattern varies from room to room and can be dynamically changed during system operation.

4. If the occupancy in a room changes from true to false or vice versa and is stable for 5 consecutive minutes, the control system adjusts the room temperature according to the following table:

Current Temp. Level	Occupancy	New Temp. Level
normal	True	normal
normal	False	below normal
below normal	True	normal
below normal	False	below normal
above normal	True	above normal
above normal	False	normal

5. There is a sensor in each room that can read the temperature at any given time.

The home heating system includes the following operations: (1) initialize the pattern; (2) activate a pattern at a given time; (3) change the occupancy in a room; and (4) control temperature in a room based on occupancy change.

Assumptions

1. The smallest time unit is a second.

The model

We first model the following data types.

Temperature: We model the temperature using real numbers. It is difficult to ensure the ordering among the temperature levels if it were to be modeled as an enumerated type. Although temperature varies continuously with time, the temperature can be observed only at discrete time points.

Room number: A room number is modeled as a natural number not exceeding a maximum value, the number of rooms in the house.

Sensors: Both temperature sensors and occupancy sensors are defined using token types because the actual description and operations of these sensors are not relevant for the current specification. However, there are functions to read the values indicated by the sensors at a given time.

Time: We model *Time* as a triple representing the hour, minute, and second of a clock. The values of these components are constrained by appropriate invariants so that their values lie within the applicable range (for example, minutes must be between 0 and 59). The reason for choosing this representation is that the pattern entries are defined on time intervals based on a 24-hour clock. The clock itself is not represented in the specification; rather, the current time is obtained by invoking the function *current-time( )* which extracts the current value of time from the clock.

Room information: In order to maintain the information on the pattern for each room and the current temperature in that room, we define the data type *Room-Information*. For each room, the information includes the current temperature in the room and the last time point at which occupancy change occurred in that room. This information helps to check the stability of the occupancy in the room for 5 consecutive minutes, and to control the temperature against the predefined pattern.

Pattern: A pattern is a collection of tuples {(t, T)}, where T is the temperature to be maintained during the interval t. It is sufficient to represent the starting time of the interval and the temperature in that interval. Therefore, a pattern is modeled as a map from time to temperature.

We define functions for obtaining current time, reading temperature from a temperature sensor and reading the occupancy status returned by an occupancy sensor. Since some operations require a metric notion of time, we define a function called *duration*.

The state of the system includes information on the rooms, the patterns for the rooms, and the temperature and occupancy sensors for the rooms. The state of the system is modeled as a collection of maps from room numbers to each of the data types *Temperature-Sensor, Occupancy-Sensor, Room-Information,* and *Pattern*. The state invariant asserts that the domains of the maps in the state are the same, thereby ensuring consistency among the maps. The state is initialized with an empty pattern for each room.

The following operations are specified for the home heating system:

set-pattern: This operation enables the control system to set the pattern for a particular room. The input for this operation consists of the room number and a pattern. The precondition ensures that the room exists in the house and the postcondition asserts that the pattern is replaced.

activate-pattern: The room number and the time at which the pattern is to be activated are passed as input to this operation. The precondition ensures that the room exists in the home, the activation time exists in the pattern for that room, and the current time matches the activation time of the pattern. The postcondition ensures that the temperature in the room is set to the level defined in the pattern for the given time.

occupied: An occupancy change occurs in a room when someone enters into an empty room or when the room becomes empty. The room number is the input to this operation. The postcondition records the change in occupancy and the time at which the occupancy change occurs.

control-temperature: This operation changes the temperature in a room depending upon the occupancy change in the room. The precondition ensures that the occupancy change is stable for 5 consecutive minutes. The postcondition asserts that the change in temperature level happens according to the requirements.

VDM-SL specification

types
    Temperature = $\mathbb{R}$;
    Room-Number = $\mathbb{N}$
    inv *rm* $\triangleq$ *rm* $\leq$ *maxrooms*;
    Temperature-Sensor = **token**;
    Occupancy-Sensor = **token**;
    Time :: *hour* : $\mathbb{Z}$
          minute : $\mathbb{Z}$
          second : $\mathbb{Z}$
    inv mk-*Time* $\triangleq$
        $(0 \leq h \wedge h \leq 23) \wedge$
        $(0 \leq m \wedge m \leq 59) \wedge$
        $(0 \leq m \wedge m \leq 59)$;
    Room-Information :: *set-temperature* : *Temperature*
                        last-occupancy-change : *Time*;
    Pattern = *Time* $\xrightarrow{m}$ *Temperature*
    inv *pat* $\triangleq$
        pat(t) = *normal* $\vee$ *pat(t)* = *below-normal* $\vee$ *pat(t)* = *above-normal*;

values
    maxrooms : $\mathbb{N}_1$:= *10*;
    stable-occupancy : *Time* := **mk-***Time* *(0,5,0)*;
    normal : *Temperature* := *28.0*;
    below-normal : *Temperature* := *25.0*;
    above-normal : *Temperature* := *31.0*;

functions
    current-time : *()* $\rightarrow$ *Time*;

read-temperature : Temperature-Sensor × *Time* → *Temperature;*

check-occupancy : Occupancy-Sensor × *Time* → $\mathbb{B}$;

normalize-time : $\mathbb{Z} \times \mathbb{Z} \times \mathbb{Z}$ → *Time*
normalize-time (h, m, s) $\triangleq$
   if *s* < *0* **then** *normalize-time (h, m–1, s+60)*
   else if *m* < *0* **then** *normalize-time (h–1, m+60, s)*
     else if *h* < *0* **then** **mk-***Time (h+24, m, s)*
      else **mk-***Time (h, m, s)*
pre
   $h \geq 0 \Rightarrow 0 \leq h \leq 23 \wedge$
   $m \geq 0 \Rightarrow 0 \leq m \leq 59 \wedge$
   $s \geq 0 \Rightarrow 0 \leq s \leq 59$;

duration : Time × *Time* → *Time*
duration (t_1, t_2) $\triangleq$
   normalize-time $(t_1.hour - t_2.hour, t_1.minute - t_2.minute, t_1.second - t_2.second)$;

state *Heating-System* **of**
   temp-sensors : Room-Number $\xrightarrow{m}$ *Temperature-Sensor*
   occ-sensors : Room-Number $\xrightarrow{m}$ *Occupancy-Sensor*
   rooms : Room-Number $\xrightarrow{m}$ *Room-Information*
   patterns : Room-Number $\xrightarrow{m}$ *Pattern*

   inv mk-*Heating-System (ts, is, rms, pts)* $\triangleq$
     dom *ts* = **dom** *is* = **dom** *rms* = **dom** *pts*

   init mk-*Heating-System (-, -, rms, pts)* $\triangleq$
     (∀ *rm* ∈ **dom** *pts* •
      pts(rm) = {↦} ∧
      rms(rm).last-occupancy-change = **mk-***Time (0, 0, 0))*
end

operations
   set-pattern (rm : Room-Number, pat : Pattern)
   ext wr *patterns : Room-Number* $\xrightarrow{m}$ *Pattern*
   pre *rm* ∈ **dom** *patterns*
   post *patterns* = $\overleftarrow{patterns}$ † {*rm* ↦ *pat*};

   activate-pattern (rm : Room-Number, at : Time)
   ext
     wr *rooms : Room-Number* $\xrightarrow{m}$ *Room-Information*

$$\textbf{rd } patterns : Room\text{-}Number \xrightarrow{m} Pattern$$

pre

$rm \in \textbf{dom } rooms \land$

$at \in \textbf{dom } (patterns(rm)) \land$

$current\text{-}time() = at$

post $rooms = \overleftarrow{rooms} \dagger \{rm \mapsto$

$\quad \textbf{mk-}Room\text{-}Information ((\overleftarrow{patterns(rm)})(at),$

$\quad\quad (\overleftarrow{rooms(rm)}).last\text{-}occupancy\text{-}change)\};$

---

occupied (rm : Room-Number)

ext

$\quad \textbf{wr } rooms : Room\text{-}Number \xrightarrow{m} Room\text{-}Information$

$\quad \textbf{rd } occ\text{-}sensors : Room\text{-}Number \xrightarrow{m} Occupancy\text{-}Sensor$

pre

$rm \in \textbf{dom } rooms \land$

$check\text{-}occupancy (occ\text{-}sensors(rm), current\text{-}time()) =$

$\quad \neg\ check\text{-}occupancy (occ\text{-}sensor(rm),$

$\quad\quad duration (current\text{-}time(), \textbf{mk-}Time (0,0,1)))$

post $rooms = \overleftarrow{rooms} \dagger \{rm \mapsto$

$\quad \textbf{mk-}Room\text{-}Information (rooms(rm).set\text{-}temperature, current\text{-}time())\};$

---

control-temperature (rm : Room-Number)

ext

$\quad \textbf{rd } temp\text{-}sensors : Room\text{-}Number \xrightarrow{m} Temperature\text{-}Sensor$

$\quad \textbf{wr } rooms : Room\text{-}Number \xrightarrow{m} Room\text{-}Information$

$\quad \textbf{rd } occ\text{-}sensors : Room\text{-}Number \xrightarrow{m} Occupancy\text{-}Sensor$

pre

$rm \in \textbf{dom } rooms \land$

$duration (current\text{-}time(), rooms(rm).last\text{-}occupancy\text{-}change)$

$\quad = stable\text{-}occupancy$

post

$\textbf{let } previous = \overleftarrow{rooms}(rm).last\text{-}occupancy\text{-}change,$

$\quad occupancy = check\text{-}occupancy (\overleftarrow{occ\text{-}sensors}(rm), current\text{-}time()) \textbf{ in}$

$\textbf{cases } read\text{-}temperature (\overleftarrow{temp\text{-}sensors}(rm), previous) :$

$\quad normal \rightarrow$

$\quad\quad \textbf{cases } occupancy :$

$\quad\quad\quad true \rightarrow rooms = \overleftarrow{rooms},$

$\quad\quad\quad false \rightarrow rooms = \overleftarrow{rooms} \dagger \{rm \mapsto$

$\quad\quad\quad\quad \textbf{mk-}Room\text{-}Information (below\text{-}normal,$

$\quad\quad\quad\quad\quad rooms(rm).last\text{-}occupancy\text{-}change)\},$

$\quad\quad\quad others \rightarrow rooms = \overleftarrow{rooms}$

$\quad\quad \textbf{end},$

$\quad below\text{-}normal \rightarrow$

cases *occupancy* :

    true → *rooms* = $\overleftarrow{rooms}$ † {*rm* ↦
        mk-*Room-Information* (*normal, rooms(rm).last-occupancy-*
                              change)},

    false → *rooms* = $\overleftarrow{rooms}$,
    others → *rooms* = $\overleftarrow{rooms}$

end,

  above-normal →

    cases *occupancy* :

      true → *rooms* = $\overleftarrow{rooms}$,
      false → *rooms* = $\overleftarrow{rooms}$ † {*rm* ↦
          mk-*Room-Information* (*normal, rooms(rm).last-occupancy-*
                                 change)},

      others → *rooms* = $\overleftarrow{rooms}$

    end,

    others → *rooms* = $\overleftarrow{rooms}$

end;

Comments

The function *normalize-time* converts a given triple of integers into a value of type *Time*. If the parameters represent positive integers that are within the limits of the three components for *Time*, the function constructs and returns a valid time value. If one of the parameters is negative, the function modifies the three parameters until the invariant for *Time* is satisfied. For example, if "seconds" is negative, it is made positive by adding 60; at the same time, "minutes" is reduced by one. Notice that after this change, "minutes" may become negative. So, the function is recursively applied until all the three parameters are in proper range. The function *duration* subtracts the second parameter from the first and returns the normalized time.

Every operation modifies some state variable, which is of map type. The postcondition ensures the modification by using the overwrite operation on map type objects. The operation *occupied* can be invoked when either an occupied room becomes empty or an empty room becomes occupied. The precondition ensures that the status of the room at the current time and at one second preceding the current time are different. There is no mechanism in VDM to specify that this operation is periodically performed, say regularly at 1-minute intervals. ∎

9.6 Case Study—Computer Network

A computer network consists of a set of nodes and a set of links connecting the nodes. Every link connects exactly two distinct nodes. A node may be active or inactive. A link is up if both the nodes connected by the link are active; otherwise, the link is down. Messages can be transmitted from an active node to any other active node in the network through a sequence of links that are up. All message transmissions are handled by a network manager. When a node wants to send a message to another node, it submits the message and the address of the recipient to the network manager. It is the responsibility of the network manager to choose a path between the sender and receiver nodes and route the message in the path. Each node maintains a buffer to hold messages deposited by the network manager. An active node periodically reads the messages in its buffer, and (1) deletes a message if it is addressed to the current node, or (2) forwards the message to the next node in the path.

Additional requirements

1. Each node has a unique address.

2. Every node on a path chosen by the network manager for message transmission remains active until the node forwards the message to the next node on the path.

3. No message is lost; every message dispatched by the network manager will eventually be received.

4. The network remains connected at all times.

5. The network manager queues all requests for sending messages based on the order in which these messages are received.

Assumptions

1. No message is corrupted.

The model

We first consider modeling the data types in the network:

Node: A node has an address, a status indicating whether it is active or inactive, and a buffer to hold the messages. Putting these requirements together, we can model a node by a record type with three fields: one for the address, another for the status, and the third one for the buffer which is a queue of messages.

Link: Since a link is uniquely identified by the two nodes connected by the link, both the nodes are included in its model. In addition, a link also includes a status variable. Therefore, a record type is chosen to model a link. The invariant for the link asserts that the two nodes are distinct and the status of the link depends on the status of the two nodes connected by the link.

Path: A path is modeled as a sequence of links. Every link, except for the first and last in the sequence, is connected to the link on either side in the path. In addition, no link appears more than once in the path. These constraints are expressed as a type invariant for the path.

Message: A message is modeled as a record consisting of the message body and the path through which the message is routed.

Request: This data type denotes records that a node uses when it submits a message to the network manager. It consists of the message body, and the sender and receiver of information.

The state of the network includes a set of nodes and a set of links and a queue of messages. The state invariant is a conjunction of the following constraints: (1) node identifiers are unique; (2) each link is uniquely identified by the two nodes it connects; (3) the network is connected; and (4) for each request submitted to the network manager, the sender and receiver nodes must be in the network.

We specify the following operations in the network:

addnode: This operation adds a new node to the network. Since the network must remain connected at all times, the new node must be connected to at least one other node in the network. The new node must have a unique identifier that must be different from the identifiers of all other nodes in the network. As a result of adding this new node, the set of nodes and links in the network are modified.

addlink: The purpose of this operation is to establish a link between two existing nodes in the network. The precondition ensures that the two nodes are present and there is no link between them. The postcondition asserts that a new link is established between the two nodes.

read-message: Every node checks its buffer periodically to read the message at the front of its buffer that must be addressed to the current node. This can be ensured by checking that the path encoded in the message is empty. The postcondition asserts that the buffer retains only those messages that are to be forwarded.

forward-message: When a node checks the message at the front of its buffer and the path associated with the message is not empty, the current node is not the receiver of the message. Consequently, the current node is expected to forward the message to the next node in the path and deletes its name from the path.

post-message: When a node wants to send a message to another node, it encodes the message text along with the sender and receiver information and submits a request to the network manager by invoking this operation. The precondition

ensures that both nodes are present in the network. The postcondition ensures that
the message is added to the queue of the network manager.

dispatch-message: This operation selects a path for each message submitted to
the network manager, encodes the path in the message, and puts it into the successor
of the first node in the path. At the time of selection, the status of all links on the
path is UP. It is assumed that this status is valid for every subpath during message
transmission.

delete-node: The delete operation accepts the node to be deleted. This node must
be present in the network. The precondition also ensures that there are at least three
nodes in the network. The postcondition asserts that the node as well as all the links
associated with the node are deleted from the network. It is assumed that a node is
deleted only when all the messages in the buffer of the node have been deleted.

VDM-SL specification

types
   Node :: nodeID : NodeAddress
            status : NodeStatus
            messages : Message;*

   NodeAddress = **token***;*

   NodeStatus = ACTIVE | INACTIVE;

   Link :: node1 : Node
          node2 : Node
          status : LinkStatus

   inv mk-*Link (n1,n2,st)* $\triangleq$ *n1.nodeID $\neq$ n2.nodeID $\wedge$*
      (n1.status = INACTIVE $\vee$ n2.status = INACTIVE) $\Rightarrow$ st = DOWN $\wedge$
      (n1.status = ACTIVE $\wedge$ n2.status = ACTIVE) $\Rightarrow$ st = UP;

   LinkStatus = UP | DOWN;

   *Path = Link**
   inv *lns* $\triangleq$ *injective (lns) $\wedge$*
      *$\forall$ i $\in$ **inds** lns $\bullet$ i $\geq$ 2 $\Rightarrow$ lns(i).node1 = lns(i–1).node2;*

   MessageBody = Char$^+$;

   Message :: text : MessageBody
             path : Path;

Request :: sender : Node
　　　　　 receiver : Node
　　　　　 text : MessageBody;

Report = SUCCESS | CONNECTING-NON-EXISTING-NODE |
　　　 NODE-ALREADY-EXISTS | LINK-ALREADY-EXISTS |
　　　 NO-MESSAGE-TO-DISPATCH | NODE-DOES-NOT-EXIST |
　　　 NO-MESSAGE | MESSAGE-IN-TRANSIT |
　　　 MESSAGE-AT-DESTINATION | NODE-HAS-MESSAGES;

state *Network* **of**
　 *nodes : Node-***set**
　 *links : Link-***set**
　 requests : Request*

　 inv mk-*Network (nodes, links, requests)*　　$\triangleq$
　　 ($\forall$ n1, n2 $\in$ nodes $\bullet$ n1.nodeID $\neq$ n2.nodeID $\Rightarrow$
　　　 connected (n1, n2, links)) $\wedge$
　　 ($\forall$ ln $\in$ links $\bullet$ ln.node1 $\in$ nodes $\wedge$ ln.node2 $\in$ nodes) $\wedge$
　　 ($\forall$ rq $\in$ requests $\bullet$ rq.sender $\in$ nodes $\wedge$ rq.receiver $\in$ nodes) $\wedge$
　　 ($\forall$ ln1, ln2 $\in$ links $\bullet$ ln1 = ln2 $\Leftrightarrow$
　　　 ln1.node1 = ln2.node1 $\wedge$ ln1.node2 = ln2.node2) $\wedge$
　　 ($\forall$ n1, n2 $\in$ nodes $\bullet$ n1 = n2 $\Leftrightarrow$ n1.nodeID = n2.nodeID)

　 init mk-*Network (nodes, links, requests)*　　$\triangleq$
　　 *nodes = {***mk-***Node(***mk-***token(1), ACTIVE, [ ]),*
　　　 mk-Node(***mk-***token(2), ACTIVE, [ ])} $\wedge$*
　　 *links = {***mk-***Link(***mk-***Node(***mk-***token(1), ACTIVE, [ ]),*
　　　 mk-Node(***mk-***token(2), ACTIVE, [ ]), UP)} $\wedge$*
　　 requests = [ ]
end

functions
　 injective : Link* $\to \mathbb{B}$
　 injective (lns)　　$\triangleq$　 **len** *lns = ***card elems** *lns;*

　 *connected : Node $\times$ Node $\times$ Link-***set** $\to \mathbb{B}$
　 connected (n1, n2, lns)　　$\triangleq$
　　 $\exists$ *p $\in$ {path | path : Path $\bullet$ ***elems** *path $\subseteq$ lns $\wedge$ ***len** *p > 0} $\bullet$*
　　　 *p(1).node1 = n1 $\wedge$ p(***len** *p).node2 = n2;*

　 *links-incident-at : Node $\times$ Link-***set** $\to$ *Link-***set**
　 links-incident-at (n, lns)　　$\triangleq$
　　 {ln | ln : Link $\bullet$ ln $\in$ lns $\wedge$ (ln.node1 = n $\vee$ ln.node2 = n)};

operations

addnode (new : Node, old : Node) rep : Report

ext

    wr *nodes : Node-***set**

    wr *links : Link-***set**

pre

    old ∈ nodes ∧

    ∀ n ∈ nodes • n.nodeID ≠ new.nodeID

post

    *nodes = $\overleftarrow{nodes}$ ∪ {***mk-***Node (new.nodeID, new.status, [ ])} ∧*

    let *up : LinkStatus := UP, down : LinkStatus := DOWN* **in**

        (new.status = ACTIVE ∧ old.status = ACTIVE) ⇒

            *links = $\overleftarrow{links}$ ∪ {***mk-***Link (old, new, up)} ∧*

        (new.status = INACTIVE ∨ old.status = INACTIVE) ⇒

            *links = $\overleftarrow{links}$ ∪ {***mk-***Link (old, new, down)} ∧*

    rep = SUCCESS

errs

    DOES-NOT-EXIST : old ∉ nodes →

        nodes = $\overleftarrow{nodes}$ ∧

        links = $\overleftarrow{links}$ ∧

        rep = CONNECTING-NON-EXISTING-NODE

    EXISTS : ∃ n ∈ nodes • n.nodeID = new.nodeID →

        nodes = $\overleftarrow{nodes}$ ∧

        links = $\overleftarrow{links}$ ∧

        rep = NODE-ALREADY-EXISTS;

addlink (from : Node, to: Node) rep : Report

ext

    rd *nodes : Node-***set**

    wr *links : Link-***set**

pre

    from ∈ nodes ∧ to ∈ nodes ∧

    ∀ ln ∈ links • ¬ (ln.node1 = from ∧ ln.node2 = to)

post

    let *up : LinkStatus := UP, down : LinkStatus := DOWN* **in**

        (from.status = ACTIVE ∧ to.status = ACTIVE) ⇒

            *links = $\overleftarrow{links}$ ∪ {***mk-***Link (from, to, up)} ∧*

        (from.status = INACTIVE ∨ to.status = INACTIVE) ⇒

            *links = $\overleftarrow{links}$ ∪ {***mk-***Link (from, to, down)} ∧*

    rep = SUCCESS

errs

    DOES-NOT-EXIST : from ∉ nodes ∨ to ∉ nodes →

$links = \overleftarrow{links} \land$
$rep = CONNECTING\text{-}NON\text{-}EXISTING\text{-}NODE$
$EXISTS : \exists\ ln \in links \bullet (ln.node1 = from \land ln.node2 = to) \rightarrow$
$links = \overleftarrow{links} \land$
$rep = LINK\text{-}ALREADY\text{-}EXISTS;$

post-message (from : Node, to : Node, msg : MessageBody) rep : Report
ext
    rd *nodes : Node*-**set**
    wr *requests : Request**
pre *from* $\in$ *nodes* $\land$ *to* $\in$ *nodes*
post *requests* $= \overleftarrow{requests}$ $\frown$ [**mk**-*Request (from, to, msg)*] $\land$
    rep = SUCCESS
errs
    DOES-NOT-EXIST : from $\notin$ *nodes* $\lor$ *to* $\notin$ *nodes* $\rightarrow$
        requests $= \overleftarrow{requests} \land$
        rep = NODE-DOES-NOT-EXIST;

dispatch-message () rep : Report
ext
    wr *nodes : Node*-**set**
    rd *links : Link*-**set**
    wr *requests : Request**
pre len *requests > 0*
post
    requests = **tl** $\overleftarrow{requests} \land$
    $\exists\ path \in \{p \mid p : Path \bullet$ **len** $p > 0 \land$ **elems** $p \subseteq links \land$
        p(1).node1 = (**hd** $\overleftarrow{requests}$).*sender* $\land$
        *p(***len** *p).node2* = (**hd** $\overleftarrow{requests}$).*receiver*$\} \land$
        $(\forall\ ln \in$ **elems** $p \bullet ln.status = UP) \bullet$
        nodes $= \overleftarrow{nodes} \setminus \{path(1).node2\} \cup$
            $\{$**mk**-*Node (path(1).node2.nodeID, path(1).node2.status,*
            path(1).node2.messages $\frown$
                [**mk**-*Message ((***hd** $\overleftarrow{requests}$).*text,* **tl** *path)*]$\} \land$
    rep = SUCCESS
errs
    NOTHING : **len** *requests = 0* $\rightarrow$
        nodes $= \overleftarrow{nodes} \land$
        requests $= \overleftarrow{requests}$
        rep = NO-MESSAGE-TO-DISPATCH;

read-message (current : Node) rep : Report
ext wr *nodes : Node*-**set**

pre

   $current \in nodes \wedge \textbf{len}\ (current.messages) > 0 \wedge$
   $(\textbf{hd}\ (current.messages)).path = [\ ]$

post

   $nodes = \overleftarrow{nodes} \setminus \{current\} \cup$
      $\{\textbf{mk-}Node\ (current.nodeID, current.status, \textbf{tl}\ current.messages)\} \wedge$
   $rep = SUCCESS$

errs

   $DOES\text{-}NOT\text{-}EXIST : current \notin nodes \rightarrow$
      $nodes = \overleftarrow{nodes} \wedge$
      $rep = NODE\text{-}DOES\text{-}NOT\text{-}EXIST$
   $NOTHING : \textbf{len}\ current.messages = 0 \rightarrow$
      $nodes = \overleftarrow{nodes} \wedge$
      $rep = NO\text{-}MESSAGE$
   $TRANSIT : (\textbf{hd}\ (current.messages)).path \neq [\ ] \rightarrow$
      $nodes = \overleftarrow{nodes}$
      $rep = MESSAGE\text{-}IN\text{-}TRANSIT;$

forward-message (current : Node) rep : Report
ext wr *nodes : Node-***set**
pre

   $current \in nodes \wedge \textbf{len}\ (current.messages) > 0 \wedge$
   $\textbf{hd}\ (current.messages).path \neq [\ ]$

post

   let $next = (\textbf{hd}\ (current.messages)).path(1).node2$ **in**
      $nodes = \overleftarrow{nodes} \setminus \{current, next\} \cup$
         $\{\textbf{mk-}Node\ (current.nodeID, current.status, \textbf{tl}\ current.messages),$
            $\textbf{mk-}Node\ (next.nodeID, next.status, next.messages \frown$
               $[\textbf{mk-}Message\ ((\textbf{hd}\ (current.messages)).text,$
                  $\textbf{tl}((\textbf{hd}\ (current.messages)).path)])\} \wedge$
   $rep = SUCCESS$

errs

   $DOES\text{-}NOT\text{-}EXIST : current \notin nodes \rightarrow$
      $nodes = \overleftarrow{nodes} \wedge$
      $rep = NODE\text{-}DOES\text{-}NOT\text{-}EXIST$
   $NOTHING : \textbf{len}\ current.messages = 0 \rightarrow$
      $nodes = \overleftarrow{nodes} \wedge$
      $rep = NO\text{-}MESSAGE$
   $DESTINATION : \textbf{hd}\ (current.messages).path = [\ ] \rightarrow$
      $nodes = \overleftarrow{nodes}$
      $rep = MESSAGE\text{-}AT\text{-}DESTINATION;$

delete-node (n : Node) rep : Report

ext

   wr *nodes : Node*-**set**

   wr *links : Link*-**set**

   wr *requests : Request**

pre

   card *nodes* ≥ *3* ∧ *n* ∈ *nodes* ∧ *n.messages* = [ ]

post

   n ∉ *nodes* ∧

   links = $\overleftarrow{links}$ \ *links-incident-at (n, $\overleftarrow{links}$)* ∧

   requests = [*$\overleftarrow{requests}$(i)* | *i* ∈ **inds** *$\overleftarrow{requests}$* •

      (*$\overleftarrow{requests}$(i).sender* ≠ *n* ∨ *$\overleftarrow{requests}$(i).receiver* ≠ *n*)] ∧

   rep = *SUCCESS*

errs

   DOES-NOT-EXIST : *n* ∉ *$\overleftarrow{nodes}$* →

      nodes = *$\overleftarrow{nodes}$* ∧

      links = *$\overleftarrow{links}$* ∧

      requests = *$\overleftarrow{requests}$* ∧

      rep = *NODE-DOES-NOT-EXIST*

   MESSAGE-EXISTS : *n.messages* ≠ [ ] →

      nodes = *$\overleftarrow{nodes}$* ∧

      links = *$\overleftarrow{links}$* ∧

      requests = *$\overleftarrow{requests}$* ∧

      rep = *NODE-HAS-MESSAGES;*

Comments

The function *injective* asserts that no link appears more than once in the sequence of links. The function *connected* specifies that two nodes are connected by a given set of links if there exists a path between them. The links comprising the path should be among those links passed as input to the function. Given a node and a set of links, the function *links-incident-at* returns the set of links incident at the node.

9.7 Rigorous Reasoning

In this section, we give a rigorous proof for the security property:

> Every message dispatched by the network manager is read only by the node to which the message is addressed.

Let a node X send a message m to a node Y; assume both X and Y exist in the network. The node X constructs a request and submits it to the network manager. When the network manager finds the record $r = (X, Y, m)$ in front of its buffer, the precondition for the operation *dispatch-message* is satisfied for the record r. The postcondition of *dispatch-message* asserts the following:

1. A path from sender to receiver exists, and the status of all links on this path are UP.

2. The first node of the first link on the path is the sender, and the second node of the last link on the path is the receiver.

3. The message and the path excluding the first link are placed in the buffer of the second node of the first link on the path.

Accordingly, the network manager chooses a path p, where

$$p(1).node1 = X, \text{ and } p(k).node2 = Y, k = \textbf{len } p, k \geq 1$$

It is also true that the status of all links in p are UP. If $p(1).node2 = Z$, the tuple $(m, \textbf{tl } p)$ is appended to the buffer of Z. For the rest of the proof, we need to assume that operations *read-message*, and *forward-message* will be eventually invoked by every node whose buffer is not empty. Note that the preconditions for the operations *read-message* and *forward-message* are independent. In particular, a node can invoke *read-message* operation only when the tuple to be processed in its buffer is of the form (m, q), where $q = [\ ]$. However, for the same node to invoke the *forward-message* operation, the second component q must be nonempty. There are two cases to consider.

Case 1: $k = 1$

Infer from the postcondition of *dispatch-message* that the message structure $(m, [\ ])$ is inserted in the buffer of $Z = p(1).node2 = p(k).node2 = Y$. When this message is at the front of $Z's$ buffer, the precondition for the operation *read-message* becomes true. The postcondition for *read-message* ensures that this tuple is deleted; that is, node Z has received the message sent from X, and no node along the path has read the message.

Case 2: $k > 1$

Infer from the postcondition of *dispatch-message* that the message structure (m, p'), where $p' = \textbf{tl } p$, is inserted in the buffer of node Z. Since $Z = p(1).node2 \neq p(k).node2 = Y$, and $p' \neq [\ ]$, when the tuple (m, p') is at the front of $Z's$ buffer, only the precondition of *forward-message* can become true. The postcondition of the operation *forward-message* ensures that the message m is encoded in the structure $(m, \textbf{tl } p')$, and placed in the buffer of node W, where $p'(1).node1 =$

$Z, p'(1).node2 = W$. Notice that **len** $p' = k' = k - 1$, and the encoded message is deleted from the buffer of node Z; that is, the message is not read by node Z. If k' = 0, then case 1 applies to node W at some future time; otherwise, case 2 applies.

Since the length of the path encoded in the message is decremented every time the message is forwarded by a node, eventually the length of the encoded path becomes zero. We observe from case 2 that when the path length is greater than zero, the message is not read. From case 1 it follows that when the path length is zero the message is read by the node to which the message is addressed. This proves that no node other than the receiver can read the message.

9.8   Refinement and Proof Obligations

In addition to providing a formalism for specification, VDM also provides the techniques for stepwise refinement of specifications. Such a systematic development approach of VDM makes it suitable for the development of large complex software systems for which the set of initial requirements continuously evolve over a period of time. VDM specifications in this case are given as a layer of models, each model being a refined version of the previous model. A lower-level model adds design and implementation details. Thus the last level of refinement will be closer to the implementation from which a program could be obtained by directly mapping the specification constructs onto those of the underlying programming language. There are two ways by which a specification in VDM can be refined—*data refinement*, and *operation decomposition*. In the former approach, abstract data types are mapped into concrete data types. A proof obligation for the refinement establishes that for every abstract data type, there exists at least one concrete type that implements it. In addition, it must be proved that every operation performed on concrete data types satisfies the constraints imposed on the abstract data types. In an operation refinement, operations in one level are refined to one or more operations in which computational details are explicit. The effect of performing the low-level operations must be proved to be consistent with the abstract operation. The following sections explain the refinement techniques in detail. For a rigorous treatment on refinement, refer [19, 20].

9.8.1   Data Refinement

In data refinement, an abstract data type is refined into one or more concrete data types. One familiar example is refining a set into a sequence with a proof that the refined data type sequence does not contain duplicate elements. A refinement should neither add more data nor lose any existing data. This requires a proof to establish that every element in the set occurs somewhere in the sequence. With these two proofs, it would be established that the sequence contains all the elements of the set, each element once, and nothing more. Hence, the length of the sequence in the refinement is equal to the size of the set. Next, it is also to be shown that for every operation performed on the set, there exists a unique operation performed on the sequence so that the constraints imposed for the set operation are still satisfied in the sequence.

In general, proof obligation for a data refinement requires (1) showing that no data is lost and no new data is introduced; and (2) for every operation that modifies data in the abstract level, the data in the refined data type is modified to yield the same effect. In the proof obligations for data refinement, we use the following notations:

$$pre\text{-}Op\ (x, \overleftarrow{state})$$
$$post\text{-}Op\ (x, \overleftarrow{state}, state)$$

where $\overleftarrow{state}$ refers to the state of the system before the operation is invoked, and *state* denotes the state of the system after the operation terminates, and *x* refers to the set of parameters of the operation *Op*. Since functions do not affect state spaces, the pre- and postconditions of a function are denoted as

$$pre\text{-}f\,(x)$$
$$post\text{-}f\,(x)$$

Proof Obligations

It is necessary to define a *retrieve function* that maps a concrete state space into its abstract state space. There are five components in a proof obligation [20].

Signature Verification   First, one must show that the retrieve function is of correct type; that is, if the abstract state is denoted as *Abs* and the concrete state is denoted as *Con*, then

$$\boxed{Signature}\vdash retrf\text{: } Con \rightarrow Abs$$

Adequacy Obligation   For every abstract state *Abs*, we show that there exists at least one concrete state *Con* that implements the abstract state using the retrieve function. Formally,

$$\boxed{Adequacy}\ \frac{Abs}{\exists\,Con \bullet retrf\,(Con) = Abs}$$

Initial State Validation   The retrieve function should match the initial concrete state $init\_C$ to the initial abstract state $init\_A$ as defined by the initialization functions in both state spaces. Formally,

$$\boxed{Init}\ \frac{init\_C}{init\_A}$$

Domain Obligation   For every concrete operation Op_C, the precondition of the corresponding abstract operation Op_A in conjunction with the retrieve function ensures the precondition of Op_C; i.e.,

$$Abs,\ Con,\ Abs = retrf(Con),\ pre\text{-}Op_A(x,\ Abs)$$

$$\boxed{Domain\ Rule}\ \overline{\hspace{1cm} pre\text{-}Op_C(x,\ Con)}$$

Informally, domain obligation ensures that the precondition of the concrete operation is weaker than that of its corresponding abstract operation.

Result Obligation For every abstract operation Op_A, the postcondition of its corresponding concrete operation Op_C, in conjunction with the retrieve function, ensures the postcondition of Op_A. That is, we show that the post-condition of the concrete operation is stronger than that of the corresponding abstract operation. Formally, if $\overleftarrow{Con}$ represents the concrete state before the operation Op_C and Con refers to the concrete state after Op_C successfully terminates, then

$$\overleftarrow{Con},\ Con,\ \overleftarrow{Abs} = retrf(\overleftarrow{Con}),\ Abs = retrf(Con),$$
$$pre\text{-}Op_A(x,\ \overleftarrow{Abs}),\ post\text{-}Op_C(\overleftarrow{Con},\ Con)$$

$$\boxed{Result\ Rule}\ \overline{\hspace{1cm} post\text{-}Op_A(\overleftarrow{Abs},\ Abs)}$$

9.8.2 Example for Data Refinement

In this section, we discuss the data refinement for the employment exchange speci-fication given in the previous section. The state variables *employed* and *unemployed* are refined into sequences. The refined specification is given below:

state *Emp-Exch₁* **of**
 employed₁ : Person*
 unemployed₁ : Person*
 inv mk_*Emp-Exch₁* (em, unem) $\triangle$
  elems *em* ∩ **elems** *unem* = {} ∧
  no-duplicates (em) ∧ *no-duplicates (unem)*
 init mk_*Emp-Exch₁* (em, unem) $\triangle$ *em* = [ ] ∧ *unem* = [ ]
end
functions
 no-duplicates : Person* $\rightarrow$ $\mathbb{B}$
 no-duplicates (plist) $\triangle$ $\forall i,j \in$ **inds** *plist* • $i \neq j \Rightarrow plist(i) \neq plist(j)$

operations
 register₁ (p : Person)
 ext
  wr *unemployed₁ : Person**
  rd *employed₁ : Person**
 pre
  $(\forall i \in$ **inds** *employed₁* • *employed₁(i)* $\neq p) \wedge$

$$(\forall\, j \in \mathbf{inds}\ unemployed_1 \bullet unemployed_1(j) \neq p)$$
$$\mathbf{post}\ unemployed_1 = \overleftarrow{unemployed_1} \curvearrowright [p];$$

$change\text{-}status_1\ (p : Person)$
ext
    wr $unemployed_1 : Person^*$
    wr $employed_1 : Person^*$
pre $\exists\ i \in \mathbf{inds}\ unemployed_1 \bullet unemployed_1(i) = p$
post
    $(\exists\ i \in \mathbf{inds}\ \overleftarrow{unemployed_1} \bullet \overleftarrow{unemployed_1}(i) = p\ \wedge$
        $(\forall\, j \in \{1,\ldots,(i-1)\} \bullet unemployed_1(j) = \overleftarrow{unemployed_1}(j))\ \wedge$
        $(\forall\, k \in \{(i+1),\ldots,\mathbf{len}\ \overleftarrow{unemployed_1}\} \bullet$
            $unemployed_1(k-1) = \overleftarrow{unemployed_1}(k))$
    $)\ \wedge$
    $employed_1 = \overleftarrow{employed_1} \curvearrowright [p];$

Signature Verification   The retrieve function for this refinement is defined as follows:

$retrf : Emp\text{-}Exch_1 \rightarrow Emp\text{-}Exch$
$retrf\,(\mathbf{mk\_}Emp\text{-}Exch_1\ (em_1,\ unem_1))\qquad \triangleq$
    $\mathbf{mk\_}Emp\text{-}Exch\ (\mathbf{elems}\ em_1,\ \mathbf{elems}\ unem_1)$

Adequacy Proof   It is shown in [20, page 40] that

$$\forall\, s \in S\text{–}\mathbf{set} \bullet \exists\ \ell \in X^* \bullet s = \mathbf{elems}\ \ell$$

This is the adequacy proof for the current example. From this proof, it can be safely concluded that

$$retrf\,(Emp\text{-}Exch_1) = Emp\text{-}Exch$$
$$retrf\,(\overleftarrow{Emp\text{-}Exch_1}) = \overleftarrow{Emp\text{-}Exch}$$

The invariant of $Emp\text{-}Exch_1$ ensures that em_1 and $unem_1$ do not contain any duplicates.

Initial State Validation   The proof is given below:

from	**init mk_***Emp-Exch*$_1$ *(em*$_1$*, unem*$_1$*); retrf*	
1	$em_1 = [\ ]$; $unem_1 = [\ ]$	**init mk_***Emp-Exch*$_1$
2	$em = \mathbf{elems}\ [\ ]$; $unem = \mathbf{elems}\ [\ ]$	*retrf*
3	$em = \{\}$; $unem = \{\}$	*sequence*
infer	**init mk_***Emp-Exch (em, unem)*	**init mk_***Emp-Exch*

Domain Obligation   For simplicity, the proof for only one operation, say, *register*, is given below; proof for the other operation is left as an exercise. For domain obligation, we have to show that

$$\forall\, p \in Person \bullet pre\text{-}register\,(p,\ \overleftarrow{Emp\text{-}Exch}) \wedge retrf\,(\overleftarrow{Emp\text{-}Exch_1})$$
$$\Rightarrow pre\text{-}register_1\,(p,\ \overleftarrow{Emp\text{-}Exch_1})$$

from   *pre-register* $(p,\ \overleftarrow{Emp\text{-}Exch})$; *retrf* $(\overleftarrow{Emp\text{-}Exch_1})$
1     $p \notin unemployed \wedge p \notin employed$ *pre-register*
2     $p \notin$ **elems** $unemployed_1 \wedge p \notin$ **elems** $employed_1$ *retrf*
3     $(\forall\, i \in$ **inds** $unemployed_1 \bullet unemployed_1(i) \neq p) \wedge$
       $(\forall\, i \in$ **inds** $employed_1 \bullet employed_1(i) \neq p)$ *sequence*
infer   *pre-register$_1$* $(p,\ \overleftarrow{Emp\text{-}Exch_1})$ 3

Result Obligation   We give the proof only for the *register* operation. It is required to prove that

$$\forall\, p \in Person \bullet pre\text{-}register\,(p,\ \overleftarrow{Emp\text{-}Exch}) \wedge retrf\,(\overleftarrow{Emp\text{-}Exch_1}) \wedge$$
$$post\text{-}register_1\,(p,\ \overleftarrow{Emp\text{-}Exch_1},\ Emp\text{-}Exch_1) \wedge \overleftarrow{Emp\text{-}Exch_1} \wedge Emp\text{-}Exch_1$$
$$\Rightarrow post\text{-}register\,(p,\ \overleftarrow{Emp\text{-}Exch},\ Emp\text{-}Exch)$$

from   *hypotheses*
1     $unemployed =$ **elems** $unemployed_1$ *retrf, Emp-Exch$_1$*
2     $unemployed =$ **elems** $(\overleftarrow{unemployed_1} \frown [p])$ *post-register$_1$*
3     $unemployed =$ **elems** $\overleftarrow{unemployed_1} \cup$ **elems** $[p]$ *sequence*
4     $unemployed =$ **elems** $\overleftarrow{unemployed_1} \cup \{p\}$ *sequence*
5     $unemployed = \overleftarrow{unemployed} \cup \{p\}$ *retrf*
infer   *post-register* $(p,\ \overleftarrow{Emp\text{-}Exch},\ Emp\text{-}Exch)$ 5, *hypotheses*

Since a map is a finite set of maplets, the proof obligation for the refinement of a map type to sequence type is quite similar to that from set type to sequence type. That is, a map can be refined into two sequences of same size, one representing the domain elements and another representing the range elements.

9.8.3   Operation Decomposition

The purpose of an *operation decomposition* process is to refine an abstract operation into a concrete operation with computational details. In order to achieve this goal, the operations in the concrete specification are chosen to reflect those operations supported by programming languages. These include *sequential composition of operations*, *control structures* (**if-then-else** and **case**), and *iterative structures* (**while**, **repeat**, and **for**). The operation decomposition process requires a proof; i.e., the combined effect of all operations in the concrete specification should be proved to satisfy the behavior of the abstract operation. Therefore, proof rules are introduced in the operation decomposition process to support formal verification.

We discuss operation decomposition technique for the *delete-node* operation of the network example given in the case study and informally justify the refinement. See [19, 21] for proof rules for operation decomposition.

9.8.4 Example for Operation Decomposition

We assume that the state variables *nodes* and *links* in the network example are refined as follows:

nodes : Node*
links : Links*

We omit the proof obligations for this data refinement. We refine the functions *connected* and *links-incident-at* for the refined data types.

connected : Node × Node × Link → $\mathbb{B}$
connected (n1, n2, lns) $\triangleq$
        $\exists$ *p* ∈ *{path | path : Path* • **elems** *path* ⊆ **elems** *lns}* •
            (p(1).node1 = n1 ∨ *p(**len** p).node2 = n2)*
pre len *lns > 0;*

links-incident-at : Node × Link → Link*
links-incident-at (n, lns) $\triangleq$
        [ln | ln : Link • *ln* ∈ **elems** *lns* ∧ *(ln.node1 = n* ∨ *ln.node2 = n)];*

We now define the refinement of the operation *delete-node*.

delete-node (n : Node) $\triangleq$
    (**dcl** *nds : Node* := [];*
    dcl *lns : Link* := [];*
    dcl *reqs : Request* := [];*

    (**let** *lnks = links-incident-at (n, links)* **in**
        for *ln* **in** *links* **do**
            if *ln* ∉ *lnks* **then**
                lns := lns ⌢ *[ln];*
        links = lns);

*(for *nd* in *nodes* do*
    if *nd ≠ n* **then**
        nds := nds ⁀ [nd];
  nodes := nds);
*(**let** upstat : LinkStatus := UP,*
    downstat : LinkStatus := DOWN **in**
  for *nd1* **in** *nodes* **do**
    for *nd2* **in** *nodes* **do**
      if *nd1 ≠ nd2 ∧ ¬ connected (nd1, nd2, links)* **then**
        if *(nd1.status = ACTIVE ∧ nd2.status = ACTIVE)* **then**
          links := links ⁀ **mk-Link** *(nd1, nd2, upstat)*
        else *links := links ⁀* **mk-Link** *(nd1, nd2, downstat));*
  *(**for** req **in** requests* **do**
    if *req.sender ≠ n ∧ req.receiver ≠ n* **then**
      reqs := reqs ⁀ [req]);
)
pre *n ∈* **elems** *nodes*

In the refined version, the links incident at the given node are deleted first; this is specified by the first **for** loop. Next, the given node under consideration is deleted from the set of nodes. By deleting the node and the links associated with the node, the network may be left with several unconnected branches. Since the network must be connected at all times as stated in the requirements, we establish links between the unconnected branches and make the network connected.

The refined operation contains a block of statements that is a sequential composition of four statements. The first statement is the **for** statement, which collects the sequence of links not associated with the node *n*. The precondition for this statement is that the node *n* must be present in the sequence of nodes. If *n* is not present in the sequence of nodes in the network, the operation fails. Since in VDM-SL an explicit operation does not specify exception, we have ignored the error conditions stated in the abstract operation *delete-node*. The postcondition of the first statement asserts that only links not associated with *n* remain in the network. The precondition for the second statement is the same as that of the first statement. The postcondition of the second statement asserts that the network no longer contains the node *n*. There is no precondition for the third statement. The postcondition asserts that new links and their respective status are created, and added to the network. The fourth statement does not depend on the sequential composition of the other three statements. It specifies that the messages submitted by the node *n* and the messages sent to the node *n* are removed from the network buffer. This is done by scanning each request in the network buffer and deleting the ones addressed by and addressed to the node *n*.

Exercises

1. In the specification for employment exchange given in Example 9.5, one of the assumptions states that registered people will not be deleted from the exchange. Remove this assumption and specify two operations: *delete-unemployed (p : Person)*, and *delete-employed (p : Person)*, which will remove persons from the *unemployed* and *employed* sets, respectively.

2. The specification for course registration system given in Example 9.4 has an assumption that the course offerings are considered for only one semester. Remove this restriction and modify the specification so that the database maintains information on course offerings for more than one semester. Include constraints such as "prerequisites for a course should not be held concurrently in the same semester."

3. This problem enriches the model in Example 9.4 with the addition of the following two types:

$$LetterGrade = \text{``}A\text{''} \mid \text{``}B\text{''} \mid \text{``}C\text{''}$$
$$Grades = Student \xrightarrow{m} LetterGrade$$

You must introduce appropriate type invariants as well. Introduce a state variable

$$grades\text{-}for\text{-}courses : Course \xrightarrow{m} grades$$

Give VDM functions and operations for the following database queries; you must justify why a particular query is modeled as a function or as an operation:

(a) Assign the course *c* to teacher *t*.

(b) Determine the set of courses that begin and end at the same time.

(c) Given a teacher *t*, determine the students currently taking the course taught by teacher *t*.

(d) List all courses that are mutually independent; that is, no two courses in the list have a common prerequisite.

(e) Find all students who have received either grade "*A*" or grade "*B*" from teacher *t*.

(f) Given a student *s*, determine the grades in courses completed by the student.

(g) Given a teacher *t*, find the grade lists for the courses taught by teacher *t*.

(h) Given a student *s* and a teacher *t*, find the set of grades given by the teacher *t* to the student *s* in the courses completed by student *s*.

(i) Determine the set of students who have grade "*C*" in all courses completed by them.

(j) Given two teachers t_1 and t_2, find the set of all students who have received the same grades from the teachers.

(k) Given two students s_1 and s_2, find the set of all teachers who awarded the same grades to them.

(l) Determine the set of courses taught by teacher t such that in every course, no more than five students received the grade "A."

(m) Find the courses taught in a given room r by a teacher t in two consecutive sessions.

4. The specification for the automated transaction machine in Example 9.6 assumes that each user has a distinct card even if the user accesses a shared account. Change this restriction and include personal details for users. Introduce mappings between personal details and card numbers so that the bank knows the users of an account. Modify the specification incorporating these changes. Add new operations if necessary. Notice that a user may have more than one account.

Specify the following new operations for the ATM example: (1) Issue a new card to a user; include more assumptions, if necessary. (2) Check the balance in an account. (3) Modify the type *Account* so that for a given time interval, the number of deposits and withdrawals can be printed when required.

5. The specification for a computer network in the case study ensures that no link appears more than once in a path. However, it does permit that a path may include a simple loop; i.e., a node can appear twice in a path, still obeying the previous invariant. Impose a restriction that a path should be linear so that no node can appear more than once in a path. Modify the specification to incorporate this change.

Set a limit to the number of messages that can be stored in the buffer of a node. Modify the specification so that if the buffer in a particular node is full, no message can be forwarded to this node until the node reads or forwards at least one message from its buffer.

Set a limit to the number of requests that can be stored in the buffer in the state space. Modify the specification so that if this buffer is full, no more requests will be accepted by the network manager until the network manager dispatches at least one message from this buffer.

6. Discuss data refinement and proof obligations for data abstractions in the network example.

7. Give a data refinement for the specification of ATM given in Example 9.6, along with proofs.

8. Specify a data type called "Line Segment" with appropriate invariant. You may need to specify "Point" first. Define the following operations on line

segments: (1) Determine whether or not two line segments are parallel to each other; (2) Determine whether or not two line segments are perpendicular to each other; (3) Determine whether or not two line segments intersect at a common point; (4) Determine whether or not two line segments share at least one common point; and (5) Determine the length of a line segment.

9. Specify a "Circle" and a "Line Segment" (you may use the specification in the previous question) and define the following operations: Determine whether (1) the circle encloses the line segment; (4) the line segment touches the circle; and (3) the line segment intersects the circle.

10. Define the *bag* data type described in Chapter 7 in VDM-SL. Specify operations to count and re-shelve books in a simple library check-out system using *bag*.

11. A simple cryptographic system uses its own code for each printable character. When a message (consisting of a sequence of printable and non-printable characters) is sent, it is encoded by the corresponding codes for each character in the message. The receiver, knowing the code dictionary, can decode the message at the other end. Notice that each station has its own coding dictionary, so the receiver must identify the sender first and then choose the appropriate dictionary. Moreover, each station must store the dictionaries of all the other stations in the system. Any change in the dictionary in any of the stations must be broadcast to all other stations.

Write a VDM-SL specification to specify this simple cryptographic system. Include appropriate operations and error messages.

12. Figure 9.1 represents homethetic polygons P_1 and P_2 in which the sides of P_1 are parallel to the sides of P_2, and the distance between every pair of parallel sides is the same. Specify a data type called "Polygon," and define a function to determine whether or not two polygons are homethetic.

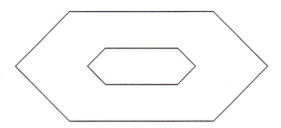

FIGURE 9.1. Homethetic polygons.

Bibliographic Notes

Peter Lucas [23] gives a historical overview of VDM, particularly describing its evolution during the last decade. The report describes the evolution of Meta-IV, the specification language associated with VDM until 1987. The standardization process then replaced Meta-IV by VDM-SL. A precise description of VDM-SL is given in [24]; its full description appears in [17].

Since the language for VDM was evolving continuously over the last decade, only a few books on VDM were published during that period. Cohen, Harwood, and Jackson describe the Meta-IV language [8] with some simple examples. Hekmatpour and Ince [16] used the same language to describe how VDM can be used for software prototyping. Dawes describes the initial concrete syntax of VDM-SL [9]. The current standard version is slightly different from the version of VDM-SL that appeared in [9]. Andrews and Ince [2], and Harry [15] also used the same version as in [9]; their book contains several examples and techniques for proving properties using VDM specifications.

In spite of the changes to the VDM specification language, VDM-SL and its predecessor Meta-IV have been used to specify a number of applications. These include a document on Message Authentication Algorithm developed by Parkin and O'Neil [25] and the Modula-2 programming language by Pronk and Schonhacker [26]. The edited monograph by Jones and Shaw [21] contains several specification case studies using VDM.

VDM originated as a software development framework and is still considered as a vehicle for software synthesis. Consequently, refinement theory has become an integral part of VDM. A number of publications have been reported in the literature on refinement of VDM specifications. Jones's work [18, 19] on refinements is a primary and relevant source of refinement theory. Others in this category include Clement's work on data refinement [6, 7] and Goldsack and Lano's work on data decomposition [14].

Reasoning about a specification and providing formal justification for refinement steps, are two important tasks in the development of a software based on a formal approach. Bicarregui and Mathews [5] compares two support systems for providing properties from formal specifications. Bicarregui and others [3] give a tutorial on the construction of proofs that are derived from a VDM specification. They give a set of proof rules based on the VDM-SL specification language and show how to use them in reasoning about VDM specifications, as well as proving refinement steps.

Several tools are available for developing specifications, refinement, and proofs using VDM. The IFAD Toolbox [27] enables one to develop a VDM-SL specification, check its syntax and type correctness, generate proof obligations, and prove some properties using its static and dynamic semantic checker. The toolbox also includes code generation facilities. The *mural* tool [4, 12, 20] supports theorem-proving using VDM specifications, but uses a different syntax of VDM. The KIDS tool [22] supports proof-based development of specifications using VDM. Agerholm [1] discusses a methodology to translate VDM specifications into PVS, a mechanical theorem prover.

The only object-oriented extension to VDM reported in the literature is the VDM++ specification language. A detailed description of VDM++ can be found in [10]. Object refinement, similar to data refinement, using VDM++ has been described in [13]. In addition, VDM++ has been used for developing specifications of real-time and concurrent systems, as reported in [11].

The Institute for Applied Computer Science in Odense, Denmark maintains an up-to-date VDM bibliography, edited by Peter Gorm Larsen. Copies of this bibliography can be obtained through anonymous ftp from hermes.ifad.dk (directory /pub/docs). A separate mailing list called vdm-forum@mailbase.ac.uk is maintained for active discussion on current developments and applications using VDM.

References

[1] S. Agerholm, "Translating Specifications in VDM-SL to PVS," in J.v. Wright, J. Grundy and J. Harrison (Eds.), *Proceedings of the International Conference on Theorem Proving in Higher Order Logics (TPHOL'96)*, Springer-Verlag, 1996.

[2] A. Andrews and D. Ince, *Practical Formal Methods Using VDM*, McGraw-Hill Book Company Europe, England, 1991.

[3] J.C. Bicarregui *et al.*, *Proof in VDM: A Practitioner's Guide*, Springer-Verlag, London, 1994.

[4] J. Bicarregui and B. Ritchie, "Reasoning about VDM Developments using the VDM Tool Support in *mural*," in S. Prehn and W.J. Toetenel (Eds.), *VDM'91: Formal Software Development Methods*; published as *Lecture Notes in Computer Science*, Vol. 552, Springer-Verlag, 1991, pp. 371–388.

[5] J. Bicarregui and B. Mathews, "Formal Methods in Practice: A Comparison of Two Support Systems for Proof," in Bartosek *et al.* (Eds.), *SOFSEM'95: Theory and Practice of Informatics*; published as *Lecture Notes in Computer Science*, Vol. 1012, Springer-Verlag, 1995.

[6] T. Clement, "Comparing Approaches to Data Reification," in M. Naftalin, T. Denvir, and M. Bertran (Eds.), *FME'94: Industrial Benefits of Formal Methods*; published as *Lecture Notes in Computer Science*, Vol. 893, Springer-Verlag, 1994, pp. 118–133.

[7] T. Clement, "Data Reification without Explicit Abstraction Functions," in M.C. Gaudel and J.C.P. Woodcock (Eds.), *FME'96: Industrial Benefits and Advances in Formal Methods*; published as *Lecture Notes in Computer Science*, Vol. 1051, Springer-Verlag, 1996, pp. 195–213.

[8] B. Cohen, W.T. Harwood, and M.I. Jackson, *The Specification of Complex Systems*, Addison-Wesley Publishing Company, Reading, MA, 1986.

[9] J. Dawes, *The VDM-SL Reference Guide*, Pitman, London, England, 1991.

[10] E.H. Dürr and N. Plat (Eds.), *VDM++: Language Reference Manual*, Afrodite (ESPRIT-III, project number 6500) document, Cap Volmac, August 1995.

[11] E.H. Dürr and S. Goldsack, "Formal Methods and Object Technology," Chapter 6 in S.J. Goldsack and S.J.H. Kent (Eds.), *Concurrency and Real-Time in VDM++*, Springer-Verlag, London, England, 1996, pp. 86–112.

[12] M. Elvang-Goransson, "Reasoning about VDM Specifications," in S. Prehn and W.J. Toetenel (Eds.), *VDM'91: Formal Software Development Methods*; published as *Lecture Notes in Computer Science*, Vol. 552, Springer-Verlag, 1991, pp. 343–355.

[13] S.J. Goldsack, E.H. Dürr, and N. Plat, "Object Reification in VDM++," in M. Wirsing (Ed.), *ICSE-17: Workshop on Formal Methods Application in Software Engineering Practice*, Seattle, WA, April 1995, pp. 194–201.

[14] S. Goldsack and K. Lano, "Annealing and Data Decomposition in VDM," *ACM SIGPLAN Notices*, Vol. 31, No. 4, April 1996, pp. 32–38.

[15] A. Harry, *Formal Methods Fact File: VDM and Z*, John Wiley & Sons, New York, NY, 1996.

[16] S. Hekmatpour and D. Ince, *Software Prototyping, Formal Methods and VDM*, Addison-Wesley Publishing Company, International Computer Science Series, 1988.

[17] P.G. Larsen *et al.*, Information Technology - Programming Languages, their environments and system software interfaces - Vienna Development Method - Specification Language - Part 1: Base Language, ISO Document, December 1996.

[18] C.B. Jones, *The Systematic Software Development using VDM*, Prentice Hall International (UK), 1986.

[19] C.B. Jones, *The Systematic Software Development using VDM* (second edition), Prentice Hall International (UK), 1990.

[20] C.B. Jones, K.D. Jones, P.A. Lindsay, and R. Moore, *mural: A Formal Development Support System*, Springer-Verlag, London, 1991.

[21] C.B. Jones and R.C. Shaw, *Case Studies in Systematic Software Development*, Prentice Hall International (UK), 1990.

[22] Y. Ledru, "Using KIDS as a Tool Support for VDM," *Proceedings of the 18th International Conference on Software Engineering*, Berlin, Germany, March 1996, pp. 236–245.

[23] P. Lucas, "VDM: Origins, Hopes and Achievements," in D. Bjørner *et al.* (Eds.) *VDM'87: VDM - A Formal Method at Work*; published as *Lecture Notes in Computer Science*, Vol. 252, Springer-Verlag, 1987, pp. 1–8.

[24] G.I. Parkin, "Vienna Development Method Specification Language (VDM-SL)," *Computer Standards and Interfaces*, Vol. 16, 1994, pp. 527–530.

[25] G.I. Parkin and G. O'Neil, "Specification of the MAA Standard in VDM," in S. Prehn and W.J. Toetenel (Eds.), *VDM'91: Formal Software Development Methods*; published as *Lecture Notes in Computer Science*, Vol. 552, Springer-Verlag, 1991, pp. 526–544.

[26] C. Pronk and M. Schonhacker, "ISO/IEC 10514-1, the Standard for Modula-2: Process Aspects," *ACM SIGPLAN Notices*, Vol. 31, No. 8, 1996, pp. 74–83.

[27] The VDM-SL Tool Group. *User Manual for the IFAD VDM-SL Toolbox*, IFAD, The Institute of Applied Computer Science, Forskerparken 10, DK-5230 Odense M, Denmark, June 1995.

10

The Z Notation

The Z notation (pronounced as *zed*, named after the German mathematician *Ernst Zermelo*) originated at the Oxford University Computing Laboratory, UK, and has evolved over the last decade into a conceptually clear and mathematically well-defined specification language. The mathematical bases for Z notation are ZF set theory and the classical two-valued predicate logic. An interesting feature of the Z specification language is the schema notation. Using schemas, one can develop modular specifications in Z and compose them using schema calculus.

This chapter presents a tutorial of the Z notation, brings out the differences between the Z notation and other model-based specification languages such as VDM-SL through informal discussions, and motivates the reader to understand the principles of modular specification supported by the Z notation. As was done in previous chapters, a number of examples are given to make the reader become familiar with basics of the Z notation and acquire skills in writing Z specifications. All the examples in this chapter have been type-checked by the *fuzz* type checker [11].

10.1 A Brief Overview of Z

The Z notation is based on set theory and first-order predicate logic. Set theory provides the foundation to construct an abstract structure of the software product being specified. The first-order predicate logic is used to express the behavior of the product. Thus, Z uses the mathematical notations that are conventional to set theory and predicate logic.

An important characteristic of the Z notation is its type system. Z is strongly typed in the sense that every object in Z must be associated with a unique type. This makes it easier to develop tools for type checking Z specifications. Types are interpreted as maximal sets. Hence, it is relatively simpler to express type compatibility as subset relations.

One of the distinguishing components of Z is the schema notation. A schema can be viewed as an encapsulated structure, associated with some properties. Using the schema notation, it is possible to specify parts of a system separately, and then compose the specifications for the parts to obtain the specification of the whole system. Schemas are commonly used in Z to represent types, state spaces and operations.

The Z notation itself can be viewed as a composition of two separate components: a base language and a mathematical toolkit. It is the mathematical toolkit that provides a majority of the notations such as operators on sets and tuples. Using the mathematical toolkit, one can add additional symbols and provide the semantics for them within the Z notation. Thus, the mathematical toolkit provides support for extensibility. Discussion on the distinction between the base language and the mathematical toolkit is beyond the scope of this chapter.

Like VDM, the Z notation supports two kinds of abstractions—*representational abstraction*, and *operational abstraction*. Representational abstraction is described by type definitions, global constants, and state space declarations. Operational abstraction is captured by operation definitions and function definitions. Sections 10.2 and 10.3 describe these two abstractions in detail.

10.2   Representational Abstraction

The syntactic structures in Z that form the basis of representational abstraction can be broadly classified into two categories: *mathematical preliminaries*, and *schemas*. The mathematical preliminaries include sets, functions, relations, and sequences which we already discussed in Chapter 7. Subsequent sections in this chapter focus only on notational differences for these structures within the Z specification language.

The distinguishing feature of Z is the *schema* notation. A schema has a unique name, a structure described by a set of declarations, and a property described by a set of predicates; these predicates express the invariant relationships among the structural components. The schema notation enables a specification to be split into small manageable pieces, allowing the development of modular specifications. Schemas can be composed using schema calculus. Thus, larger specifications are obtained from smaller specification pieces. Later subsections in this section describe in detail the syntax for schema notation and that for composing schemas.

10.2.1   Types

Types are interpreted as sets in Z. The set of values associated with a type is called *the carrier set* of that type. This set describes the collection of values that an object of the concerned type can assume. Thus, an object of a type in Z is actually a member of the carrier set of that type.

The Z notation is strongly typed. That is, every variable, constant, and expression in a Z specification must be associated with a type. Such a strict type system brings out two major advantages [10]: (1) it is easier to spot errors in a specification, and (2) the type system enforces a discipline in writing good specifications. Moreover, the notion of strong typing enables type checking of a Z specification to be automated.

Types in Z fall into two categories: *simple types*, and *composite types*. Composite types are derived from simple types using type constructors. The type of a composite structure such as a schema or that of a compound expression is generally derived from the types of its constituents.

Simple types

There are two kinds of simple types in type Z—*primitive types* (already defined in Z), and *basic types* (user defined). Integer type ($\mathbb{Z}$) is the only primitive type defined in Z. Basic types are assumed to be defined for the current specification (the specification in which they are declared) and are not further elaborated. The assumption is that these basic types will be defined later. As an example, the users of an automated teller machine in a banking system can be modeled as a basic type. The syntax for this basic type is

[USERS]

The square parentheses are part of the syntax. Several basic types may be introduced in one line as in

[USERS, STAFF, CLIENTS]

Several basic type definitions may be introduced in a specification.

Since types are treated as sets in Z, equality ($=$) and membership ($\in$) operators are defined for all types. Hence, objects of basic types can be compared for equality and membership:

$[USERS]$
$\forall u_1, u_2 : USERS \bullet u_1 \neq u_2 \Rightarrow \ldots$
$\ldots$
$u \in USERS \Rightarrow \ldots$

The arithmetic operators $+$, $-$, $*$, div, and mod, and the relational operators $<$, $>$, $\leq$, and $\geq$ are defined for integers.

Operator	Synopsis	Meaning
$\in$	$x \in S$	set membership
$\cup$	$S_1 \cup S_2$	set union
$\cap$	$S_1 \cap S_2$	set intersection
$\setminus$	$S_1 \setminus S_2$	set difference
$\#$	$\#S$	cardinality of a set
$\subseteq$	$S_1 \subseteq S_2$	subset
$\subset$	$S_1 \subset S_2$	proper subset
$=$	$S_1 = S_2$	set equality
$\bigcup$	$\bigcup SS$	generalized union of sets SS
$\bigcap$	$\bigcap SS$	generalized intersection of sets SS
$\mathbb{P}$	$\mathbb{P}\,S$	power set of the set S
$\mathbb{F}$	$\mathbb{F}\,S$	finite subsets of the set S

TABLE 10.1. Set operators in Z.

Composite types

There are three composite types in Z: *powerset types, Cartesian product types,* and *schema types*. Other composite types can be built from them and from simple types.

Sets and powerset types   In Z, a set can be declared in three ways: set as a type, set by enumeration, and set by comprehension. These notations have been introduced in Chapter 7. Set operators built into Z are given in Table 10.1. The symbol $\mathbb{F}$ is used to denote finite subsets of a set, while the symbol $\mathbb{P}$ is used to define the set of all subsets of a set. Mathematically speaking, a finite set is the one whose members can be put into one-to-one correspondence with the elements of the set $\{1,\ldots,n\}$ for some natural number, n. Whether to use $\mathbb{F}$ or $\mathbb{P}$ in a specification depends on the application. As an example, to denote a subset of natural numbers without any indication of how it is to be used, one would choose $\mathbb{P}\,\mathbb{N}$, whereas if it is used to denote a finite subset such as a set of room numbers in a building, the declaration $\mathbb{F}\,\mathbb{N}$ must be used.

Tuples and Cartesian product types   The notation for Cartesian product type, as defined in Chapter 7, is used in Z. In the declaration,

book: *Title* × *Author* × *CallNumber* × *Year*

the variable *book* is a quadruple (t, a, c, y) indicating respectively the title, author, call number, and year of publication of a book. Thus, if t_1, a_1, c_1, and y_1 are variables of type *Title*, *Author*, *CallNumber*, and *Year* respectively, then the following equality holds:

$$book = (t_1, a_1, c_1, y_1)$$

10.2.2   Abbreviation

Often, it is convenient to introduce a new name for a complex expression so that the new name can be used in place of the complex expression. For example, a type such as

Title × Author × CallNumber × Year

can be renamed as *Book*, which is easier to use. This is achieved in Z by the following syntax:

Book == Title × Author × CallNumber × Year

The notation *==* is called *abbreviation*, meaning that the expression to the right side of *==* is abbreviated to the name on the left side. The semantics of the abbreviation

$X == Y$

is that X is of type $\mathbb{P}\, Y$. Generally, abbreviation definition is used for defining a type, as in

RoomNumber $== \mathbb{N}_1$

Here, *RoomNumber* defines a new type which is represented by a subset of $\mathbb{N}_1$. This new type can further be constrained to assume only a finite subset of values using global constraints, as in the following:

$\forall r : RoomNumber \bullet 100 \leq r \leq 199$

10.2.3   Relations and Functions

Relations and functions are composite mathematical objects, described using sets and Cartesian products. The formal definitions of relations and functions introduced in Chapter 7 are the basis for Z specifications. The kinds of functions supported in Z and their corresponding notations are listed in Table 10.2. The operators on functions and relations and their corresponding notations in Z are given in Table 10.3. The meanings of these operators are the same as discussed in Chapter 7. Mathematical functions in Z are different from computable functions in programming languages, even though during refinement, the mathematical functions are generally implemented using computable functions. Since a function is synonymous to a relation and has a type $\mathbb{P}(X \times Y)$, one can think of a function as a precomputed set of ordered pairs. Consequently, the values of the function are assumed to be known. In fact, both constant definitions and functions use the same syntax in Z, as shown below:

Symbol	Meaning
$\rightarrow$	total function
$\nrightarrow$	partial function
$\rightarrowtail$	total injective function
$\rightarrowtail\!\!\!\!\!\rightarrow$	partial injective function
$\twoheadrightarrow$	total surjective function
$\twoheadrightarrow$	partial surjective function
$\rightarrowtail\!\!\!\!\!\twoheadrightarrow$	partial bijective function
$\rightarrowtail\!\!\!\twoheadrightarrow$	total bijective function
$\nrightarrow\!\!\!\rightarrow$	finite partial function
$\rightarrowtail\!\!\!\!\nrightarrow$	finite partial injective function

TABLE 10.2. Notations for functions.

Operator	Synopsis	Meaning
$\leftrightarrow$	$X \leftrightarrow Y$	declaration of a binary relation between X and Y
$\mapsto$	$x \mapsto y$	maplet
dom	dom R	domain of the relation R
ran	ran R	range of the relation R
id	id X	identity relation
$\fatsemi$	$R_1 \fatsemi R_2$	relational composition
$\circ$	$R_1 \circ R_2$	backward relational composition
$\lhd$	$S \lhd R$	domain restriction
$\rhd$	$R \rhd S$	range restriction
$\ntriangleleft$	$S \ntriangleleft R$	domain subtraction (domain anti-restriction)
$\ntriangleright$	$R \ntriangleright S$	range subtraction (range anti-restriction)
$\sim$	$R^\sim$	relational inverse
$-(\!\vert-\vert\!)$	$R (\!\vert S \vert\!)$	relational image
$\oplus$	$R_1 \oplus R_2$	relational overriding
	R^k	relational iteration
	R^+	transitive closure of the relation R
	R^*	reflexive transitive closure of the relation R

TABLE 10.3. Operators on relations and functions in Z.

$$\begin{array}{|l}
\hline
maximum : \mathbb{N} \\
\hline
maximum = 1000
\end{array}$$

$$\begin{array}{|l}
\hline
half : \mathbb{N} \rightarrow \mathbb{N} \\
\hline
half = \{n : \mathbb{N} \bullet n \mapsto n \text{ div } 2\}
\end{array}$$

Function types such as

$$password : UserId \nrightarrow Password$$

may be used in declarations.

10.2.4 Sequences

The mathematical basis for sequences has been discussed in Chapter 7. Below, we mention their syntax and specific built-in operations defined in Z. A sequence is treated as a function from $\mathbb{N}_1$ (representing the indexes of the sequence) to the type of objects in the sequence. Hence, the operators defined for functions (in fact, those defined for relations) can be equally applied to sequences.

Sequences can be specified in two ways. A sequence, empty or nonempty, can be declared using the keyword *seq* (e.g., seq $\mathbb{N}$). Nonempty sequences can be explicitly declared using the keyword seq_1 (e.g., seq_1 *Char*). Sequences with no duplicate elements (also called *injective sequences*) are declared using the special keyword *iseq* (e.g., iseq *Person*). A sequence can also be enumerated by explicitly introducing the objects and their relative positions within the sequence.

The notation $S(i)$ denotes the ith element of the sequence S. Empty sequence is represented by $\langle \rangle$. Table 10.4 lists the notations and the meanings of operators on sequences. The following example illustrates the application of some of these operators.

Example 10.1   *Operators on sequences.*
Let $S_1 = \langle a, b, c, d \rangle$, $S_2 = \langle a, b \rangle$, $S_3 = \langle f, g, h \rangle$,
     $S_4 = \langle b, c \rangle$, $S_5 = \langle c, d \rangle$, $SS = \langle S_1, S_2, S_3 \rangle$.

$S_1 \frown S_2 = \langle a, b, c, d, a, b \rangle$
$rev\ S_1 = \langle d, c, b, a \rangle$
$\frown / SS = \langle a, b, c, d, a, b, f, g, h \rangle$
S_2 prefix S_1 is true
S_4 suffix S_1 is false
S_5 in S_1 is true
$\{2, 3\} \upharpoonright S_1 = \langle b, c \rangle$
$S_1 \restriction \{b, d, f, g\} = \langle b, d \rangle$
disjoint $\langle \{a, b\}, \{c, d\}, \{f, g\} \rangle$ is true
disjoint $\langle \{a, b\}, \{c, d\}, \{f, g, a\} \rangle$ is false
$\langle \{a, b, c\}, \{d\}, \{f, g, h\} \rangle$ partition $\{a, b, c, d, f, g, h\}$ ∎

10.2.5 Bags

Like the *schema notation* (to be discussed shortly), *bag* is another distinguishing feature of the Z notation, which is not included in many model-based specification

Operator	Synopsis	Meaning
#	# S	length of the sequence S
⌢	$S_1 \frown S_2$	concatenation of the sequence S_1 with S_2
rev	*rev* S	reverse of the sequence S
head	*head* S	first element of the sequence S
last	*last* S	last element of the sequence S
tail	*tail* S	sequence S with its first element removed
front	*front* S	sequence S with its last element removed
⌢/	⌢/ SS	distributed concatenation of the sequence of sequences SS
prefix	S prefix T	S is a sequence forming the prefix of the sequence T
suffix	S suffix T	S is a sequence forming the suffix of the sequence T
in	S in T	S is a segment inside the sequence T
↿	U ↿ S	extract the elements from the sequence S corresponding to the index set U; the result is also a sequence, maintaining the same order as in S
↾	S ↾ V	extract the elements of the set V from the sequence S; the result is also a sequence, maintaining the same order as in S
disjoint	disjoint SeqSet	SeqSet is an indexed family of mutually distinct sets
partition	SeqSet partition T	the indexed family of mutually disjoint sets whose distributed union is T

TABLE 10.4. Operators on sequences in Z.

languages including VDM-SL. However, it can be easily modeled using functions or maps. The introduction of *bag* and the set of operators on bags simply provides additional modeling facility.

A bag is a set of elements that also encodes the number of occurrences of each element in the bag. Formally, a bag is defined as a partial function from the type of elements to the number of occurrences of the elements.

$$\text{bag}\, X == X \nrightarrow \mathbb{N}_1$$

Notice that the range of a bag is denoted by positive numbers ($\mathbb{N}_1$). This is to indicate that a bag does not maintain the information about those elements that are not in the bag.

As an example, consider a bag of coins with varying denominations: 2 pennies, 7 nickels, and 12 quarters. Let the type *coins* be defined as

$$coins == \{penny, nickel, dime, quarter\}$$

The coin bag under consideration is then denoted as

$$coinbag = \{penny \mapsto 2, nickel \mapsto 7, quarter \mapsto 12\}$$

Operators on bags

The following operators on bags are available in Z.

Count

The operator *count* is actually a higher-order function that accepts a bag as input and returns a total function from the type of elements in the bag to their corresponding number of occurrences. Typically, *count* elaborates the partial function in the formal definition of the bag into a total function by explicitly checking each element in the domain and associating a zero as the number of occurrences to those elements that are not present in the domain.

The application of the *count* operator is illustrated below:

$$count\ coinbag\ quarter = 12$$
$$count\ coinbag\ dime = 0$$

The infix notation $\sharp$ for *count* may also be used in Z. Using $\sharp$, we can rewrite the example as

$$coinbag \sharp quarter = 12$$
$$coinbag \sharp dime = 0$$

Membership

The presence of an element in a bag is checked by the bag membership operator $\sqsubseteq$, whose semantics is similar to the set membership operator. The following example illustrates the application of the bag membership operator:

$$nickel \sqsubseteq coinbag$$
$$dime \not\sqsubseteq coinbag$$

Union, difference, and sub-bag operators

Similar to sets, there are three operators to compose bags: bag union operator ($\uplus$), bag difference operator ($\uplus$), and sub-bag operator ($\sqsubseteq$). These three operators are binary infix operators and require that both operands be of the same type of bag.

When two bags are joined under the bag union operator, the domain of the new bag includes all the elements in both bags. The number of occurrences of common elements in both bags are summed up in the new bag. Elements that are not common to the two bags are retained as such in the new bag.

For the difference operator, the domain of the new bag is a subset of the domain of the bag on the left side of the operator. The number of occurrences of elements in the new bag is decreased from that in the left operand according to the count in the right operand. It becomes zero if the result of subtraction is negative. As a result, those elements whose counts become zero due to the difference operation will be eliminated from the bag since the bag does not retain count for elements that are not present.

The sub-bag operator returns true if the domain of the left operand is a subset of the domain of the right operand, and the number of occurrences of each element in the left operand is the same or less than that of the same element in the right operand.

The example below illustrates the application of these operators:

Let two new bags be defined as

$$newbag_1 = \{dime \mapsto 3, penny \mapsto 1\}$$
$$newbag_2 = \{nickel \mapsto 2, quarter \mapsto 2\}$$

Some bag expressions are

$$coinbag \uplus newbag_1 = \{penny \mapsto 3, nickel \mapsto 7, dime \mapsto 3, quarter \mapsto 12\}$$
$$coinbag \uplus newbag_2 = \{penny \mapsto 2, nickel \mapsto 5, quarter \mapsto 10\}$$
$$newbag_2 \sqsubseteq coinbag$$

Bag from a sequence

A sequence represents an ordered collection of elements emphasizing the position of each element in the sequence. Given a sequence, therefore, it is possible to count the number of occurrences of each distinct element in the sequence, thus obtaining a bag. The prefix operator *items* performs this operation. Thus, if *coinseq* is a sequence defined as

$$coinseq = \langle nickel, nickel, penny, nickel, dime, quarter, quarter, dime, penny \rangle$$

then

$$items\ coinseq = \{penny \mapsto 2, nickel \mapsto 3, dime \mapsto 2, quarter \mapsto 2\}$$

10.2.6 Free Types

The primary purpose of a free type definition is to introduce enumerated constants and recursive type definitions. Like type abbreviation, every free type definition introduces a new type name into the current specification.

The syntax of a free type definition is

$$FreeType ::= constant_1 \mid \ldots \mid constant_n \mid$$
$$constructor_1 \langle\!\langle source_1 \rangle\!\rangle \mid \ldots \mid constructor_m \langle\!\langle source_m \rangle\!\rangle$$

The symbols "::=", "|", "$\langle\!\langle$" and "$\rangle\!\rangle$" are part of the full syntax. The terms $constant_1$, ..., $constant_n$ refer to distinct constants that belong to the carrier set of the free type. The symbols for these constants, as given in the free type definition, stand for their values, and they are similar to enumerated type definition in programming languages such as Pascal. The term $constructor_i \langle\!\langle source_i \rangle\!\rangle$ refers to an injective function that accepts an object of type $source_i$ as input and returns an object of type $FreeType$. The definition for $FreeType$ is said to be closed, in the sense that

$$\langle \{constant_1\}, \ldots, \{constant_n\}, \text{ran } constructor_1, \ldots, \text{ran } constructor_m \rangle$$
$$\text{partition } FreeType$$

That is, the sets $\{constant_1\}, \ldots, \{constant_n\}$, ran $constructor_1, \ldots$, ran $constructor_m$ are pairwise disjoint and their union makes up the entire set $FreeType$. Thus, a free type definition explicitly defines all the members of its carrier set.

The following examples illustrate the application of free type definitions in several contexts:

Example 10.2   The different types of coins in a currency system can be defined as an enumerated type.

$$Coins ::= Penny \mid Nickel \mid Dime \mid Quarter \qquad \blacksquare$$

Example 10.3   The users of an automated banking system are drawn from three categories of people:

$$Users ::= cust \langle\!\langle Customer \rangle\!\rangle \mid stf \langle\!\langle Staff \rangle\!\rangle \mid mgr \langle\!\langle Manager \rangle\!\rangle \qquad \blacksquare$$

Notice that the above definition is similar to the union type definition in VDM-SL, except for the notation for constructor functions.

Example 10.4   The abstract data type "List" can be defined using the syntax for free type definition. Following is the recursive definition for a list of natural numbers.

$$List ::= nil \mid cons \langle\!\langle \mathbb{N} \times List \rangle\!\rangle \qquad \blacksquare$$

In the definition $List$, the symbol nil stands for a unique value of $List$ (similar to quote types in VDM-SL); $cons$ is a constructor function that adds an element to a list. Notice that the definition *List* does not indicate whether *cons* adds the element to the front or to the back of the list. Such constraints must be specified separately outside the free type definition, possibly as global constraints.   ∎

10.2.7 Schemas

A *schema* is a formal mathematical text describing some aspect of the software system being developed. A schema has a *unique name*, a *declaration part*, and a *predicate part*. The name of a schema can be used anywhere in the document after its declaration to refer to the text. This name can also serve as a type name (to be discussed in detail shortly). The declaration part introduces some variables along with their types, which are local to the schema. The predicate part describes some invariant relationships between the local variables themselves, and/or some relationships between the local variables, and global constants and global variables that are declared before the schema.

As an example, a user of a computer system can be specified by the schema:

[*Char*]

$$
\begin{array}{|l}
\hline
\_\,User\_1 \,\underline{\hspace{8cm}} \\
name : \text{seq } Char \\
password : \text{seq } Char \\
storage\_limit : \mathbb{N} \\
\hline
\end{array}
$$

Generally, schemas are defined using the box notation, as shown above. The name of the box (in this case *User_*1) is the name of the schema. A schema of this style without any additional constraints is a simple schema. If there are constraints imposed on components of the schema, then these constraints are listed below the declaration part, separated by a horizontal line.

$$
\begin{array}{|l}
\hline
\_\,User\_2 \,\underline{\hspace{8cm}} \\
name : \text{seq } Char \\
password : \text{seq } Char \\
storage\_limit : \mathbb{N} \\
\hline
name \neq password \\
\hline
\end{array}
$$

The constraints are generally expressed as well-formed formulas in predicate logic. Alternatively, several well-formed formulas, one on each separate line in the predicate part of the schema, can be given. In this case, an implicit conjunction is assumed between the predicates. For example, the predicate in the schema

```
┌─ User_3 ────────────────────────────────────────────────────
│ name : seq Char
│ password : seq Char
│ storage_limit : ℕ
├──────────────────────────────────────────────────────────────
│ name ≠ password
│ #password < 8
└──────────────────────────────────────────────────────────────
```

is equivalent to

$$name \neq password \land \#password < 8$$

A schema can also be specified in a horizontal style as

$$User\_4 \mathrel{\widehat{=}} [name : \text{seq } Char; password : \text{seq } Char; storage\_limit : \mathbb{N} \mid$$
$$name \neq password \land \#password < 8]$$

The variables in the declaration part of a horizontal schema must be separated by semicolons, and all constraints in one schema should be stated as one well-formed formula. The square brackets on the right side of '$\widehat{=}$' are part of the syntax.

Signature and properties   A *signature* is a collection of variables, each variable being associated with a type. For example,

$$name : \text{seq } Char; \quad age : \mathbb{N}_1$$

is a signature with two variables *name* and *age*; the type of *name* is a sequence of characters and the type of *age* is $\mathbb{N}_1$. The *property* of a schema is a predicate that is obtained from the predicate part of the schema and the predicate implicit in the declaration part. Thus, the property of the schema *User_3* is the following predicate:

$$name \in \text{seq } Char \land password \in \text{seq } Char \land storage\_limit \in \mathbb{N} \land$$
$$name \neq password \land \#password < 8$$

Schema types and bindings

The definition of schema *User_3* introduces the name *User_3* as a type. A *schema type* is an association or a *binding* between names (derived from the schema name and the names of the local variables) and types of the local variables. The type of a schema is completely determined by the names and types in the declaration part. The predicate part is irrelevant in establishing the type of the schema. Two schema types are regarded as identical if they differ only in the order of presentation of their signatures. Thus, the schemas *User_1* and *User_2* define the same type, even though their predicate parts are different. The schema *User_3* defines a type different from *User_1* (and *User_2*), since the signatures are different. An object *u* with the schema type *User_3* has components *u.name*, *u.password*, and *u.storage_limit*.

If N, P, and S are objects of types seq *Char*, seq *Char*, and $\mathbb{N}$, respectively, we can establish a binding between the component names of the schema *User_3* and the objects N, P, and S as

$$\theta \; User\_3 \equiv (name \Rrightarrow N, \; password \Rrightarrow P, \; storage\_limit \Rrightarrow S)$$

which assigns the objects N, P, and S to the schema components *u.name*, *u.password*, and *u.storage_limit*, respectively. The symbol $\Rrightarrow$ is used to describe bindings in Z, but is not part of the Z notation. The expression $\theta \; S$, where S is a schema, has a binding as its value. That is, $\theta \; S$ is an instance of S with its components as declared in S. The set comprehension expression $\{User\_3\}$ is interpreted to mean $\{User\_3 \bullet \theta \; User\_3\}$, which denotes a set of users, and its type is $\mathbb{P} \; User\_3$.

Type compatibility of signatures

Two signatures are said to be *type compatible* if and only if every variable common to both signatures has the same type. Thus, the signature

name : seq *Char*
password : seq *Char*

is type compatible with the signature

name : seq *Char*
social_insurance_number : $\mathbb{N}_1$

since the only common variable *name* has the same type in both signatures. As another example, the two signatures

$x, y : \mathbb{N}$ and
$x, t : \mathbb{Z}$

are also type compatible. Here, the type of the common variable x in both signatures is $\mathbb{Z}$. The term $\mathbb{N}$ denotes a set of non-negative integers with a constraint that

$$\forall n \bullet \mathbb{N} \bullet n \geq 0$$

The type of $\mathbb{N}$ is $\mathbb{Z}$, the maximal set.

Schema inclusion

Schema inclusion is a mechanism by which a previously defined schema definition can be reused in the definition of another schema. This could be done in two ways: (1) a schema S_1 can be included in the declaration part of another schema S_2; (2) S_1 can be included in the predicate part of S_2.

When a schema S_1 is included in the declaration part of another schema S_2, the signature of S_2 includes that of S_1 and the newly declared <variable, type> pairs introduced in the declaration part of S_2. The signature of S_1 must be type compatible with that of S_2. The predicate part of S_1 is conjoined with the newly declared predicates of S_2. As an example, consider the definition of a schema *Student*, which includes the schema *User_3*.

```
┌─ Student ────────────────────────────────────
│  User_3
│  idnumber : ℕ₁
├──────────────────────────────────────────────
│  storage_limit ≤ 1000
└──────────────────────────────────────────────
```

This is equivalent to the schema

```
┌─ Student ────────────────────────────────────
│  name : seq Char
│  password : seq Char
│  storage_limit : ℕ
│  idnumber : ℕ₁
├──────────────────────────────────────────────
│  name ≠ password
│  #password < 8
│  storage_limit ≤ 1000
└──────────────────────────────────────────────
```

A schema S_1 can be included in the predicate part of another schema S_2 in two ways: (1) the name S_1 can be placed on a separate line in the predicate part of S_2; (2) S_1 can be included using a quantified expression. In both cases, the signature of S_1 must be type compatible with that of S_2. See the two examples below, which illustrate these concepts.

The schema

```
┌─ Student_0 ──────────────────────────────────
│  name : seq Char
│  password : seq Char
│  storage_limit : ℕ
│  idnumber : ℕ₁
├──────────────────────────────────────────────
│  User_3
│  storage_limit ≤ 1000
└──────────────────────────────────────────────
```

is equivalent to the schema

$$
\begin{array}{|l}
\_\_Student\_0 _____ \\
\quad name : \text{seq } Char \\
\quad password : \text{seq } Char \\
\quad storage\_limit : \mathbb{N} \\
\quad idnumber : \mathbb{N}_1 \\
\hline
\quad name \neq password \\
\quad \#password < 8 \\
\quad storage\_limit \leq 1000 \\
\end{array}
$$

The schema

$$
\begin{array}{|l}
\_\_Student\_1 _____ \\
\quad idnumber : \mathbb{N}_1 \\
\hline
\quad \exists\, User\_3 \bullet storage\_limit \leq 1000 \\
\end{array}
$$

is equivalent to the schema

$$
\begin{array}{|l}
\_\_Student\_1 _____ \\
\quad idnumber : \mathbb{N}_1 \\
\hline
\quad \exists\, name : \text{seq } Char;\ password : \text{seq } Char;\ storage\_limt : \mathbb{N} \bullet \\
\qquad name \neq password \wedge \#password < 8 \wedge storage\_limit \leq 1000 \\
\end{array}
$$

Remarks Notice that the constraints defined in the three schemas *Student*, *Student_0*, and *Student_1* are the same as seen from their expanded definitions. However, the three schemas are not identical. The subtle differences are the following:

- The types of the schemas *Student* and *Student_0* are the same, namely the bindings defined by
  $\langle name : \text{seq } Char;\ password : \text{seq } Char;\ idnumber : \mathbb{N}_1;\ storage\_limit : \mathbb{N}\rangle$
- The type of the schema *Student_1* is $\langle idnumber : \mathbb{N}\rangle$, which is different from the types of *Student* and *Student_0*.
- The declaration and predicate parts of *User_3* are automatically brought into the respective declaration and predicate parts of *Student*, whereas to create *Student_0* we have to retype the declarations of *User_3* in *Student_0* in order to bring the variables in scope; only the predicate part of *User_3* is automatically conjoined with the newly declared predicate of *Student_0*.

Schema as a type

As stated earlier, a schema can be used as a type name after it has been introduced. The carrier set of this type is the set of all instances of the schema satisfying the binding of the schema. To illustrate, consider the schema *Users* defined below:

```
┌─ Users ──────────────────────────────────────────────────
│ all : ℙ User_3
├──────────────────────────────────────────────────────────
│ ∀ u₁, u₂ : User_3 | u₁ ≠ u₂ ∧ u₁ ∈ all ∧ u₂ ∈ all •
│     u₁.name ≠ u₂.name
└──────────────────────────────────────────────────────────
```

The predicate part of *Users* asserts that the names of users of type *User_3* must all be unique. A variable *u* of type *Users* is an instance of *Users* schema. To refer to a particular component of a schema, the _ . _ operator is used; thus, the name *u.all* refers to the instance in *u* of the variable *all* in *Users*.

Generic schemas

The generic constructs in Z allow a family of concepts to be captured in a single definition. For example, a table can be defined as a generic schema:

```
┌─ Table[T, X] ────────────────────────────────────────────
│ first_column : seq T
│ second_column : seq X
└──────────────────────────────────────────────────────────
```

The schema *Table* defines a two-column table pattern with entries of type T in the first column and entries of type X in the second column. The structure of a specific table can be described as an instance of this generic pattern. For example,

[*Person, PhoneNumber*]
PhoneBook == *Table*[*Person, PhoneNumber*]

defines tables with objects of type *Person* in the first column and objects of type *PhoneNumber* in the second column. The instantiation of the generic parameters T and X by the actual parameters *Person* and *PhoneNumber*, respectively, provides a strict binding defined as

⟨first_column : seq *Person*; second_column : seq *PhoneNumber*⟩

Notice that the two columns in *Table*[T, X] need not be of the same length. If there is a restriction, such as

#first_column = #second_column

it will be stated in the predicate part of *Table*[T, X]. This restriction will be carried over when *Table*[T, X] is instantiated with actual parameters. Thus, *PhoneBook* has the same restriction as that of *Table*[T, X]. One may further constrain the instantiation. For example, if the phone book is required to be sorted on alphabetical ordering of *Person*, then a global constraint such as

$$\forall \, phb : PhoneBook \bullet$$
$$\forall \, i, j : 1 \,.. \, \#(phb.first\_column) \bullet$$
$$i \leq j \Rightarrow (phb.first\_column)(i) \leq_p (phb.first\_column)(j)$$

is used. The operator $\leq_p$ is assumed to be defined for objects of type *Person*.

Schema expressions

Type compatible schemas can be composed using the logical operators $\neg$, $\vee$, $\wedge$, $\Rightarrow$, and $\Leftrightarrow$. When the unary operator $\neg$ is applied to a schema S, the result is a schema denoted by $\neg \, S$ whose signature is the same as that of S and whose predicate part is obtained by negating the property of S. As an example, consider the schema S defined as

┌─ S ────────────────────────
│ $x, y : \mathbb{N}$
├────────────────────────────
│ $x > y$
└────────────────────────────

Before considering $\neg \, S$, we should rewrite S so that the implicit predicates of S are visible. Thus, S can be rewritten as

┌─ S ────────────────────────
│ $x, y : \mathbb{Z}$
├────────────────────────────
│ $x \geq 0$
│ $y \geq 0$
│ $x > y$
└────────────────────────────

Now, $\neg \, S$ can be defined as

┌─ $\neg \, S$ ────────────────────────
│ $x, y : \mathbb{Z}$
├────────────────────────────
│ $\neg \, (x \geq 0 \wedge y \geq 0 \wedge x > y)$
└────────────────────────────

As another example, consider the schema S_1 defined as

┌─ S_1 ────────────────────────
│ $x : 1 \,.. \, 10$
│ $y : \mathbb{N}_1$
├────────────────────────────
│ $y > x * x$
└────────────────────────────

S_1 has an implicit predicate in its declaration part. To obtain its negation, S_1 is first rewritten as

$$
\begin{array}{|l|}
\hline
\_S\_1 \\\\
\hline
x, y : \mathbb{Z} \\\\
\hline
1 \le x \le 10 \\\\
y > 0 \\\\
y > x * x \\\\
\hline
\end{array}
$$

and then $\neg\, S\_1$ is obtained:

$$
\begin{array}{|l|}
\hline
\neg\, S\_1 \\\\
\hline
x, y : \mathbb{Z} \\\\
\hline
\neg\, (1 \le x \le 10)\ \vee \\\\
\neg\, (y > 0)\ \vee \\\\
\neg\, (y > x * x) \\\\
\hline
\end{array}
$$

The signature of the schema $S \wedge T$ is the union of the signatures of S and T. The predicate part of $S \wedge T$ is the conjunction of the predicate parts of S and T. Similar definitions are given for $S \vee T$, $S \Rightarrow T$, and $S \Leftrightarrow T$. In all the four cases, the signatures of S and T must be type compatible. The following example illustrates schema composition operations:

Example 10.5 *Logical operators applied to schemas.*
Let $S \triangleq [x, y : \mathbb{N} \mid x > y]$ and $T \triangleq [x : \mathbb{Z} \mid x > 100]$

$$
\begin{aligned}
S \vee T &\triangleq [x : \mathbb{Z}; y : \mathbb{N} \mid x > y \vee x > 100] \\
S \wedge T &\triangleq [x : \mathbb{Z}; y : \mathbb{N} \mid x > y \wedge x > 100] \\
S \Rightarrow T &\triangleq [x : \mathbb{Z}; y : \mathbb{N} \mid x > y \Rightarrow x > 100] \\
S \Leftrightarrow T &\triangleq [x : \mathbb{Z}; y : \mathbb{N} \mid x > y \Leftrightarrow x > 100]
\end{aligned}
$$

∎

Schemas can appear in quantified expressions. Given two schemas S and T, each one of the expressions $\exists T \bullet S$, $\exists_1 T \bullet S$, and $\forall T \bullet S$ results in a new schema. In all these cases, the signatures of S and T must be type compatible. The resulting schema in each case has its signature as the signature of S with components of T removed from S. The property of the new schema is true under all the bindings for which the property of S is true constrained by the property of T. This requires that the components of T that are not present in the signature of the resulting schema be brought back into the predicate part of the result through the same quantifier. The example below illustrates this concept.

Example 10.6 *Schemas in quantified expressions.*
Let $S \triangleq [x, y : \mathbb{N} \mid x > y]$, $T \triangleq [x : \mathbb{Z} \mid x > 100]$ and $U \triangleq [x, w : \mathbb{Z} \mid x > w]$

$$
\begin{aligned}
\exists T \bullet S &\triangleq [y : \mathbb{N} \mid (\exists x : \mathbb{Z} \mid x > 100 \bullet x > y)] \\
\exists_1 T \bullet S &\triangleq [y : \mathbb{N} \mid (\exists_1 x : \mathbb{Z} \mid x > y \bullet x > 100)]
\end{aligned}
$$

$$\exists_1 U \bullet S \cong [y : \mathbb{N} \mid (\exists_1 x : \mathbb{Z}; w : \mathbb{Z} \mid x > w \bullet x > y)]$$
$$\forall T \bullet S \cong [y : \mathbb{N} \mid (\forall x : \mathbb{Z} \mid x > 100 \bullet x > y)]$$ ∎

We next define a schema expression. A schema expression SE is a member of the smallest set generated by the following rules:

1. A schema S is a SE.

2. If SE_1 and SE_2 are schema expressions, then their compositions through the logical operators $\neg$, $\vee$, $\wedge$, $\Rightarrow$, and $\Leftrightarrow$ are also schema expressions; i.e., $\neg SE_1$, $SE_1 \vee SE_2$, $SE_1 \wedge SE_2$, $SE_1 \Rightarrow SE_2$, $SE_1 \Leftrightarrow SE_2$ are all schema expressions.

3. If SE is a schema expression and T is a schema, then the quantified expressions $\exists T \bullet SE$, $\exists_1 T \bullet SE$, $\forall T \bullet SE$ are schema expressions.

Schema renaming

The variables $x_1, \ldots, x_n$ of a schema S can be renamed using the notation $S[y_1/x_1, \ldots, y_n/x_n]$, where $y_1, \ldots, y_n$ are new identifiers replacing the existing identifiers $x_1, \ldots, x_n$. The new identifiers y_i's need not be distinct from one another and may even be the same identifiers already present in S. The following conditions must be true for the validity of schema renaming:

- The signature of S and that of $S[y_1/x_1, \ldots, y_n/x_n]$ must be type compatible.
- For every binding under which the property of S is true, the property of $S[y_1/x_1, \ldots, y_n/x_n]$ must also be true after renaming. Thus, if S is defined as
  $$S \cong [x, y : \mathbb{N} \mid x > y]$$
  then the renaming $S[p/x, q/y]$ results in a valid schema
  $$S[p/x, q/y] \cong [p, q : \mathbb{N} \mid p > q]$$
  whereas the renaming $S[y/x]$ results in an invalid schema
  $$S[y/x] \cong [y : \mathbb{N} \mid y > y]$$
  because the property $y > y$ is false under all bindings.[1]
- Schema renaming is merely a process of changing identifiers; hence, substitution of expressions to replace components of a schema using schema renaming is invalid.

Schema hiding and projection

The purpose of schema hiding is to hide some components of a schema from its declaration part. However, these components will be reintroduced in the predicate

---

[1] Strictly speaking, this condition is not mandatory. Thus, the schema $S[y/x]$ is a valid Z specification for which there is no model. However, we impose this restriction for the usefulness of schema renaming.

part of the schema through the existential quantifier. The reason is to bring these components in scope so that the property of the new schema will be true under all bindings for which the property of the original schema is true. Since these components are removed from the declaration part, the type of the resulting schema will be different from the original schema.

The notation $S \setminus (x_1, \ldots, x_n)$ is used to hide the components $x_1, \ldots, x_n$ from the schema S. As an example, $User\_3 \setminus (name)$ is the schema

$$
\begin{array}{|l}
\hline
\_User\_3 \setminus (name) _____ \\
password : \text{seq } Char \\
storage\_limit : \mathbb{N} \\
\hline
\exists\, name : \text{seq } Char \mid name \neq password \bullet \#password < 8 \\
\hline
\end{array}
$$

For schema hiding such as $S \setminus (x_1, x_2, \ldots, x_n)$ to be valid, the variables $x_1, x_2, \ldots, x_n$ must be present in the declaration part of S.

A schema S can be projected into another schema T using the schema projection operator. The result is a schema written as $S \upharpoonright T$, whose signature is the same as that of T. The property of $S \upharpoonright T$ is satisfied by exactly those bindings under which the property of $S \wedge T$ is true, but are restricted by the components $x_1, \ldots, x_n$ such that $x_1, \ldots, x_n$ are in S but not in T. Typically,

$$S \upharpoonright T \equiv (S \wedge T) \setminus (x_1, \ldots, x_n)$$

For the schema projection to be valid, the signatures of S and T must be type compatible; see the following example.

Example 10.7   *Type compatibility.*
Let $S \mathrel{\widehat{=}} [x, y : \mathbb{N} \mid x > y \wedge x > 100]$ and $T \mathrel{\widehat{=}} [y, z : \mathbb{Z} \mid y > z]$

$$S \upharpoonright T \mathrel{\widehat{=}} [y, z : \mathbb{Z} \mid y > z \wedge y \geq 0 \wedge (\exists x : \mathbb{N} \bullet x > y \wedge x > 100)]$$

Notice that the variable y in T is an integer, whereas y in $S \upharpoonright T$ is a natural number because y is declared as a natural number in S. In order to maintain type compatibility, the constraint $y \geq 0$ is introduced in $S \upharpoonright T$. ∎

10.2.8 State Representation

A schema can be used to describe the abstract state of a software system in Z. The declaration part of the schema contains the state space variables and the predicate part describes the state invariant. Unlike VDM, substates can be independently specified and combined using schema calculus. Modularity, achieved in this fashion, promotes comprehension, analysis, and reuse of schemas.

The instances or snapshots of a state representation in Z correspond to the bindings of the state components to various objects, which satisfy the state invariant. For illustration, consider the state space schema

```
ComputerSystem
valid, active, inactive : ℙ UserId
password : UserId ⇸ Password

active = dom password
active ∩ inactive = ∅
valid = active ∪ inactive
```

The state *ComputerSystem* describes three types of users. The variable *valid* denotes the set of users who have registered with the system. This set is partitioned into two groups, *active* users who are currently using the system, and *inactive* users whose accounts are frozen and therefore are not used. The state variable *password* in *ComputerSystem* stands for a file that maintains the names and respective passwords of the users. The state invariant of *ComputerSystem* asserts the following: (1) The variable *password* maintains the passwords of active users only; notice that it is defined as a partial function; (2) A user's account will not be active and inactive at the same time. Stated otherwise, the set of active users and the set of inactive users are mutually exclusive; (3) The valid users of the system include the sets of active and inactive users.

Table 10.5 shows some snapshots of the state specified by *ComputerSystem* (in this table, John, Mary, and Tom refer to distinct objects of type *UserId*; animal, clown and crazy refer to distinct objects of type *Password*).

10.3   Operational Abstraction

The operational abstraction formalizes operations and functions on an abstract state. The major difference between operations and functions is, as in VDM-SL, that operations access state space variables while functions do not.

valid	active	inactive	password
∅	∅	∅	∅
{John, Mary}	{John}	{Mary}	{John ↦ animal}
{John, Mary, Tom}	{Mary, Tom}	{John}	{Mary ↦ clown, Tom ↦ crazy}

TABLE 10.5. Some bindings of the state represented by *ComputerSystem*.

10.3.1 Operations

An operation, defined over an abstract state space, may or may not change the state space and unlike functions, does not return any value explicitly. The schema notation is used to define operations. The declaration part of an operation schema includes the names of the state variables before and after the operation, and input and output parameters for the operation. The predicate part describes how the values of variables in the declaration part are constrained.

Let us consider how to specify the state and operations for a simplified model of a store that issues credit cards to its customers. For each customer, the store maintains the information such as the name of the customer, the card number issued to the customer, and the current balance in the customer's account. The schema *Customer* defined below specifies the type of customers for this store.

[*STRING*]

```
┌─ Customer ────────────────────────────────────
│ name : STRING
│ cardnumber : ℕ
│ balance : ℕ
└────────────────────────────────────────────────
```

The state space of the system consists of the set of all customers of the store. The schema *Company* describes this state space. It has only one state variable, *customers*, which is defined as a set of *Customer*. The state invariant asserts that card numbers issued to customers are unique.

```
┌─ Company ─────────────────────────────────────
│ customers : ℙ Customer
│───────────────────────────────────────────────
│ ∀ c₁, c₂ : Customer | c₁ ∈ customers ∧ c₂ ∈ customers •
│     c₁ = c₂ ⇔ c₁.cardnumber = c₂.cardnumber
└────────────────────────────────────────────────
```

To enroll a new customer, we need an operation *AddCustomer*, which ensures that the card number for the new customer is different from any other card that has already been issued. This is the precondition for the operation. The postcondition asserts that the database of customers has been modified to include the new customer's information.

```
┌─ AddCustomer ─────────────────────────────────
│ customers, customers′ : ℙ Customer
│ new_customer? : Customer
│───────────────────────────────────────────────
│ (∀ cust : Customer | cust ∈ customers •
│     cust.cardnumber ≠ new_customer?.cardnumber)
│ customers′ = customers ∪ {new_customer?}
└────────────────────────────────────────────────
```

The declaration part of *AddCustomer* consists of three components: *customers* represents the set of customers before the operation, *customers'* represents the customers after the operation successfully terminates, and *new_customer?* is the input parameter to the operation. Unprimed names like *customers* are used to denote the values of the components of the state before the operation, the prestate. Names with primes like *customers'* are used to denote the values of the same components of the state after the operation, the poststate. Names like *new_customer?* denote input parameters to the operation. Names like *result!* with a "!" at the end are used to denote output parameters of the operation. These decorations are conventionally used for the intended purposes, although the Z notation does not prevent a specifier from using the decorations for other purposes. For example, if the state space schema *Company* contains a variable *customer?*, it is still valid. However, experienced Z users may find such declarations unconventional.

The predicate part of *AddCustomer* consists of two predicates: the first one is the precondition for the operation, which asserts that the card number of the new customer must not be the same as the card number of any other customer in the system. The second predicate is the postcondition which ensures that the new customer is added to the database of the system.

Recall that the specification of an operation in VDM-SL may include an error clause; the error clause asserts the conditions that must be satisfied when the precondition fails. In Z, such error conditions may be specified as separate schemas and then they may be combined with the operation schema using schema composition. In the store example discussed above, we may wish to include messages indicating a successful or an unsuccessful addition of a new customer to the store. So, we first define a message type:

$$Message ::= CUSTOMER\_ADDED \mid CARD\_NUMBER\_EXISTS$$

AddCustomer_0
customers, customers' : $\mathbb{P}$ *Customer*
new_customer? : *Customer*
message! : *Message*

$(\forall cust : Customer \mid cust \in customers \bullet$
$\quad cust.cardnumber \neq new\_customer?.cardnumber)$
customers' = *customers* $\cup$ {*new_customer?*}
message! = *CUSTOMER_ADDED*

The operation *AddCustomer_0* is enriched with a message in *AddCustomer*.

```
 ┌─ Customer_Exists ──────────────────────────────────────
 │ customers : ℙ Customer
 │ new_customer? : Customer
 │ message! : Message
 ├──────────────────────────────────
 │ (∃ cust : Customer | cust ∈ customers •
 │       cust.cardnumber = new_customer?.cardnumber)
 │ message! = CARD_NUMBER_EXISTS
 └────────────────────────────────────────────────────────
```

The operation *Customer_Exists* affirms the presence of a customer in the database whose card number matches the card number of the new customer.

$$AddCustomer\_new \;\widehat{=}\; AddCustomer\_0 \lor Customer\_Exists$$

The operation *AddCustomer_new* composes *AddCustomer_0* and *Customer_Exists* to incorporate both messages into one single operation.

Remarks It should be noted that both *AddCustomer* and *AddCustomer_new* assert only the conditions that must be true of the state variables before and after the operation. However, they do not guarantee the validity of the state invariant after the termination of the operation. It requires a proof obligation; see Section 10.4.

10.3.2 Schema Decorators and Conventions

The conventions for schema decorations allow specifications to be written with clarity and reused in other schemas. Among the three decorators (prime, question mark, and exclamation mark) discussed earlier for variable names, the use of prime deserves further elaboration. When an operation schema includes the variables of a state, it should include all the variables in that state plus their primed counterparts. This is in contrast to the specification of an operation in VDM-SL where only those state variables that are modified by the operation are specified through the **ext** clause. An important consequence of including all the state variables and their primed counterparts in a schema is that the specifier must explicitly show what state variables are changed by the operation (by specifying how they are modified) and must also report that all other state variables remain unchanged. In order to simplify the writing of all the state variables and their primed counterparts in an operation schema, Z has two conventions: the Δ and the Ξ notations.

The Δ notation

The Δ notation is used as an abbreviation to include schemas S and S' into a single schema ΔS. Note that Δ is part of a schema name, and not an operator.

$$
\begin{array}{|l}
\hline
S \\
\hline
x : X \\
y : Y \\
\hline
P(x, y) \\
\hline
\end{array}
$$

$$
\begin{array}{|l}
\hline
S' \\
\hline
x' : X \\
y' : Y \\
\hline
P[x'/x, y'/y] \\
\hline
\end{array}
$$

$$
\begin{array}{|l}
\hline
\Delta S \\
\hline
S \\
S' \\
\hline
\end{array}
$$

Having defined ΔS, we can include it in an operation schema to introduce all state variables of S before and after the operation. We illustrate below the Δ convention by rewriting *AddCustomer* operation defined previously:

$$
\begin{array}{|l}
\hline
AddCustomer\_1 \\
\hline
\Delta Company \\
new\_customer? : Customer \\
\hline
(\forall\ cust\ :\ Customer\ |\ cust \in customers\ \bullet \\
\quad cust.cardnumber \neq new\_customer?.cardnumber) \\
customers' = customers \cup \{new\_customer?\} \\
\hline
\end{array}
$$

The above operation definition is equivalent to

$$
\begin{array}{|l}
\hline
AddCustomer\_1 \\
\hline
customers : \mathbb{P}\ Customer \\
customers' : \mathbb{P}\ Customer \\
new\_customer? : Customer \\
\hline
(\forall\ c_1, c_2\ :\ Customer\ |\ c_1 \in customers \wedge c_2 \in customers\ \bullet \\
\quad c_1 = c_2 \Leftrightarrow c_1.cardnumber = c_2.cardnumber) \\
(\forall\ c_1, c_2\ :\ Customer\ |\ c_1 \in customers' \wedge c_2 \in customers'\ \bullet \\
\quad c_1 = c_2 \Leftrightarrow c_1.cardnumber = c_2.cardnumber) \\
(\forall\ cust\ :\ Customer\ |\ cust \in customers\ \bullet \\
\quad cust.cardnumber \neq new\_customer?.cardnumber) \\
customers' = customers \cup \{new\_customer?\} \\
\hline
\end{array}
$$

Notice that the operation *AddCustomer_1* includes the state invariant before and after the operation as part of its meaning. This ensures the validity of state invariant before and after the operation.

The Ξ notation

When the Δ notation is used in an operation schema, the intention is that the operation changes the values of some of the state variables. This is synonymous to read/write operation in programming languages. If the operation is an inquiry operation such as to find or to read the value of a state variable, then the Ξ notation is used. The formal definition of Ξ*S* is given below:

$$
\begin{array}{|l}
\underline{\Xi S} \\
\quad \underline{\Delta S} \\
\quad S = S'
\end{array}
$$

Following is a revised specification of the operation *Customer_Exists*:

$$
\begin{array}{|l}
\underline{Customer\_Exists} \\
\quad \Xi Company \\
\quad new\_customer? : Customer \\
\quad message! : Message \\
\hline
\quad (\exists\, cust : Customer \mid cust \in customers \bullet \\
\qquad cust.cardnumber = new\_customer?.cardnumber) \\
\quad message! = CARD\_NUMBER\_EXISTS
\end{array}
$$

Unlike VDM-SL, an operation in Z can act on several state spaces at the same time. These state spaces will be included in the definition of the operation schema using the Δ or Ξ notations. The semantics for schema inclusion will be applied to merge common declarations in these state spaces. The invariants of the state spaces are conjoined with the predicate part of the operation schema.

10.3.3 Sequential Composition

Schema calculus uses logical connectives on predefined schemas to create new schemas. In addition, there is a *sequential composition operator* denoted by "⨾" which is primarily used to compose operation schemas.

The sequential composition of operations describes the combined effect of the operations, applied in the specified sequence, on the state of the system. The sequential composition $S \; \hat{=} \; S_1 \; ; \; S_2$ defines S as an operation for which the input is the input of S_1 and the result is that from S_2 when the result of S_1 is fed as input to S_2. That is to say, the postcondition of S_1 implies the precondition of S_2. For sequential composition to remain meaningful, the signatures of the two schemas S_1 and S_2 must be type compatible and both S_1 and S_2 should address the same abstract state. If this abstract state is represented as T, then S_1 will describe the states T and T'. Since T' is fed as input to S_2, S_2 describes the states T' and T''; all the Ts are of the same type. S will contain T and T'' as its initial and final states. The signature of S consists of the unprimed components of S_1, the primed components of S_2, and the input and output parameters of both S_1 and S_2.

The sequential composition operator can be used to specify the changes in profile of a customer in the database of a credit card company, an example discussed earlier. The following operation deletes a customer record:

$$
\begin{array}{|l}
\hline
\_DeleteCustomer \rule{3cm}{0pt} \\
\Delta Company \\
old\_customer? : Customer \\
\hline
(\exists\, cust : Customer \mid cust \in customers \; \bullet \\
\quad\quad cust.cardnumber = old\_customer?.cardnumber) \\
customers' = customers \setminus \{old\_customer?\} \\
\hline
\end{array}
$$

Assuming that the operation *AddCustomer* is the same as defined earlier, we can now define the *ChangeCustomer* operation as a sequential composition of *Delete-Customer* and *AddCustomer*:

$$ChangeCustomer\_0 \; \hat{=} \; DeleteCustomer \; ; \; AddCustomer$$
$$ChangeCustomer \; \hat{=} \; [ChangeCustomer\_0 \mid$$
$$old\_customer?.cardnumber = new\_customer?.cardnumber]$$

The syntax of Z does not allow constrained sequential composition. So, we first introduce the operation *ChangeCustomer_0* and then introduce the additional constraint that the card numbers of *old_customer?* and *new_customer?* are the same.

The fully expanded version of the operation *ChangeCustomer_0* is given below:

```
__ ChangeCustomer_0 _____
customers, customers' : ℙ Customer
old_customer? : Customer
customers', customers'' : ℙ Customer
new_customer? : Customer
_____
```

$(\forall c_1, c_2 : Customer \mid c_1 \in customers \wedge c_2 \in customers \bullet$
$\quad c_1 = c_2 \Leftrightarrow c_1.cardnumber = c_2.cardnumber)$
$(\forall c_1, c_2 : Customer \mid c_1 \in customers' \wedge c_2 \in customers' \bullet$
$\quad c_1 = c_2 \Leftrightarrow c_1.cardnumber = c_2.cardnumber)$
$(\exists cust : Customer \mid cust \in customers \bullet$
$\quad cust.cardnumber = old\_customer?.cardnumber)$
$customers' = customers \setminus \{old\_customer?\}$
$(\forall c_1, c_2 : Customer \mid c_1 \in customers' \wedge c_2 \in customers' \bullet$
$\quad c_1 = c_2 \Leftrightarrow c_1.cardnumber = c_2.cardnumber)$
$(\forall c_1, c_2 : Customer \mid c_1 \in customers'' \wedge c_2 \in customers'' \bullet$
$\quad c_1 = c_2 \Leftrightarrow c_1.cardnumber = c_2.cardnumber)$
$(\forall cust : Customer \mid cust \in customers' \bullet$
$\quad cust.cardnumber \neq new\_customer?.cardnumber)$
$customers'' = customers' \cup \{new\_customer?\}$

Next, we simplify the schema: the state implied by single primed variables is first merged; to maintain consistency with the Δ notation, the single primed variables are removed and the double primed variables are changed into single primed variables. Thus, the simplified definition of *ChangeCustomer_0* is

```
__ ChangeCustomer_0 _____
ΔCompany
old_customer? : Customer
new_customer? : Customer
_____
```

$(\exists cust : Customer \mid cust \in customers \bullet$
$\quad cust.cardnumber = old\_customer?.cardnumber)$
$(\forall cust : Customer \mid cust \in customers \bullet$
$\quad cust.cardnumber \neq new\_customer?.cardnumber)$
$customers' = customers \setminus \{old\_customer?\} \cup \{new\_customer?\}$

10.3.4 Functions

The specification of a function has two parts—signature and definition. The signature consists of names and types of input and output parameters. Like VDM-SL, one can define a function in two ways in Z: using *explicit style*, or using *implicit style*. The definition of an explicit function is constructive in the sense that the function definition explicitly shows how the output parameter is obtained. For example, the function *Sqr* which squares its input parameter can be explicitly stated as follows:

$$Sqr : \mathbb{N} \longrightarrow \mathbb{N}$$
$$\forall n : \mathbb{N} \bullet Sqr(n) = n * n$$

An implicit function states the relationships between the input parameters and the result of the function, as shown in the example below:

$$max : \mathbb{F}_1 \mathbb{N} \longrightarrow \mathbb{N}$$
$$\forall nset : \mathbb{F}_1 \mathbb{N}; n : \mathbb{N} \bullet max(nset) = n \Leftrightarrow$$
$$n \in nset \wedge (\forall i : \mathbb{N} \bullet i \in nset \Rightarrow i \leq n)$$

A function definition can also be recursive. For example, the function *sum_list* defined below sums up all integers in an integer list and returns the sum. It uses the free type definition *List*, defined as

$$List ::= nil \mid cons \langle\!\langle \mathbb{Z} \times List \rangle\!\rangle$$

$$sum\_list : List \longrightarrow \mathbb{Z}$$
$$\forall n : \mathbb{Z}; l : List \bullet$$
$$sum\_list(nil) = 0 \wedge$$
$$sum\_list(cons(n, l)) = n + sum\_list(l)$$

The definition of *sum_list* asserts that the sum of integers of an empty integer list is zero. If the list is nonempty, then the list has been constructed by adding an integer n to a sublist l. In this case, the resulting sum is the sum of integers in l and the integer n.

Generic functions

Generic functions are those that produce results for arguments of arbitrary types. We have seen examples of generic functions in Chapter 7. The syntax for defining a generic function in Z is a box with a double line at the top containing the name of the generic parameters. The generic function *length* defined below recursively determines the length of a sequence (of elements of some type).

$$[T]$$
$$length : \text{seq } T \longrightarrow \mathbb{N}$$
$$\forall inseq : \text{seq } T \bullet$$
$$inseq = \langle\rangle \Rightarrow length(inseq) = 0 \wedge$$
$$inseq \neq \langle\rangle \Rightarrow length(inseq) = 1 + length(tail \, inseq)$$

10.4   Specification Examples

A Z specification consists of a series of paragraphs, where each paragraph can be a type definition, global constant, global constraint, state space declaration, or an operation. Z follows the principle of "define before use"; accordingly, every entity (type declaration, operation, function) must be defined before being used. The scope of an entity starts from the point at which it is declared and extends to the end of the current specification (except for the structural components of a schema, whose scope ends at the end of the schema definition itself). A specifier can introduce any Z paragraph as and when it is needed. In addition, each paragraph can be augmented with informal descriptions. This helps the specifier to explain the purpose of a piece of specification immediately after it is introduced. The reader should note how this feature differs from VDM-SL syntax, where an entire specification must be written in one piece, under one state space.

In this section, three Z specification examples are given to illustrate the syntactic structures discussed so far. In all examples, the specifications are accompanied by informal descriptions.

Example 10.8   Login subsystem management.

Problem description

A login subsystem maintains a set of accounts, one for each user of the system. Each account consists of a user name and a password. It is required that the names of users must be unique in the system. A user can have multiple accounts in the system with different user names. It should be possible to (1) add a new account to the system (2) delete an existing account, and (3) change the password of an account.

Additional requirement

   1. Suitable error messages must be given.

The model

User names and passwords are modeled as basic types. The rationale for this decision is that user attributes are neither stated in the problem nor are they required to specify the operations. An account is a composite entity that consists of a user name and a password. This can be modeled either as a Cartesian product or as a schema. We have chosen the schema notation to model an account. The state space is represented by a schema that consists of only one component: the set of accounts. Since no ordering is implied by the problem description, the state variable can be modeled as a set. The state invariant ensures that no two accounts have the same user name. Operations to add an account, to delete an account, and to change the password of an account, are given.

Z specification

An account in the login subsystem consists of a user name and a password.

[*Username, Password*]

```
┌─ Account ──────────────────────────────────────
│ name : Username
│ password : Password
└────────────────────────────────────────────────
```

The state space is described by the schema *LoginSubsystem*.

```
┌─ LoginSubsystem ───────────────────────────────
│ users : ℙ Account
├────────────────────────────────────────────────
│ ∀ u₁, u₂ : Account | u₁ ∈ users ∧ u₂ ∈ users •
│     u₁.name = u₂.name ⇔ u₁ = u₂
└────────────────────────────────────────────────
```

The state invariant in the above schema asserts that if two accounts have the same name, then the two accounts are identical. That is, no two users in the system have the same name.

It is possible to rewrite the state invariant as

$$\forall u_1, u_2 : users \bullet u_1.name = u_2.name \Leftrightarrow u_1 = u_2$$

We follow the former style in this book so that the types of variables are explicit from their declarations.

The operation *AddAccount* accepts a new account as input. It modifies the state space to include the new account, if the precondition is satisfied.

```
┌─ AddAccount ───────────────────────────────────
│ ΔLoginSubsystem
│ a? : Account
├────────────────────────────────────────────────
│ (∀ a : Account | a ∈ users • a.name ≠ a?.name)
│ users' = users ∪ {a?}
└────────────────────────────────────────────────
```

The precondition ensures that there is no user in the system having the same name as that of the user name in the new account. The postcondition asserts that the state space is modified to include the new account.

To delete an existing account, it is sufficient to present the user name of that account since user names are unique in the system.

```
 __DeleteAccount _____
 ΔLoginSubsystem
 uname? : Username
 _____
 users' = users \ {a : Account | a ∈ users ∧ a.name = uname? • a}
```

The predicate in *DeleteAccount* asserts that the user's account whose name matches with the input parameter is deleted from the database.

In order to change the password of an existing account, the user name of the account to be modified and the new password must be presented.

```
 __ChangePassword _____
 ΔLoginSubsystem
 uname? : Username
 pnew? : Password
 _____
 ∃ a : Account | a ∈ users ∧ a.name = uname? ∧ a.password ≠ pnew? •
     users' = users \ {a} ∪
            {(μ acc : Account | acc.name = uname? ∧
            acc.password = pnew?)}
```

The operation *ChangePassword* first checks whether the new password is different from the old password. If this condition is satisfied, the account corresponding to the old password is deleted from the database and a new account having the same user name and the new password is created.

The operation *ChangePassword* uses a μ expression which has the following syntax in Z:

$$(\mu < \text{declaration} > | < \text{predicate} > \bullet < \text{expression} >)$$

The parentheses at both ends of the μ expression are part of the syntax. The semantics of a μ expression is the same as that of set comprehension except that a μ expression returns only one value. This value is determined by the expression after the "•" symbol in the μ expression. If the expression after "•" is omitted, then the result of the μ expression is the same as that of the declaration constrained by the predicate after the "|" symbol.

The types of error messages for the chosen problem are

$$Message ::= Success \mid UsernameAlreadyExists \mid$$
$$UsernameUnknown \mid SamePassword$$

The success of an operation will be prompted by the message *Success*; this is given by the schema *Successful*.

```
┌─ Successful ──────────────────────────────────────────
│ message! : Message
├───────────────────────────────────────────────────────
│ message! = Success
```

The operation *AlreadyExists* returns the message *UsernameAlreadyExists* when a match for the name in the input is found in the database. The operation *Unknown* returns the message *UsernameUnknown* if no match for the given input name is found. Finally, the operation *Repeated* returns the message *SamePassword* when a user invokes *ChangePassword* and inputs the same password instead of a new one.

```
┌─ AlreadyExists ───────────────────────────────────────
│ ΞLoginSubsystem
│ a? : Account
│ message! : Message
├───────────────────────────────────────────────────────
│ (∃ a : Account | a ∈ users • a.name = a?.name)
│ message! = UsernameAlreadyExists
```

```
┌─ Unknown ─────────────────────────────────────────────
│ ΞLoginSubsystem
│ uname? : Username
│ message! : Message
├───────────────────────────────────────────────────────
│ ¬ (∃ a : Account | a ∈ users • a.name = uname?)
│ message! = UsernameUnknown
```

```
┌─ Repeated ────────────────────────────────────────────
│ ΞLoginSubsystem
│ uname? : Username
│ pnew? : Password
│ message! : Message
├───────────────────────────────────────────────────────
│ (∃ a : Account | a ∈ users ∧ a.name = uname? ∧ a.password = pnew?)
│ message! = SamePassword
```

The seven operations described so far can be combined to produce three new operations corresponding to the required functionalities of the problem description.

$CAddAccount \mathrel{\widehat{=}} (AddAccount \wedge Successful) \vee AlreadyExists$
$CDeleteAccount \mathrel{\widehat{=}} (DeleteAccount \wedge Successful) \vee Unknown$
$CChangePassword \mathrel{\widehat{=}} (ChangePassword \wedge Successful) \vee Unknown \vee Repeated$

The meaning of each one of these operations will be best understood if we expand them using the semantics for schema composition. For example, the operation *CAddAccount* can be viewed as

$\underline{CAddAccount}$

$\Delta LoginSubsystem$
$a? : Account$
$message! : Message$

$((\forall a : Account \mid a \in users \bullet a.name = a?.name) \land$
$\quad users' = users \cup \{a?\} \land$
$\quad message! = Success)$
$\lor ((\exists a : Account \mid a \in users \bullet a.name = a?.name) \land$
$\quad message! = UsernameAlreadyExists)$

■

Example 10.9   University accounts office.

Problem description

An accounts office in a university is required to maintain a database of information on courses in which students are registered and enrolled. A student pays a fee for each course taken during a semester. In addition, each student also pays a fixed fee for administration and student activity. Graduate students are required to pay additional fees towards thesis registration and graduation. Only after full payment of fees will students be registered in courses. The accounts office expects to perform three operations: (1) enroll a student, (2) register a student in a course, and (3) collect fees.

Additional requirement

1. A student cannot register for the same course more than once.

The model

A student's record can be modeled as a schema consisting of *identification number, status* (undergraduate or graduate), and *the courses registered*. The courses registered by a student is modeled as a set of course numbers. The details of a course such as course name, instructor, and time at which the course is offered are irrelevant for the current problem. Therefore, courses can be uniquely represented by course numbers.

The state space is represented by a schema that consists of two state variables, one representing the collection of students who have already paid their fees, and the other representing the collection who have not yet paid the fees. These collections can be modeled either as sets or sequences. We choose sequences to model them. This choice enables us to modify the specification, if necessary, later; for example, the student records can be sorted based on their identification numbers. The state invariant ensures that no student is included in both collections at the same time.

Z specification

The course numbers are derived from the basic type *COURSENO*.

[*COURSENO*]

We declare *IDNUMBER* as a finite nonempty subset of natural numbers.

$$IDNUMBER : \mathbb{F}_1 \, \mathbb{N}$$

Notice that *COURSENO* is defined as a basic type, while *IDNUMBER* is declared as a global variable. In particular, *IDNUMBER* has been declared as of type $\mathbb{Z}$. The reason for this choice is that identification numbers must be compared when ordering the students' records. However, no such comparison is necessary for course numbers.

The free type *Status* declares the two student categories managed by the system.

$$Status ::= Ugrad \mid Grad$$

A student's record is modeled by the schema *Student*.

```
┌─ Student ──────────────────────────────
│ id : IDNUMBER
│ status : Status
│ courses : ℙ COURSENO
└────────────────────────────────────────
```

Following is a global constraint that asserts that no two students have the same identification number.

$$\forall s_1, s_2 : Student \bullet s_1.id = s_2.id \Leftrightarrow s_1 = s_2$$

The state space is represented by the schema *Accounts*.

```
┌─ Accounts ──────────────────────────────
│ paid, unpaid : iseq Student
├──────────────────────────────────────────
│ ran paid ∩ ran unpaid = ∅
│ (∀ i, j : 1 .. #paid • i ≤ j ⇒ (paid i).id ≤ (paid j).id)
│ (∀ k, l : 1 .. #unpaid • k ≤ l ⇒ (unpaid k).id ≤ (unpaid l).id)
└──────────────────────────────────────────
```

The sequence *paid* is the collection of enrolled students who have paid the fee. The sequence *unpaid* is the collection of enrolled students who have not registered in any course. Since these are injective sequences, no student is included more than once in a sequence. The state invariant asserts that (1) the two collections are mutually exclusive; and (2) each sequence is ordered on the identification numbers of the students. The term *paid i* uses a functional notation and is equivalent to *paid*(*i*).

The operation *Enrol* accepts a student, who has not been previously enrolled, and puts the student in the *unpaid* list of students so that the ordering in the sequence is maintained. To simplify the writing of the *Enrol* operation, the function *insert* has been introduced; this function places a student's record at an appropriate location in an injective sequence of student records maintaining the ordering on identification numbers. The operation *Enrol* will use this function in the postcondition.

---
insert : iseq *Student* × *Student* ⇸ iseq *Student*

∀ *inseq*, *outseq* : iseq *Student*; *s* : *Student* • *outseq* = *insert*(*inseq*, *s*) ⇔
  (∃ *prior*, *after* : iseq *Student* |
      prior **prefix** *inseq* ∧
      after **suffix** *inseq* ∧
      inseq = *prior* ⌢ *after* •
          (*last prior*).*id* < *s.id* ∧
          s.id < (*head after*).*id* ∧
          outseq = *prior* ⌢ ⟨*s*⟩ ⌢ *after*)

The function *insert* splits the input sequence *inseq* into two subsequences *prior* and *after*, such that *s* is greater than the last element in *prior* and *s* is smaller than the first element in *after*. It constructs a new sequence by concatenating *prior*, *s*, and *after*. The function assumes that *inseq* is a non-decreasing sequence and does not check whether or not *s* occurs in *inseq*. The function *insert* must be rewritten to take care of boundary conditions. The operation *Enrol* and the nature of sequencing are separated in this design.

The definition for *Enrol* is

_Enrol _____
ΔAccounts
new? : *Student*

¬ (∃ *s* : *Student* | *s* ∈ (ran *paid* ∪ ran *unpaid*) • *s.id* = *new*?.*id*)
unpaid′ = *insert*(*unpaid*, *new*?)
paid′ = *paid*

An enrolled student may register for one or more courses. A student cannot register for a course after fees for one set of registered courses have been paid. So, at the time of registration the student record must belong to *unpaid* sequence. The operation *Register* modifies the sequence *unpaid* reflecting course registration. This operation uses the function *update*, which modifies the set of courses in one student record.

---
update : iseq *Student* × *Student* ⇸ iseq *Student*

∀ *inseq*, *outseq* : iseq *Student*; *snew* : *Student* •
    outseq = *update*(*inseq*, *snew*) ⇒
        (∃ *prior*, *after* : iseq *Student*; *sold* : *Student* | *sold.id* = *snew.id* •
            inseq = *prior* ⌢ ⟨*sold*⟩ ⌢ *after* ∧
            outseq = *prior* ⌢ ⟨*snew*⟩ ⌢ *after*)

The schema for *Register* follows:

```
┌─ Register ─────────────────────────────────────────────
│ ΔAccounts
│ s? : Student
│ c? : COURSENO
├─────────────────────────────────────────────────────────
│ s? ∈ ran unpaid
│ unpaid' = update(unpaid, (μ s : Student | s.id = s?.id ∧
│       s.status = s?.status ∧ s.courses = s?.courses ∪ {c?}))
│ paid' = paid
└─────────────────────────────────────────────────────────
```

The operation *PayFees* calculates the fee to be paid by a student, deletes the student record from *unpaid*, and inserts it in *paid*. The fee calculation is based on the student's status and the number of courses registered. The tuition fee for each course, administration fee and thesis fee are defined as global constants:

$$
course\_fee, admin\_fee, thesis\_fee : \mathbb{N}_1
$$

The delete function removes a student record from a sequence.

```
│ delete : iseq Student × Student ⤖ iseq Student
├─────────────────────────────────────────────────────────
│ ∀ inseq, outseq : iseq Student; s : Student • outseq = delete(inseq, s) ⇔
│     (∃ prior, after : iseq Student | prior ⌢ ⟨s⟩ ⌢ after = inseq •
│         outseq = prior ⌢ after)
```

Notice that the *delete* operation does not depend on the sequence type. It depends only on the ordering of elements in the sequence. Therefore, it can be defined as a generic function, as shown below:

```
╔═ [X] ═══════════════════════════════════════════════════
║ delete_from_sequence : iseq X × X ⤖ iseq X
╠═════════════════════════════════════════════════════════
║ ∀ inseq, outseq : iseq X; x : X •
║     outseq = delete_from_sequence(inseq, x) ⇔
║         (∃ prior, after : iseq X | prior ⌢ ⟨x⟩ ⌢ after = inseq •
║             outseq = prior ⌢ after)
╚═════════════════════════════════════════════════════════
```

```
┌─ PayFees ──────────────────────────────────────────────
│ ΔAccounts
│ paid_by? : Student
│ total! : ℕ
├────────────────────────────────────────────────────────
│ paid_by? ∈ ran unpaid ∧ paid_by?.courses ≠ ∅
│ (paid_by?.status = Ugrad ⇒
│     total! = #(paid_by?.courses) * course_fee + admin_fee)
│ (paid_by?.status = Grad ⇒
│     total! = #(paid_by?.courses) * course_fee + admin_fee + thesis_fee)
│ paid' = insert(paid, paid_by?)
│ unpaid' = delete(unpaid, paid_by?)
└────────────────────────────────────────────────────────
```

The precondition for *PayFees* ensures that the student *paid_by?* has already reg-istered for some courses. The postcondition asserts that (1) the fee is calculated; and (2) the student's record is moved from *unpaid* to *paid*.   ∎

Example 10.10   Resource allocation in a computer system.

Problem description

Every computer system manages the allocation and deallocation of resources to processes. A process, when created, is assumed to indicate the resource types and the number of resources for each type that it will require in fulfilling its task. Process creation fails if (1) resource types unknown to the system are requested by a process; and (2) the number of resources of any one type exceeds the number of resources of that type available in the system. The resource allocator maintains information on the resources allocated to processes, and resources requested by processes. Based on the availability of resources, either resources are allocated to the process and the process is executed, or the request is queued. Upon release of resources, queued requests are serviced on first-in-first-out basis.

Additional requirements

There are two additional requirements: (1) Process and resource instances have unique identifications. (2) When a process is destroyed, all resources that were held by the process must be returned to the system.

Assumptions

The following assumptions are made: (1) The types of resources and the number of instances of each type are fixed. (2) Processes are created and destroyed dynam-ically during the operation of the system. (3) All processes have equal privileges in acquiring the resources.

The model

There are two basic types, one for process identifiers and another for resource identifiers. A free type, called *ResourceType*, enumerates the resource types. A resource has a unique type, a unique identifier, and a status (free or in use). Since a process requests a resource by type, we model *resources* as a function from *ResourceType* to the power set of *ResourceInstance*, where *ResourceInstance* is a schema containing the *id* and *status* of the resource being modeled. In this model, resource instances of a given type can be looked up efficiently.

All requests that have not been met are queued. Since different resource types may have been requested by a process, an appropriate model would be a total function *waiting_queues* from *ResourceType* to iseq *PROCESS_ID*. The injective sequence will ensure that no process is added more than once to any queue.

A process has a unique identifier, status (running or waiting), and information on resources needed to complete its task. The structure of a process is modeled by a schema *ProcessStructure* with two components: *status*, and *resources_needed*. The variable *resources_needed* is a total function from *ResourceType* to $\mathbb{N}$ giving the number of resources of each type required by the process. Since process identifiers are unique, the set of all processes in the system is a partial function *processes* from *PROCESS_ID* to *ProcessStructure*.

A resource instance can be allocated to at most one process. So, all resource allocations can be modeled by a partial injective function *allocated* from *RESOURCE_ID* to *PROCESS_ID*. Being injective, it asserts that no resource instance will be allocated to more than one process.

The state of the computer system includes the declarations of *resources*, *processes*, *waiting_queues*, and *allocated*.

Z specification

[*PROCESS_ID*, *RESOURCE_ID*]

We define three distinct types of resources:

ResourceType ::= *Terminal* | *Printer* | *Disk*
ProcessStatus ::= *Running* | *Waiting*
ResourceStatus ::= *Free* | *In_Use*

┌─ *ResourceInstance* ─────────────────────────────
│ *id* : *RESOURCE_ID*
│ *status* : *ResourceStatus*
└──

Every resource instance is unique, irrespective of its type; this condition is ensured by the following global constraint:

$$\forall \, rins_1, rins_2 : ResourceInstance \bullet rins_1.id = rins_2.id \Leftrightarrow rins_1 = rins_2$$

A process structure is a schema containing the status and resource requirements of a process.

```
__ ProcessStructure _____
  status : ProcessStatus
  resources_needed : ResourceType ⟶ ℕ
```

Notice that a process identification is not part of the process structure since a process is a dynamic entity. It is assigned a unique identification as and when it is created. The schema *ComputerSystem* given below describes the state space of the computer system.

```
__ ComputerSystem _____
  resources : ResourceType ⤚⤚ ℙ ResourceInstance
  waiting_queues : ResourceType ⟶ iseq PROCESS_ID
  processes : PROCESS_ID ⤚↠ ProcessStructure
  allocated : RESOURCE_ID ⤚↠ PROCESS_ID
 _____
  (∀ r₁, r₂ : ResourceType | r₁ ∈ dom resources ∧ r₂ ∈ dom resources •
      resources r₁ ∩ resources r2 = ∅)
  (∀ r : ResourceType | r ∈ dom waiting_queues •
      ran(waiting_queues r) ⊆ dom processes)
  ran allocated ⊆ dom processes
  (∀ rid : RESOURCE_ID | rid ∈ dom allocated •
      (∃ rinset : ℙ ResourceInstance | rinset ∈ ran resources •
          rid ∈ {rins : ResourceInstance | rins ∈ rinset ∧
              rins.status = In_Use • rins.id}))
  (∀ pid : PROCESS_ID | pid ∈ dom processes •
      (processes pid).status = Running ⇒
          ¬ (∃ r : ResourceType | r ∈ dom waiting_queues •
              pid ∈ ran(waiting_queues r)))
```

The state invariant asserts the following:

- Each resource instance belongs to a unique type. Stated otherwise, the sets of resource instances in the range of *resources* are pairwise disjoint.

- The set of processes waiting for a resource type r must be a subset of the processes that already exist in the system.

- The set of processes currently holding some resources must be a subset of the processes already existing in the system.

- The status of every resource instance that is allocated to some process is *In_Use*.

- If the status of a process is *Running*, then the process should not be waiting for any resource. Stated otherwise, the process's identifier should not appear in the range of the waiting queues.

Initialization

The initialization of a software system is specified by a separate state schema that has the same components as that of the state space of the system. The initial state schema, named as *InitComputerSystem*, is defined below:

$$
\begin{array}{|l}
\underline{\quad InitComputerSystem} \\
ComputerSystem' \\
\hline
\forall\, r : ResourceType \mid r \in \mathrm{dom}\; resources' \bullet \#(resources'\; r) > 0 \\
\forall\, r : ResourceType \mid r \in \mathrm{dom}\; waiting\_queues' \bullet waiting\_queues'\; r = \langle\rangle \\
\mathrm{dom}\; processes' = \varnothing \\
\mathrm{dom}\; allocated' = \varnothing
\end{array}
$$

The predicate part of *InitComputerSystem* asserts the following conditions: (1) Every resource type must have at least one instance. (2) The waiting queues of all resource types are initially empty. (3) Initially, there is no process in the system. (4) All resources are initially free.

The schema *CreateProcess* given below describes the creation of a process:

$$
\begin{array}{|l}
\underline{\quad CreateProcess} \\
\Delta ComputerSystem \\
pstruct? : ProcessStructure \\
\hline
\mathrm{dom}(pstruct?.resources\_needed) \subseteq \mathrm{dom}\; resources \\
(\forall\, r : ResourceType \mid r \in \mathrm{dom}(pstruct?.resources\_needed) \bullet \\
\quad (pstruct?.resources\_needed)\, r \le \#(resources\; r)) \\
(\exists\, pid : PROCESS\_ID \mid pid \notin \mathrm{dom}\; processes \bullet \\
\quad processes' = processes \cup \{pid \mapsto (\mu\, ps : ProcessStructure \mid \\
\qquad ps.status = Running\; \wedge \\
\qquad ps.resources\_needed = pstruct?.resources\_needed)\}) \\
resources' = resources \\
waiting\_queues' = waiting\_queues \\
allocated' = allocated
\end{array}
$$

The *CreateProcess* operation accepts a process structure (denoted by *pstruct?*) as input. The processor identifier is internally generated (not specified) within this operation. The precondition for *CreateProcess* ensures that the types of resources and the number of instances of each type required by the new process are available in the system. The postcondition for the operation asserts that the new process is added to the set of processes after a new identifier was assigned to it and its status is set to *Running*. Other state variables are not modified by *CreateProcess*.

When a process is destroyed, all the resources held by the process are returned to the system. The process identifier of the deleted process will be removed from the waiting queues, in which the process has registered. The entire process description is also removed from the set of processes in the system. To simplify the writing of this operation and several others to follow, three functions are introduced.

Given a set of resource instances, the function *set_status* sets the status of one particular instance to *In_Use*; others in the set are not modified.

$$
\begin{array}{l}
\textit{set\_status} : \mathbb{P}\,\textit{ResourceInstance} \times \textit{RESOURCE\_ID} \nrightarrow \mathbb{P}\,\textit{ResourceInstance} \\
\hline
\forall\,\textit{rinset} : \mathbb{P}\,\textit{ResourceInstance};\ \textit{rid} : \textit{RESOURCE\_ID} \bullet \\
\quad \textit{set\_status}(\textit{rinset}, \textit{rid}) = (\textit{rinset} \setminus \\
\qquad \{\textit{rins} : \textit{ResourceInstance} \mid \textit{rins} \in \textit{rinset} \wedge \textit{rins.id} = \textit{rid}\}) \cup \\
\qquad \{\textit{rnew} : \textit{ResourceInstance} \mid \textit{rnew.id} = \textit{rid} \wedge \textit{rnew.status} = \textit{In\_Use}\}
\end{array}
$$

Unlike *set_status*, the function *reset_status* resets a subset of resource instances among a given set of resource instances to *Free*. The reason for this subtle change is that the computer system might set the status of only one resource instance at a time. However, when a process is deleted, all resource instances held by the process need to be reset. Therefore, it would be appropriate to define *reset_status* in such way to reset a set of resource instances. Even when a particular resource instance is required to be reset individually (for example, when a resource instance is released by a process), *reset_status* can still be used with a singleton set as the parameter.

$$
\begin{array}{l}
\textit{reset\_status} : \mathbb{P}\,\textit{ResourceInstance} \times \mathbb{P}\,\textit{RESOURCE\_ID} \nrightarrow \mathbb{P}\,\textit{ResourceInstance} \\
\hline
\forall\,\textit{rinset} : \mathbb{P}\,\textit{ResourceInstance};\ \textit{rids} : \mathbb{P}\,\textit{RESOURCE\_ID} \bullet \\
\quad \textit{reset\_status}(\textit{rinset}, \textit{rids}) = (\textit{rinset} \setminus \\
\qquad \{\textit{rins} : \textit{ResourceInstance} \mid \textit{rins} \in \textit{rinset} \wedge \textit{rins.id} \in \textit{rids}\}) \cup \\
\qquad \{\textit{rnew} : \textit{ResourceInstance} \mid \textit{rnew.id} \in \textit{rids} \wedge \textit{rnew.status} = \textit{Free}\}
\end{array}
$$

The third function, *delete_process*, is defined to remove a process identification from an injective sequence of process identifiers. Typically, this function will be used to delete a process from a waiting queue.

$$
\begin{array}{|l}
\hline
delete\_process : \mathrm{iseq}\, PROCESS\_ID \times PROCESS\_ID \longrightarrow \mathrm{iseq}\, PROCESS\_ID \\
\hline
\forall procids : \mathrm{iseq}\, PROCESS\_ID;\ pid : PROCESS\_ID \bullet \\
\quad (procids = \langle\rangle \Rightarrow delete\_process(procids, pid) = \langle\rangle) \land \\
\quad (procids \neq \langle\rangle \Rightarrow \\
\qquad (pid = head\, procids \Rightarrow delete\_process(procids, pid) = \\
\qquad\quad tail\, procids \land \\
\qquad pid \neq head\, procids \Rightarrow delete\_process(procids, pid) = \\
\qquad\quad \langle pid \rangle \frown delete\_process(tail\, procids, pid)))
\end{array}
$$

The operation *DestroyProcess* uses both *reset_status* and *delete_process*.

$$
\begin{array}{|l}
\underline{\quad DestroyProcess \quad}\\
\Delta ComputerSystem \\
pid? : PROCESS\_ID \\
\hline
pid? \in \mathrm{dom}\, processes \\
processes' = \{pid?\} \vartriangleleft processes \\
allocated' = allocated \vartriangleright \{pid?\} \\
(\mathbf{let}\ rids == \{rid : RESOURCE\_ID \mid allocated(rid) = pid?\} \bullet \\
\quad resources' = resources \oplus \{r : ResourceType \mid r \in \mathrm{dom}\, resources \bullet \\
\qquad r \mapsto reset\_status(resources\, r, rids)\}) \\
waiting\_queues' = waiting\_queues \oplus \\
\quad \{r : ResourceType;\ ps : \mathrm{iseq}\, PROCESS\_ID \mid (r \mapsto ps) \in \\
\qquad waiting\_queues \bullet (r \mapsto delete\_process(ps, pid?))\}
\end{array}
$$

The schema *DestroyProcess* uses the **let** clause, which needs further explanation. The **let** clause is used in Z to dynamically introduce local variables whose scope ends with the current paragraph (a paragraph may contain a schema, an axiomatic definition, a generic definition, or a global constraint). The general form of a **let** clause is

let *variable* == *expression* • ...

In this case, *expression* is abbreviated to *variable* and thereafter *variable* is used in the paragraph. In essence, *variable* stands for a textual substitution of *expression* wherever *variable* is used in the rest of the paragraph. The type of *variable* is power set of the type of the expression, following the semantics of type abbreviation. In the schema *DestroyProcess*, the variable *rids* stands for a set of resource identifiers that are allocated to the process *pid?* (indicated by the constraint *allocated*(*rid*) = *pid?*).

When a process *P* requests a resource, it specifies the type *rtype* of the resource. If at least one instance *rins* of *rtype* is free, then *rins* is allocated to *P*. If no such instance can be found, *P* is placed at the end of the waiting queue for *rtype*. The allocation is defined by the schema *Allocate*.

Allocate

Δ*ComputerSystem*
pid? : *PROCESS_ID*
rtype? : *ResourceType*

---
pid? $\in$ dom *processes*
rtype? $\in$ dom *resources*
($\exists$ *rins* : *ResourceInstance* |
    rins $\in$ *resources rtype*? $\wedge$ *rins.status* = *Free* •
    allocated′ = *allocated* $\cup$ {*rins.id* $\mapsto$ *pid*?} $\wedge$
    (*resources*′ = *resources* $\oplus$ {*r* : *ResourceType* | *r* $\in$ dom *resources* •
        if *r* = *rtype*? **then** *r* $\mapsto$ *set_status*(*resources r*, *rins.id*)
        else *r* $\mapsto$ *resources r*}) $\wedge$
    waiting_queues′ = *waiting_queues* $\wedge$
    processes′ = *processes*)
$\neg$ ($\exists$ *rins* : *ResourceInstance* •
    rins $\in$ *resources rtype*? $\wedge$ *rins.status* = *Free*) $\Rightarrow$
    resources′ = *resources* $\wedge$
    allocated′ = *allocated* $\wedge$
    (*waiting_queues*′ = *waiting_queues* $\oplus$
        {*rtype*? $\mapsto$ (*waiting_queues rtype*?) $\frown$ $\langle$*pid*?$\rangle$}) $\wedge$
    (*processes*′ = *processes* $\oplus$
        {*pid*? $\mapsto$ (μ *ps* : *ProcessStructure* |
            ps.status = *Waiting* $\wedge$
            ps.resources_needed =
            (*processes pid*?).*resources_needed*)})

The operation *Allocate* has two preconditions: the process requesting a resource must exist in the system, and the resource type that the process requests must be known to the system. The first part of the postcondition of *Allocate* is for the case when a free instance is found. The state variables *allocated* and *resources* are modified to indicate that the resource instance has been allocated to the requesting process, and the status of the allocated resource is set to *In_Use*. The other two variables *waiting_queues* and *processes* are not modified.

The second part of the postcondition for *Allocate* is for the condition that no instance of the resource type is free. The state components *waiting_queues* and *processes* are modified to indicate that the requesting process must be placed in the waiting queue of the resource type and that the status of the requesting process is set to *Waiting*. The other two state variables are not modified.

Note the following facts regarding the specification of *Allocate*: When a resource instance *rins* is allocated to a process, the status of *rins* is updated. This modification does not affect the status of any other resource instance in the system. Such a modification on a portion of a state variable (in this case *resources*) cannot be specified in isolation because the primed variables in an operation schema correspond to only state variables. Therefore, it becomes necessary to specify the effect of the change in one resource instance on the whole set of resource instances that are collectively referred to by *resources'*.

The expression

$$(resources' = resources \oplus \{r : ResourceType \mid r \in \text{dom } resources \bullet$$
$$\textbf{if } r = rtype? \textbf{ then } r \mapsto set\_status(resources\ r, rins.id)$$
$$\textbf{else } r \mapsto resources\ r)$$

in the postcondition asserts that the function *resources* is overwritten (indicated by $\oplus$) by the changes in the resource instances of one particular resource type (indicated by $r = rtype?$); instances of other resource types are not modified (indicated by $r \mapsto resources\ r$).

Finally, the *DeAllocate* operation is specified. When a resource instance is released by a process, it is returned to the pool of resources in the system.

```
__ DeAllocate _____
ΔComputerSystem
rid? : RESOURCE_ID
_____
rid? ∈ dom allocated
allocated' = {rid?} ⊲ allocated
processes' = processes
waiting_queues' = waiting_queues
(∃ rtype : ResourceType; rins : ResourceInstance |
      rtype ∈ dom resources ∧
      rins ∈ resources rtype ∧
      rins.id = rid? •
          resources' = resources ⊕
              {rtype ↦ reset_status(resources rtype, {rid?})})
```

It would be appropriate to allocate a deallocated resource *rins* belonging to a resource type *rtype* to the process at the front of the waiting queue for *rtype*. This can be specified by the sequential composition of three operations

DeAllocate ⨾ *SelectProcess* ⨾ *Allocate*

where the operation *SelectProcess* retrieves the first process in the waiting queue of *rtype* whose instance is deallocated in *DeAllocate*. Specification of *SelectProcess* is left as an exercise for the reader. ∎

10.5   Proving Properties from Z Specifications

A specification must be inspected by the specifiers and developers to ensure that it captures all the requirements of the software system being specified. The inspection process, also called *consistency checking*, includes the following steps: (1) Check the syntactic and type correctness of the specification. Ensure that all operations strictly use the state model. (2) Ensure that the specification captures the required functionalities and properties. (3) Analyze the formal text to bring out inconsistent and missing information in the documented requirements.

In this section, we illustrate how we could ensure consistency of Z specifications and how some properties can be derived by formal analysis. The consistency of a Z specification is established (1) by showing that there exists a valid initial state for the state space of the system, and (2) by showing that every operation respects the state invariant (that is, if the state invariant is true before the operation, then it must be true after the operation as well).

10.5.1   Initial State Validation

The validity of an initial state is established by the *initialization theorem*, which asserts that

$$\exists\, S' \bullet InitS$$

where S refers to the state space schema and *InitS* is the initial state schema. Informally, the initialization theorem asserts that it is possible to find a state S' with the initialization asserted by *InitS*. The proof obligation in this case is to show that the initialization is type correct and it indeed satisfies the state invariant. We illustrate the initialization theorem for the two examples: login subsystem and resource allocation system. Generally, the proof for initialization theorem uses a technique called the *one-point-rule* in order to eliminate the quantifier in the initialization theorem.

One-point-rule

The one-point-rule eliminates the existential quantifier from a quantified statement if the bound variables in the existentially quantified statement can be substituted by other terms in the same statement, and the types of the substituting terms are compatible with those of the bound variables. Formally, the one-point-rule may be stated as

$$\exists\, x : X \bullet P \wedge (x = y) \quad \equiv \quad y \in X \wedge P[y/x]$$

The right side of the equivalence asserts that y can be substituted for x, provided that (1) y is of the same type as that of x, and (2) the property P inside the quantified expression must still be satisfied even after substituting y for x. An important constraint for the application of the one-point-rule is that x should not be a free variable in the expression y.

Example 10.11   *Login subsystem—revisited.*
One of the possible initial states for the login subsystem (not given earlier) is

$$
\begin{array}{l}
\underline{\;InitLoginSubsystem\;}\\
\;LoginSubsystem'\\
\hline
\;users' = \varnothing
\end{array}
$$

The corresponding initialization theorem would be

$$\exists\, LoginSubsystem' \bullet InitLoginSubsystem$$

By expanding *LoginSubsystem'*, we get

$$
\vdash \exists\, users' : \mathbb{P}\,Account \mid (\forall u_1, u_2 : Account \mid u_1 \in users' \wedge u_2 \in users' \bullet \\
u_1.name = u_2.name \Leftrightarrow u_1 = u_2) \bullet \\
users' = \varnothing
$$

The symbol $\vdash$ denotes syntactic derivation, as explained in Chapter 6. Using the one-point-rule, the above statement is simplified to

$$
\vdash \varnothing \in \mathbb{P}\,Account \wedge \\
\forall u_1, u_2 : Account \mid u_1 \in \varnothing \wedge u_2 \in \varnothing \bullet \\
u_1.name = u_2..name \Leftrightarrow u_1 = u_2
$$

The first conjunct is true because the formal definition of $\varnothing$ in the mathematical toolkit for Z [12] is defined as

$$\varnothing[X] == \{x : X \mid false\}$$

The above definition asserts that $\varnothing$ is defined as a generic type that can be instantiated for any type X. Accordingly,

$$\varnothing[Account] \in \mathbb{P}\,Account$$

The second conjunct in the proof is vacuously true because the predicate $u_1 \in \varnothing \wedge u_2 \in \varnothing$ is false, and hence the quantified statement as a whole is true. Therefore, the initial state *InitLoginSubsystem* is valid.   ∎

Example 10.12   *Resource allocation in a computer system—revisited.*
For convenience, the initial state of the computer system given earlier is repeated here:

```
┌─ InitComputerSystem ──────────────────────────────────────
│ ComputerSystem'
├──────────────────────────────────────────────────────────
│ ∀ r : ResourceType | r ∈ dom resources' • #(resources' r) > 0
│ ∀ r : ResourceType | r ∈ dom waiting_queues' • waiting_queues' r = ⟨⟩
│ dom processes' = ∅
│ dom allocated' = ∅
└──────────────────────────────────────────────────────────
```

The initialization theorem for this example would be

$$\exists\, ComputerSystem' \bullet InitComputerSystem$$

which when expanded gives rise to the following derivation:

$$\vdash \exists\, resources' : ResourceType \rightarrowtail \mathbb{P}\, ResourceInstance;$$
$$waiting\_queues' : ResourceType \longrightarrow \text{iseq}\, PROCESS\_ID;$$
$$processes' : PROCESS\_ID \nrightarrow ProcessStructure;$$
$$allocated' : RESOURCE\_ID \nrightarrow PROCESS\_ID \mid$$
$$\quad (\forall r : ResourceType \mid r \in \text{dom}\, waiting\_queues' \bullet$$
$$\quad\quad \text{ran}(waiting\_queues'\, r) \subseteq \text{dom}\, processes') \wedge$$
$$\quad \text{ran}\, allocated' \subseteq \text{dom}\, processes' \wedge$$
$$\quad (\forall rid : RESOURCE\_ID \mid rid \in \text{dom}\, allocated' \bullet$$
$$\quad\quad (\exists rinset : \mathbb{P}\, ResourceInstance \mid rinset \in \text{ran}\, resources' \bullet$$
$$\quad\quad\quad rid \in \{rins : ResourceInstance \mid rins \in rinset \wedge$$
$$\quad\quad\quad\quad rins.status = In\_Use \bullet rins.id\})) \wedge$$
$$\quad (\forall pid : PROCESS\_ID \mid pid \in \text{dom}\, processes' \bullet$$
$$\quad\quad (processes'\, pid).status = Running \Rightarrow$$
$$\quad\quad\quad \neg\, (\exists r : ResourceType \mid r \in \text{dom}\, waiting\_queues' \bullet$$
$$\quad\quad\quad\quad pid \in \text{ran}(waiting\_queues'\, r))) \bullet$$
$$\quad (\forall r : ResourceType \mid r \in \text{dom}\, resources' \bullet \#(resources'\, r) > 0) \wedge$$
$$\quad (\forall r : ResourceType \mid r \in \text{dom}\, waiting\_queues' \bullet$$
$$\quad\quad waiting\_queues'\, r = \langle\rangle) \wedge$$
$$\quad \text{dom}\, processes' = \varnothing \wedge \text{dom}\, allocated' = \varnothing$$

With regard to type correctness, it must be shown that

$$\langle\rangle \in \text{iseq}\, PROCESS\_ID \wedge \varnothing \in \mathbb{P}\, PROCESS\_ID \wedge \varnothing \in \mathbb{P}\, RESOURCE\_ID$$

From the definition of $\varnothing$, the last two conjuncts are trivial. The formal definitions of "$\langle\rangle$", "seq", and "iseq" are

$$\text{seq}\, X == \{f : \mathbb{N} \nrightarrow X \mid \text{dom}\, f = 1 .. \#f\}$$
$$\langle\rangle\, X == \{f : \mathbb{N} \nrightarrow X \mid \text{dom}\, f = \varnothing\}$$
$$\text{iseq}\, X == \text{seq}\, X \cap (\mathbb{N} \rightarrowtail X)$$

From these formal definitions, one can infer that the type of $\langle\rangle$ is the same as that of seq X and so is the type of iseq X. Therefore, the first conjunct in the derivation, namely

$$\langle\rangle \in \text{iseq } PROCESS\_ID$$

is type correct. Next, it must be shown that the initializations satisfy the state invariant. The state invariant is defined by four conjuncts. Using the initializations, the state invariant can be rewritten as

$$(\forall r : ResourceType \mid r \in \text{dom } waiting\_queues \bullet \text{ran } \varnothing \subseteq \varnothing) \land$$
$$\varnothing \subseteq \varnothing \land$$
$$(\forall rid : RESOURCE\_ID \mid rid \in \varnothing \bullet$$
$$\quad (\exists rinset : \mathbb{P} ResourceInstance \mid rinset \in \text{ran } resources \bullet$$
$$\qquad rid \in \{rins : ResourceInstance \mid rins \in rinset \land$$
$$\qquad\quad rins.status = In\_Use \bullet rins.id\})) \land$$
$$(\forall pid : PROCESS\_ID \mid pid \in \varnothing \bullet$$
$$\quad (processes\, pid).status = Running \Rightarrow$$
$$\qquad \neg\, (\exists r : ResourceType \mid r \in \text{dom } waiting\_queues \bullet$$
$$\qquad\quad pid \in \text{ran}(waiting\_queues\, r)))$$

The four conjuncts are vacuously true for the same reason explained in proving the initialization theorem for the login subsystem example. Therefore, the initial state for the computer system is valid.   ∎

10.5.2   Consistency of Operations

The specification for an operation is ensured to be consistent if it can be shown that the pre- and postconditions of the operation respect the state invariant. That is, the property "if the state invariant is true before the operation is invoked, the invariant remains true after the operation terminates" should be proved for every operation. Formally, for every operation Op, if S and S' refer to the states before and after the operation, respectively, and $inv\,(S)$ and $inv\,(S')$, refer to the invariant evaluated at S and S', respectively, the consistency of Op is established by proving

$$pred\,(Op) \land inv\,(S) \Rightarrow inv\,(S')$$

where $pred\,(Op)$ denotes the predicate part of the operation schema Op.

We prove the consistency of the $AddAccount$ operation given in the $LoginSubsystem$ example. In this case, it must be shown that

$$(\forall u_1, u_2 : Account \mid u_1 \in users \land u_2 \in users \bullet$$
$$\quad u_1.name = u_2.name \Leftrightarrow u_1 = u_2) \land$$
$$(\forall a : Account \mid a \in users \bullet a.name \neq a?.name) \land$$
$$users' = users \cup \{a?\}$$
$$\Rightarrow$$
$$(\forall u_1, u_2 : Account \mid u_1 \in users' \land u_2 \in users' \bullet$$
$$\quad u_1.name = u_2.name \Leftrightarrow u_1 = u_2)$$

By replacing *users′* in the right side of the implication by $users \cup \{a?\}$, the right side is rewritten as

$$(\forall u_1, u_2 : Account \mid u_1 \in users \cup \{a?\} \wedge u_2 \in users \cup \{a?\} \bullet$$
$$u_1.name = u_2.name \Leftrightarrow u_1 = u_2)$$

Three possibilities must be considered: (1) both u_1 and u_2 are identical and refer to $a?$; (2) one of them refers to $a?$ and the other is different from $a?$; and (3) both of them are different from $a?$.

<u>Case 1:</u> $u_1 = a? \wedge u_2 = a?$ Hypothesis

In this case, both u_1 and u_2 have been selected to denote the same account, namely the input parameter. The formal proof below shows that the invariant is true after the operation.

1.1	**from**	$u_1 = a?$	
		$u_1.name = a?.name \wedge$	*schema equality*
		$u_1.password = a?.password$	
	infer	$u_1.name = a?.name$	$\wedge$-*elimination*
1.2	**from**	$u_2 = a?$	
		$u_2.name = a?.name \wedge$	*schema equality*
		$u_2.password = a?.password$	
	infer	$u_2.name = a?.name$	$\wedge$-*elimination*
1.3	**from**	1.1, 1.2	
	infer	$u_1.name = u_2.name$	equality
1.4	**from**	$u_1 = a?$	
		$u_1.name = a?.name \wedge$	schema equality
		$u_1.password = a?.password$	
	infer	$u_1.password = a?.password$	$\wedge$-elimination
1.5	**from**	$u_2 = a?$	
		$u_2.name = a?.name \wedge$	schema equality
		$u_2.password = a?.password$	
	infer	$u_2.password = a?.password$	$\wedge$-elimination
1.6	**from**	1.1, 1.2	
	infer	$u_1.password = u_2.password$	equality
1.7	**from**	1.3, 1.6	
	infer	$u_1.name = u_2.name \wedge$	$\wedge$-introduction
		$u_1.password = u_2.password$	
1.8	**from**	1.7	
	infer	$u_1 = u_2$	schema equality
1.9	**from**	1.3, 1.7, Hypothesis	
	infer	$u_1.name = u_2.name \Rightarrow u_1 = u_2$	
1.10	**from**	Hypothesis	
	infer	$u_1 = u_2$	

1.11 **from** 1.10
    infer $u_1.name = u_2.name$ schema equality
1.12 **from** 1.10, 1.11
    infer $u_1 = u_2 \Rightarrow u_1.name = u_2.name$ $\Rightarrow$-introduction
1.13 **from** 1.9, 1.12
    infer $u_1.name = u_2.name \Leftrightarrow u_1 = u_2$ $\Leftrightarrow$-introduction

<u>Case 2:</u> $u_1 = a? \wedge u_2 \neq a?$ Hypothesis

The variable u_1 denotes the input parameter and u_2 denotes some other account
already existing in the system. One expects u_1 and u_2 to be different because the
system does not maintain duplicate accounts. The formal proof below not only
assures this fact, but also shows that accounts are compared based on user names.

2.1 **from** $u_1 = a?$
            $u_1.name = u_2.name \wedge$ schema equality
            $u_1.password = a?.password$
    infer $u_1.name = a?.name$ $\wedge$-elimination
2.2 **from** $u_1 = a?$
            $u_1.name = u_2.name \wedge$ schema equality
            $u_1.password = a?.password$
    infer $u_1.password = a?.password$ $\wedge$-elimination
2.3 **from** $u_2 \in users \cup \{a?\}$ and $u_2 \neq a?$
            $u_2 \in users$ set union
    infer $u_2.name \neq a?.name$ precondition of *AddAccount*
2.4 **from** $u_2 \neq a?$
            $\neg\ (u_2.name = a?.name \wedge$ schema inequality
            $u_2.password = a?.password)$
            $u_2.name \neq a?.name \vee$ DeMorgan's law
            $u_2.password \neq a?.password$
    infer $u_2.name \neq a?.name$ 2.3
2.5 **from** 2.1, 2.4
    infer $u_1.name \neq u_2.name$ inequality
2.6 **from** 2.5
    infer $u_1 \neq u_2$ schema inequality
2.7 **from** 2.5, 2.6
    infer $u_1.name \neq u_2.name \Rightarrow u_1 \neq u_2$ $\Rightarrow$-introduction
2.8 **from** Hypothesis
    infer $u_1 \neq u_2$ inequality
2.9 **from** 2.8
            $u_1.name \neq u_2.name \vee$ schema inequality
            $u_1.password \neq u_2.password$
    infer $u_1.name \neq u_2.name$ 2.5
2.10 **from** 2.8, 2.9
    infer $u_1 \neq u_2 \Rightarrow u_1.name \neq u_2.name$ $\Rightarrow$-introduction

2.11 **from**   2.7, 2.10
    infer $u_1.name \neq u_2.name \Leftrightarrow u_1 \neq u_2$ $\Leftrightarrow$-introduction

A similar proof applies for the case $u_1 \neq a? \wedge u_2 = a$.

<u>Case 3:</u> $u_1 \neq a? \wedge u_2 \neq a?$ Hypothesis

Since both u_1 and u_2 are different from the input parameter $a?$, they denote two
accounts that already exist in the system. Since the invariant is true before the
operation, it is trivial to prove that u_1 and u_2 are equal if and only if the user names
in these two accounts are the same.

3.1 **from** $u_1 \in users \cup \{a?\}$ and $u_1 \neq a?$
    infer $u_1 \in users$ set union
3.2 **from** $u_2 \in users \cup \{a?\}$ and $u_2 \neq a?$
    infer $u_2 \in users$ set union
3.3 **from**   3.1, 3.2
    infer $u_1.name = u_2.name \Leftrightarrow u_1 = u_2$ invariant before

Formal proofs, as seen from the above example, require a number of proof steps
where in each step an inference rule is used to derive a new fact. For most non-
trivial applications, formal proofs are very hard to produce. Even with the help of
a proof assistant, deriving a formal proof can be a tedious and difficult process.
The major difficulty lies in managing the large number of proof steps and in the
generation of intermediate inference rules.

To alleviate the problems in deriving formal proofs but still support reasoning based
on formal specifications, software developers use a *rigorous approach*. A rigorous
proof is not formal, but it is not informal either. A rigorous proof resembles a
mathematical proof.

In this approach, proofs include rigorous arguments and informal descriptions. The
rigorous arguments are justified by quoting the formal specification components.
The inference rules are ignored and fundamental properties of basic types are
assumed. Below, we rigorously prove that the operation *ChangePassword* in the
LoginSubsystem example is consistent.

Example 10.13   *Login subsystem—revisited.*
The operation *ChangePassword* in the *LoginSubsystem* example should not modify
any account other than the account selected for modification. Formally stated:

$$ChangePassword \vdash \forall u : Account \mid u \in users' \bullet$$
$$u.name \neq uname? \Rightarrow (\exists v : Account \mid v \in users \bullet v = u)$$

In the expression above, u denotes any account in the state after the operation
terminates (indicated by $u \in users'$). There are two cases to be considered for the
proof:

<u>Case 1</u>: $u \in users' \land u.name = uname?$

The variable u refers to the account being modified. Since $u \in users'$ and $u.name = uname?$ is the negation of the constraint given in the quantified expression

$$\forall u : Account \mid u \in users' \bullet u.name \neq uname? \Rightarrow \dots$$

the implication is vacuously true. This means that the stated property is derivable from *ChangePassword*. Notice that the variables and their types in the hypothesis are derived from the declaration of the schema *ChangePassword*, as indicated by the semantics of the notation $\vdash$.

<u>Case 2</u>: $u \in users' \land u.name \neq uname?$

The predicate part in *ChangePassword* has been reproduced below for the sake of understanding:

$$
\begin{array}{|l}
\quad ChangePassword \underline{} \\
\Delta LoginSubsystem \\
uname? : Username \\
pnew? : Password \\
\hline
\exists a : Account \mid a \in users \land a.name = uname? \land a.password \neq pnew? \bullet \\
\quad users' = users \setminus \{a\} \cup \{(\mu\, acc : Account \mid acc.name = uname? \land \\
\qquad acc.password = pnew?)\} \\
\end{array}
$$

ChangePassword describes the construction of *users'*: i.e., a is removed from *users* and *acc* is inserted in *users*. From

$u.name \neq uname?$ (hypothesis)
$a.name = uname?$ (precondition),

we conclude

$u.name \neq a.name$

From the state invariant

$$\forall u_1, u_2 : Account \mid u_1 \in users \land u_2 \in users \bullet$$
$$u_1.name = u_2.name \Leftrightarrow u_1 = u_2$$

one can derive

$u \neq a$

Therefore, u is not the account that is being deleted by *ChangePassword*. Since u exists in the state after the operation terminates (indicated by $u \in users'$), either it exists in the state before the operation or it is the newly created account (i.e., $u = acc$).

From *ChangePassword*, infer $acc.name = uname?$

From hypothesis, infer $u.name \neq uname?$

Therefore $u.name \neq acc.name$.

From the state invariant, conclude that

$u \neq acc$

Therefore, u is not changed by the operation *ChangePassword*.   ■

10.6 Case Study—An Automated Billing System

In this section, we describe the specification of an automated billing system for work schedule in a software firm. Most of the Z notation discussed so far is used in this specification.

Problem description

Software consulting firms generally deal with several clients where each client contracts out a project to the firm and receives a set of services related to the project. An employee in the firm may work on multiple projects at any one time, with an interleaved work schedule. A customer is billed at an hourly rate and an employee is paid at another hourly rate. The focus of the problem is to develop an automated billing system that can be used both for billing the customers for their projects and for calculating the salaries of employees.

Additional requirements

1. A project employs one or more employees.
2. The hourly rate charged for projects is the same for all the projects and is assigned at the initiation of the project.
3. The hourly salary is the same for all employees in the firm. The salary is independent of the project(s) assigned to the employee.
4. The estimated number of hours for completing a project is fixed for billing purposes, whether or not the project is completed by the deadline. If a project is not completed within its estimated time, the customer who initiated this project will not be billed for the extra hours required by the firm to complete the project. However, employees who work on this project during the extra hours will be paid according to their salary rate.
5. Depending on the rate of progress and the nature of a project, employees may be assigned to a project or be removed from a project.
6. A project, once initiated, will not be terminated until it is completed.
7. It must be possible to perform the following operations: (1) Add a new employee to the firm. (2) Add a new customer. (3) Initiate a project (by

a known customer). (4) Assign an employee to a project. (5) Release an employee from a project. (6) Report the work done by an employee. (7) Calculate the salary of an employee for a given month and year. (8) Bill a customer for a given month and year.

The model

The requirements reveal that *Employee*, *Customer*, and *Project* are three composite data types to be modeled with a number of static and dynamic relationships among them. For example, "a project is initiated by a customer" is a static relationship between *Project* and *Customer*, while "an employee is assigned to a particular project" defines a dynamic relationship between *Employee* and *Project*. These relationships must be captured succintly in their models.

Schema type or Cartesian product type may be used to construct the data model for *Employee*, *Project*, and *Customer*. However, they may lead to a clumsy specification. For example, a schema for *Employee* would have to include project information as well. This necessitates using expressions of the form *e.project* in operation specifications. If the Cartesian product type were to be used, as in

$$Customer == CUSTOMER\_ID \times \mathbb{P}(PROJECT\_ID \times DATE \times HOURS)$$

two projection operations are required to select the number of hours spent on a project initiated by a customer. So we avoid these two modeling approaches and instead use a modular approach to building data types required for the problem. First, primitive types and operations on them are defined. Next, composite types are constructed and curried functions (higher-order functions) are defined to capture the relationships among the composite types. Finally, these are used to form aggregates modeling the three types *Employee*, *Customer*, and *Project*.

Z specification

We first define several basic types and auxilary functions that are necessary in the system specification.

Basic types

The identifiers for employees, customers, and projects are represented by three distinct basic types.

$$[EMPLOYEE\_ID, CUSTOMER\_ID, PROJECT\_ID]$$

Date

The requirements state that salaries of employees and customer invoices are based on the number of hours devoted to the projects on a daily basis. So we need to model *Date*. *Date* is a triple *(day, month, year)*, so Cartesian product is an appropriate model for it.

$Day == 1..31$
$Month ::= January \mid February \mid March \mid April \mid May \mid June \mid July \mid$
$\qquad\qquad August \mid September \mid October \mid November \mid December$
$Year == 1949..2999$
$Date == Day \times Month \times Year$

The enumerated values for *Year* are chosen arbitrarily. We next specify three projection functions *day*, *month*, and *year* to select the fields of a date.

$day : Date \longrightarrow Day$
$month : Date \longrightarrow Month$
$year : Date \longrightarrow Year$

$\forall dt : Date \bullet$
$\qquad \exists d : Day;\ m : Month;\ y : Year \mid (d, m, y) = dt \bullet$
$\qquad\qquad day(dt) = d \wedge month(dt) = m \wedge year(dt) = y$

The following global constraint asserts the validity of instances of type *Date*.

$\forall dt : Date \bullet$
$\qquad (month(dt) \in \{April, June, September, November\} \Rightarrow day(dt) \le 30) \wedge$
$\qquad (month(dt) = February \Rightarrow$
$\qquad\qquad ((year(dt) \bmod 4 = 0 \wedge year(dt) \bmod 100 \ne 0) \Rightarrow day(dt) \le 29) \wedge$
$\qquad\qquad ((year(dt) \bmod 4 \ne 0 \vee year(dt) \bmod 100 = 0) \Rightarrow day(dt) \le 28))$

Work hours
An employee may work for a maximum of 24 hours during a 24-hour day. We therefore define *Hours* as an enumerated type.

$Hours == 0..24$

Time sheet
Combining *Date* and *Hours*, we define the data type *TimeSheet*, which shows the dates and the number of hours worked by an employee during each day on a particular project. A time sheet cannot show two different work hours for a given date, since a *TimeSheet* is a function from *Date* to *Hours*.

$TimeSheet == Date \nrightarrow Hours$

A *TimeSheet* may also be used as part of a customer's record to enter the work hours completed on a particular project.

Two time sheets may be combined into one. The resulting time sheet will show the number of hours worked by an employee on two different projects on a given day.

$$
\begin{array}{|l}
\hline
update\_timesheet : TimeSheet \times TimeSheet \nrightarrow TimeSheet \\
\hline
\forall tsh_1, tsh_2, tsh : TimeSheet \bullet update\_timesheet(tsh_1, tsh_2) = tsh \Rightarrow \\
\quad \mathrm{dom}\, tsh = \mathrm{dom}\, tsh_1 \cup \mathrm{dom}\, tsh_2 \wedge \\
\quad (\forall dt : Date \mid dt \in \mathrm{dom}\, tsh \bullet \\
\quad\quad (dt \in \mathrm{dom}\, tsh_1 \wedge dt \in \mathrm{dom}\, tsh_2 \Rightarrow \\
\quad\quad\quad tsh\, dt = tsh_1\, dt + tsh_2\, dt) \wedge \\
\quad\quad (dt \in \mathrm{dom}\, tsh_1 \wedge dt \notin \mathrm{dom}\, tsh_2 \Rightarrow tsh\, dt = tsh_1\, dt) \wedge \\
\quad\quad (dt \in \mathrm{dom}\, tsh_2 \wedge dt \notin \mathrm{dom}\, tsh_1 \Rightarrow tsh\, dt = tsh_2\, dt)) \\
\hline
\end{array}
$$

Given a time sheet, we can sum up all the entries in the second column, which is the number of hours worked by an employee on different dates. This sum can be used to calculate the salary of an employee (or to prepare a bill for the customer). The function *sum_timesheet* computes this sum for a given time sheet.

$$
\begin{array}{|l}
\hline
sum\_timesheet : TimeSheet \longrightarrow \mathbb{N} \\
\hline
\forall tsh : TimeSheet \bullet \\
\quad tsh = \varnothing \Rightarrow sum\_timesheet(tsh) = 0 \wedge \\
\quad tsh \neq \varnothing \Rightarrow (\exists dt : Date \mid dt \in \mathrm{dom}\, tsh \bullet \\
\quad\quad sum\_timesheet(tsh) = (tsh\, dt) + sum\_timesheet(\{dt\} \lhd tsh)) \\
\hline
\end{array}
$$

Notice that the expression

$$sum\_timesheet(\{dt\} \lhd tsh)$$

recursively defines the sum on the time sheet entries after deleting the entry corresponding to *dt* from the domain of *tsh*. Since there can be only finitely many entries in a time sheet, the terminating condition stated in the postcondition will eventually be satisfied.

Work sheet

There is at most one (logical) time sheet for a project. A work sheet records for each project the time sheet associated with that project.

$$WorkSheet == PROJECT\_ID \nrightarrow TimeSheet$$

The number of work hours completed for a project can be calculated from a work sheet by projecting the project identifier and the work hours in the work sheet. The function *project_hours* discards the date component in the *TimeSheet* of a work sheet and returns the project identification with the number of hours completed for that project.

$$
\begin{array}{|l}
\hline
project\_hours : WorkSheet \nrightarrow (PROJECT\_ID \nrightarrow \mathbb{N}) \\
\hline
\forall work : WorkSheet \bullet project\_hours(work) = \\
\quad \{pid : PROJECT\_ID; \ hrs : Hours \mid \\
\quad\quad pid \in \mathrm{dom}\, work \wedge hrs = sum\_timesheet(work\, pid) \bullet \\
\quad\quad (pid \mapsto hrs)\} \\
\hline
\end{array}
$$

The function *sum_workhours* accepts a work sheet as input and returns the total number of hours in all the time sheets contained in the work sheet. This function is necessary to calculate the salary of an employee as well as the amount to be billed to a customer.

$$sum\_workhours : WorkSheet \nrightarrow \mathbb{N}$$
$$\forall work : WorkSheet \bullet$$
$$\quad work = \varnothing \Rightarrow sum\_workhours(work) = 0 \wedge$$
$$\quad work \neq \varnothing \Rightarrow (\exists pid : PROJECT\_ID \mid pid \in \mathrm{dom}\, work \bullet$$
$$\quad\quad sum\_workhours(work) = sum\_timesheet(work\, pid) +$$
$$\quad\quad\quad sum\_workhours(\{pid\} \lhd work))$$

In order to know the monthly salary of an employee or cost on a project to a customer, we need to select the time sheets corresponding to the particular month under consideration from the set of time sheets given in a work sheet.

$$select\_timesheets : WorkSheet \times Month \times Year \nrightarrow WorkSheet$$
$$\forall work : WorkSheet; m : Month; y : Year \bullet$$
$$\quad select\_timesheets(work, m, y) =$$
$$\quad\quad \{pid : PROJECT\_ID; tsh : TimeSheet \mid pid \mapsto tsh \in work \wedge$$
$$\quad\quad (\forall dt : Date \mid dt \in \mathrm{dom}\, tsh \bullet month(dt) = m \wedge year(dt) = y) \bullet$$
$$\quad\quad (pid \mapsto tsh)\}$$

Like the function *update_timesheet*, we also define another function *update_worksheet* to update a worksheet.

$$update\_worksheet : WorkSheet \times WorkSheet \nrightarrow WorkSheet$$
$$\forall work_1, work_2, work : WorkSheet \bullet update\_worksheet(work_1, work_2) =$$
$$\quad work \Rightarrow \mathrm{dom}\, work = \mathrm{dom}\, work_1 \cup \mathrm{dom}\, work_2 \wedge$$
$$\quad (\forall pid : PROJECT\_ID \mid pid \in \mathrm{dom}\, work \bullet$$
$$\quad\quad (pid \in \mathrm{dom}\, work_1 \wedge pid \in \mathrm{dom}\, work_2 \Rightarrow$$
$$\quad\quad\quad work\, pid = update\_timesheet(work_1\, pid, work_2\, pid)) \wedge$$
$$\quad\quad (pid \in \mathrm{dom}\, work_1 \wedge pid \notin \mathrm{dom}\, work_2 \Rightarrow work\, pid = work_1\, pid) \wedge$$
$$\quad\quad (pid \in \mathrm{dom}\, work_2 \wedge pid \notin \mathrm{dom}\, work_1 \Rightarrow work\, pid = work_2\, pid))$$

State of the system

There are three constants in the state model: *project_rate*, denoting the hourly rate used to charge a customer; *employee_rate*, denoting the hourly rate for calculating the salaries of employees; and *bill_charge*, indicating the fixed monthly charge to be added to the bill for each customer.

$$project\_rate : \mathbb{N}_1$$
$$employee\_rate : \mathbb{N}_1$$
$$bill\_charge : \mathbb{N}_1$$

$\begin{array}{|l}
__Organization_____ \\
employees : EMPLOYEE_ID \nrightarrow WorkSheet \\
customers : CUSTOMER_ID \nrightarrow WorkSheet \\
projects : PROJECT_ID \nrightarrow (\mathbb{N}_1 \times \mathbb{N}) \\
\hline
(\forall\, eid : EMPLOYEE_ID \mid eid \in \mathrm{dom}\ employees \bullet \\
\quad \mathrm{dom}(employees\ eid) \subseteq \mathrm{dom}\ projects \wedge \\
\qquad (\forall\, pid : PROJECT_ID \mid pid \in \mathrm{dom}(employees\ eid) \bullet \\
\qquad\quad second(projects\ pid) \geq sum_timesheet((employees\ eid)\ pid))) \wedge \\
(\forall\, cid : CUSTOMER_ID \mid cid \in \mathrm{dom}\ customers \bullet \\
\quad \mathrm{dom}(customers\ cid) \subseteq \mathrm{dom}\ projects \wedge \\
\qquad (\forall\, pid : PROJECT_ID \mid pid \in \mathrm{dom}(customers\ cid) \bullet \\
\qquad\quad second(projects\ pid) = sum_timesheet((customers\ cid)\ pid))) \wedge \\
(\forall\, pid : PROJECT_ID \mid pid \in \mathrm{dom}\ projects \bullet \\
\quad second(projects\ pid) \leq first(projects\ pid))
\end{array}$

The state space schema *Organization* defines three entities: *employees*, a function from employee identifiers to worksheet; *customers*, a function from customer identifiers to worksheet; and *projects*, a function from project identifiers to a pair of integers, where the first integer denotes the estimated time for the completion of a project, and the second denotes the actual number of hours put in.

The state invariant is a conjunction of the following constraints:

- Every project assigned to an employee is a project contracted out to the firm:
  $$\mathrm{dom}(employees\ eid) \subseteq \mathrm{dom}\ projects$$

- The number of work hours reported by an employee on a project cannot exceed the total number of hours completed on that project:
  $$second(projects\ pid) \geq sum\_timesheet((employees\ eid)\ pid)$$

- The number of hours completed on a project must agree with the number of hours reported to the customer of that project:
  $$second(projects\ pid) = sum\_timesheet((customers\ cid)\ pid)$$

- For every project, the number of work hours completed must be less than or equal to the number of work hours estimated for the project:
  $$second(projects\ pid) \leq first(projects\ pid)$$

Initialization

The initial state for the organization is one in which there is no employee, customer, or project.

$\begin{array}{|l}
__InitOrganization_____ \\
Organization' \\
\hline
employees' = \varnothing \\
customers' = \varnothing \\
projects' = \varnothing
\end{array}$

Operations

The operation *AddEmployee* adds a new employee to the organization, who is not yet assigned to any project.

```
┌─ AddEmployee ────────────────────────────────────
│ ΔOrganization
├──────────────────────────────────────────────────
│ (∃ eid : EMPLOYEE_ID | eid ∉ dom employees •
│     employees' = employees ⊕ {eid ↦ ∅})
│ customers' = customers
│ projects' = projects
└──────────────────────────────────────────────────
```

The identifier for the new employee is generated by the *AddEmployee* operation and ensures that the identifier is unique.

The operations *InitiateProject* and *AddCustomer* are similar; however, there are some minor differences between them. Only a customer of the organization can initiate projects. That is, a project initiation by a customer happens only after the customer has been included in the database of customers in the organization. When a customer is added to the database, the customer is assigned a unique identification number and no project has been initiated at that instant. Below, the *InitiateProject* operation is shown; *AddCustomer* is left as an exercise.

```
┌─ InitiateProject ────────────────────────────────
│ ΔOrganization
│ cid? : CUSTOMER_ID
│ estimate? : ℕ₁
├──────────────────────────────────────────────────
│ cid? ∈ dom customers
│ (∃ pid : PROJECT_ID | pid ∉ dom projects •
│     customers' = customers ⊕ {cid? ↦
│         (customers cid?) ⊕ {pid ↦ ∅}} ∧
│     projects' = projects ⊕ {pid ↦ (estimate?, 0)})
│ employees' = employees
└──────────────────────────────────────────────────
```

```
┌─ AssignEmployee ─────────────────────────────────
│ ΔOrganization
│ eid? : EMPLOYEE_ID
│ pid? : PROJECT_ID
├──────────────────────────────────────────────────
│ eid? ∈ dom employees
│ pid? ∈ dom projects
│ ¬ (pid? ∈ dom(employees eid?))
│ employees' = employees ⊕ {eid? ↦ (employees eid?) ⊕ {pid? ↦ ∅}}
│ customers' = customers
│ projects' = projects
└──────────────────────────────────────────────────
```

The operation *AssignEmployee* assigns an employee to a project (or a project to an employee). The employee identifier *eid* and the project identifier *pid* are input parameters. The precondition checks the validity of these identifiers. In addition, the precondition ensures that the project *pid*? has not been assigned previously to the employee *eid*? The postcondition asserts that the employee has been assigned the project.

The operation *ReleaseEmployee*, a complement of the operation *AssignEmployee*, is left for the exercises.

```
┌─ ReportWork ─────────────────────────────────────────────────
│ ΔOrganization
│ eid? : EMPLOYEE_ID
│ work? : WorkSheet
├──────────────────────────────────────────────────────────────
│ eid? ∈ dom employees
│ dom work? ⊆ dom(employees eid?)
│ employees' = employees ⊕ {eid? ↦
│       update_worksheet(employees eid?, work?)}
│ customers' = customers ⊕ {cid : CUSTOMER_ID | cid ∈ dom customers •
│       cid ↦ update_worksheet(customers cid, work?)}
│ (let updates == project_hours(work?) •
│       projects' = projects ⊕ {pid : PROJECT_ID | pid ∈ dom updates •
│             pid ↦ (first(projects pid), second(projects pid)+
│             (updates pid))})
└──────────────────────────────────────────────────────────────
```

Since the date/time at which the employee reports the completion of work has not been modeled, the operation *ReportWork* only specifies the functionality of updating the work sheet for a particular employee without regard to the date and time of update. The precondition checks for the validity of the employee identification and the legitimacy of the work reported. The postcondition uses the two functions *update_worksheet* and *project_hours* to modify the state variables.

```
┌─ CalculateSalary ────────────────────────────────────────────
│ ΞOrganization
│ eid? : EMPLOYEE_ID
│ month? : Month
│ year? : Year
│ salary! : ℕ
├──────────────────────────────────────────────────────────────
│ eid? ∈ dom employees
│ (let worksheet == select_timesheets((employees eid?), month?, year?) •
│       salary! = sum_workhours(worksheet) * employee_rate)
└──────────────────────────────────────────────────────────────
```

The salary for an employee is calculated for a given month, so the operation *CalculateSalary* receives three input parameters: the employee identifier *eid* whose salary is to be calculated, and the month and year for which the salary is to be calculated. The **let** clause in the predicate part of *CalculateSalary* projects only those time sheets that correspond to the selected month from the employee's record. Since *CalculateSalary* does not modify the state (indicated by Ξ), it is not necessary to include those constraints that assert that the state variables are not changed by this operation.

The operation *BillCustomer* is similar to the operation *CalculateSalary*, and is left for the exercises.

10.7   Additional Features in Z

In this section, we discuss *precondition calculation* and *promotion*, two additional features in Z. The predicate part of a schema consists of several predicates, some denoting preconditions and some denoting postconditions for the specified operation. However, the Z notation does not explicitly separate the precondition from the postcondition. Therefore, a procedure to calculate the precondition is introduced. Promotion effectively describes the influence of an operation defined for a local state space on a global state space; the local state space must be part of the global state space.

10.7.1   Precondition Calculation

The precondition of an operation describes the set of possible assignments of values to the state variables and input variables such that the operation terminates in a consistent state and generates an expected output. If the precondition of an operation fails, the consequences of invoking that operation are unpredictable or are unacceptable. Unlike in VDM-SL, there is no explicit notation to denote the precondition of an operation in Z. Instead, one has to calculate the precondition from the definition of the operation. The notation *pre op* will be used to denote the schema derived by the precondition calculation on the schema *op*.

The main question to be answered in a precondition calculation is "for what combinations of inputs and starting states can one find the ending states and outputs that satisfy the predicates?" Informally, the answer to the above question is to assert the existence of outputs and ending states such that the predicate part of the *op* schema is satisfied for the unprimed variables. So the precondition calculation is done as follows: from the given schema, remove the outputs and ending states (primed variables) from the declaration part and bind them in the predicate part with an existential quantifier.

As an example, consider the operation *AddAccount* in the specification *LoginSubsystem*. For convenience, we reproduce the specification of *AddAccount* here with its declaration and predicate parts expanded.

$$
\begin{array}{|l}
\_AddAccount\_\! \\
users, users' : \mathbb{P}\,Account \\
a? : Account \\
\hline
(\forall\, u_1, u_2 : Account \mid u_1 \in users \land u_2 \in users \bullet \\
\quad u_1.name = u_2.name \Leftrightarrow u_1 = u_2) \\
(\forall\, u_1, u_2 : Account \mid u_1 \in users' \land u_2 \in users' \bullet \\
\quad u_1.name = u_2.name \Leftrightarrow u_1 = u_2) \\
(\forall\, a : Account \mid a \in users \bullet a.name \neq a?.name) \\
users' = users \cup \{a?\}
\end{array}
$$

No implicit predicate arises from the declaration. We need to remove the outputs and ending states from the declaration and bind them with existential quantifier in the predicate part. The expression *pre AddAccount* results in the following unnamed schema:

$$
\begin{array}{|l}
\_\! \\
users : \mathbb{P}\,Account \\
a? : Account \\
\hline
\exists\, users' : \mathbb{P}\,Account \bullet \\
\quad (\forall\, u_1, u_2 : Account \mid u_1 \in users \land u_2 \in users \bullet \\
\quad\quad u_1.name = u_2.name \Leftrightarrow u_1 = u_2) \land \\
\quad (\forall\, u_1, u_2 : Account \mid u_1 \in users' \land u_2 \in users' \bullet \\
\quad\quad u_1.name = u_2.name \Leftrightarrow u_1 = u_2) \land \\
\quad (\forall\, a : Account \mid a \in users \bullet a.name \neq a?.name) \land \\
\quad (users' = users \cup \{a?\})
\end{array}
$$

The application of *pre* always results in an unnamed schema because the result is neither a state space schema nor an operation schema. It is generally used in proofs or part of another schema expression. The predicate part of the precondition schema can be further simplified by applying predefined inference rules [16] and techniques such as the *one-point-rule*.

Precondition simplification

Using the one-point-rule, *pre AddAccount* can be further simplified. The term *users'* will be substituted by *users* $\cup$ $\{a?\}$ and the existential quantifier in $\exists$ *users'* : $\mathbb{P}\,Account$... will be removed. The constraint *users* $\cup$ $\{a?\} \in \mathbb{P}\,Account$ will be conjoined with the predicate part. The modified schema is shown below:

$$
\begin{array}{|l}
\hline
users : \mathbb{P}\,Account \\
a? : Account \\
\hline
(\forall u_1, u_2 : Account \mid u_1 \in users \wedge u_2 \in users \bullet \\
\quad u_1.name = u_2.name \Leftrightarrow u_1 = u_2) \\
(\forall u_1, u_2 : Account \mid u_1 \in users \cup \{a?\} \wedge u_2 \in users \cup \{a?\} \bullet \\
\quad u_1.name = u_2.name \Leftrightarrow u_1 = u_2) \\
(\forall a : Account \mid a \in users \bullet a.name \neq a?.name) \\
users \cup \{a?\} \in \mathbb{P}\,Account \\
\hline
\end{array}
$$

The predicate

$$users \cup \{a?\} \in \mathbb{P}\,Account$$

can be removed because it is easily provable from the declarations of *users* and *a?* and from set union. The constraint

$$
\forall u_1, u_2 : Account \mid u_1 \in users \wedge u_2 \in users \bullet \\
u_1.name = u_2.name \Leftrightarrow u_1 = u_2
$$

can be removed because it is subsumed by the other two constraints. Therefore, *pre AddAccount* will effectively reduce to

$$
\begin{array}{|l}
\hline
users : \mathbb{P}\,Account \\
a? : Account \\
\hline
(\forall u_1, u_2 : Account \mid u_1 \in users \cup \{a?\} \wedge u_2 \in users \cup \{a?\} \bullet \\
\quad u_1.name = u_2.name \Leftrightarrow u_1 = u_2) \\
(\forall a : Account \mid a \in users \bullet a.name \neq a?.name) \\
\hline
\end{array}
$$

Since the universally quantified statement in *pre AddAccount* is the state invariant that is inherent in every operation schema, we specify only the other constraint as precondition when we write the specification for *AddAccount*.

10.7.2 Promotion

Promotion is a technique by which an operation on a component (referred to as local state space) of a large system (referred to as global state space) is promoted or upgraded to the large system. The major advantage of promotion is the reuse of smaller notations in more elaborate situations.

Consider the following schema definitions:

$$
\begin{array}{|l}
\hline
\textit{User} \underline{\hspace{11cm}} \\
\textit{name} : \textit{STRING} \\
\textit{id} : \mathbb{N}_1 \\
\hline
\end{array}
$$

$$
\begin{array}{|l}
\hline
\textit{AllUsers} \underline{\hspace{10.5cm}} \\
\textit{all} : \mathbb{P}\,\textit{User} \\
\hline
\forall\, u_1, u_2 : \textit{User} \mid u_1 \neq u_2 \land u_1 \in \textit{all} \land u_2 \in \textit{all} \bullet \\
\qquad u_1.\textit{name} \neq u_2.\textit{name} \\
\hline
\end{array}
$$

In this case, the local state space is defined by the schema *User*. An operation such as *ChangeName* can be defined to change the name of a user. The schema *AllUsers* defines the global state space in which *User* is a component. In order to change the name of one user within the set of users defined by *AllUsers*, one can make use of the operation *ChangeName* and promote it to the global state *AllUsers*.

Let *Local* denote a local state space, and *Global* denote a global state space that contains *Local*. Let $\textit{Local}_{op}$ denote an operation on *Local*. Let $\textit{Global}_{op}$ denote an operation on *Global* that has the same effect as that of $\textit{Local}_{op}$ (modifying only *Local* in *Global* and the rest of *Global* being unaffected). We can now define an operation called *Promote* such that

$$
\textit{Global}_{op} \;\equiv\; \exists\, \Delta\textit{Local} \bullet \textit{Local}_{op} \land \textit{Promote}
$$

For promotion to be valid, the global state must be an aggregate of the local state space; that is, there must exist a component of *Global* whose type is *Local*. The following example illustrates the concept of promotion.

Consider the operation *Register* in the accounts system example, which is reproduced below:

$$
\begin{array}{|l}
\hline
\textit{Register} \underline{\hspace{10cm}} \\
\Delta\textit{Accounts} \\
s? : \textit{Student} \\
c? : \textit{COURSENO} \\
\hline
s? \in \mathrm{ran}\ \textit{unpaid} \\
\textit{unpaid}' = \textit{update}(\textit{unpaid}, (\mu\, s : \textit{Student} \mid s.id = s?.id \land \\
\qquad s.\textit{status} = s?.\textit{status} \land s.\textit{courses} = s?.\textit{courses} \cup \{c?\})) \\
\textit{paid}' = \textit{paid} \\
\hline
\end{array}
$$

Register is a global operation that operates on the global state *Accounts*. The local state in this case is *Student*. We now introduce the operation *Register_Local* that operates on *Student* and updates the set of courses included in *Student*. Finally, we define the promotion operation called *Promote*.

$\underline{\quad Register\_Local \quad\rule{5cm}{0.4pt}}$
$\Delta Student$
$c? : COURSENO$

$id' = id$
$status' = status$
$courses' = courses \cup \{c?\}$

$\underline{\quad Promote \rule{6cm}{0.4pt}}$
$\Delta Accounts$
$\Delta Student$
$s? : Student$

$\exists s : Student \mid s \in \operatorname{ran} unpaid \wedge s.id = s?.id \bullet \theta Student = s$
$unpaid' = update(unpaid, \theta Student')$
$paid' = paid$

In principle, the operation *Promote* establishes a binding between the global state *Accounts* and local state *Student*. The expression

$$\exists s : Student \mid s \in \operatorname{ran} unpaid \wedge s.id = s?.id \bullet \theta Student = s$$

asserts that the local state before the operation corresponds to a copy of a student record already existing in the system. The expression

$$unpaid' = update(unpaid, \theta Student')$$

indicates that the global state variable *unpaid'* is updated using the modified local state $\theta Student'$. The change in local state is established by the operation *Register_Local*. Therefore, the equation

$$Register \equiv \exists \, \Delta Student \bullet Register\_Local \wedge Promote$$

confirms that the operation *Register_Local* is promoted to the global state.

The use of the θ operator in *Promote* has significance. The term $\theta Student$ refers to any instance of the schema *Student*, which in this case is bound to the input student record. That is, the connection between the local state and the global state is established through the input variable *s?*. The term $\theta Student'$ refers to the same instance of *Student* after being updated by an operation on a local state, which in this case is bound to *Register_Local* through the equation for promotion. By the use of the θ operator, *Promote* asserts that whenever the local state is updated, the global state is also modified. But *Promote* does not specify which local operation causes this change. Therefore, the same *Promote* operation can be conjoined with another local operation to promote it to the global state. For example, if there is an operation *Withdraw_Local* on *Student*, which is defined as

$$
\begin{array}{|l}
\_\,Withdraw\_Local \underline{} \\
\Delta Student \\
c? : COURSENO \\
\hline
id' = id \\
status' = status \\
courses' = courses \setminus \{c?\} \\
\end{array}
$$

then it can be promoted to *Accounts* in the same way as *Register_Local*. Thus,

$$Withdraw \equiv \exists\, \Delta Student \bullet Withdraw\_Local \wedge Promote$$

10.8   Refinement and Proof Obligations

The goal of a refinement process is to develop a detailed design and/or implementation from formal specification of requirements. A refinement process requires a proof obligation to ensure that successive designs are consistent. We use the term "abstract specification" to denote the specification that is the source of refinement (the one that is supposed to be refined) and the term "concrete specification" for the specification obtained after refinement.

Morgan and Vickers discuss refinement calculus for model-based specification techniques with sufficient rigor [9]. In this section, we describe refinement of Z specifications as described by Spivey in [12].

The two possible refinements of a Z specification are *data refinement* and *operation refinement*. In data refinement, a data type in an abstract state space is refined into another data type in the concrete state space. The data type in the concrete state space is selected in such a way that it is more easily implementable. One of the obligations for data refinement is that every operation that uses the abstract data type must be proved to be correct if it also uses the concrete data type. Operation refinement, on the other hand, focuses on mapping an operation in the abstract state space to one or more operations in the concrete state space. In particular, operation refinement describes algorithmic details of concrete operations, thereby justifying that the specification is implementable. Unlike VDM-SL, the Z notation does not directly support programming language-like constructs. Hence, there is a semantic gap between Z and a programming language implementing specifications in Z. For this reason, we do not consider operation refinement in this book.

10.8.1   Data Refinement

In data refinement, three possible mappings exist between abstract and concrete state spaces:

- There exists exactly one concrete state space for every abstract state space. This is the ideal situation. Proof obligations in this case are easy and straightforward.

- For every abstract state space, there exist possibly many concrete state spaces. This is the most general case. The proof obligations for this case are very similar to those of the ideal case.

- One concrete state space serves as the refinement of several abstract state spaces. Such a situation occurs only when some aspects of each one of the abstract state spaces are not implementable. The concrete state space implements those features that are common to all the abstract state spaces. Naturally, any feature of an abstract state space that is not implementable is not interesting and hence is not worthy of refinement.

We now consider proof obligations for the first two cases. A data refinement process requires an abstraction schema that maps concrete state spaces to abstract state spaces. For the rest of the discussion in this chapter, we use the following terminology:

AbsState	An abstract state space.
ConState	The concrete state space mapped to AbsState.
AbsOp	An operation on the abstract state space AbsState.
ConOp	The operation on the concrete state space ConState that implements AbsOp.
Refine	The abstraction schema that maps ConState to AbsState.
AbsInit	An initial state for the abstract specification.
ConInit	An initial state for the concrete specification that implements AbsInit.

A data refinement process must satisfy the following three conditions:

- Every initial state for the concrete state space corresponds to a valid initial state for the abstract state space. Formally, for the ideal case,

$$\forall AbsState; ConState \bullet ConInit \wedge Refine \Rightarrow AbsInit$$

and for the general case,

$$\forall ConState; ConInit \Rightarrow (\exists AbsState \bullet Refine \wedge AbsInit)$$

- A concrete operation terminates whenever the corresponding abstract operation is guaranteed to terminate. That is to say, the precondition of the concrete operation must be weaker than that of the abstract operation. This can be formally stated for the ideal case as follows:

$$\forall AbsState; ConState; x? : X \bullet pre\ AbsOp \wedge Refine \Rightarrow pre\ ConOp$$

The term $x? : X$ denotes the set of input parameters to the operation. The formal expression for the general case is the same as that of the ideal case.

- Every state in which a concrete operation terminates corresponds to a member of those abstract states in which the corresponding abstract operation could terminate. This condition indirectly asserts that the postcondition of the concrete operation is stronger than that of the abstract operation. The formal expression describing this condition for the ideal case is,

$$\forall AbsState; AbsState'; ConState; ConState'; x? : X; y! : Y \bullet$$
$$pre\,AbsOp \wedge Refine \wedge ConOp \wedge Refine' \Rightarrow AbsOp$$

and the formal expression for the general case is,

$$\forall AbsState; ConState; ConState'; x? : X; y! : Y \bullet$$
$$pre\,AbsOp \wedge Refine \wedge ConOp \Rightarrow$$
$$(\exists AbsState' \bullet Refine' \wedge AbsOp)$$

Notice that both these formal expressions contain the subexpression

$$pre\,AbsOp \wedge Refine$$

which denotes that *pre ConOp* is satisfied according to the second condition. Therefore, the left side of the implication asserts that *ConOp* is invoked in *ConState*, resulting in *ConState'*. The refinement schema *Refine'*, when conjoined with *ConState'*, results in *AbsState'* which is one of the terminating states obtained from *AbsState*. The existence of *AbsState* and *AbsState'* thereby indicates the presence and validity of *AbsOp*.

It is interesting to notice that the three conditions for data refinement in Z correspond to *initial state validation*, *domain obligation*, and *result obligation* for data refinement in VDM. The only difference is that the mapping of concrete state spaces to abstract state spaces is defined as a function (*retrieve function*) in VDM, whereas it is defined by a schema in Z. By including the abstract and concrete states in the declaration part of the refinement schema, the latter satisfies the *signature* and *adequacy* obligations warranted by data refinement. Thus, the refinement theory for VDM and Z specifications are one and the same, except for notational differences.

Example 10.14   *Personal phonebook.*
A simple model of a personal phonebook contains pairs of names and phone numbers. It is assumed that every name is associated with only one phone number. Two names, however, may be associated with the same phone number.

Abstract specification

For simplicity, *Name* and *Phone* are assumed to be basic types in this specification.

[*Name, Phone*]

The state of the phonebook contains only one variable, *entries*, which denotes the mapping between names and phone numbers.

```
┌─ PhoneBook ──────────────────────────────────
│  entries : Name ⇸ Phone
│
└──────────────────────────────────────────────
```

There is no state invariant for this abstract state. A possible initial state is given below.

```
┌─ InitPhoneBook ──────────────────────────────
│  PhoneBook
│ ─────────────────────────────────────────────
│  entries = ∅
│
└──────────────────────────────────────────────
```

We illustrate data refinement on only one operation, *AddPhone*. This operation adds a new pair of name and phone number to the book. The precondition for this operation ensures that the new name does not already exist in the book.

```
┌─ AddPhone ───────────────────────────────────
│  ΔPhoneBook
│  n? : Name
│  ph? : Phone
│ ─────────────────────────────────────────────
│  n? ∉ dom entries
│  entries' = entries ∪ {n? ↦ ph?}
│
└──────────────────────────────────────────────
```

The postcondition asserts that the new pair is added to the book.

Concrete specification

In the refined specification, each entry is modeled as a record. This record is described by the schema *Entry*, as shown below:

```
┌─ Entry ──────────────────────────────────────
│  name : Name
│  phone : Phone
│
└──────────────────────────────────────────────
```

Since the names are assumed to be unique in the phonebook, we introduce a global constraint on entries asserting that two entries are equal if and only if their names are equal.

$$\forall e_1, e_2 : Entry \bullet e_1.name = e_2.name \Leftrightarrow e_1 = e_2$$

In the refined version of the phonebook, the entries are arranged in a sequence. The ordering of entries depends on the order in which they are entered in the phonebook. It is therefore clear that a new entry will be placed at the end of the sequence.

```
┌─ PhoneBook_1 ────────────────────────────────
│  entries_1 : iseq Entry
│
└──────────────────────────────────────────────
```

Like the abstract state, there is no state invariant for the concrete state. The declaration "iseq" in the concrete state *PhoneBook_1* denotes an injective sequence and hence there are no duplicate entries in the concrete state. This declaration, in conjunction with the global constraint defined earlier, asserts that the names in the concrete state are unique.

A possible initial state for the concrete specification is shown in the schema *InitPhoneBook_1*.

$$
\begin{array}{|l}
\_\textit{InitPhoneBook\_1}_____ \\
\hline
\textit{PhoneBook\_1} \\
\hline
\textit{entries\_1} = \langle\rangle \\
\end{array}
$$

We now specify the concrete operation *AddPhone_1*.

$$
\begin{array}{|l}
\_\textit{AddPhone\_1}_____ \\
\hline
\Delta \textit{PhoneBook\_1} \\
n? : \textit{Name} \\
ph? : \textit{Phone} \\
\hline
\neg\ (\exists\, e : \textit{Entry} \mid e \in \mathrm{ran}\ \textit{entries\_1} \bullet e.name = n?) \\
\textit{entries\_1}' = \textit{entries\_1} \frown \langle(\mu\, e : \textit{Entry} \mid e.name = n? \wedge e.phone = ph?)\rangle \\
\end{array}
$$

The precondition for *AddPhone_1* ensures that the new name does not exist in the book before the operation is invoked. The postcondition ensures that a new record is constructed with the input parameters and is concatenated to the sequence of entries in the book.

Refinement schema

The refinement schema for the above example is given below:

$$
\begin{array}{|l}
\_\textit{Refine}_____ \\
\hline
\textit{PhoneBook} \\
\textit{PhoneBook\_1} \\
\hline
\mathrm{dom}\ \textit{entries} = \{e : \textit{Entry} \mid e \in \mathrm{ran}\ \textit{entries\_1} \bullet e.name\} \\
\forall\, i : 1 \mathinner{\ldotp\ldotp} \#\textit{entries\_1} \bullet \\
\quad (\textit{entries\_1}\ i).phone = \textit{entries}((\textit{entries\_1}\ i).name) \\
\end{array}
$$

The schema *Refine* maps the concrete space *PhoneBook_1* to the abstract space *PhoneBook*. The first predicate in *Refine* asserts that both *PhoneBook* and *PhoneBook_1* contain the same set of names. The second predicate ensures that the phone number associated with each name in *PhoneBook* and that associated with the same name in *PhoneBook_1* are identical.   ∎

10.8.2 Proof Obligations

We give a rigorous proof that *PhoneBook_1* implements *PhoneBook*. The proof shows that the refinement described by *Refine* satisfies all the three conditions for data refinement.

Initial state validation

For the initial state validation, it must be proved that

$$\forall PhoneBook;\ PhoneBook\_1 \bullet$$
$$InitPhoneBook\_1 \wedge Refine \Rightarrow InitPhoneBook$$

Since there is no state invariant both in *PhoneBook* and in *PhoneBook_1*, we need to consider only the predicate parts of *InitPhoneBook_1*, *Refine* and *InitPhoneBook*. Expanding the predicate parts of all the three schemas, the left side of the implication becomes

$$entries\_1 = \langle\rangle\ \wedge$$
$$\text{dom } entries = \{e : Entry \mid e \in \text{ran } entries\_1 \bullet e.name\}\ \wedge$$
$$(\forall\, i : 1 .. \#entries\_1 \bullet$$
$$(entries\_1\ i).phone = entries((entries\_1\ i).name))$$

Since $entries\_1 = \langle\rangle$, there is no entry in $entries\_1$. Hence,

$$\{e : Entry \mid e \in \text{ran } entries\_1 \bullet e.name\} = \varnothing$$

From the second predicate, we can therefore infer that

$$\text{dom } entries = \varnothing$$

which is the same as

$$entries = \varnothing$$

This is the predicate part of *InitPhoneBook*, which is the right side of the implication. Therefore, every initial state of *PhoneBook_1* also serves as an initial state for *PhoneBook*.

Domain obligation

For the second condition, we have to prove that the precondition of *PhoneBook* in conjunction with *Refine* implies the precondition of *PhoneBook_1*. That is,

$$\forall PhoneBook;\ PhoneBook\_1;\ n? : Name;\ ph? : Phone \bullet$$
$$\text{pre } AddPhone \wedge Refine \Rightarrow \text{pre } AddPhone\_1$$

Since the specifications are simple, we do not show the precondition evaluation of *AddPhone* and that of *AddPhone_1*. Instead, we directly use the results. Thus, we need to prove

$$n? \notin \mathrm{dom}\, entries \land$$
$$\mathrm{dom}\, entries = \{e : Entry \mid e \in \mathrm{ran}\, entries\_1 \bullet e.name\} \land$$
$$(\forall i : 1 .. \#entries\_1 \bullet$$
$$\quad (entries\_1\, i).phone = entries((entries\_1\, i).name) \Rightarrow$$
$$\quad\quad \neg\, (\exists e : Entry \mid e \in \mathrm{ran}\, entries\_1 \bullet e.name = n?))$$

From

$$n? \notin \mathrm{dom}\, entries \land$$
$$\mathrm{dom}\, entries = \{e : Entry \mid e \in \mathrm{ran}\, entries\_1 \bullet e.name\}$$

we can infer that

$$n? \notin \{e : Entry \mid e \in \mathrm{ran}\, entries\_1 \bullet e.name\}$$

Using the semantics of set membership, we can rewrite this expression as

$$\forall e : Entry \mid e \in \mathrm{ran}\, entries\_1 \bullet e.name \neq n?$$

which is the same as

$$\neg\, (\exists e : Entry \mid e \in \mathrm{ran}\, entries\_1 \bullet e.name = n?)$$

Result obligation

Finally, we have to prove that the postcondition of *AddPhone_1* is stronger than that of *AddPhone*. Formally,

$$\forall PhoneBook; PhoneBook'; PhoneBook\_1; PhoneBook\_1';$$
$$\quad n? : Name; ph? : Phone \bullet$$
$$\quad\quad \mathrm{pre}\, AddPhone \land Refine \land AddPhone\_1 \land Refine' \Rightarrow AddPhone$$

By expanding the predicate parts of the respective schemas, we obtain

$$n? \notin \mathrm{dom}\, entries \land$$
$$\mathrm{dom}\, entries = \{e : Entry \mid e \in \mathrm{ran}\, entries\_1 \bullet e.name\} \land$$
$$(\forall i : 1 .. \#entries\_1 \bullet$$
$$\quad (entries\_1\, i).phone = entries((entries\_1\, i).name)) \land$$
$$\neg\, (\exists e : Entry \mid e \in \mathrm{ran}\, entries\_1 \bullet e.name = n?) \land$$
$$entries\_1' = entries\_1 \,\frown\, \langle(\mu\, e : Entry \mid e.name = n? \land e.phone = ph?)\rangle \land$$
$$\mathrm{dom}\, entries' = \{e : Entry \mid e \in \mathrm{ran}\, entries\_1' \bullet e.name\} \land$$
$$(\forall i : 1 .. \#entries\_1' \bullet$$
$$\quad (entries\_1'\, i).phone = entries'((entries\_1'\, i).name)) \Rightarrow$$
$$\quad (n? \notin \mathrm{dom}\, entries \land entries' = entries \cup \{n? \mapsto ph?\})$$

The right side of the implication contains two conjuncts, of which the first one occurs as one of the conjuncts on the left side of the implication. Hence, it is sufficient to derive only the second conjunct from the left side of the implication. This conjunct asserts that the new name and phone number are added to the entries of the phone book in the abstract state. We prove this conjunct in two parts: (1) $n?$ is in the domain of *entries'*, and (2) the phone number corresponding to $n?$ in *entries'* is $ph?$.

<u>Part 1:</u> To prove that $n? \in$ dom *entries'*

In the predicate

$$\text{dom } entries' = \{e : Entry \mid e \in \text{ran } entries\_1' \bullet e.name\}$$

substitute for *entries_1'*. For ease of understanding, we rename the bound variables in the expression.

$$\text{dom } entries' = \{e : Entry \mid e \in \text{ran}(entries\_1 \frown \langle(\mu\, e_1 : Entry \mid e_1.name = n? \wedge e_1.phone = ph?))) \bullet e.name\}$$

Using the semantics of sequence concatenation, we infer that the right side of the equality contains an entry corresponding to $n?$ and so does the left side. Therefore, we can conclude that $n? \in$ dom *entries'*.

<u>Part 2:</u> To prove that $entries'(n?) = ph?$

From Part 1 and from the predicate

$$(\forall\, i : 1 .. \#entries\_1' \bullet$$
$$(entries\_1'\, i).phone = entries'((entries\_1'\, i).name))$$

we can infer that

$$entries'(n?) = \{i : 1 .. \#entries\_1' \mid (entries\_1'\, i).name = n? \bullet$$
$$(entries\_1'\, i).phone\} \tag{1}$$

From the predicate

$$entries\_1' = entries\_1 \frown \langle(\mu\, e : Entry \mid e.name = n? \wedge e.phone = ph?))$$

we can conclude—using one-point-rule—that

$$\exists\, i : 1 .. \#entries\_1' \bullet e.name = n? \wedge e.phone = ph? \tag{2}$$

From equations (1) and (2), we assert that the phone number corresponding to $n?$ in *entries'* is $ph?$.

Exercises

1. Given two sequences s_1 and s_2, prove

   (a) $items\,(s_1 \frown s_2) = items\,s_1 \uplus items\,s_2$

   (b) if s_2 in s_1, then $items\,s_2 \sqsubseteq items\,s_1$

   (c) if $s_2 = I \upharpoonright s_1$ for some $I \subseteq 1 \ldots \#s_1$, then $items\,s_2 \sqsubseteq items\,s_1$

2. Modify the specification for the login subsystem given in Example 10.8, as stated below:

   (a) Instead of the schema definition *Account*, use the function definition *Username* $\nrightarrow$ *Password* in *LoginSubsystem* schema.

   (b) The specification in the text considers only one class of users. Introduce at least two different categories of users: *normal* and *system* users. With this change, modify the specification for the login subsystem example to satisfy the following requirements:

      i. A user belongs to only one category.

      ii. Adding and deleting accounts can be performed only by a system user.

      iii. The password of an account can be changed either by the owner of that account or by a system user. A normal user who is not the owner of a particular account cannot access that account.

3. In the specification for a university accounts office in Example 10.9, introduce a schema called *Course* that contains course number, prerequisites for a course, and the maximum number of seats available in that course. Modify the specification to reflect these changes. It should accommodate the following condition: *a student registering for a course must have completed all the prerequisites for that course.*
   Modify the specification such that the information for more than one semester can also be maintained by the registration system.

4. The operation *SelectProcess* in the specification for resource allocation in a computer system (Example 10.10) is not given in the text. Complete the specification by introducing an operation schema *SelectProcess*.
   If it is assumed that there is only one instance for each resource type, what changes are required in the specification?

5. Give the specification for an initial state for the university accounts office example, and prove its validation.

6. Prove the consistency of operations *Enrol*, *Register*, and *PayFees* given in the specification for the university accounts office.

7. One of the requirements for the accounts office example is that a student cannot register for the same course more than once. Prove that the operation *Register* satisfies this requirement.

8. Do the following for the specification discussed in the case study:

   (a) Give the specification for the following additional operations:

   - *ListProject*, which will list all the projects initiated by a particular customer.

   - *DeleteProject*, which will delete a particular project.

   - *ListEmployees*, which determines all the employees working on projects initiated by a particular customer.

   (b) Consider the following new set of requirements for the billing system:

   i. There are three categories of employees: *programmer*, *supervisor*, and *manager*. Employees in each category have the same hourly rate, but the hourly rate will be different for the three categories.

   ii. There are three categories of customers: *individual*, *corporation*, and *government*.

   iii. There are three categories of projects: *small*, *medium*, and *large*.

   iv. A project is charged differently depending on the category of the project and the category of the customer who initiates that project.

   Discuss necessary changes in the data types, state space, and operations in the specification of the billing system given in the text, and rewrite the specification to capture the requirements mentioned above, in addition to the original requirements.

9. Calculate the preconditions for the following operations:

   (a) *PayFees* in the specification for university accounts office (Example 10.9).

   (b) *DeAllocate* in the specification for resource allocation (Example 10.10).

   (c) *ReportWork* in the specification for the automated billing system (case study).

10. In the specification for the login subsystem, define a local operation called *ChangePassword_Local* that operates on *Account* and changes the password for that account. Promote this operation to the global state *LoginSubsystem*.

11. Model *TimeSheet* and *WorkSheet* as schemas in the specification for the automated billing discussed in the case study. Define all functions on time sheets and worksheets as local operations to the respective state spaces defined by *TimeSheet* and *WorkSheet*. Promote these operations to the global state *Organization*. Notice that you may want to promote operations defined on *TimeSheet* to the state space defined by *WorkSheet* and then promote them again to *Organization*.

12. The specification for the login subsystem models accounts as sets. Refine the data type *users* using sequences and modify the specification accordingly. Prove the correctness of this refinement.

13. The *waiting_queues* in the specification of the resource allocation system is modeled using a partial function. Refine this model using sequences, modify the specification accordingly, and prove the correctness of the refinement.

14. (Project) A post office handles three types of mail: *Regular mail*, *Express mail*, and *Fast or Courier mail*. Mail may arrive from different locations at different times, including the mail handed over in person at the post office itself. Mail is sorted by three different processes: the first process sorts mail based on the zone to which the mail is to be delivered (may be identified by the first three letters of the postal code), the second process sorts mail based on the location within that zone (may be identified by the last three letters of the postal code), and the third process sorts mail based on the street number. After the third sorting process, mail is classified based on the type of mail. At the end of this classification, the mail is sent out from the post office for delivery.

Model the mail handling subsystem in the post office. You may introduce additional requirements and assumptions, if necessary.

Bibliographic Notes

Much of the earlier work on Z can be found in [6]. The syntax of the Z notation evolved continuously over several years; a somewhat more stable version has been described by Spivey, which can be found in [10, 12]. Currently, the Z notation is being standardized by the International Standards Organization (ISO). The most recent version of the Z notation described in [16] is slightly different from the earlier version described in [10, 12]. We have used the earlier version [12] in this book.

Spivey's version includes the notion of piping, which is discarded in the Standard version. We have not discussed piping in this chapter.

Woodcock and Davies [14] discuss refinement theory for Z specifications, which is not dealt with in such great detail in this book. A somewhat simple refinement method for both data refinement and operation refinement can be found in [15]. The readers can also find a detailed and formal treatment of the precondition calculation in [14].

Among all the books for Z, Spivey's book [12] seems to be the only one that describes formal definitions of symbols in Z; these are collectively described as the *mathematical toolkit*. The ISO Standards draft [16] also includes formal definitions of the symbols in the mathematical toolkit, but with minor modifications.

Several object-oriented extensions to the Z notation have been reported in the literature. These include the languages MooZ [8], Object-Z [5], and Z++ [13]. All these extensions are based on Spivey's version. A comprehensive overview of these can be found in [13]. As a result of the standardization process, these object-oriented languages are also evolving.

Coombes and McDermid [4], and Baumann and Lermer [2] discussed real-time specifications using Z, without extending the syntax of Z. Mahony and Hayes [7] have described extensions to the Z notation to specify real-time systems. Carrido [3], and Alagar and Periyasamy [1] have extended Object-Z towards real-time specifications; in both these cases, the semantics of the extensions have been developed as extensions of the semantics for the Z language.

The Computing Laboratory at Oxford University in the U.K. maintains a Web site for the Z notation: http://www.comlab.ox.ac.uk/zforum. This Web site contains a current Z bibliography, information on tool support for Z notation, and pointers to work achieved by the standardization process. A separate moderated newsgroup called comp.specification.z is also maintained by the Oxford Computing Laboratory, which is a useful source for beginners to find out more about the Z notation. In addition, proceedings of the annual conference called *The Z Users Meeting* is also an invaluable source for up-to-date developments in Z.

References

[1] V.S. Alagar and K. Periyasamy, "Real-Time Object-Z: A Language for the Specification and Design of Real-Time Reactive Systems," Technical Report, Department of Computer Science, Concordia University, Montreal, Canada, June 1996.

[2] P. Baumann and K. Lermer, "A Framework for the Specification of Reactive and Concurrent Systems in Z," *Proceedings of the Fifteenth Conference on Foundations of Software Technology and Theoretical Computer Science*; published as *Lecture Notes in Computer Science Series*, Vol. 1026, Springer-Verlag, 1995, pp. 62–79.

[3] J.M. Carrido, "Specification of Real-Time Systems with Extensions to Object-Z," *Proceedings of Technology of Object-Oriented Languages and Systems (TOOLS USA)*, Santa Barbara, CA, 1995, pp. 167–179.

[4] A.C. Coombes and J.A. McDermid, "Specifying Temporal Requirements for Distributed Real-Time Systems in Z," Technical Report YCS176, Computer Science Department, University of York, Heslington, York, England, 1992.

[5] R. Duke, G. Rose, and G. Smith, "Object-Z: A Specification Language for the Description of Standards," *Computer Standards & Interfaces*, Vol. 17, 1995, pp. 511–533.

[6] I.J. Hayes (Ed.), *Specification Case Studies*, Prentice Hall International (UK), 1987.

[7] B.P. Mahony and I.J. Hayes, "A Case-Study in Timed Refinement: A Mine Pump," *IEEE Transactions on Software Engineering*, Vol. 18, No. 9, September 1992, pp. 817–826.

[8] S.L. Meira and A.L.C. Cavalcanti, "The *MooZ* Specification Language," Technical Report, Departamento de Informática, Universidade Federal de Pernambuco, Recife – PE, Brasil, 1992.

[9] C. Morgan and T. Vickers (Eds.), *On the Refinement Calculus*, Springer-Verlag, London, England, 1994.

[10] B. Potter, J. Sinclair, and D. Till, *An Introduction to Formal Specification and Z*, Prentice Hall International (UK), 1991.

[11] J.M. Spivey, *The fuzz Reference Manual*, J.M. Spivey Computing Science Consultancy, Oxford OX44 9AN, U.K., 1992.

[12] J.M. Spivey, *The Z Notation - A Reference Manual* (second edition), Prentice Hall International (UK), 1992.

[13] S. Stepney, R. Barden, and D. Cooper (Eds.), *Object-Orientation in Z*, Workshops in Computing Series, Springer-Verlag, London, England, 1992.

[14] J.C.P. Woodcock and J. Davies, *Using Z: Specification, Refinement and Proof*, Prentice Hall International (UK), 1996.

[15] J.B. Wordsworth, *Software Development with Z*, Addison-Wesley Publishing Company, International Computer Science Series, 1992.

[16] *The Z Notation*, ISO/IEC JTC 1/SC22 CD 13568, September 1995.

11

Larch

A specification of the system under development must include a description of the boundary between the system and its environment. This boundary characterizes the *interface* of the system. The components in a system interact with each other through their interfaces. It is crucial that each interface specification describes precisely the forms of communications that are permitted at the interface, their causes and effects. Understanding the interface of a component should provide insight into the nature of the system being specified. This is particularly important for systems exhibiting similar behavior, with different interfaces.

Each interface language is designed to deal with information that can be observed by client programs written in a particular programming language. Formal specification languages studied in the previous three chapters are general-purpose languages; they are suitable for design specifications. The refinement techniques associated with model-oriented specification languages provide a methodology for deriving a detailed specification, close to the final implementation. However, to be able to use Z or VDM-SL as an interface language, an interface refinement relation is required to bridge the semantic gap between the specification language and the programming language to be used to implement the refined module. This refinement relation must express assertions about program states, and implementation-specific notions such as exceptions. It is unlikely that all features of a programming language can be captured in such an interface refinement relation. To describe the behavioral characteristics of a software system, we need a language in which the interfaces of the system components and the externally observable behavior of each system component can be formally specified. The works of Wing [11, 12], and Guttag and Horning [6] on Larch specification languages are geared towards this goal.

11.1 The Two Tiers of Larch

Larch provides a two-tiered approach to specification of program interfaces:

- In the *interface tier*, a Larch Interface Language (LIL) is used to describe the behavior of a program module written in a specific programming language. LIL specifications provide the information needed to understand and use a module interface. LIL refers to a family of specification languages. Each specification language in the LIL family is designed for a specific programming language. Specifications are written in a predicative language using assertions on the pre- and poststates.

- In the *shared tier*, the Larch Shared Language (LSL) is used to specify state-independent, mathematical abstractions that can be referred to in the interface tier. These underlying abstractions are called *traits*; a trait defines a multi-sorted first-order theory, and is written in the conventional style of equational algebraic specification.

The philosophy behind this two-tiered approach is best summarized by Wing [12, page 3]:

> We believe that for specifications of program modules, the environment in which a module is embedded, and hence the nature of its observable behavior, is likely to depend in fundamental ways on the semantic primitives of the programming languages .... Thus we intentionally make an interface language dependent on a target programming language, and keep the shared language independent of any programming language. To capitalize on our separation of a specification into two tiers, we isolated programming language dependent issues—such as side effects, error handling, and resource allocation—into the interface language component of a specification.

Larch's two-tiered approach makes it possible to express programming language dependent properties using syntax and semantics that corroborate with the underlying programming language. Constructs are provided for expressing programming language dependent properties such as parameter passing, side effects, exceptions, and concurrency using the syntax and semantics of the underlying programming language. Each LIL has a mechanism for referencing the formal parameters in the specification of an operation using the same syntax and semantics as in the underlying language. The semantics for the primitive terms used in the interface specification is provided by traits in the shared tier.

Larch's two-tiered approach has the advantage of providing separation of concerns between the two tiers. According to Guttag and Horning [6], the complex parts of the specification are to be kept in the shared tier, where mathematical abstractions necessary for the interface specifications are defined. Although some of these abstractions may be very specific to applications, a large number of them will exhibit general characteristics. Such abstractions may be reused in various applications. The semantics of LSL is simpler than most of the interface specification languages. Consequently, specifiers are less likely to make mistakes in LSL traits. The Larch proof assistant (LP) [6] can be used to verify the validity of claims about semantic properties of LSL traits. The interface tier may be specialized for use with a particular programming language. The concepts and constructs of the chosen programming language may be used to describe resources provided to the module, state changes, computed results, and exceptions. By understanding the interface specification and overlooking its implementation, a class can be reused in a black-box fashion. From the experience reported by Alagar et al. [1] Larch has the potential for unintrusively integrating into current industrial processes for effective reuse of commercial class libraries such as Rogue Wave [10].

Several specification languages for the interface tier have been proposed in recent literature. These include

- LCL [6] tailored to the C language,
- LM3 [7] tailored to Modula-3,
- Larch/Smalltalk [3] for Smalltalk,
- Larch/Ada [5] for Ada, and
- Larch/C++ [8] for C++.

We present a brief tutorial on Larch Shared Language and discuss some of the salient features of Larch/C++ in this chapter. There are some pragmatic considerations in introducing Larch/C++. The language C++ provides support for data abstraction, encapsulation, polymorphism, and inheritance. The widespread use of C++ in industry warrants that any effort to unintrusively integrate formal methods in software development as well as to reuse specifications are most likely to succeed if targeted at C++.

11.2 LSL—Larch Shared Language

This section introduces LSL, Larch Shared Language. The founders of Larch, Guttag and Horning [6], give an excellent exposé of LSL; we conform to their style and liberally add several examples.

11.2.1 Equational Specification

The unit of encapsulation in LSL is a trait, which introduces some operators and specifies some of their properties. There are two kinds of symbols in such a description: *operators* and *sorts*. An operator is similar to the programming language concepts procedure, function, and method. A sort is analogous to the notion of type in programming languages. When we discuss a trait, the terms *operators* and *sorts* will be used; in the context of discussing programming language issues, we use the term type. Sorts are disjoint sets of values, and are used to denote the domain and range of operators. LSL operators are *total* functions.

Traits are constructed in a *monotonic* fashion: we first define basic traits and then use them in constructing larger ones. A trait, once constructed, can be put in an LSL library and reused in contexts where their properties are meaningful. The LSL handbook of Guttag and Horning [6] contains a collection of traits, many of which we reuse in our examples. Two basic traits that are often required are Boolean and Integer, which respectively define a theory for boolean values and a theory for integers. The logic operators *true, false,* ¬, ∨, ∧, ⇒, and ⇔, as well as some overloaded operators such as *if_then_else_* and =, are predefined in the language; that is, the traits defining these operators are implicitly included in every trait.

Figure 11.1 shows an LSL trait *SetTrait* specifying the properties of a set. The example is similar to a conventional algebraic specification as introduced in Chapter 8. The name of a trait is distinct from the names of all sort and operator identifiers defined in the trait, for example, *Set*.

A trait contains a collection of operator declarations, or *signatures*, which follow the keyword **introduces**, and a collection of *equations*, which follow the keyword **asserts**. Each operator is a total function that maps a tuple of values from its domain sorts to a value from its range sort. Every operator used in a trait must have been declared. Signatures are used to type check the terms in a trait. Sorts are not explicitly declared; they are implicitly introduced through the signature of the trait.

The specification of *SetTrait* includes the trait *Integer*, which is defined in the LSL handbook [6]. The included *Integer* trait gives information about the operators +, −, 0, and 1, which are used in the right-hand side of equations. The *body* of the specification is composed of the set of equations, the **implies**, **converts**, and **exempting** clauses following the reserved word **asserts**.

An equation is of the form $x == y$, where x and y are terms of the same sort. An equation of the form $x == true$ can be abbreviated by simply writing x. Equation 1 in *SetTrait* is an abbreviation for ¬*(member(x,emptyset))* == *true*. Similarly, equation 5 is an abbreviation for *subset(emptyset,s)* == *true*. Equations 10 and 11 affirm the essential property that a nonempty set can contain only distinct elements. Equations 2 to 9 define the mathematical properties of set membership for sets constructed using the basic constructor *insert*, and nonbasic constructors *delete*, and *unionn* (set union).

The semantics of = and == are exactly the same; only their syntactic precedence differs to ensure that expressions are parsed in an expected manner without the use of parentheses. The operator = binds more tightly than ==.

All operators in *SetTrait* are in *prefix* notation, the familiar notation for function definition in mathematics. Operators can also be defined in *mixfix* notation. When

SetTrait(Set, E): **trait**
    includes *Integer*
    introduces
        emptyset: $\rightarrow$ *Set*
        insert: E, Set $\rightarrow$ *Set*
        delete: E, Set $\rightarrow$ *Set*
        unionn: Set, Set $\rightarrow$ *Set*
        member: E, Set $\rightarrow$ *Bool*
        subset: Set, Set $\rightarrow$ *Bool*
        size: Set $\rightarrow$ *Int*
  asserts
    Set **generated by** *emptyset, insert*
    Set **partitioned by** *member*
    $\forall$ *x, y : E, s, t : Set*
        $\neg$*(member(x, emptyset))*
        member(x, insert(y,s)) == (x = y) $\vee$ *member(x,s)*
        member(x, delete(y,s)) == (x $\neq$ y) $\wedge$ *member(x,s)*
        member(x, unionn(s,t)) == member(x,s) $\vee$ *member(x,t)*
        subset(emptyset, s)
        subset(insert(x,s),t) == member(x,t) $\wedge$ *subset(s,t)*
        subset(delete(x,s),t) == subset(s,t)
        unionn(s, emptyset) == s
        unionn(s, insert(x,t)) == insert(x, unionn(s,t))
        size(emptyset) == 0
        size(insert(x,s)) == if member(x,s) then size(s) else 1 + size(s)
  implies
    Set **partitioned by** *subset*
    $\forall$ *x, y: E, s, t: S*
        insert(x, insert (x,s)) == insert(x,s)
        insert(x, insert(y,s)) == insert(y, insert(x,s))
        subset(s,t) $\Rightarrow$ *(member(x,s)* $\Rightarrow$ *member(x,t))*
    converts *delete, unionn, member, subset*
      exempting $\forall$ *i : E*
        delete(i, emptyset)

FIGURE 11.1. An LSL trait for finite sets.

defining an operator in mixfix notation, the symbol "_" is used to indicate an argument placeholder. For example, the operator *member* in *SetTrait* could also be defined using the binary infix operator $\in$. The signature for this infix operator is

$\_\in\_$: *E, Set* $\rightarrow$ *Bool*

Using this signature, the second equation can be rewritten as

$$x \in insert(y,s) == (x = y) \lor x \in s.$$

Mixfix operators can be used to enhance the readability of specifications; for example, it is preferable to use $\_+\_$ than to use *plus* as an operator. Precedence rules in Larch ensure that terms are parsed as expected. The precedence scheme for operators is given below; operators are listed such that the most tightly bound come first:

- postfix operators consisting of a period followed by an identifier, such as $\cdot$ *front*,
- all other user-defined operators and built-in boolean negation,
- the built-in equality operators, $=$ and $\neq$,
- the built-in propositional connectives, $\lor$, $\land$, $\Rightarrow$, and $\Leftrightarrow$,
- the built-in conditional connective *if_then_else_*,
- the equation connective $==$.

Infix terms with multiple occurrences of an operator at the same level, and without parenthesis, associate the operators from left to right. For example, the equation

$$x == y \cdot a \cdot b \cdot c + front(z) = u \land v$$

is equivalent to the term

$$x == (((((y \cdot a) \cdot b) \cdot c) + front(z)) = u) \land v$$

A trait is *well-formed* if it is syntactically correct and the terms in the equations are legal and are successfully parsed. The semantics of Larch traits is based on multisorted first-order logic with equality, rather than on an initial, terminal or loose algebra semantics as used by algebraic specification languages. A *theory* is a set of logical formulas with no free variable. A well-formed trait denotes a theory in multisorted first-order logic with equality. The theory contains the equations of the trait, the conventional axioms of first-order logic with equality, and the logical consequences that follow from the axioms. Formulas in the theory follow only from the presence of assertions in the trait—never from their absence. The theory associated with a trait including other traits corresponds to the union of its theory and those of the included traits. For instance, the theory associated with *SetTrait* contains all consequences of the equations given in Figure 11.1 and of the equations defined for *Integer* and the traits that implicitly define the logic operators.

SetTrait does not provide all information about sets:

1. It does not state how sets are to be represented.
2. Procedures to implement the operators are not stated.
3. It does not explicitly state all the mathematical properties of sets—some of them can be inferred from the equations and others cannot be inferred.

The first issue can be settled at the implementation stage. The second issue is taken up during the development of interface specifications. The claims made in an LSL specification can be checked; if they are proved to follow from the specification, then it brings out the extent of completeness intended by the specifier.

A trait definition need not correspond to the definition of an abstract data type definition since an LSL trait can define any arbitrary theory of multisorted first-order equational logic. For example, a trait can be used to define abstract states of an object, or a first-order theory of mathematical abstractions such as partial orders and equivalence relations. Figure 11.4 shows specifications for preordered sets, partially ordered sets, and totally ordered sets. The mathematical concept of Abelian group, a set with a binary operation "+" and its inverse "–", having 0 as the identity element, is specified in Figure 11.2. The algebraic structure of rings having a unit element 1 is specified in Figure 11.3. This specification includes the trait characterizing the Abelian group and adds a binary operation "*", which is transitive and distributive with respect to the binary operation "+". Notice that 0 is the identity element for the "+" operation, and 1 is the identity element for the "*" operation. The operation "+" is commutative, while the operation "*" is not defined to be commutative.

11.2.2 More Expressive Specifications and Stronger Theories

Equational theories are not adequate to specify abstract data types. A trait defining an abstract data type introduces a *distinguished sort*, also called the *principal sort* or *data sort*. In such traits, an explicit reference to the operator symbols that generate values of the data sort and a mechanism to recognize equivalent terms of the data

$$Abegroup(\_+\_, \_-\_, T):\ \textbf{trait}$$
$$\textbf{introduces}$$
$$0 : \rightarrow T$$
$$\_ + \_: T, T \rightarrow T$$
$$- \_: T \rightarrow T$$
$$\_ - \_: T, T \rightarrow T$$
$$\textbf{asserts}$$
$$\forall\, x,\, y,\, z : T$$
$$x + (-x) == 0$$
$$x - y == x + (-y)$$
$$x + 0 == x$$
$$x + y == y + x$$
$$x + (y + z) == (x + y) + z$$

FIGURE 11.2. Specification of Abelian groups.

$Ring(\_*\_, T)$: **trait**
    includes *Abegroup*
    introduces
        $1 : \rightarrow T$
        $\_*\_: T, T \rightarrow T$
    asserts
        $\forall x, y, z : T$
            $x * (y + z) == (x * y) + (x * z)$
            $x * 0 == 0$
            $x * 1 == x$
            $x * (y * z) == (x * y) * z$

FIGURE 11.3. Specification of rings.

sort can be provided. These are achieved in LSL by adding **generated by** and **partitioned by** clauses.

In *SetTrait*, the **generated by** clause states that all values of the sort *Set* can be represented by terms composed solely of the two operator symbols *emptyset* and *insert*. Asserting that sort S is generated by a set of operators *Ops* means that each term of sort S is equal to a term whose outermost operator is in *Ops*. This corresponds to the "no junk" principle of the initial algebra semantics of algebraic specification languages. The operators in *Ops* are referred to as the *generators* of sort S. The **generated by** clause justifies a *generator induction schema* for proving properties of the distinguished sort. In the case of natural numbers, *0* and *succ* are the generators. These generators combined with the total ordering property for natural numbers provide the induction scheme. Similarly, the **generated by** clause strengthens the theory of *SetTrait* by adding an inductive rule of inference that can be used to prove properties for all *Set* values.

The **generated by** clause of *SetTrait* asserts that any value of the sort *Set* can be constructed from the operator *emptyset* by a finite number of applications of the operator *insert*. We can thus use induction to prove the following property:

$\forall s : Set \bullet size(s) \geq 0$

Basis of induction:

$size(emptyset) = 0$ is true.

Induction step:

$\forall s: Set, x:E \bullet size(s) \geq 0 \Rightarrow size(insert(x, s)) \geq 0$

This claim is proved using the last equation from the theory of *SetTrait*.

The operators of an abstract data type in Larch can be categorized as *generators*, *extensions*, and *observers*. Generators produce all the values of the abstract data type. Extensions are the other operators whose range is the distinguished sort. Observers are those operators whose domain includes the distinguished sort and

$Preorder(\_\diamond\_, T)$: **trait**
   includes *Boolean*
   introduces
     $\_\diamond\_: T, T \rightarrow Bool$
   asserts
     $\forall\, x, y, z : T$
      $x \diamond x$
      $(x \diamond y \wedge y \diamond z) \Rightarrow x \diamond z$

$Poset(T)$: **trait**
   includes *Boolean*
   introduces
     $\_ < \_: T, T \rightarrow Bool$
     $\_ \leq \_: T, T \rightarrow Bool$
   asserts
     $\forall\, x, y, z : T$
      $\neg\,(x < x)$
      $x \leq x$
      $(x < y \wedge y \leq z) \Rightarrow x < z$
      $(x \leq y \wedge y < z) \Rightarrow x < z$
      $x \leq y \wedge y \leq x == x = y$
      $x \leq z == x < z \vee x = z$
  implies
    $Preorder(\_\leq\_\textbf{for}\ \diamond)$
    $\forall\, x, y, z : T$
     $(x \leq y \wedge y \leq z) \Rightarrow x \leq z$

$TotalOrder(T)$: **trait**
   includes *Poset*
   asserts
     $\forall\, x, y : T$
      $x < y \vee y \leq x$

FIGURE 11.4. Specifications for ordering relations.

whose range is some other sort. As remarked in Chapter 8, a good heuristic for writing axioms is to write one equation defining the result of applying each observer or extension to each generator. This provides a sufficient coverage of the abstract data types as it assumes all possible values.

A **partitioned by** clause asserts that the operators listed in that clause form a complete set of observers for the trait. Intuitively, it states that two terms are equal if they cannot be distinguished by any of the observers. All equal terms form one equivalence class. Observers partition the set of all terms into equivalence classes so that for any two terms, observers can determine whether or not they belong to the same equivalence class. For the *SetTrait* example, this property can be used to show that the order of insertion in the set is immaterial. The terms $insert(x, insert(y, s))$ and $insert(y, insert(x, s))$ are equal for all values $x, y : E, s : Set$. A **partitioned by** clause gives a new axiom justifying a deduction rule in proving properties about the trait. Hence, the **partitioned by** clause in *SetTrait* adds the deduction rule

$$\forall x : E \bullet (x \in s = x \in t) \Rightarrow s = t$$

This deduction rule can be used to prove the property

$$\forall x : E, s : Set \bullet insert(x, insert(x, s)) == insert(x, s)$$

To prove this property, we need to discharge the proof

$$\forall y : E \bullet member(y, insert(x, insert(x, s))) = member(y, insert(x, s))$$

The proof steps are as follows:

1. From Equation (2) in *SetTrait*, infer
   $member(y, insert(x, s)) == (x = y) \vee member(y, s)$

2. From Equation (2) in *SetTrait*, infer
   $member(y, insert(x, insert(x, s))) == (x = y) \vee member(y, insert(x, s))$

3. Applying Equation (2) again to the right-hand side, we obtain
   $member(y, insert(x, insert(x, s))) ==$
   $(x = y) \vee ((x = y) \vee member(y, s))$

4. The right-hand side of step 3 can be further reduced to
   $(x = y) \vee member(y, s)$

5. The result follows from step 4 and the right-hand side of step 1.

11.2.3 Composing Traits

LSL traits can be composed using the **includes** clause. A trait that includes another trait is textually expanded to contain all operator declarations, constraints clauses, **generated by** clauses, and axioms of the included trait. The meaning of operations and equations in the including trait are made clear by the meanings of operations and equations in the included traits. The constants 0, and 1, and the operation "+" in *SetTrait* are defined in the included trait *Integer*. The operator *size* cannot be defined without this inclusion.

Traits describing specific theories and defined separately can be reused within other traits where such theories are appropriate. For example, the trait *TotalOrder* becomes more structured by including the trait *Poset*. This is consistent with the mathematical property "if every pair of elements of a partially ordered set is comparable, then it is a totally ordered set." Thus when an ordering such as set inclusion is needed in a theory, the trait *Poset* can be included, whereas when a total ordering theory is to be imposed on structures, the trait *TotalOrder* can be included. When both partial order and total order theories are required in another theory, both *Poset* and *TotalOrder* can be included. The LSL library available in Guttag and Horning [6] contains traits built by reusing simpler traits in a monotonic fashion.

11.2.4   Renaming

While reusing traits, sort names and operator names can be renamed as in parametric substitutions. The trait *Poset* shown in Figure 11.4 is included in the trait *TotalOrder*. There is an implicit dependency on the operators $<$ and $\leq$. Since there are different partial orders for different sorts, we can rewrite the header of the *Poset* trait as

   Poset$(T, \_<\_, \_\leq\_)$: **trait**.

Now the reference

   includes *Poset*(*int* **for** T, $<$ **for** $<$, $\leq$ **for** $\leq$)

in the trait *TotalOrder* gives the theory of a total ordering on integers. Note that the operators $<$ and $\leq$ are overloaded—for any trait T, and for the trait *Integer*.

Using renaming, a set of integers can be obtained from the trait *SetTrait* shown in Figure 11.1 as follows:

   includes *SetTrait(S, int* **for** *E)*

In addition, the operator *subset* can be replaced by the customary mathematical symbol $\subseteq$, using the following statement:

   includes *SetTrait(S, int* **for** *E) (*$\subseteq$ **for** subset*)*

In general, the syntax for renaming is *Tr(x* **for** *y)*, denoting the trait *Tr* in which every occurrence of *y* is replaced by *x*, where *y* is a sort or an operator. The renaming is propagated in the signature of *Tr* to the operators where *y* appears. The theory of a trait is not changed due to renaming, because the theory is a logical consequence of the assertions in the trait.

11.2.5   Stating Checkable Properties

An LSL trait is a precise formal description of a specifier's intended object that is an abstract structure or an abstract data type. When an object is not properly conceptualized, its specification may not faithfully reflect the intended behavior of the object. An LSL trait, which is syntactically correct, may have semantic errors. These errors cannot be detected in the way that programs are debugged, for LSL traits cannot be executed. Consequently, specifiers are provided with LP, the Larch proof assistant, using which LSL traits can be debugged. Nevertheless, there is no basis against which correctness of an LSL trait can be established.

To gain confidence in LSL traits, these should be checked for the satisfaction of intended properties. Three important properties that should be checked are *consistency*, *theory containment*, and *completeness*.

Consistency

An LSL trait is consistent if and only if its theory does not contain a *contradiction*; that is, the theory must not contain the equation *true == false*. In general, consistency is hard to prove and is undecidable. The inconsistency of a trait is often much easier to detect. When an inconsistency is detected, the trait must be debugged for errors. However, when no inconsistency is detected, we cannot assume the specification to be consistent.

Theory containment

If a property, that is not explicitly stated as an equation can be shown to be a logical consequence of the equations in a trait, then that property is contained in the theory of the trait. LSL traits can be augmented with checkable claims in order to verify whether intended consequences actually follow from the axioms of a trait. These checkable claims are specified in the form of assertions that are included in the **implies** clause of the trait and that can be verified using LP. For example, the property

$$\forall s, t : S, x : E \bullet subset(s, t) \Rightarrow ((member(x, s) \Rightarrow member(x, t))$$

can be claimed for the trait *SetTrait* shown in Figure 11.1. The assertion can be added to the trait in the **implies** clause. Proving this claim increases the confidence in the predictive capability of the theory associated with the trait. It also helps to establish properties in other traits that include this trait. The **implies** clause can be used to specify a theory with equations, generator clauses, partitioning clauses, and references to other traits.

Completeness

A theory is complete if every sentence in the theory can be reduced to either *true* or *false*. LSL trait theories need not be complete—sometimes, some characteristics of certain operators may be deliberately omitted. Such intentional incompleteness may provide some flexibility in writing interface specifications. However, it is useful to state verifiable claims about completeness; this is done in the **converts** clause. The claim **converts** *top, pop, isEmpty* states that the equations in Figure 11.5 fully define the operators *top, pop*, and *isEmpty* of *StackTrait*.

However, the meaning of the terms *pop(new)*, and *top(new)* are not defined. The **exempting** clause documents the absence of equations for these terms; that is, it lists the terms that are not claimed to be defined. The **converts** and **exempting**

StackTrait(E, Stack): **trait**
    introduces
        new: → Stack
        push: Stack, E → Stack
        top: Stack → E
        pop: Stack → Stack
        isEmpty: Stack → Bool
    asserts
        Stack **generated by** new, push
        Stack **partitioned by** top, pop, isEmpty
        ∀ s: Stack, e: E
            top(push(s,e)) == e
            pop(push(s,e)) == s
            isEmpty(new)
            ¬ isEmpty(push(s,e))
    implies
        converts top, pop, isEmpty
            exempting top(new), pop(new)

FIGURE 11.5. LSL trait for stack.

clauses together provide a means of stating that an LSL trait is *sufficiently* complete. For the *SetTrait* example, intuitively, the **converts** and **exempting** clauses assert that the specification of each of the operators *delete*, *union*, *member*, and *subset* is complete in the sense that any term involving these operators can be reduced to a term not involving these operators. The only exception to this rule is the term *delete(x,emptyset)*. For example, any term *t* whose outermost operator is *unionn* can be reduced to a term *s* involving only the operators *emptyset* and *insert*, provided that *t* has no subterms of the form *delete(x,emptyset)*.

11.2.6   Stating Assumptions

Recall that in VDM every operation has pre- and postconditions. The satisfaction of the precondition is essential for invoking the operation. In Larch, we document the precondition for proper usage of a trait with the **assumes** clause. Assumptions stated in the **assumes** clause must be *discharged* by a formal proof.

The specification of a stack given in Figure 11.5 is quite general. It can be specialized to specify an integer stack by renaming the sorts in its definition. For example, the specification

    IntegerStack : **trait**
    includes Integer, StackTrait(Int, Stack)

introduces a stack of integers. The operators defined in the *Integer* trait are quite distinct from the operators in *StackTrait*. Consequently, there is no inheritance of

RStackTrait(E, Stack): **trait**
    includes *StackTrait, Integer*
    introduces
        count: E, Stack → Int
        $\_ \leq \_: E, E → Bool$
    asserts
        ∀ *s : Stack, a,b : E*
            count(a, new) == 0
            count(a, push(s, b)) == count(a, s) + (if $b \leq a$ then 1 else 0)

FIGURE 11.6. A specialization of stack.

integer properties in *StackTrait*. Therefore, *StackTrait(Int, Stack)* needs no assumptions on integers.

Let us consider the specification of a stack of integers in which the elements that do not exceed the integer on top of the stack is of interest. This requires an extension to *StackTrait* dealing with integers and an operator for counting the number of elements in the stack having the stated property. Writing the specification as shown in Figure 11.6, the operator $\leq$ is used in defining *count*; however, the properties of $\leq$ are not stated within the specification. We should not define $\leq$ within *RStackTrait* because the properties would be required by the trait that includes *RStackTrait*. The properties of the operator $\leq$ are "assumed" in *RStackTrait*, with an explicit statement in the **assumes** clause.

The specification in Figure 11.7 states in the **assumes** clause that the theory of *TotalOrder(E)* is assumed. Since *TotalOrder(T)*, shown in Figure 11.4, defines the properties of $\leq$ through its **includes** clause and its equation, we do not have to introduce the operator $\leq$ in *NStackTrait*. With the assumption that *E* is totally

NStackTrait(E, Stack): **trait**
    assumes *TotalOrder(E)*
    includes *StackTrait, Integer*
    introduces
        count: E, Stack → Int
    asserts
        ∀ *s : Stack, a,b : E*
            count(a, new) == 0
            count(a, push(s, b)) == count(a, s) + (if $b \leq a$ then 1 else 0)
    implies
        ∀ *a,b : E, s : Stack*
            $a \leq b \Rightarrow count(a,s) \leq count(b,s)$

FIGURE 11.7. A specialization of stack with assumption clause.

ordered, one can state and prove properties for the operator *count*; for example, *count* is monotonic in its first argument. This is stated in the **implies** clause.

The theory of the trait *NStackTrait* is the same as if *TotalOrder* were included in the trait. The only difference is that whenever *NStackTrait* is included or assumed in another trait, the assumption on *TotalOrder* must be discharged with a proof. For example, consider defining another stack trait that includes *NStackTrait* and introduces the operator *height*, which counts the number of elements in the stack. Intuitively, it is clear that

$$\forall \, a : E, \, s : Stack, \, count(a, s) \leq height(s)$$

is true. The proof of this claim requires discharging the proof obligation on the assumed total order property for integers. Proofs become simpler when included traits include assumed traits—that is, no separate proof is necessary. For example, using the trait *TotalOrder* from Guttag and Horning [6], we notice that it is also used in the trait *Integer* which is included in *NStack(E,Stack)*, and can therefore discharge the proof syntactically. In other situations, LP can be used to discharge the proof.

11.2.7 Operator Overloading

In mathematics, operators such as =, ≤, and + are often used to denote operations on different kinds of objects: for example, A + B, where A and B are integers, reals, rationals, or matrices. The operators have precise meanings in their contexts of usage. One of the advantages of operator overloading is to avoid excessive proliferation of operators, as this may limit the extent of understanding and clarity. LSL has several built-in overloaded operators and these operators can also be overloaded by users.

The operators =, ≠, and *if_then_else* are built-in and overloaded; they have consistent meaning in all traits where they can be used. Users can introduce overloaded operators in the **introduces** clause and provide equations in the **asserts** clause to disambiguate their meaning. For example, consider the trait *Rational* shown in Figure 11.8.

The operator ≤ is introduced in the **introduces** clause; it takes two rational numbers and returns *true* or *false*. Equation 3 in the **asserts** clause defines the ordering on rationals. The symbol ≤ on the right-hand side of the equation relates integers. The context of usage unambiguously provides the meaning of ≤. However, it is also possible to state the context in assertions: for example, equation 3 could be written as

$$(r \leq s) : Rat == (deno(r) \neq 0) \, \land$$
$$(deno(s) \neq 0) \, \land$$
$$((nume(r) * deno(s)) : Int \leq (nume(s) * deno(r)) : Int)$$

Rational(Int,Int): **trait**
    includes *Integer, TotalOrder(Int)*
    introduces
        cons: Int, Int → *Rat*
        deno: Rat → *Int*
        nume: Rat → *Int*
        $\_ \leq \_$: *Rat, Rat* → *Bool*
    asserts
        ∀ *x, y : Int, r, s : Rat*
          deno(cons(x,y)) == *y*
          nume(cons(x,y)) == *x*
          $r \leq s$ == $(deno(r) \neq 0) \wedge (deno(s) \neq 0) \wedge$
              $((nume(r) * deno(s)) \leq (nume(s) * deno(r)))$
          $deno(cons(x,y)) \neq 0$
    implies
        IsTO($\leq$, Rat)

FIGURE 11.8. LSL trait for rationals.

The operators +, −, and ∗ can be overloaded to define addition, subtraction, and multiplication, respectively, for rationals.

11.2.8   In-line Traits

LSL provides a shorthand for writing traits in-line. Three such examples are *enumerations*, *tuples*, and *union*. The trait *Flavor* shown in Figure 11.9 defines three distinct constants, and an operator to enumerate them. This trait can be succintly defined as

    Flavor **enumeration of** *chocolate, vanilla, strawberry*

The tuple notation is similar to the notation used for the fixed-size record type in Pascal. It introduces fixed-size tuples of a sort. The *Point* trait in Figure 11.10 introduces a tuple with three fields.

There are two operators associated with each field, one for extracting the field from the tuple, and another to change the value of the field. A shorthand definition for this trait is

    Point **tuple of** *xcoord, ycoord, zcoord: Int*

The union notation introduces a discriminated union of two sorts, as in the definition of union types in some programming languages. For a variable of union sort, we need a tag to identify its individual sort. Consequently, the union sort is finitely generated by the components of an enumerated sort. The sort *TransModes*

Flavor: **trait**
    introduces
        chocolate: $\rightarrow$ *Flavor*
        vanilla: $\rightarrow$ *Flavor*
        strawberry: $\rightarrow$ *Flavor*
        $\_ \leq \_$: *Flavor, Flavor* $\rightarrow$ *Bool*
    asserts
        $\forall$ *a : Flavor*
            chocolate $\neq$ *vanilla*
            chocolate $\neq$ *strawberry*
            vanilla $\neq$ *strawberry*
            chocolate $\leq$ *vanilla*
            vanilla $\leq$ *strawberry*

FIGURE 11.9. An enumeration trait.

Point: **trait**
    introduces
        [_,_,_]: Int, Int, Int $\rightarrow$ *Point*
        _.xcoord: Point $\rightarrow$ *Int*
        _.ycoord: Point $\rightarrow$ *Int*
        _.zcoord: Point $\rightarrow$ *Int*
    asserts
        Point **generated by** *[_,_,_]*
        Point **partitioned by** *_.xcoord, _.ycoord, _.zcoord*
            $\forall$ *x,y,z: Int*
        ([x,y,z]).xcoord $==$ *x*
        ([x,y,z]).ycoord $==$ *y*
        ([x,y,z]).zcoord $==$ *z*

FIGURE 11.10. A tuple trait.

in Figure 11.11 is the union of two sorts *A* and *L*. The name *atomic_trans* of
sort *A* and the name *long_trans* of sort *L* serve as the two field names for the sort
TransModes. That is, a transaction type *TransModes* is either an atomic transaction
or a long transaction. A shorthand definition for this trait is

    TransModes **union of** *atom_trans: A, long_trans: L*

11.3   More LSL Examples

We discuss four LSL trait examples to illustrate the features of Larch shared tier.
The first example develops a theory of files; the second builds a theory of iterators

TransModes: **trait**
    includes
        Mode_tag **enumeration of** *atomic_trans, long_trans*
    introduces
        atomic_trans: A → TransModes
        long_trans: L → TransModes
        _.atomic_trans: TransModes → A
        _.long_trans: TransModes → L
        tag: Transmodes → Mode_tag
    asserts
        TransModes **generated by** *atomic_trans, long_trans*
        TransModes **partitioned by** *_.atomic_trans, _.long_trans*
          $\forall \, t : A, \, T : L$
            atomic_trans(t).atomic_trans == *t*
            long_trans(T).long_trans == *T*
            tag(atomic_trans(t)) == *atomic_trans*
            tag(long_trans(T)) == *long_trans*

FIGURE 11.11. A union trait.

that can be used in specifying different C++ collection classes; the last two examples are related to *internationalization* issues in software engineering, wherein accommodating different cultural conventions for representing and dealing with time and date are addressed.

These examples require the LSL library trait *String* given in Guttag and Horning [6]; for reference, it is reproduced in Figure 11.12. The trait *String* models a string as a list of elements. The sort of string is *C*, and the sort for elements is *E*. The trait implicitly includes the properties of the sort *Int*, and includes the trait *List* shown in Figure 11.14, in which the operators *empty, tail, head*, and $\dashv$ are defined. The operator $\dashv$ inserts an element to the front of a given list; the rest of the operators have meanings similar to the list operators defined in Chapter 8. The operator *_[_]* extracts the element from a given position of a string; the other operations have their intuitive meanings.

11.3.1   File

The trait in Figure 11.13 specifies properties common to text files. A text file in disk storage or in memory can be modeled as a string of bytes. We consider *Byte* as a basic abstraction to model fixed-length sequences of characters. The **includes** clause mentions the trait *String* with two parameters of the sorts *Byte*, and *Data* as a string of bytes to abstract file data. A disk file is described by the **tuple** trait *File* with three fields, *name : Name, data : Data, mode : Mode*. The trait *Mode* is defined by the **enumeration** of three distinct constants *READ, WRITE, READ_WRITE*. The abstraction of a file in memory is introduced in the trait *Openfile*, as a tuple with

String(E, C): **trait**
  includes *List*
  introduces
    _[_] : C, Int → E
    prefix : C, Int → C
    removePrefix : C, Int → C
    substring : C, Int, Int → C
  asserts
    $\forall$ *e : E, s : C, i, n : Int*
      ¬(member(e, emptyset))
      tail(empty) == empty
      s[0] == head(s)
      n ≥ 0 ⇒ s[n + 1] = tail(s)[n]
      prefix(empty, n) == empty
      prefix(s, 0) == empty
      n ≥ 0 ⇒ prefix(e ⊣ s, n + 1) = e ⊣ prefix(s, n)
      removePrefix(s, 0) == s
      n ≥ 0 ⇒ removePrefix(s, n + 1) = removePrefix (tail(s), n)
      substring(s, 0, n) == prefix(s, n)
      i ≥ 0 ⇒ substring(s, i + 1, n) = substring(tail(s), i, n)
  implies
    IndexOp(⊣ **for** *insert)*
    C **partitioned by** *len, _[_]*
  converts *tail*

FIGURE 11.12. LSL trait for string.

four fields: *file* refers to the disk file, *data* refers to the contents of the file, *mode* refers to the mode enumeration, and *fpointer* corresponds to a position in the file. The trait *readeffect* abstracts the effect of reading a file in memory, by resetting the position in the file to the last byte read. The sorts and operations are

- File on disk corresponds to the sort *File*.
- File in memory corresponds to the sort *Openfile*.
- The data in a file is abstracted as a string of bytes, *Data*.
- When a file is opened, the data in the file in memory is a copy of the data in the corresponding disk file.
- *create*—creates a disk file.
- *open*—opens a disk file in memory with its proper mode set.
- *flush*—updates a disk file with the data from the corresponding memory file.
- *error*—returns true if an I/O error occurred in a memory file.
- *read*—describes the effect of reading a file in memory.
- *write*—describes the effect of writing a file from memory onto disk.

11.3.2   Iterator

An iterator is an object associated with a list, a basic container type. By specializing a list and its iterator, one can obtain iterators for hash-dictionaries, bags, and tree-dictionaries. The goal of this example is to construct a theory of iterators. We first extract a simple theory of finite lists from the theory given in Guttag and Horning [6]; we then construct a richer theory of lists; finally, we develop a theory of iterators associated with this list type. The first two steps are motivated by the need for iterator operations in C++ classes in the Rogue Wave library [10].

List Trait   Figure 11.14 shows the LSL trait for a finite list. It has operations to construct a list by concatenation, and by adding elements at the front or rear of the list. The element at one end can be extracted and the list following this element can be identified.

Enriching List Trait   The trait *ListOp* shown in Figure 11.15 includes *List*(*E*, *C*) and introduces the following additional operations:

- *isequal*—compares two lists for identical elements occurring in the same order.
- *movepos*—removes a number of elements from the front of the list and returns the rest of the list; this operation is equivalent to a finite number of successive applications of the *tail* operation.
- *occurrencesof*—determines the number of occurrences of an element in a given list.
- *findonlist*—returns *true* if a given element is in the given list; otherwise returns *false*.
- *lastnode*—returns the list containing the last node of a given list.
- *tailrem*—returns the list after removing a given number of elements from the rear of the list.
- *sublist*—extracts a sublist from the given list.

The iterator trait, as shown in Figures 11.16 and 11.17, is represented as a tuple composed of the fields *Col* and *Head*, where *Col* is a pointer to the collection that is to be iterated, and *Head* points to the current item in the collection. Consequently, the iterator is modeled as a pair of lists. The following operations are provided:

- *create*—returns an iterator to traverse the list in the *Col* field; the *Head* field is undefined.
- *sizecol*—returns the number of items in the collection *Col*.
- *moveiterator*—returns the iterator after moving *Head* by a specified number of positions; when *Head* is undefined or when the number of positions is greater than the number of unvisited elements in the list, the result is undefined.
- *reset*—returns the iterator as it was at its creation time.

File: **trait**

> **includes** *String(Byte, Data)*
> *File* **tuple of** *name : Name, data : Data, mode : Mode*
> *Openfile* **tuple of** *file : File, data : Data, mode : Mode, fpointer : Int*
> *Mode* **enumeration of** *READ, WRITE, READ_WRITE*
> *readeffect* **tuple of** *ofile : OpenFile, reddata : Data*
> **introduces**
>> *create: Name, Mode → File*
>> *open: File, Mode → OpenFile*
>> *flush: OpenFile → OpenFile*
>> *error: OpenFile → Bool*
>> *read: OpenFile, Int, Int → readeffect*
>> *write: OpenFile, Data, Int → OpenFile*
>
> **asserts**
>> ∀ *f : File, opf : OpenFile, mode, m : Mode, nm : Name, i, p : Int, dat : Data*
>> *create(nm, m) == [nm, empty, m]*
>> *open(f, READ) == [f, f.data, READ, 1]*
>> *open(f, READ_WRITE) == [f, f.data, READ_WRITE, 1]*
>> *open(f, WRITE) == [f, f.data, WRITE, len(f.data)]*
>> ¬*(error(flush(opf)))* ⇒ *(opf.data = opf.file.data)*
>> *read(opf, i, p).reddata == prefix(removePrefix(opf.data, p), i)*
>> *read(opf, i, p).ofile == [opf.file, opf.data, opf.mode, p + i]*
>> *write(opf, dat, p) == [opf.file, prefix(opf.data, p) ‖ dat ‖*
>>> *removePrefix(opf.data, p + len(dat)),*
>>> *opf.mode, p + len(dat)]*

implies

> ∀ *opf : OpenFile, dat : Data, i, p : Int*
>> *read(write(opf, dat, p), len(dat), p).reddata == dat*
>
> **converts** *create, open*
>> **exempting**
>
> ∀ *nm : Name, f : File, dat : Data, p : Int*
>> *write(open(f, READ), dat, p),*
>> *open(create(nm,READ), WRITE),*
>> *open(create(nm, READ), READ_WRITE)*

FIGURE 11.13. LSL trait for file.

- *itemat*—returns the element in the list *Col* at the current position pointed to by *Head*.

- *isfirst*—returns *true* if the current element, as pointed to by *Head*, is the first element of *Col*.

- *islast*—returns *true* if the current element, as pointed to by *Head*, is the last element of the list *Col*.

$List\ (E,C)$: **trait**
    includes *Integer*
    introduces
        empty: $\rightarrow C$
        $\_ \dashv \_: E,\ C \rightarrow C$
        $\_ \vdash \_: C,\ E \rightarrow C$
        head: $C \rightarrow E$
        tail: $C \rightarrow C$
        len: $C \rightarrow Int$
        $\{\_\}: E \rightarrow C$
        $\_ \parallel \_: C,\ C \rightarrow C$
    asserts
        C **generated by** *empty*, $\vdash$, $\parallel$
        C **partitioned by** *len, head, tail*
        $\forall e, e_1, e_2 : E, c, c_1, c_2 : C$
          $e \dashv empty == empty \vdash e$
          $e_1 \dashv (c \vdash e_2) == (e_1 \dashv c) \vdash e_2$
          $head(e \dashv c) == e$
          $tail(e \dashv c) == c$
          $len(empty) == 0$
          $len(e \dashv c) == 1 + len(c)$
          $\{e\} == empty \dashv e$
          $c \parallel empty == c$
          $(e \dashv c_1) \parallel c_2 == e \dashv (c_1 \parallel c_2)$
    implies
        $\forall c : C$
           $c = empty \vee (c = head(c) \dashv tail(c))$
        converts *head, tail, len,* $\parallel$, $\{\_\}$
          exempting *head(empty), tail(empty)*

FIGURE 11.14. An LSL trait for finite lists.

- *first*—returns the iterator with *Head* pointing to the first element of the list *Col*.

- *last*—returns the iterator with *Head* pointing to the last element of the list *Col*.

- *nextitem*—returns the iterator with *Head* pointing to the next item in the list *Col*, equal to a given value.

- *remove*—returns an iterator after removing the item pointed to by the Head.

- *removenext*—returns an iterator after removing the item next to a given element.

- *insertat*—returns an iterator after inserting a given element at the position pointed to by the Head.

ListOp(E, C): **trait**
    includes *List(E, C)*
    introduces
        isequal: C, C → Bool
        movepos: C, Int → C
        occurrencesof: C, E → Int
        findonlist: C, E → Bool
        lastnode: C → C
        sublist: C, Int, Int → C
        tailrem: C, Int → C
    asserts
        $\forall c_1, c_2 : C, n, n_1, n_2 : Int, e, e_1, e_2 : E$
            isequal(empty, empty)
            $isequal(e_1 \dashv c_1, e_2 \dashv c_2) == e_1 = e_2 \wedge isequal(c_1, c_2)$
            $movepos(c_1, n) ==$ *if* $n = 0$ *then* c_1
                else if $n > 0 \wedge n \leq len(c_1)$ *then*
                    $movepos(tail(c_1), n - 1)$
                else empty
            occurrencesof(empty, e) == 0
            $occurrencesof(e_1 \dashv c, e) ==$ *if* $e = e_1$ *then* $1 + occurrencesof(c, e)$
                else occurrencesof(c, e)
            $\neg$ *findonlist(empty, e)*
            $findonlist(e_1 \dashv c, e) == (e_1 = e) \vee findonlist(c, e)$
            $lastnode(c) == movepos(c, len(c) - 1)$
            tailrem(empty, n) == empty
            tailrem(c, 0) == c
            $tailrem(c \vdash e, n) ==$ *if* $n > 0$ *then* $tailrem(c, n - 1)$ *else empty*
            $sublist(c, n_1, n_2) ==$ *if* $(n_1 + n_2) \leq len(c)$ *then*
                $tailrem(movepos(c, n_1 - 1), n_2)$
                else empty

FIGURE 11.15. LSL trait for an enrichment of list trait.

11.3.3   Date and Zone

Database and network programs use date and zone types. A theory for these data types is described in the traits *Date*, and *Zone*. The trait *Zone* shown in Figure 11.21 defines the standard and daylight saving zones and their relationship. The trait *Date* shown in Figures 11.19 and 11.20 models the dates in a Julian calendar, and operations on the dates. A date is abstracted by a fixed length tuple of *Day, Month, Year*, all of type *Int*. Constraints on the fields, converting the numeric value of a month to a string to denote its name, and the relationship between number of days and month are specified in equations shown in Figure 11.20. The formatting convention for date is abstracted in the trait *Locale* shown in Figure 11.18. Date

Iterator(Iter, C, E): **trait**
   includes *ListOp(E, C)*
   Iter **tuple of** *Col : C, Head : C*
   introduces
      create: C → Iter
      sizecol: Iter → Int
      moveiterator: Iter, Int → Iter
      reset: Iter → Iter
      itemat: Iter → E
      UND: → E
      isfirst: Iter → Bool
      islast: Iter → Bool
      first: Iter → Iter
      last: Iter → Iter
      nextitem: Iter, E → Iter
      remove: Iter → Iter
      removenext: Iter, E → Iter
      insertat: Iter, E → Iter
   asserts
      $\forall$ *i : Iter, c : C, n : Int, e : E*
         create(c).Head == empty
         create(c).Col == c
         reset(i).Head == empty
         reset(i).Col == i.Col
         moveiterator(i,0) == i
         n > 0 ⇒ (moveiterator(i,n).Head =
            (if len(i.Head) = 0 ∧ len(i.Col) > 0
            then movepos(i.Col, n − 1)
            else if len(i.Col) = 0 then empty
               else movepos(i.Head,n)))
         n < 0 ⇒ (moveiterator(i,n).Head =
            (if len(i.Head) = 0 ∧ len(i.Col) > 0
            then moveiterator(last(i), n − 1).Head
            else if isequal(i.Head, i.Col) ∧ len(i.Col) > 0 then empty
            else if len(i.Col) = 0 then empty
            else if ((−n) ≤ (len(i.Col) − len(i.Head))) then
               movepos(i.Col, (len(i.Col) − len(i.Head)) + n)
               else empty))

FIGURE 11.16. An LSL trait for iterators—Part I.

$moveiterator(i,n).Col == i.Col$

$itemat(i) == head(i.Head)$

$sizecol(i) == len(i.Col)$

$isfirst(i) == isequal(i.Col, i.Head)$

$islast(i) == isequal(tail(i.Head),empty)$

$first(i).Col == i.Col$

$first(i).Head == i.Col$

$last(i).Col == i.Col$

$last(i).Head == lastnode(i.Col)$

$nextitem(i,e).Head == if\ (itemat(moveiterator(i,1)) = e$
$\quad \vee\ itemat(moveiterator(i,1)) = UND)\ then$
$\qquad moveiterator(i,1).Head$
$\quad else\ nextitem(moveiterator(i,1),e).Head$

$nextitem(i,e).Col == i.Col$

$i.Head = empty \Rightarrow itemat(i) = UND$

$remove(i).Col == sublist(i.Col,\ 1,\ (len(i.Col) - len(i.Head)))\ \|\ tail(i.Head)$

$remove(i).Head == movepos(remove(i).Col,\ (len(i.Col) - len(i.Head) - 1))$

$removenext(i,e).Head == remove(nextitem(i,e))$

$insertat(i,e).Col == (sublist(i.Col,\ 1,\ len(i.Col) - len(i.Head))) \vdash e)\ \|\ i.Head$

$insertat(i,e).Head == movepos(remove(i).Col,\ (len(i.Col) - len(i.Head)))$

FIGURE 11.17. An LSL trait for iterators—Part II.

Locale: **trait**
  includes *Integer*
  introduces
    Localformat: → *Int*

FIGURE 11.18. LSL trait for local format.

can also be represented as a natural number, the number of days elapsed since *startDay*. The operations in *Date* have the following significance.

- *today*—constructor; creates the current date.
- *date*—constructor; composes a date from the given values.
- *totalDays*—returns the number of days elapsed since *startDay* until the given date.
- *dayConvert*—converts the given number of days into date.
- *isValid*—returns *true* if the given date is valid.
- *week_day*—determines which day of the week the given date is.

- *startDay*—defines which day of the week the starting date is.
- *leap*—returns *true* if the given year is a leap year.
- *ConvertY*—determines the number of days elapsed since *startDay*, including the current day.
- *ConvertM*—determines the number of days elapsed in a given year up to the given month, including the given month.
- *ConvertD*—determines which day of the month the given date is.
- *yConvert*—converts a given year into the number of days, that is, 366 for a leap year, and 365 otherwise.
- *mConvert*—determines the number of days in the given month during the given year.
- *dYconvert*—converts the given day in a given year into the corresponding date; for example, 32 corresponds to February 1.
- *dtConvert*—converts the given date into the number of days elapsed in the given year.
- *validDay*—returns *true* if the given day is valid.
- *validMonth*—returns *true* if the given month is valid.
- *validYear*—returns *true* if the given year is valid.
- *date_string*—converts the given date into a string.
- *string_date*—converts the given string into a date.
- *name_month*—converts the given name of a month into the corresponding number.
- *month_name*—converts the given number corresponding to a month into its name.
- *name_date*—converts the given name of a day into the corresponding number.
- *day_name*—converts the given number corresponding to a day into its name.
- *toLocale*—transforms the given date into the given local format.

The trait *Zone* in Figure 11.21 abstracts the time zones of the world as a tuple with four fields. The first two fields assign names to the zone and the daylight saving time (DST) of that zone; the next two fields refer to the standard time offset and the DST offset.

- *standardOffset*—an offset from the Greenwich time with no daylight saving time correction.
- *DSTOffset*—an offset from the Greenwich time with daylight saving time correction.
- *utc*—Greenwich time zone.
- *local*—local time zone with respect to the daylight saving time, if there is any.

Date : **trait**
includes *Boolean, Integer, Locale, Zone*
Weekday **enumeration of** *mon, tue, wed, thu, fri, sat, sun*
Date **tuple of** *Day, Month, Year : Int*
introduces
    today: $\rightarrow$ *Date*
    date: Int, Int, Int $\rightarrow$ *Date*
    totalDays: Date $\rightarrow$ *Int*
    dayConvert: Int $\rightarrow$ *Date*
    isValid: Date $\rightarrow$ *Bool*
    week_day: Date $\rightarrow$ *Int*
    startDay: $\rightarrow$ *Int*
    leap: Int $\rightarrow$ *Bool*
    ConvertY: Int $\rightarrow$ *Int*
    ConvertM: Int, Int $\rightarrow$ *Int*
    ConvertD: Int $\rightarrow$ *Int*
    yConvert: Int $\rightarrow$ *Int*
    mConvert: Int, Int $\rightarrow$ *Int*
    dYconvert: Int, Int $\rightarrow$ *Date*
    dtConvert: Date $\rightarrow$ *Int*
    validDay: Int $\rightarrow$ *Bool*
    validMonth: Int $\rightarrow$ *Bool*
    validYear: Int $\rightarrow$ *Bool*
    date_string: Date $\rightarrow$ *Str*
    string_date: Str $\rightarrow$ *Date*
    name_month: Str $\rightarrow$ *Int*
    month_name: Int $\rightarrow$ *Str*
    name_day: Str $\rightarrow$ *Int*
    day_name: Int $\rightarrow$ *Str*
    toLocale: Date, Locale $\rightarrow$ *Date*
    min: Date, Date $\rightarrow$ *Date*
    max: Date, Date $\rightarrow$ *Date*

FIGURE 11.19. LSL trait for date—Part I.

- *standard*—local time zone without daylight saving time correction.

11.3.4 Time

Time stamping information is mandatory for legal contracts and communication protocols. The LSL trait *Time* provides necessary abstractions for programming tasks in such applications. Time is abstracted as observed according to daylight saving conventions in the Julian calendar. We have abstracted the notion of time

asserts

   Date **generated by** *date*

   ∀ *d : Int, m : Int, y : Int, dt, dt_1 : Date, dn : Int*

     ConvertY(dt.Year) == if (dt.Year = 1) then yConvert(dt.Year)
      else yConvert(dt.Year) + ConvertY(dt.Year − 1)

     mConvert(m,y) == if (m = 1 ∨ m = 3 ∨ m = 5 ∨ m = 7 ∨
      m = 8 ∨ m = 10 ∨ m = 12) then 31
      else if (m = 4 ∨ m = 6 ∨ m = 9 ∨ m = 11) then 30
      else if leap(y) then 29 else 28

     yConvert(y) == if leap(y) then 366 else 365

     ConvertM(m, y) == if m = 1 then 31
      else mConvert(m, y) + ConvertM(m − 1, y)

     dtConvert(dt) == ConvertM(dt.Month − 1, dt.Year) + ConvertD(dt.Day)

     validDay(dt.Day) == dt.Day ≤ 31 ∧ dt.Day > 0

     validMonth(dt.Month) == dt.Month ≤ 12 ∧ dt.Month > 0

     validYear(dt.Year) == dt.Year > 1900

     leap(y) == if (y = 1900) then true
      else if (y > 1903) then leap(y − 4) else false

     week_day(dt) == mod(totalDays(dt) + startDay, 7)

     totalDays(dt) = ConvertY(dt.Year − 1) +
      ConvertM(dt.Month − 1, dt.Year) + ConvertD(dt.Day)

     isValid(dt) == dt.Month = 1 ∨ dt.Month = 3 ∨ dt.Month = 5 ∨
      dt.Month = 7 ∨ dt.Month = 8 ∨ dt.Month = 10 ∨ dt.Month = 12 ∧
      dt.Day > 0 ∧ dt.Day ≤ 31

     isValid(dt) == dt.Month = 4 ∨ dt.Month = 6 ∨ dt.Month = 9 ∨
      dt.Month = 11 ∧ dt.Day > 0 ∧ dt.Day ≤ 30

     isValid(dt) == leap(dt.Year) ∧ dt.Day > 0 ∧ dt.Day ≤ 29
      ∧ dt.Month = 2

     isValid(dt) == ¬ leap(dt.Year) ∧ dt.Day > 0 ∧ dt.Day ≤ 28 ∧
      dt.Month = 2

     min(dt, dt_1) == if totalDays(dt) ≥ totalDays(dt_1) then dt_1 else dt

     max(dt, dt_1) == if totalDays(dt) ≤ totalDays(dt_1) then dt_1 else dt

     d < ConvertM(1, y) ⇒ date(d, 1, y) = dYconvert(d, y)

     d < ConvertM(m, y) ⇒ date(d − ConvertM(m − 1, y), m, y) =
      dYconvert(d, y)

implies

   ∀ *d_1 : Date, d, m, y : Int*
     validMonth(2) ⇒ ¬ validDay(30)

FIGURE 11.20. LSL trait for date—Part II.

Zone : **trait**
    includes *Integer, String*
    Zone **tuple of** *standardName, DSTName : String,*
       standardOffset, DSTOffset : Int
    introduces
       utc: → *Zone*
       local: → *Zone*
       standard: → *Zone*
       daylightObserved: Zone → *Bool*
    asserts
       Zone **partitioned by** *daylightObserved*
       ∀ *zn : Zone*
          utc.DSTOffset == 0
          utc.standardOffset == 0
          ¬ *daylightObserved(local)* ⇒ *local.DSTOffset = standard.DSTOffset*
          local.standardOffset == standard.standardOffset
          ¬ *daylightObserved(zn)* ⇒ *zn.DSTOffset = zn.standardOffset*
          ¬ *daylightObserved(standard)*

FIGURE 11.21. LSL trait for zone.

zones and dates in the previous example. These traits are included in the **includes** clause.

The sort *Time* shown in Figure 11.22 models time as a tuple of *date, hour, minute, second*, and *zone*. The local convention for stating time is abstracted in the trait *Locale*. From the local format, time is converted to an integer and converted again to the structure imposed by the sort *Time*. In order to do this conversion, we need to know the *origin* of time. This *origin* is fixed at midnight of *startDay*, the abstraction of the first day of the last millenium. The abstraction for daylight saving time depends on the *Zone* and *Date* abstractions. The operations introduced in *Time* are the following:

- *makeStr*—returns a string representation of a given time according to the format specified by the *Locale* parameter.
- *makeTime*—converts a given string to time.
- *toZone*—converts the given time to time in a different zone.
- *observedDST*—returns AHEAD if the clock is changed forward.
- *observedDST*—returns BEHIND if the clock is changed backward.
- *observedDST*—returns NON if there is no daylight saving clock change in the given zone for a given year.
- *beginDST*—returns the time when clock is changed forward.
- *endDST*—returns the time when clock is changed backward.

Time : **trait**

> **includes** *TotalOrder(Time), Date, Integer, Locale, Zone, String(E for E, Str for C)*
> *Time* **tuple of** *date : Date, hour, minute, second : Int, zone : Zone*
> *DSTmethod* **enumeration of** *AHEAD, BEHIND, NON*
> **introduces**
>> *current_time:* → *Time*
>> *convert: Time* → *Int*
>> *reconvert: Int* → *Time*
>> *suc: Time* → *Time*
>> *pred: Time* → *Time*
>> *inc: Time, Int* → *Time*
>> *dec: Time, Int* → *Time*
>> *max: Time, Time* → *Time*
>> *min: Time, Time* → *Time*
>> ≤*: Time, Time* → *Bool*
>> ≥*: Time, Time* → *Bool*
>> *makeStr: Time, Locale* → *Str*
>> *makeTime: Str, Locale* → *Time*
>> *isValid: Time* → *Bool*
>> *toZone: Time, Zone* → *Time*
>> *observedDST: Year, Zone* → *DSTmethod*
>> *beginDST: Year, Zone* → *Time*
>> *endDST: Year, Zone* → *Time*

FIGURE 11.22. LSL trait for time—Part I.

- *convert*—takes a time representation and converts it to number of seconds.

- *reconvert* - takes a number of seconds and converts it to a valid time expression.

Figure 11.22 shows the signature of the trait *Time*, and Figure 11.23 shows the equations constraining its operations.

11.4   Larch/C++ : A Larch Interface Specification Language for C++

An interface is the place where two independent systems meet and communicate with each other. An interface specification defines an interface between program components. Larch/C++ is a formal specification language for specifying C++ program components. A Larch/C++ specification suggests how to use C++ program modules within C++ programs. The version of Larch/C++ discussed in this chapter is based on the work of Gary Leavens [8].

asserts

　　Time **partitioned by** *convert*

　　∀ *t*, t_1 : *Time, d : Date, y : Year, h , m , s : Int, zn, zn_1 : Zone,*

　　i : Int, locale : Locale

　　　isValid(current_time)

　　　current_time.zone == local

　　　isValid(t) == isValid(t.date) ∧ convert(t) > 0

　　　convert(t) == (3600 * 24 * totalDays (t.date)) + (3600 * t.hour) +

　　　　(60 * t.minute) + t.second

　　　reconvert(convert(t)) == t

　　　suc(t) == reconvert(convert(t) + 1)

　　　pred(t) == reconvert(convert(t) − 1)

　　　inc(t, i) == reconvert(convert(t) + i)

　　　dec(t, i) == reconvert(convert(t) − i)

　　　$t \geq t_1 == convert(t) \geq convert(t_1)$

　　　$t \leq t_1 == convert(t) \leq convert(t_1)$

　　　$max(t, t_1) = t == t \geq t_1$

　　　$min(t, t_1) = t == t \leq t_1$

　　　$toZone(t, zn_1).zone == zn_1$

　　　toZone(toZone(t, zn), t.zone) == t

　　　makeTime(makeStr(t, locale), locale) == t

　　　(observedDST(y, zn) = AHEAD) ⇒

　　　　convert(beginDST(y, zn)) < convert(endDST(y, zn))

　　　(observedDST(y, zn) = BEHIND) ⇒

　　　　convert(beginDST(y, zn)) > convert(endDST(y, zn))

　　　(observedDST(y, zn) = NON) ⇒

　　　　beginDST(y, zn) = endDST(y, zn)

implies

　　∀ *t : Time*

　　　suc(pred(t)) == t

FIGURE 11.23. LSL trait for time - Part II.

An interface specification is written from the point of view of clients who will use the module. A C++ class has three interfaces: *public, protected*, and *private*. Figure 11.24 shows the public, protected, and private interfaces for a simple module implementing a data structure for time.

A public interface is used by all clients, including subclasses, member functions of the class, and friends. A public interface of a class *Y* derived from the base class *X* under a public subclass relationship includes the public members of *X*; however, the private and protected members of *X* maintain their access level in *Y*. For example, the public members of `display` are also the public members of `time`; however, the private and protected members of `display` maintain their access level in `time`.

```
class time : public display, protected date, private zone {
    public:
        time(int hours, int minutes, int seconds);
        int get_hour();
        int get_min();
        int get_sec();
        void display();
    protected:
        set_hour(int hours);
        set_min(int minutes);
        set_sec(int seconds);
    private:
        int hr,min,sec;
};
```

FIGURE 11.24. C++ class for time.

If a class Y is derived from the base class X under a protected subclass relationship, then the protected interface of class Y consists of the protected members of class Y and all public and protected members of class X. This interface can be used only by member functions of the class, friends, and subclasses of this class. The public and private members of date become protected members of time; however, the private members of date retain their access level in `time`.

If a class Y is derived from the base class X under a private subclass relationship, then the private interface of class Y consists of the private members of class Y and all the members of class X. For example, all members of class zone become private members of the class `time`. A private interface can be accessed by member functions and friends only.

Documenting the functions in the public interface of a C++ module provides a clean separation between the interface and the implementation of the module. Detailed design decisions can be captured by giving specifications for protected and private interfaces. For example, the specification of a protected interface is useful for programs based on subclasses. However, it is very important to specify public interfaces so that the behavior of public members can be understood independent of the specifications of other interfaces. Henceforth, we focus on the specification of public members.

11.4.1   Relating Larch/C++ to C++

Each Larch/C++ specification is structured similar to a C++ module. It contains the names of imported modules, traits used from the LSL tier, and specifications.

The formal model of Objects, Values, and States

A C++ object is a region of storage or a reference to a storage location. Every object has an identifier corresponding to the *address* of the object. Every variable identifier has a type and is associated with a location of that type. *Values* stored in memory locations can be complex or simple, such as the integer 13 or character "x". Complex values can be

- values of data structures constructed; for example, *date(2,10,1995)*.

- values of set expressions, such as *insert(3, insert(2, emptyset))*.

- values of attributes that are themselves objects or references to objects; for example, **X*, where * indicates that *X* is a pointer to an object.

Formal parameters passed by value in Larch/C++ are not objects; only formal parameters passed by reference are objects. Pointers passed by value are not objects, but may point to objects. An object in Larch/C++ is either mutable or a constant (immutable). Mutable objects include variables and reference parameters. Objects of sort S are referred to as Obj[S]; that is, Obj[S] is the object of sort S.

A formal model of objects in Larch/C++ has been developed by Leavens [8]. The trait *MutableObj* describes the formal model of mutable objects by adding the mutability to the trait *TypedObj*. The trait *TypedObj* handles the translation between typed objects and values, and untyped objects and values used in the trait *state*. The trait *ConstObj* gives the formal model of constant objects. Constant objects are modeled by sorts with names of the form ConstObj[T], the sort of a constant object containing abstract values of sort *T*. Traits of interest for Larch/C++ can be built hierarchically by including this library of traits. For example, the trait specifying a dictionary of items, where each item is a tuple of Obj[K] and Obj[V], includes *MutableObj(K)*, *MutableObj(V)*, and *Iterator(Iter[item]* **for** Iter, C, item **for** E).

States are mappings from objects to values. During execution, a program creates objects and binds values to them. A state captures the set of objects and their bindings that exist at a specific point in time. The trait *State* given by Chen [2] gives the formal model of states used in Larch/C++. It defines the sort State as a mapping between untyped objects of sort Obj and abstract values of sort Val.

Declarations and Declarators

C++ provides various kinds of declarators for every possible declaration. Larch/C++ has incorporated these declarators both in syntax and semantics. A declaration in Larch/C++ implies that the C++ module that implements the specification must have a matching declaration. There are some minor differences between the syntax of Larch/C++ for declarators and that of C++; these have been deliberately included in Larch/C++ to resolve some ambiguities in the C++ grammar.

In a declaration, a declarator defines a single object, a function or a type, giving it a name. The semantics of each declarator is described by identifying the sort associated with the variables in the declaration. For instance, when declaring a global variable of type integer, Larch/C++ implicitly uses the LSL trait *Integer*. A declarator may refine an object's type using the following operators:

pointer	*
pointer to member	:: *
reference	&
array	[ ]
function	()

A variable declared globally, a formal parameter passed to a function, or a quantified variable is of a specific sort. Larch/C++ uses sort generators to automatically introduce certain auxiliary sorts for modeling some features of C++. An example of a sort generator is `Obj`, which can be used to generate the auxiliary sort `Obj[int]`, whose abstract values are of the sort `int`. Other sort generators in Larch/C++ include `Ptr` for pointers, `Arr` for arrays, and `ConstObj` for constants and for functions. Tables 11.1 and 11.2 give a summary of the sorts that correspond to global variables, and formal parameters. Larch/C++ describes the semantics of these sorts using LSL traits.

In these tables a term x of sort `Ptr[Obj[T]]` is a pointer that points to an object that contains an abstract value of sort `T`. To obtain the object pointed to, the operator $*$ must be used. Therefore, $*x$ is of the sort `Obj[T]`. A term x of sort `Arr[Obj[T]]` is an array of objects that contains abstract values of sort T. To obtain any of these objects, the operator [ ] and the integer index of the particular object are used. A *structure* or a *union* declared globally is an object. Since C++ parameters are passed by value (except for reference parameters), a *structure* or

Declaration	Sort of x (x is global)
T x	Obj[T]
const T x	ConstObj[T]
T & x	Obj[T]
const T & x	ConstObj[T]
T & const x	Obj[T]
T * x	Obj[Ptr[Obj[T]]]
const T * x	Obj[Ptr[ConstObj[T]]]
T * const x	ConstObj[Ptr[Obj[T]]]
T x[3]	Arr[Obj[T]]
const T x[3]	Arr[ConstObj[T]]
IntList x	ConstObj[IntList]
int x(int i)	ConstObj[cpp_function]

TABLE 11.1. Sorts of global variables.

Declaration	**Sort of x (x is formal parameter)**
T x	T
const T x	T
T & x	Obj[T]
const T & x	ConstObj[T]
T & const x	ConstObj[T]
T * x	Ptr[Obj[T]]
const T * x	Ptr[ConstObj[T]]
T * const x	Ptr[Obj[T]]
T x[]	Ptr[Obj[T]]
const T x[]	Ptr[ConstObj[T]]
IntList x	Val[IntList]

TABLE 11.2. Sorts of formal parameters.

a *union* passed as a parameter to a function is not an object but simply a tuple of the respective fields. Thus, in Table 11.1 the sort of the global variable of type IntList is ConstObj [IntList], and in Table 11.2 the sort of the formal parameter of type IntList is Val [IntList].

State functions

An object can be in an infinite number of states through its lifetime. Some states may not be visible to the client of a class interface; in particular, only a limited number of states are visible. States that are not visible to a client are *internal object states*. States that are of particular interest to the class interface are

- the *prestate*, which maps objects to their values just before the function body is run, but after parameter passing
- the *poststate*, which maps objects to their values at the point of returning from the function call, or signalling an exception, but before the function parameters go out of scope.

A state function must be used to obtain an object's abstract value in a particular state, provided the object is assigned a value in that state. There are four state functions in Larch/C++ :

- \pre or ^ : gives the abstract value of an object in the prestate.
- \post or ' : gives the abstract value of an object in the poststate.
- \any : gives the abstract value of an object without reference to any particular state. This state function is usually used when the object is immutable with the same abstract value in both the prestate and the poststate.
- \obj : is used to explicitly refer to an object itself, instead of its abstract value. It is only used for emphasis.

```
class IntSet
{
    uses SetTrait(IntSet for S, int for E);
public:
    IntSet() {
        modifies self;
        ensures self' = emptyset;
    }
    ~IntSet() {
        modifies self;
        ensures trashed(self);
    }
    void add(int i) {
        modifies self;
        ensures self' = insert(i, self^);
    }
    void remove(int i) {
        requires member(i, self^);
        modifies self;
        ensures self' = delete(i, self^);
    }
    IntSet* unionn(IntSet* pS) {
        ensures (*result) = unionn(self^, (*pS)^);
    }
    bool isIn(int x) {
        ensures result = member(x, self^);
    }
};
```

FIGURE 11.25. Larch/C++ specification for integer set.

State functions can only be applied to terms that denote objects and sorts that are either `Obj[T]` or `ConstObj[T]` for some type `T`. The sort of any object of type `T` to which one of the three state functions `\pre, \post, \any` has been applied is the same as the sort of the object but without the leading `Obj` or `ConstObj` sort generator. When the `\any` state function is applied to an object, the sort of the expression is the same as the sort of the object. For example, if the sort of `x` is `Obj[int]`, then the sort of `x'` is `int` and the sort of `x\any` is `Obj[int]`.

A type in the interface layer is associated with a sort in the shared layer. The abstract values of a type are the equivalence classes of the sort with which the type is associated. For example, the types `int, int[5]` are mapped to sorts *Int, Arr[Int]*. However, there may be no type corresponding to a sort. For instance, there is no C++ type corresponding to the sort `Obj[int]`.

Larch/C++ syntax—an example

Figure 11.25 shows a Larch/C++ interface specification for *IntSet*, a module implementing sets of integers. For each *IntSet* operation, the specification consists of a *header* and a *body*. The header specifies the name of the operation, the names and types of parameters, as well as the return type; it uses the same notation as used in C++. The body of the specification consists of an **ensures** clause as well as optional **requires** and **modifies** clauses. We discuss the body of the specification in the next section.

The link between the *IntSet* interface specification and the LSL tier specification for *SetTrait* is indicated by the clause **uses** *SetTrait (IntSet* **for** *Set, int* **for** *E)*. The trait used in *IntSet* provides the names and meanings of the operators *emptyset, insert, delete, unionn, member*, and *subset*, as well as the meaning of the equality symbol, "=", which are referred to in the pre- and poststates of the operations of *IntSet*. The **uses** clause also specifies the *type* to *sort* mapping that indicates the abstract values over which the objects involved in the specification range. For example, the abstract values of *IntSet* objects are represented by terms of the sort *Set*. In summary, the **uses** clause defines the mapping from interface types to LSL sorts; the interface specification is written based on types and values; the used trait gives the names and meanings of the operators referred to in the interface specifications, thus providing meaning to values.

11.4.2 Function Specification

The specification of a function in the interface documents its behavior. This can be understood without reference to other functions in the interface. The body of a function consists of a number of clauses. Most function specifications contain **requires, modifies**, and **ensures** clauses. Other clauses are discussed in the next section.

The **requires** clause defines constraints on the state and parameters at the instance of function invocation. From the point of view of clients, a function must be invoked only when the program state satisfies the predicate in the **requires** clause. Otherwise, the behavior of the function is unconstrained. The **modifies** and **ensures** clauses state the behavior of the function when it is invoked properly. If a function is called when the program state satisfies the predicate in the **requires** clause, the function will terminate in a state that satisfies the predicate in the **ensures** clause. Moreover, the program is allowed to change only those visible objects listed in the **modifies** clause. Thus, the behavior of a function is described relative to two states: the state before the function is entered and the state after the function returns. A **requires** clause refers to variables in the prestate. An **ensures** clause may refer to variables in both the pre- and the poststate. The **modifies** clause states that no location visible to the user other than those listed in the **modifies** clause may be changed. All these clauses in the function specification are optional. Omitting either the **requires** or the **ensures** clause is equivalent to including the predicate *true* in the corresponding clause. If there is no **modifies** clause, then nothing visible to the client may be changed.

When a client wants to use the program module implementing a function, then it is the responsibility of the client to make the **requires** clause true in its prestate. Once this is done, the client may assume the behavior as expressed in the **ensures** and **modifies** clauses upon termination of the function. The implementation must ensure that this behavior is achieved.

In Figure 11.25, the identifier *self* denotes the object that receives the message corresponding to the specified method. The operations *add* and *remove* are allowed to change the state of an *IntSet* object, but the operations *unionn* and *isIn* are not. The predicate in the **requires** clause of the *remove* procedure states that the set object from which the integer *i* should be deleted must contain it. The names and meaning of the operators in **requires** and **ensures** clauses come from the LSL trait *SetTrait*.

It is important to note the following points about a Larch/C++ interface specification:

1. The keyword *self* is a shorthand for *(*(this/any))*, which is dereferencing the pointer value of *this* in some visible state. The state function *any* stands for either the *pre-* or the *post*state. In C++, *this* represents a pointer to the receiving object, so that

    $$self = (*(this/any))$$

    is a name representing a pointer to the receiving object itself in some visible state. The keyword *self* can be used only in specifications of member functions.

2. A distinction is made between an object and its value. An identifier, such as x, denotes an object. A superscripted object identifier such as x' or $x^\wedge$ denotes a value of x; the identifier x' denotes the value of x in a poststate, and $x^\wedge$ denotes the value of x in a prestate. Thus, the assertion $self' = self^\wedge$ says that the value of object *self* is not changed by the operation.

3. The **modifies** clause specifies which objects are changed. The changes are asserted in the **ensures** clause.

4. Modules defining abstract data types have constructor and destructor functions. For module *IntSet*, these are *IntSet()* and *~IntSet()*, respectively. The constructor function creates an instance of the abstract data type. The destructor function deallocates the storage space associated with the instance of the abstract data type.

5. The keyword *result* denotes the result of a function call. The type of function *unionn* is a pointer to an *IntSet* object. The argument to the function is a pointer *pS* to object *IntSet*. The predicate in the **ensures** clause asserts the union as

```
typedef int *ratl;
ratl make_ratl(int num, int den)
    requires den ≠ 0;
    ensures assigned(result, post) ∧ size(locs(result)) = 2 ∧
        (result[0])' = n ∧ (result[1])' = d ∧
        fresh(result[0], result[1]);
```

FIGURE 11.26. Use of fresh in Larch/C++.

defined by the LSL trait operator *unionn* to be an object whose pointer is *result*. The keyword *result* cannot be used in functions with return type *void*.

11.4.3 Additional Function Specification Features

Keywords recently added to Larch/C++ include allocated, assigned, and fresh. The keyword allocated can be used in a predicate for the **requires** and **ensures** clauses, in order to specify that an object is allocated in a certain state. An object can be defined without being allocated. The keyword assigned can be used in a predicate for the **requires** and **ensures** clauses, in order to specify that an object has a well-defined value. The keyword fresh can only appear within a predicate of an ensures clause; it is used to specify that an object was not allocated in the prestate, and it is allocated in the poststate. The example in Figure 11.26 illustrates the use of fresh in function specifications.

Several new clauses have been added lately to Larch/C++. Some of these allow recording implementation design decisions, and some others provide notational convenience.

The **constructs** clause is the equivalent of the **modifies** clause. Larch/C++ provides this clause for reading convenience. The clause is used in constructor functions in order to express that an object is not only modified but there is memory allocated for it, and its attributes are initialized.

The **trashes** clause is used for any function that trashes objects. In Larch/C++ the trashing of an object is done whenever the object was assigned in the prestate and not assigned in the poststate, or when the object was allocated in the prestate and not allocated in the poststate. The **trashes** clause lists a set of objects that may be trashed from the function.

The **claims** clause contains a predicate that does not affect the meaning of a function specification, but rather describes redundant properties that can be checked by a theorem prover. This is quite similar to the **implies** clause in LSL tier.

The **let** clause can appear in any function specification. It can be used to abbreviate expressions that will be used many times in the **requires**, **ensures**, and **example**

```
void student_account(gpa & g);
    requires assigned(a, pre) ∧ allocated(g, pre);
    modifies g;
    trashes a;
    ensures
        let new = cumulative(g) in
        if new < 2.5 then trashed(a) else set_gpa(a^, a^.new);
        claims new > 2.5 ⇒ ¬isTrashed(a, pre, post);
```

FIGURE 11.27. Use of allocated, assigned, trashed, let, and claims in Larch/C++.

clauses of the function specification. The example in Figure 11.27 illustrates the use of these clauses.

11.5   Proofs in LSL

All assertions stated in the **implies** and **converts** clauses of a trait require proof. When specifications are composed, the resulting specification must be consistent. The various proof obligations, proof methods, and the features of LP, the Larch proof assistant, are briefly outlined in this section.

11.5.1   Proof Obligations

In general, an LSL specification T consists of a hierarchy of traits. The hierarchy is formed by the **includes** and **assumes** relationships on the traits. These relationships are irreflexive and transitive. If the **implies** clause of a trait T mentions a trait S, then T implies S, and T cannot transitively include S. Consequently,

- the *assertions* of T consist of the equations in the **asserts** clause of T and those in the **asserts** clause of the traits transitively included in T.

- the *assumptions* of T are those transitively assumed by it.

- the *axioms* of T consist of its assertions and its assumptions.

- the *theory* of T consists of the logical consequence of its axioms.

As mentioned earlier, the **generated by** clause of the **asserts** section adds induction rules, and the **partitioned by** clause of the **asserts** section adds deduction rules. The claims made in the **implies** and **converts** clauses of an LSL trait require proof obligations. The assertions made in the **implies** clause must follow from the stated axioms. The **converts** clause must follow from its axioms, assertions in its **implies** clause, and assertions in the **implies** clauses of the included traits and implied traits.

The proof techniques for LSL traits include the natural deduction method and proof by implication, both discussed in Chapter 6, and proof by structural induction discussed in Chapter 7. The proofs can be developed using LP, the Larch proof assistant, which has several built-in proof strategies. Below, we demonstrate how to develop a proof for the specifications given in Section 11.2.1. The proof steps are not strictly formal.

Example 11.1   The **implies** clause in the trait $Poset(T)$ shown in Figure 11.4 consists of the two assertions

$$(x \le y \wedge y \le z) \Rightarrow x \le z$$
$$Preorder(\_\le\_ \textbf{ for } \diamond)$$

The proof steps for the first claim are

$$x \le y == x < y \vee x = y, \qquad\qquad\qquad \textit{from equation (6)}$$
$$y \le z == y < z \vee y = z, \qquad\qquad\qquad \textit{from equation (6)}$$
$$x \le y \wedge y \le z \equiv [(x < y \wedge y < z) \vee (x = y \wedge y < z)]$$
$$\qquad \vee [(x < y \wedge y = z) \vee (x = y \wedge y = z)] \qquad \textit{distributive law}$$
$$\Rightarrow (x < z \vee x < z) \vee (x < z \vee x = z) \qquad\qquad \textit{equation(4)}$$
$$\equiv (x < z \vee x = z)$$
$$\equiv x \le z$$

To prove the second claim, we write the axioms after ignoring the operator $<$ from the specification $Poset(T)$:

$$x \le x$$
$$x \le y \wedge y \le x == x = y$$

Substituting $\diamond$ for $\le$ in the above assertions and in the implication, we get the assertions

$$x \diamond x$$
$$x \diamond y \wedge y \diamond x == x = y$$
$$x \diamond y \wedge y \diamond z \Rightarrow x \diamond z$$

Hence, $Poset(T, \le) \Rightarrow Preorder(\le, T)$; that is, if $\le$ is a partial order on T, then $\le$ is also a preordering on T. ∎

Example 11.2   The claim that *Set* is **partitioned by** *subset* is made in the **implies** clause of the trait *SetTrait*. To prove this claim, we must show that two sets S and T are equal if they have the same subsets. Formally stated, it is required to prove the following assertion

$$\forall X \bullet X \subseteq S = X \subseteq T \Rightarrow S = T$$

Let X, S, and T denote nonempty sets. Use the fact that *insert* is a generator of *SetTrait* to rewrite the left-hand side of the assertion to obtain

$$subset(insert(e, X'), S) = subset(insert(e, X'), T)$$

Using equation (6) of *SetTrait*, we rewrite the above equation as

$$member(e, S) \wedge subset(X', S) = member(e, T) \wedge subset(X', T)$$

From this we infer that $member(e, S)$, $member(e, T)$, $subset(X', S)$, and $subset$ (X', T) are true. Continuing with the above two rewriting steps for an element of the set X', and repeating until all the elements of X are accounted, the assertion to be proved can be rewritten as

$$\forall X \bullet \forall e : X \bullet member(e, S) = member(e, T) \Rightarrow S = T$$

This result has already been proved in Section 11.2.2. This completes the proof.

Notice that in the first step of the proof, it is shown that

$$subset(s, t) \Rightarrow (member(x, s) \Rightarrow member(x, t))$$

which is another claim made in the **implies** clause of *SetTrait*.   ∎

The **implies** clause of a trait may include a **generated by** clause, in which case a proof is required to show that the set of elements generated by the given operators in the **generated by** clause contains all the elements of the sort. We use induction on the set of generators defined in the **generated by** clause of the trait. For example, we may introduce { } as a unary operator in *SetTrait* with the signature

$$\{\,\}: E \rightarrow S$$

and an equation

$$\{e\} == insert(e, \{\}).$$

The operator constructs a singleton set for every element from E. The claim

> **generated by** { }, *emptyset, unionn*

can be included in the **implies** clause of the the trait *SetTrait*. The proof of this claim is left as an exercise.

11.5.2   LP: Larch Proof Assistant

LP [6] is a proof assistant for a subset of multisorted first-order logic with equality. The basis for proofs in LP is a logical system, consisting of a set of operators, rewrite rules, operator theories, induction rules, and deduction rules. LP is intended as an interactive proof assistant rather than an automatic theorem prover. LP is designed with the assumption that initial attempts to state a theorem correctly, and to prove it usually fail. As a result, LP provides useful information about the reasons for the failure of a proof. This feature of LP is especially important when used for verification of properties not explicitly stated in the **implies** clause.

LP theories

Each axiom of LP has two semantics, a definitional semantics in first-order logic, and an operational semantics that is sound with respect to the definitional semantics but not necessarily complete.

The LP sort, operator and variable declarations in LP are semantically the same as those in LSL. LP has the built-in sort *Bool*, as well as the operators *true*, *false*, *if*, *not*, $=$, $\&(and)$, $|$ (or), $=>$ *(implies)*, and $<=>$ *(if and only if)*. During a proof, LP can generate local variables, constants, and operators.

A term in multisorted first-order logic consists of either a variable or an operator with a sequence of terms as arguments. The number of arguments in a term and their sorts agree with the declaration of the operator.

Equations

A theory in LP consists of equations. An equational theory as defined in Section 11.2.1 is a theory axiomatized by a set of equations. The set of terms constructed from a set of variables and operators is called *a free-word algebra* or *term algebra*. A set S of equations defines a congruence relation on a term algebra. This is the smallest relation containing the equations in S and that is closed under reflexivity, symmetry, transitivity, instantiation of free variables, and substitution of terms by their equals. An equation $t_1 == t_2$ is in the equational theory of S, or is an equational consequence of S, if t_1 is congruent to t_2. The notion of congruence is related to reduction to canonical forms and equality of such reduced terms.

Rewrite rules

LP inference mechanisms require that equations are oriented into rewrite rules. The logical meaning of the rewrite rules is identical to that of equations; however, the operational behavior is different. A rewrite rule is an ordered pair (u, v) of terms, usually written as $u \rightarrow v$, such that u is not a variable and that every variable that occurs in v also occurs in u. A *rewriting system* is a set of rewrite rules. LP orients equations into rewrite rules and uses these rules to reduce terms to *normal* forms.

Informally, starting from a rewrite rule $u \rightarrow v$ and a substitution q that matches u with a subterm w of t, we can replace w by $q(v)$ to reduce t to a new term t'. This reduction process, starting with some term t, can continue until no more reduction is possible. A term t is *irreducible* if there is no term t' to which it can be reduced using the rewrite rules; an irreducible term is in normal form.

A term can have many different normal forms; a term with only one normal form, is a *canonical* term. It is usually essential that the rewriting system is terminating. Although in general it is undecidable whether the set of rewrite rules is terminating, LP provides mechanisms that orient a subset of the equations into the terminating rewrite system. A terminating rewrite system in which all terms have a canonical form is said to be *convergent*. If a rewrite system is convergent, its rewriting theory, that is, the equations that can be proved by reducing them to identities, is identical to its equational theory. Most rewriting systems are not convergent. In these systems, the rewriting theory is a proper subset of the equational theory.

Operator theories

Some equations cannot be oriented into terminating rewrite rules; these include associativity and commutativity statements. For example, attempting to orient the commutativity equation $a + b == b + a$ into rewrite rules will produce a non-terminating system:

$$a + b \rightarrow b + a;$$
$$b + a \rightarrow a + b.$$

To avoid this, LP uses *equational term-rewriting* to match and unify terms modulo associativity and commutativity. In equational term-rewriting, a substitution q matches $t1$ and $t2$ modulo a set S of equations if $q(t1) = t2$ is in the equational theory of S. For example, if $*$ is associative and commutative, the rewrite rule $a * b \rightarrow c$ will reduce the term $a * c * b$ to $c * c$.

Inductive rules

Inductive rules increase the number of theories that can be axiomized using a finite set of assertions. Their syntax and semantics are similar to those of the inductive statements in LSL. An example is *Set* **generated by** *emptyset, insert*. The equation

$$delete(insert(s, e), e) == s$$

in *SetTrait* (see Figure 11.1) produces an infinite number of equations:

$$delete(insert(emptyset, e), e) == new;$$
$$delete(insert(insert(emptyset, b), e), e) == insert(emptyset, b)$$

Thus, the **generated by** clause is equivalent to the infinite set of first-order formulas:

$$(E[emptyset] \wedge (\forall s : Set, b : element \bullet E[s] \Rightarrow E[insert(s, b)])) \Rightarrow$$
$$(\forall s : Set) \bullet E[s],$$

for any well-formed equation E.

Deduction rules

LP uses deduction rules to deduce new equations from existing equations and rewrite rules. LP produces deduction rules from the LSL **partitioned by** clause. For example, the LSL statement *Stack* **partitioned by** *isEmpty, top, pop* is reflected in LP theory as

assert when
top(s1) == top(s2),
pop(s1) == pop(s2),
isEmpty(s1) == isEmpty(s2)
yield *s1 == s2*

Proof methods

LP provides mechanisms for proving theorems using both forward and backward inference. Forward inferences produce consequences from a logical system; backward inferences produce a set of subgoals from a goal whose proof will suffice to establish a conjecture.

Normalization Whenever a new rewrite rule is added to its logical system, LP normalizes all equations, rewrite rules, and deduction rules all over again. If an equation or rewrite rule normalizes to an identity, it is discarded. LP uses normalization in forward inference. If a new conjecture is to be proved, LP tries to normalize it to an identity. If successful, the conjecture is proved by normalization; this action is a backward inference applying normalization.

Critical-pair equations A common problem arises when a set of equations is oriented into a rewriting system that is not convergent, and hence, there is more than one way to normalize the logical system. Thus, reduction to normal form does not provide a decision procedure for the equational theory. As a consequence, LP can fail, for example, to reduce term v and term u to the same normal form, even if v and u are reducible. The **critical-pair** command provides a method of extending the rewriting theory to approximate its equational theory more closely. Each critical-pair equation captures a way in which a pair of rewrite rules might be used to reduce a single term in two different ways. For example, the critical-pair equation between $(x * y) * z \rightarrow x * (y * z)$ and $i(w) * w \rightarrow e$ produces the equation $e * z == i(y) * (y * z)$, when the substitution $\{i(y) \mid x, y \mid w\}$ unifies $i(w) * w$ with the subterm of $(x * y) * z$.

Instantiation Explicit instantiation of variables in equations, rewrite rules, and deduction rules may lead to establishing that the conjecture is an identity. For example, to establish the identity of the theorem $x == x \cup x$ in a logical system that contains the deduction rule

when $(\forall e)\ e \in x = e \in y$ **yield** $x == y$

and the rewrite rule

$e \in (x \cup y) \rightarrow e \in x \mid e \in y,$

we instantiate y by $x \cup x$ in the deduction rule.

Proof by case   A conjecture can often be simplified by dividing a proof into cases. When a conjecture reduces to an identity in all cases, it is a theorem. For example, the command **prove** $0 < f(c)$ by case $c = 0$ will make LP consider three cases: $c = 0$, $c < 0$, and $c > 0$. If in all three cases the conjecture is true, then it is a theorem.

Proof by induction   A proof by induction is based on the induction rules. The command **prove** e **by induction on** x **using** IR directs LP to prove the equation e by induction on variable x using the induction rule IR. LP generates subgoals for the basic and inductive steps in a proof by induction as follows. The basic subgoals involve the equations that result from substituting the basic generators of IR for x in e. Basis generators are those with no variables of the sort of x. Induction subgoals generate one or more hypotheses by substituting one or more new constants for x in e. Each induction subgoal involves proving an equation that results from substituting a nonbasic generator of IR for x in e. For example, consider an induction proof over the sort *Nat*:

> **prove** $i \leq j => i \leq (j + k)$ **by induction on** j

> Conjecture *lemma*.1: Subgoals for proof by induction on 'j'
> Basis subgoal:
>   *lemma*.1.1 : $(i < 0) => (i < (0 + k)) == true$
> Induction constant : *jc*
> Induction hypothesis:
>   *lemma*.*InductHyp*.1 : $(i < jc) => (i < (jc + k)) == true$
> Induction subgoal:
>   *lemma*.1.2 : $(i < s(jc)) => (i < (s(jc) + k)) == true$

Proof by implication   The command **prove** $t1 => t2$ **by** $=>$ directs LP to prove the subgoal $t'2$ using the hypothesis $t'1 == true$. In general $t'1 = t1$ and $t'2 = t2$, but in some cases LP has to generate new constants instead of variables in $t1$ and $t2$ to form $t'1$ and $t'2$ and preserve the soundness of proof. For example, given the axioms $a => b \rightarrow true$ and $b => c \rightarrow true$, the command **prove** $a => c$ **by** $=>$ uses the hypothesis $a \rightarrow true$ to normalize the axiom and to reduce it to identity.

11.6   Case Study—Two Examples from Rogue Wave Library

Rogue Wave Tools.h++ class library [10] is a rich, robust, and versatile C++ foundation class library of industrial standard. The library classes are well-structured and well-documented.

Tools.h++ consists of a large set of C++ classes that are usable in isolation independent of other classes. The set consists of simple classes, such as date, zone, time,

```
typedef int Zone;
typedef int RWCString;
imports typedefs;
struct RWDaylightRule;
extern Zone local;
extern Zone standard;
enum DstRule {NoDST, NoAm, WeEu};
extern RWDaylightRule *rules[3];
enum StdZone {NewZealand = −12, Japan, Greenwich, Hawaii,
    Europe, USEastern} zone;
abstract class RWZone
{
uses Zone, Time(RWBoolean for Bool), string(RWCString for C);
public:
virtual int timeZoneOffset() {
        ensures result = self^.standardOffset;
    }
virtual int altZoneOffset() {
        ensures result = self^.DSTOffset;
    }
virtual RWBoolean daylightObserved() {
        ensures result = daylightObserved(self^);
    }
virtual RWBoolean isDaylight(const struct tm* tspec) {
        requires daylightObserved(self^) ∧ (*tspec)^.tm_wday =
            week_day(date((*tspec).tm_day, (*tspec)^.tm_month,
                (*tspec)^.tm_year));
        ensures ∃ t : Time (result = (t = get((*tspec)^)) ∧
            observedDST(t.year, self^) <> NON ∧
            (observedDST(t.year, self^) = AHEAD ⇒
            (convert(t) ≥ convert(beginDST(t.year, self^)) ∧
            convert(t) ≤ convert(endDST(t.year, self^)))) ∧
            (observedDST(t.year, self^) = BEHIND ⇒
            (convert(t) ≤ convert(beginDST(t.year, self^)) ∧
            convert(t) ≥ convert(endDST(t.year, self^))))));
    }
```

FIGURE 11.28. Larch/C++ interface specification for RWZone—Part I.

and string, and three families of collection classes, namely collection classes based on templates, collection classes that use preprocessor facilities, and "Smalltalk-like" classes for heterogeneous collections. The library also includes a set of abstract data types and corresponding specialized classes that provide a frame-

```
virtual void getBeginDaylight(struct tm* tspec) {
      requires validYear((*tspec)^.tm_year);
      modifies (*tspec);
      ensures ∃ t : Time ((daylightObserved(self ) ⇒
            (t = beginDST((*tspec)^.tm_year, self^) ∧ (*tspec)' = fill(t))) ∧
            (¬ daylightObserved(self^) ⇒ (*tspec)'.all' < 0));
}
virtual void getEndDaylight(struct tm* tspec) {
      requires validYear((*tspec)^.tm_year);
      modifies (*tspec);
      ensures ∃ t : Time ((daylightObserved(self ) ⇒
            (t = endDST((*tspec)^.tm_year, self^) ∧ (*tspec)' = fill(t))) ∧
            (¬ daylightObserved(self^) ⇒ (*tspec)'.all' < 0));
}
virtual RWCString timeZoneName() {
      ensures result = self^.standardName;
}
virtual RWCString altZoneName() {
      ensures result = self^.DSTName;
}
static const RWZone& local() {
      ensures result = local;
}
static const RWZone& standard() {
      ensures result = standard;
}
static const RWZone& utc() {
      ensures result = utc;
}
static const RWZone& local(const RWZone* zn) {
      modifies local;
      ensures local' = (*zn)^;
}
```

FIGURE 11.29. Larch/C++ interface specification for RWZone—Part II.

work for persistence, localization, and other issues. All collection classes have a corresponding iterator.

RWZone is a simple Rogue Wave abstract base class, whose operations are imported into *RWDate* and *RWTime*. We give the interface specifications for the classes *RWFile* and *RWZone* in this section.

static const RWZone& standard(const RWZone* zn) {
    modifies *standard;*
    ensures *standard' = (*zn)^;*
}
static const RWDaylightRule* dstRule(DstRule x = NoAm) {
    ensures *result = rules[x];*
}}

FIGURE 11.30. Larch/C++ Interface Specification for RWZone—Part III.

11.6.1 RWZone Specification

RWZone is an abstract base class for user-defined zones and accommodates the necessary methods for the derived class when used with *RWTime* and *RWDate* classes. It defines an interface for issues pertaining to various time zones, such as whether or not daylight saving time is in use in a specific zone, the offset from GMT (Greenwich Meridian Time) to the time in a zone, and the starting and ending dates for daylight saving time. The Rogue Wave library provides rules for constructing zone objects for North American (NoAm) and Western Europe (WeEu). This feature is modeled as the values of an enumerated type in the specification. A class such as *RWTime*, which defines operations on time across different time zones in the world, inherits these properties.

The informal descriptions of virtual functions of RWZone abstract class are given in [10]. The basic abstractions for Greenwich time zone, *standard* and *daylight saving time* are defined in the LSL trait *Zone* shown in Figure 11.21. Interface specification for RWZone is given in Figures 11.28, 11.29, and 11.30. This specification is consistent with the intended purpose of the virtual functions informally described in [10], and are adequate for specifying the classes *RWTime* and *RWDate*.

11.6.2 RWFile Specification

The class *RWFile* encapsulates binary file operations, using Standard C stream library. Since this class is intended to encapsulate operations on binary files, it is required that the file be opened in a binary mode. An adequate formal model is to specify a file as a sequence of bytes. The memory copy of a file is captured by *Open_file*, whereas the disk copy of the file is considered as a global structure. The specification models the memory copy to be identical to the disk copy when the file is opened. Proper encapsulation in the class hides the logic of file creation. Different data structures are used to write and read a file. Since LSL is strongly typed, explicit type casting from a sequence of bytes to the target type and vice versa is needed. A parameterized function is used to improve readability of the specification. The LSL trait *File* shown in Figure 11.13 introduces and defines all the abstract operators.

typedef unsigned size_t;
typedef char* String;
enum MODE {READ, WRITE, READ_WRITE};
struct Mode {MODE create_mode; MODE open_mode};
typedef int RWBoolean;
class RWFile
{
uses *File(RWFile for OpenFile, String for Name), Types(char for S);*
public:
RWFile(const char* filename, const char* mode = 0) {
    modifies *self;*
    ensures if *mode = 0*
      then ∃ *f : File, of : OpenFile*
        if *f.name=filename* ∧ *of = open(f, READ_WRITE)* ∧ ¬ *error(of)*
        then *self' = of*
        else *self' = open(create(filename,*
          READ_WRITE), READ_WRITE)
      else *self' = open(create(filename, create_mode), open_mode);*
  }
RWFile() {
    modifies *self;*
    ensures *trashed(flush(self^));*
  }
long CurOffset() {
    ensures *result = self^.fpointer;*
  }
RWBoolean Eof() {
    ensures *result = (self^.fpointer = len(self^.date));*
  }
RWBoolean Erase() {
    modifies *self;*
    ensures *self'.data = empty* ∧ *result = ¬ error(self');*
  }
RWBoolean Error() {
    ensures *result = error(self^);*
  }

FIGURE 11.31. Larch/C++ interface specification for RWFile—Part I.

RWBoolean Exists() {
>   **ensures** ∃ *file : File, name : Name, mode : Mode*
>   *(result = ((self^= open(file, mode)) ∧*
>   *file = create(name, READ_WRITE)));*

}
RWBoolean Flush() {
>   **ensures** *result = ¬ error(flush(self^));*

}
const char GetName() {*
>   **ensures** *result' = self^.file.name;*

}
RWBoolean ISEmpty() {
>   **ensures** *result = (self^.data = empty);*

}
RWBoolean isValid() const {
>   **ensures** ∃ *f : File, m : Mode (result = (self^ = open(f, m)));*

}
RWBoolean Read(char& c) {
>   **requires** *(len(self^.data) − self^.fpointer ≥ len(toByte(c^)));*
>   **modifies** *self.fpointer, c;*
>   **ensures** *result = ¬ error(self') ∧*
>   *(result ⇒ (toByte(c') = read(self^, len(toByte(c^)), self^.fpointer)));*

}
RWBoolean Read(char i, size_t count) {*
>   **requires** *len(self^.data) − self^.fpointer ≥ count * len(toByte((*i)^))*
>   *∧ maxIndex(i) + 1 ≥ count;*
>   **modifies** *self.fpointer, *i;*
>   **ensures** *result = ¬ error(self') ∧ ∀ ind : Int (¬ error(self')*
>   *∧ ind ≥ 0 ∧ ind ≤ count ⇒ toByte((*(i + ind))') =*
>   *read(self^, len(toByte((*String)^)), self^.fpointer +*
>   *ind * len(toByte((*i)^))));*

}

FIGURE 11.32. Larch/C++ interface specification for RWFile—Part II.

The interface specification for *RWFile* is shown in Figures 11.31, 11.32, 11.33, and 11.34.

```
RWBoolean Read(char* string) {
    requires ∃ l : Int(nullTerminated(substring(self^,self^.fpointer, l)))
        ∧ (maxIndex(string) + 1 ≥ l * len((*string)^));
    modifies self.fpointer, *string;
    ensures result = ¬ error(self') ∧
        ∀ ind : Int (ind ≥ 0 ∧ ind ≤ l ∧ result ⇒
            toByte((*(string + ind))') =
                read(self^, len(toByte((*string)^)),
                    self^.fpointer + ind * len((*string)^)));
}
RWBoolean SeekTo(long offset) {
    modifies self.fpointer;
    ensures result = (self'.fpointer = offset);
}
RWBoolean SeekToBegin() {
    modifies self.fpointer;
    ensures result = (self'.fpointer = 1);
}
RWBoolean SeekToEnd() {
    modifies self.fpointer;
    ensures result = (self'.fpointer = len(self^));
}
RWBoolean Write(char i) {
    requires ∃ f : File (self^ = open(f, WRITE) ∨
        self^ = open(f, READ_WRITE));
    modifies self;
    ensures result = ¬ error(self') ∧ (¬ error(self') ⇒
        self' = write(self^, toByte(i), self^.fpointer));
}
RWBoolean Write(char* i, size_t count) {
    requires maxIndex(i) + 1 ≥ count ∧
        ∃ f : File (self^ = open(f, WRITE) ∨
        self^ = open(f, READ_WRITE));
    modifies self;
    ensures result = ¬ error(self') ∧ (result ⇒
        ∀ ind : Int ((ind ≥ 0) ∧ (ind ≤ count) ∧ toByte((*(i + ind))^) =
            read(self', len(toByte((*i)^)),
                self^.fpointer + ind * len(toByte((*i)^)))));
}
```

FIGURE 11.33. Larch/C++ interface specification for RWFile—Part III.

        RWBoolean Write(const char* string) {
          requires $\exists f$: *File ((self^ = open(f, WRITE) ∨*
            self^ = open(f, READ_WRITE)) ∧
            ($\exists l$: Int (nullTerminated(prefix((*string)^, l)))));
          modifies *self;*
          ensures *result = ¬ error(self') ∧*
            ∀ ind : Int (ind ≥ 0 ∧ ind ≤ l ∧
            result ⇒ toByte((*(string + ind))^) =
                read(self', len(toByte((*string)^)),
                    self^.fpointer + ind * len((*string)^)));
        }
      RWBoolean Exists(const char* filename) {
          ensures $\exists f$: *File(result =*
           (filename = f.name ∧ file = create(filename, READ_WRITE)));
        }
      }

FIGURE 11.34. Larch/C++ interface specification for RWFile—Part IV.

Exercises

In the following exercises, use the traits defined in this chapter wherever possible.

1. Give an LSL theory for finite directed line segments. A directed line segment is a *vector*, with a *position* and a *direction*. Include operations so that (1) two vectors can be compared; (2) the position and orientation of a vector may be obtained; (3) a vector may be translated to a new position while maintaining its orientation; and (4) the inner product of two vectors can be calculated. Define simple traits and compose them to construct a trait for directed line segments.

2. Define an LSL theory for triangles; it should include the theory of vectors defined in Question 1. Include an operation for moving a triangle to a new position without changing the orientation of its sides. Derive specialized theories for (1) right-angled triangles; (2) equilateral triangles; and (3) isosceles triangles.

3. Give a Larch/C++ specification of the C++ class `Triangle`, which uses the traits developed in Question 2.

4. Enrich the theory of *Rational* given in Section 11.2.7 by adding the arithmetic operators +, and ∗ for rational numbers. Provide a sufficient number of equations.

5. Prove the claims made in the **implies** clause of the following LSL traits:
   (a) *Rational* shown in Figure 11.8.
   (b) *NStackTrait* shown in Figure 11.7.

   (c) *String* shown in Figure 11.12.

   (d) *File* shown in Figure 11.13.

6. Use the traits discussed in Section 11.3 to construct the following Larch traits:

   (a) The trait *DictIterObj* specifies iterators for dictionaries. An item in the dictionary is an ordered pair *Obj[K], Obj[V]*. Include operations for (1) advancing the iterator to the next position where an item with its key matching the given key is found; and (2) advancing the iterator to the next position where an item equal to the given item is found.

   (b) The trait *Crypt* encrypts a string to another string such that no two different strings have the same image.

   (c) The trait *Filecrypt*, which includes the *File* and *Crypt* traits, creates an encrypted copy of a given file on disk.

7. Give a Larch/C++ specification of the C++ class `Intstack`, which uses the *StackTrait* given in Figure 11.5.

8. Give Larch/C++ specifications for the following C++ classes:

   (a) The class `IntDate` has the following constructors and member functions:

      i. `IntDate(unsigned day, unsigned year)`—constructs a date with the given day and the year.

      ii. `IntDate(unsigned day, char* month, unsigned year, const locale)`—constructs a date with the given day of the month, the month, and the year. The locale argument is used to convert the month name.

      iii. `IntDate(const IntTime& t, const IntZone& zone = LocalZone)`—constructs a date from a time and zone in `IntTime`.

      iv. `between(const IntDate& a, const IntDate& b) const`—returns true if *this* `IntDate` is between a and b.

      v. `previous(const char* dayName, const Locale& locale = LocalFormat) const`—returns the date of the previous dayName, for example, the date of the previous Saturday. The weekday name is interpreted according to the local conventions in `locale`.

      vi. `leapyear(unsigned year)`—returns true if a given year is a leap year.

      vii. `firstdayofmonth(unsigned month)`—returns the day of the year corresponding to the first day of the month in this `IntDate`'s year.

   (b) The class `IntTime` has the following constructors and member functions:

     i. `IntTime(unsigned long x)`—constructs a time with x seconds since *00:00:00 January 1, 1901 UTC.*

    ii. `IntTime(unsigned date, unsigned hour = 0, unsigned minute = 0, unsigned second = 0, const RWZone& local)`—constructs the time for the given date, hour, minute, and second, relative to the time zone `local`, which defaults to local time.

   iii. `compare(const IntTime* t)`—returns 0 if `self ==* t`, returns 1 if `self > *t`, and returns −1 if `self < *t`.

   iv. `isDST(const RWZone& zone = local) const`—returns `true` if `self` is during daylight saving time in the time zone given by `zone`, `false` otherwise.

    v. `beginDST(unsigned year, const RWZone& zone= local)`—returns the start of daylight savings time for the given `year` in the given time `zone`. Returns a message if DST is not observed in that time zone in that year.

   vi. `seconds() const`—returns the number of seconds since *00:00:00 January 1, 1901.*

9. The topology of a communication network may be abstracted as a directed graph with a finite number of nodes and links; the network is connected. Typical operations on the network include (1) adding a link between two nodes; (2) adding a node and linking it to some node in the network; (3) deleting a node in the network; and (4) deleting a link in the network. Deletions must preserve the connectedness property. Write a Larch/C++ interface specification that provides these functionalities. Define a mathematical model of the network in the LSL layer, and use it in the interface specification. Hint: See the computer network example in Chapter 9.

Bibliographic Notes

The Larch family of languages originated from the works of Wing [11, 12], and Guttag and Horning [6]. A specifier can design theories by using and composing theories in the mathematical toolkit provided by Guttag and Horning [6]. LP, the Larch proof assistant, provides an interactive verification support for checking properties of LSL traits. There are several interface specification languages, each tailored to a specific programming language. Larch/C++ was designed by Gary Leavens [8].

In a Larch/C++ interface specification, implementation design details that are tailored to the C++ programming language can be specified. This feature makes Larch/C++ suitable for industrial applications, where black-box specifications of

C++ classes can enhance their effective reuse. Larch/C++ interface specifications for several classes taken from Rogue Wave *tools.h++* [10] can be found in Alagar et al. [1]. The report summarizes the incompleteness of informal class descriptions in the Rogue Wave Library and the experience gained in understanding and writing the interface specifications and the corresponding LSL traits.

A classified Larch bibliography can be found at the Larch home page:

    http://larch.lcs.mit.edu:8001/larch/index.html

References

[1] V.S. Alagar, P. Colagrosso, A. Loukas, S. Narayanan, and A. Protopsaltou, "Formal Specifications for Effective Black-Box Reuse," Technical Reports (2 volumes), Department of Computer Science, Concordia University, Montreal, Canada, February 1996.

[2] J. Chen, "The Larch/Generic Interface Language," S.B. Thesis, Department of Electrical Engineering and Computer Science, Massachusettes Institute of Technology, Boston, MA, 1989.

[3] Y. Cheon, "Larch/Smalltalk: A Specification Language for Smalltalk," M.Sc. Thesis, Department of Computer Science, Iowa State University, Iowa, 1991.

[4] P. Colagrosso, "Formal Specification of C++ Class Interfaces for Software Reuse," M.Comp.Sci. Thesis, Department of Computer Science, Concordia University, Montreal, Canada, 1993.

[5] D. Guaspari, C. Marceau, and W. Polak, "Formal Verification of Ada Programs," *IEEE Transactions on Software Engineering*, Vol. 16, No. 9, September 1990, pp. 1058–1075.

[6] J.V. Guttag, J.J. Horning, with S.J. Garland, K.D. Jones, A.Modet, and J.M. Wing, *Larch: Languages and Tools for Formal Specification*, Springer-Verlag, New York, NY, 1993.

[7] K. Jones, *LM3: A Larch Interface Language for Modula-3: A Definition and Introduction: Version 1.0*, Technical Report 72, DEC/SRC, Digital Equipment Corporation, MA, 1991.

[8] G.T. Leavens, *Larch/C++ Reference Manual, Draft: Revision 5.1*, February 1997.

[9] G.T. Leavens and Y. Cheon, "Preliminary Design of Larch/C++," in U. Martin and J. Wing (Eds.), *Proceedings of the First International Workshop on Larch*, Workshops in Computer Science Series, Springer-Verlag, London, 1992.

[10] Rogue Wave, *Tools.h++ Class Library*, Version 6.0, Rogue Wave Software, 1993.

[11] J. Wing, "A Two-Tiered Approach for Specifying Programs," Technical Report TR_299, Laboratory for Computer Science, Massachussets Institute of Technology, Boston, MA, 1983.

[12] J. Wing, "Writing Larch Interface Language Specifications," *ACM Transactions on Programming Languages and Systems*, Vol. 9, No. 1, 1987, pp. 1–24.

Index